explorer

ISRAEL

Andrew Sanger

AA Publishing

Cover: Jerusalem
Page 3: the Dome of
the Rock, Jerusalem
Page 4: olives
Page 5 (top): Jews
praying at the Western
Wall
Page 5 (left): poppies,
Galilee
Page 5 (right): Russian
Orthodox Church,
Jerusalem
Page 6 (bottom): Old
City, Akko
Page 7 (bottom): reli-
gious artist, Safed
Page 9: detail from the
Dome of the Rock, a
Greek Orthodox priest
and the national flag
with Star of David

Page 29: the Western
Wall, Alexander the
Great
Page 46: Tower of
David
Page 162: mosaic, Beit
Alpha Synogogue,
Galilee

Written by Andrew Sanger
Additional writing by Deborah Wald and Geraldine Dunham
Original photography by Jon Arnold and Pat Athie

Revised second edition 1998
First published 1996

Edited, designed and produced by AA Publishing
Maps © The Automobile Association 1996
Distributed in the United Kingdom by AA Publishing,
Norfolk House, Priestley Road, Basingstoke, Hampshire,
RG24 9NY.

The contents of this publication are believed correct at the
time of printing. Nevertheless, the publishers cannot be held
responsible for any errors or omissions or for changes in the
details given in this guide or for the consequences of any
reliance on the information provided by the same.
Assessments of attractions, hotels, restaurants and so forth
are based upon the author's own personal experience and,
therefore, descriptions given in this guide necessarily contain an element of subjective opinion which may not reflect
the publishers' opinion or dictate a reader's own experiences on another occasion.
   We have tried to ensure accuracy in this guide, but things
do change and we would be grateful if readers would advise
us of any inaccuracies they may encounter.

A CIP catalogue record for this book is available from the
British Library.
ISBN 0 7495 1611 9

Published by AA Publishing (a trading name of Automobile
Association Developments Limited, whose registered
office is Norfolk House, Priestley Road, Basingstoke,
Hampshire RG24 9NY. Registered number 1878835).

Colour separation by Fotographics Ltd
Printed and bound in Spain by Graficas Estella S.A.

Titles in the Explorer series...
Australia • Boston & New England • Britain • Brittany
California • Caribbean • China • Costa Rica • Crete • Cyprus
Egypt • Florence & Tuscany • Florida • France • Germany
Greek Islands • Hawaii • Indonesia • Ireland • Italy • Japan
London • Mexico • Moscow & St Petersburg • New York
New Zealand • Paris • Portugal • Prague • Provence
Rome • San Francisco • Scotland • Singapore & Malaysia
South Africa • Spain • Thailand • Turkey • Venice • Vietnam

AA World Travel Guides publish nearly 300 guidebooks to a
full range of cities, countries and regions across the world.
Find out more about AA Publishing and the wide range of
services the AA provides by visiting our Web site at
www.theaa.co.uk.

How to use this book

This book is divided into five main sections:

❏ **Section 1: *Israel Is***

discusses aspects of life and living today, from the rôle of religion in Israeli society to the concept of Israel as a homeland

❏ **Section 2: *Israel Was***

places the country in its political and historical context, and examines the past events whose influences are felt to this day

❏ **Section 3: *A to Z Section***

covers places to visit within five regional chapters, including walks and drives. This section also includes the Focus-on articles, which consider a variety of subjects in greater detail

❏ **Section 4: *Travel Facts***

contains the practical information that is vital for a successful trip

❏ **Section 5:
*Hotels and Restaurants***

lists recommended establishments throughout Israel, giving an indication of price and a brief résumé of what each offers

How to use the star ratings
Most of the places described in this book have been given a separate rating:

▶▶▶   **Do not miss**

▶▶   **Highly recommended**

▶   **Worth seeing**

  Not essential viewing

Map references
To make the location of a particular place easier to find, every main entry in this book is given a map reference, such as176B3. The first number (176) indicates the page on which the map can be found; the letter (B) and the second number (3) pinpoint the square of the map in which the main entry is located. The maps on the inside front cover and inside back cover are referred to as IFC and IBC respectively.

Contents

Quick reference

This quick-reference guide highlights the features of the book you will use most often: the maps; the introductory features; the Focus-on articles; the walks; and the drives.

6

Quick reference

7

Andrew Sanger is a well-established and award-winning travel writer who has contributed to many British newspapers and magazines, including the *Guardian,* the *Telegraph* and *Woman's Journal*. He is the editor of French Railway's holiday magazine *Top Rail*, series editor of a number of travel books and the author of a dozen guidebooks to France, Ireland and other European countries. After a long fascination with Israel, and frequent visits, this is his first book about the country.

My Israel by Andrew Sanger

Scratch the present and you'll find the past. Look at the past and you'll see the future. There's something about this place that thrills me. Places, like people, are all unique. But with Israel it's different – it just *isn't* like *anywhere* else.

Of course, certain comparisons are tempting, and inevitable. For example, I often see how Israel and Israelis fit into the warm, lively, noisy, out-of-doors Eastern Mediterranean culture that runs from, say, Italy to the Levant. And in its efforts to restore itself after years of Ottoman domination, there's an obvious similarity to Greece.

But in Israel there's something else going on. There's a dizzying, exciting sensation, like falling through time, like being at the vortex of human experience, living in a vibrant, emphatic here-and-now which yet looks with passion to both the past and the future.

The land itself mirrors this. Everything converges here. Not only all human life, not only the old and the new are fused, but the climate and topography – from sweet Galilee to searing Negev – are fantastically varied, and the flora and fauna of Europe, Asia and Africa combine at this spot.

Once upon a time, we are told, this was a land of forests and fields, rich with milk and honey, or at least, olives and grapes. Now as its people return and clear the dust from their heritage, they plant, irrigate and rebuild. Every day in Israel, travelling from ancient site, to beach resort, to hardworking town or kibbutz, I am astonished, impressed and delighted by what is happening here.

This little patch of Mediterranean landscape, which already has taught so much to the rest of humanity, now offers another inspiration. Exploring the strange, tiny, kaleidoscopic country which is modern Israel is not just tourism or research: here I catch a glimpse of the potential of human beings, if they are willing to cling to their dreams, to overcome even the most extraordinary obstacles, and make dreams come true at last.

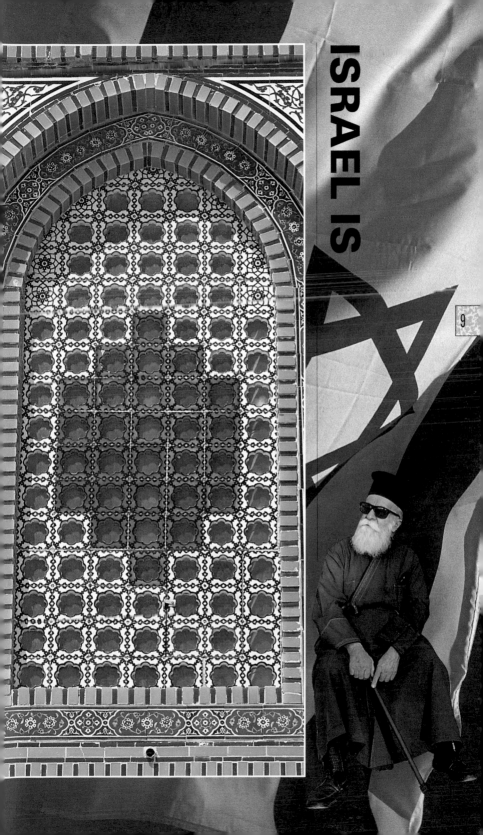

■ The story of Israel has many beginnings. The creation of the modern state was just one step along a road that reaches back into the first pages of the Bible. Since the nation's rebirth on 14 May, 1948, there have been many more new beginnings. Israel today is marked by excitement and a strange, dizzying sensation of moving both ways in time: retrieving the past, and creating the future. ■

Under the spotlight The gaze of the world often focuses on Israel. It is a place that exists deep in the psyche of the western world but that, for many, is more myth than reality. For anyone with Sunday School notions about 'the Holy Land', the dynamic, restless, abrasively energetic modern nation of Israel will come as a big surprise. Many Israelis just wish theirs could be a 'normal' country. But normal countries do not encourage waves of large scale immigration when they already have an unemployment problem. In normal countries, vibrant capitalism would not thrive within a monolithic socialist infrastructure where the state owns almost all the land. But then, normal countries do not have Israel's problems. And somehow, the world does not expect Israel to find normal solutions.

Matters of opinion People hold strong views about Israel. It is hard to grasp that a place only the size of Wales or Massachusetts can be so crucial to world politics and to world religion. The problems have

Above right: Roman-era menorah
Below: timeless architecture –
Jerusalem's Islamic Museum

❑ The official emblem of the State of Israel is the Golden Menorah, the seven-branched ritual candelabrum once used in the Temple in Jerusalem. ❑

an old-new look about them, too. Those ancient Assyrians, Egyptians and Babylonians who once vied for control over the land of the Hebrews have modern inheritors. Those Canaanite tribes who made life difficult for conquering Israelites might almost have been the prototype for today's West Bank militants.

As always, different people lay claim to the same patch of earth. Can such deep and intractable conflicts ever be resolved? The world's press certainly has plenty of easy answers, as do governments around the globe. Politicians and pundits, concerned more about their own national interest, are all too ready to instruct Israel in the error of its ways. Visitors often come up with quick solutions. Israelis know it is not so simple, and that their whole survival is at stake. They, more than anyone, want to be

free to enjoy life in peace. Would it be better to hand over the whole West Bank to the PLO? Some of it? What if Hamas or Islamic Jihad took over? The PLO itself contains elements at odds with Arafat. Parts of the West Bank are almost in the Tel Aviv suburbs. Would it have been better to hang on to it for ever? Was it a mistake to do a deal with Arafat? But then, Arab states made peace because of that. The country is alive with debate, a kaleidoscope of opinions, ideas, choice, diversity.

The land That diversity of opinions is just one other facet of Israel's extraordinary spectrum of peoples and landscapes. For sheer physical variety, the country is phenomenal, with four climate zones and four types of terrain, ranging from handsome and verdant Mediterranean hills in the north to parched desert in the south; from majestic snow-capped Mount Hermon to the salty Dead Sea at the lowest point on the earth. Journeying between the two, you will pass vineyards and olive groves mentioned in the Bible, apple orchards, fields of corn and banana plantations, tomatoes and strawberries – truly a bewildering range of crops. Today, after just a century of labour and reclamation, Israel looks again like a land of milk and honey. This is the ancient-modern 'Eretz Israel' – literally, Land of Israel. Some call it the Promised Land, some the Holy Land, some the Zionist Entity. Most Israelis call it simply, HaAretz: the Land.

History and heritage Past, present and future seem to converge here. Uninspired apartment blocks in well-ordered planned towns give an impression of modernity, but builders digging the foundations usually have to call in the archaeologists. Every walk or drive involves an encounter with Israel's long and dramatic history. Almost every Israeli family has its own story of events that span the globe – but that started here.

Unchanging desert landscapes which the Children of Israel crossed thousands of years ago

11

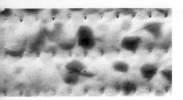

■ **Israel's population has been growing fast – most recently by around 10 per cent a year – and has shot past the 5 million mark. The bulk of the growth comes from immigration. From all over the world, Jews are still arriving to make a home in the Land of Israel.** ■

12

Many migrants are motivated by religious or cultural zeal, many by the simple promise of food, a roof and a regular job, and many by the longing to escape persecution. The service which Jewish families read together over the annual Passover meal, celebrating the Exodus from Egypt, concludes 'Next year in Jerusalem.' Daily that wish is made a reality.

No ordinary homeland The cornerstone of Israel's existence is the Zionist dream of gathering in all the Jews who have been exiled across the globe and bringing them back to their true home, an idea that was even set down in the book of Genesis. Yet any country that willingly promotes a policy of mass immigration must seem at best foolishly philanthropic, at worst, suicidal. The economic logistics alone appear formidable. To an Israeli, however, the case looks

Top: Matza, unleavened bread eaten during Passover
Below: a Hasidic Jew wearing traditional dress

different. Israel is a nation born of new immigrants: they are its life force.

Since 1948 more than two million have 'made *aliyah*' – literally, gone up – to Israel. These *olim* (new arrivals) will face hard times – not just in terms of adjustment to a new language and alien culture but also due to the fact that their new country is itself at risk. Nevertheless, their decision to make a life in Israel is greeted with joy and continuing wonder by Israelis as evidence that the creation of a Jewish homeland really is working as its founders planned.

Who can come? In 1950 the Israeli parliament passed the Law of Return. This enshrined as a right what had, until then, been an unwritten tenet: namely, that any person who could claim Jewish descent would be welcomed to the country. Migrants have since arrived in waves from eastern Europe, north Africa, the Gulf states, the former Soviet Union and Ethiopia. For some of them, Israel was seen as their only hope of survival.

Making it happen Often these 'exiles' were in such difficult circumstances that they could not afford to make their own way to Israel. Some were not even in a position to let anyone know of their plight.

So the job of finding and retrieving the exiles goes on. The task of bringing to Israel any Jew who wishes to come is planned, if need be, with military precision – often capturing the attention of the world in the process. One such operation was Israel's daring airlift of 30,000 Ethiopian Jews, rescued in two phases in Operation Moses in the mid-1980s and early 1990s.

Refugees from the former Soviet Union in Tel Aviv

Contrast this with the arrival of a well-to-do family of South Americans who simply want to be closer to their heritage. Either way, each new arrival is channelled through a welter of absorption processes: language school, location and housing choices, educational options, career guidance, health service registration. Those who arrive with few possessions, such as refugees from the former Soviet Union, receive welfare bene-fits to help ease the first months, and all immigrants receive start-up assis-tance, such as tax rebates on the essentials of a new home.

The induction process takes six months, but full integration may take longer. It may not be until the next generation that people feel thoroughly Israeli. Among the immigrant

❑ All new immigrants attend *ulpan*, an intensive Hebrew lan-guage school with daily lessons for every standard, from total beginners to advanced. Since an *ulpan* may comprise as many as 45 different nationalities, all lessons are in Hebrew. By the end of the five-month course, most immigrants can read, write and converse in the language of the Bible. ❑

generation, some groups, like the Yemenites, see no reason to abandon all their old ways. Some, like the Ethiopians, find it almost too hard to adapt to the Israeli lifestyle. Some, like the new Russians, are criticised for their lack of Jewishness and their unwillingness to contribute to the country. Yet, as Jews, all are entitled to make their escape to Israel, and the belief is that all will eventually play their part in Israel's destiny.

A jeweller at work in the Jewish Quarter of Jerusalem

Hopes and dreams

■ Israel came into being through the efforts of idealists. Not for nothing is its national anthem called *The Hope* (*HaTikvah*). The greatest hope is still the old one: for the Jewish state to be accepted as a country like any other, yet without losing its Biblical imperative to be 'a Light unto the Nations'. Underlying that is the simpler hope of the pioneers: that the Jewish homeland will survive. ■

All for one If you listen to Israelis discussing the most innocent topic it is easy to get the impression that divisions burn deep. Everyone has individual goals, but all that is forgotten when the country is under threat. War has been Israel's jailer since 1948 and you would not need to be religious to say a morning prayer for peace sometimes. What Israelis crave more than anything is the ordinariness of daily life enjoyed by other nations, and an end to lost lives. Yet the demanding and tense pattern of daily life in Israel – begun by early settlers who fought adversity with undaunted optimism – has created a unique national character. In Israelis you will find a rare pride and a sense of achievement that relishes the differences, feeds off stresses and outshines any disagreement.

Top: pioneers
Below: Jews from Ethiopia

Redemption of the land No matter what their politics or attitude to religion, Israelis all have a bond with the earth of Israel – the land of their origin, of their identity, faith and history. Since the Jews fled the Romans in AD 70, religious belief has fuelled the hope of all Jews that they will be able to return to their homeland. In the 19th century, when Diaspora Jews (those living outside Palestine) were the target of persecution, that ambition took on a political dimension and became known as Zionism. In Israel, Jews of whatever affiliation believe that reclaiming the land is a fundamental responsibility, metaphorically and literally: for the religious, to see the Promised Land bloom with the life of returned Jews, and for the secular, to see it flourish again with the fruits of their labours.

The kibbutz One of Israel's least exportable triumphs is simple communal living in hardworking rural

❏ *HaTikvah* (*The Hope*), Israel's poignant national anthem, was composed by Naftali Herz Imber more than 60 years before the founding of the state. It includes the words: 'As long as...the soul of a Jew yearns, our hope is not yet lost, the hope of two thousand years, to be a free people in our land, the land of Zion and Jerusalem.' ❏

settlements where members possess nothing of their own, share equally the burden of work and put back all the profits. Kibbutzim may not have taken off around the world, but they were in the vanguard of the creation of the state. They took on much of the responsibility for immigrants, defence and agriculture and most importantly advocated an ethos of community care. The legacy of the kibbutz movement to the country could hardly be over-estimated. One of the most potent forces in Israel is still the commitment to a dream, the sharing of burdens and of rewards, which has its seeds in these early socialist communities.

The price of peace Turning 18 in most parts of the world means entering adulthood, with unrestricted access to all its risks and rewards. In Israel, it is also the time when girls and boys hold a gun for the first time. Compulsory army service, when you are technically at war with your neighbours, is a frightening prospect. But the desire for peace is matched equally by the desire to defend the

Sentiment motivates many Israelis to achieve near-impossible dreams

country, which would literally be eradicated by losing a war. Paradoxically, were peace ever fully to envelop the Middle East, and end the need to have a fit, young army on standby all the time, Israel might well lose a vital part of its character.

■ **One nation, a hundred nationalities – that's Israel. People from all over the world have poured their influence into this tiny state. Then there are the country's non-Jews, a significant minority. Israel manages to accommodate – and celebrate – all their diversity under a single unifying flag. ■**

The typical Israeli The average Israeli is hard to define. He or she may be dark-eyed and olive-skinned. Then again you can find pale-skinned blondes, brunettes and red-heads, and black skin too. The Jewish majority may (or may not) share a common faith, but each person is coloured by their background and maintains traditions from the 'old country', be it in food, music or family structure.

Israelis of eastern-European origin are called Ashkenazim. Those from the Mediterranean, many of whose ancestors were expelled from Spain in 1492, are Sephardim while Jews from the other Islamic states are Oriental or Mizrahim.

Israel's non-Jews, totalling more than one in six of the population, are found mainly in Jerusalem, Akko, Haifa and the smaller northern towns. They consist of Muslim and

Top: native Israelis are called sabras (prickly pears): spiky on the outside but sweet within
Below: every generation contributes to the Israeli identity

❑ About half of the population of Israel are Sabras – Israeli-born Jews. It is interesting that they do have, already, a distinct character. Like the fruit from which they take their name (also known as prickly pear), Sabras are said to be spiky on the outside, but sweet inside. Israelis do sometimes appear rude, unpolished and peremptory. The direct, forthright speech and abrasive manner really comes from a dislike for pretence, combined perhaps with the effects of living a knife-edge existence. After all, Sabras are also noted for their astonishing informality, irreverence, spontaneous warmth and unexpected generosity. ❑

Christian Arabs and east Mediterraneans, Druze and various other religious groups, as well as Bedouin in the south, and a plethora of other cultures which have set up home here.

Israeli legislation aspires to full equality of all citizens regardless of race or creed, and each group has had a distinctive cultural impact on Israel. As these backgrounds mix and matchmake (about a quarter of Jewish marriages are between Ashkenazim and Sephardim), exciting combinations emerge. With each new wave of immigration, the typical Israeli is constantly reinvented.

Power play Chaim Weizmann, David Gruen (better known as David Ben-Gurion), Isaac Shimshelevitz (Moshe Sharett), Zakam Rubashov (Zalman Shazar), Levi Shkolnik (Levi Eshkol),

Sephardi Jews came to Israel from Mediterranean countries

Golda Meir – the names of the first prime ministers and presidents of Israel reveal that they were all of east European origin. For decades this sector of society, for whom Hebrew was a second language, dominated all important areas of life, from commerce and politics to education and defence. The Sephardic and Oriental communities, which now constitute over 40 per cent of society, came from lands where democracy was unheard of and education optional. Only recently have they made strides into the power zones of life in Israel, taking government positions, wielding industrial clout and spicing up public debate. Eventually, Israelis say, every group and community will be equally involved.

Language and culture If speaking Hebrew and English does not work with your interlocutor, try French, Arabic, Portuguese, Romanian, Russian or a mix of tongues. Not only did most older Israelis master Hebrew only after settling here, many already spoke more than one language when they arrived. Every facet of Israeli culture – music, theatre, literature, politics – has become textured with the threads of other lands. Ethnic variations mean diverse cuisines and there are restaurants to reflect each one: Moroccan, Indian, Italian, American, Argentinian, French, Russian and native Israeli to name a few. Most towns have a 'Chinese' restaurant – often in fact Vietnamese, since Israel gave haven to a number of boat people.

The diverse landscape Israel also packs a great deal into its borders. A short drive can begin in a mountain range and end at lush, fertile plains; it is a quick journey from the urban metropolis to the stillness of the desert; where Tel Aviv is humid, Jerusalem, an hour away, is dry; you can ski in the north, then fly south for an hour to scuba-dive in the tropics.

Israeli soldiers in training. All single women undergo two years service

■ **Israel teems with the passion of its believers. In few other places is devotion so concentrated as in the country which bequeathed monotheism to the world. For Jews, Christians, Muslims and their many offshoots, the land is filled with holy sites which are a great source of inspiration for living faiths.** ■

18

Three parallel roads Israel's five million plus population is roughly 82 per cent Jewish. Of the others, 78 per cent are Sunni Muslim Arabs. There are 100,000 Christians, too – Maronite, Greek Orthodox, Roman and Greek Catholic. The land has been the spiritual home of Jews since the time of Joshua (the 12th century BC). King David founded Jerusalem as the Jewish capital in 1004 BC. The 'Common Era' (as Israelis call it) starts with Christianity's presence in the Holy Land. Since Byzantine times (the 4th century AD), Bethlehem and Nazareth have ranked close behind Rome as spiritual centres for Christians. Though Mecca is holiest for Islam, with Medina a runner-up,

Jerusalem's Muslim Dome of the Rock

the legend was born in the 8th century AD that Muhammad ascended to heaven from the rock now enclosed within Jerusalem's Dome of the Rock. Thus Israel brings together three monotheistic religions, all with unbreakable links: yet those who practise these faiths live remarkably separate and antagonistic lives.

City centre of faith The skyline of Jerusalem's old city reveals the hold it has on the hearts of millions. At sunset the rosy light throws into relief the cross atop the church of the Holy Sepulchre; the golden Dome of the Rock glistens as muezzins call the Muslim quarter to prayer; below stand the immense, immutable stones of the Western Wall – remains of the Jews' Second Temple. In the noisy, confused maze of old city streets that divide it into four sectors – Jewish, Muslim, Christian and Armenian – nuns, priests, rabbis and imams hurry past each other to fulfil God's work.

Each faith has jurisdiction over its own religious sites, and, at festival time, Jerusalem swells with millions more devoted pilgrims. But 'the eternal city' bears the scars of such divisions and heightened atmosphere. Though Judaism and Islam meet in Jerusalem, Jew and Arab do not easily converse. It is often said that the meaning of the word Jerusalem is 'City of Peace'. If so, the name is an expression of hope rather than of any kind of reality.

Sects and secrecy The Biblical Good Samaritan has descendants. Six hundred altogether, who live in Holon, south of Tel Aviv, and Nablus, in Samaria, and treat the Torah (the first

five books of the Old Testament) and the Book of Joshua as their scripture. Their first language is Arabic. The Karaites, a separate group who believe in the Torah but reject all later writings, number 15,000. Up in the Galilee are 3,000 Sunni Muslim Circassians. Neither Arab nor Islamic in origin, they maintain an independent identity, even speaking the Circassian language. Elsewhere, over 70,000 Druze populate 22 villages in the north. Little is known about their religion, except that they have a small caste of learned initiates, though the concept of loyalty to the ruling power is one precept.

Israel is also the world centre of the Baha'i faith, a religion of universal love and equality, whose magnificent headquarters are to be found in Haifa.

Christian pilgrims pray at Solomon's Pools, near Bethlehem

Would-be Jews Many non-Jews see Israel as a place of divinity, and seek to live there. One group are the Black Hebrews, African-Americans with a communal, brotherly-love type of creed, who decided to regard themselves as Jewish, came to Israel during the 1970s and set up home in the southern town of Dimona. Since they are not genetically or culturally Jewish, and do not practise Judaism, it is not surprising that their status as Jews is not recognised! Meanwhile in India, a reported 4 million people believe they have a religious connection to the Holy Land.

The many forms of Judaism

Visitors sometimes think that only Hasids (with sidelocks, long black coats and wide black hats) are Jews. Others may realise that these are only the most observant of the orthodox. Few appreciate that even non-religious Jews tend to be observant to a degree – for example, in having sons circumcised.

Judaism comes in many forms, with differences based on attitudes to the Jewish books of law (the Torah), subsequent prophetic writings, the codified oral law and the Talmud (rabbinic commentary). The Orthodox purport to believe that the scriptures were all physically handed down by the Divine already written. Conservative (or Masorti) Jews take the view that the scriptures are divinely inspired, but written by human beings. Reform and Liberal Jews prefer to emphasise Judaism's ethical tenets, seeing the scriptures as inspired but not binding. Some secular Jews adopt a humanist version of Judaism that rejects the authority of the scriptures completely.

■ **Israel works hard and plays hard. The country fairly bursts with *joie de vivre*, the very picture of an energetic, upbeat nation hurtling towards 21st-century success. Eager for income and rewards, Israelis put in long hours and struggle for promotion. But they generally take the view that the real point of life is what money can buy: leisure, pleasure, fun and freedom.** ■

Wanting it all Almost anything you care to name is available in Israel. A combination of enterprise and acquisitiveness has made it the consumer country *par excellence*. Since the early days, the price of imported goods has been sky-high, so Israelis are used to supporting their lifestyle by working ferociously hard. With salaries roughly one third lower than in most western countries, and with the constant tension of war, the population has learned to extract the maximum intensity from every experience. Israelis will not miss an opportunity to enjoy themselves, yet they still manage to be 'up and at it' early next morning.

The working day starts at 7am or 8am and can last till 8pm or later. All the while, the bars and restaurants quench the Israeli thirst for social interaction virtually 24 hours a day. Many Israelis work a six-day week, as set down in Biblical law, resting only on the sabbath (Saturday). Sunday is a regular weekday in Israel, though working on Friday, when the sabbath starts, is increasingly on the way to becoming optional.

Workers' rights Despite the long hours many Israelis put in, the labour union, Histadrut, is powerful and active – indeed it is part of the bedrock of Israeli society. Almost all workers are members, and it takes a cradle-to-grave approach to its role. It runs a vast health insurance scheme, with its own hospitals, as well as offering social and welfare services to its members.

Some question Histadrut's position, and many workers feel obliged to stay within its health scheme when

Israelis are great readers of newspapers – in several languages

they might prefer an alternative. This monolithic organisation, in an apparent possible clash of interests, is also the nation's largest non-government employer. Yet Histadrut has been the strongest ally for both Jewish and Arabic workers since it was established in the 1920s, with formidable leverage. Striking is not uncommon in Israel, but Histadrut has, on the whole, been a positive force in ensuring that wages and working conditions reach a consistently high standard.

Love of life With their free time, Israelis head for the seaside, to the streets, to sportsgrounds, pools, national parks, and picnic places in the country, or to open-air cafés in the cities. On the beaches they swim and play interminable games of

20

beachball and *matkot* – a simple bat and ball game. Israel has a vibrant cultural life, in which opera, theatre and classical concerts are not viewed as elitist or remote but are tremendously popular: Tel Aviv and Haifa are the main cultural centres. Tel Aviv is also the focal point for late-night entertainment, discos and nightclubs. But even people who are not going out anywhere special will spend the evening hours strolling in the open air, meeting and talking.

Speak up! Conversation is easy to strike up in Israel: all you need is split-second eye contact and you're made. People are friendly and outgoing even though sometimes desperately short on politeness and pleasantries. The ease with which people get together is a lesson in human relations. Explanations for this, perhaps, lie in the crowded apartment blocks, the group ethos of schools and institutions, and the universal army experience – a great leveller and dumping ground for

The varied climate even allows for winter sports

prejudices and vanities. The downside is that it is hard to find privacy or peace and quiet. Surprisingly, Israel is a country of erotic encounters, too. Though immodest behaviour is frowned on for people above a certain age, youngsters – who seem to radiate health and energy – have an unashamed physical confidence and are not shy of parading themselves. Coyness is certainly not an Israeli characteristic!

Why stay indoors? The sun is usually shining somewhere in Israel – even in the brief winter, the temperature in the southern city of Eilat is likely to be around 20°C. And when the sun is out in Israel, so are the people. At the end of the day, in the balmy sweet-scented evenings, the balconies of the ubiquitous Israeli apartment blocks are used as informal dining rooms and lounges. Entertainment of every kind is available under the Mediterranean sky – from spontaneous beach parties to classical concerts at ancient amphitheatres, from craft markets to weddings. In this respect, Israelis enjoy a superb quality of life.

■ **Having an opinion is not optional for Israelis – it is inevitable. Passions run high on every side, on every issue. It is often said that Israel is the only democracy in the Middle East. That understates the case. While the rest of the region consists largely of feudal dictatorships, Israel is bursting with debate. Thanks to its system of proportional representation, almost every viewpoint finds expression.** ■

The system The Knesset (literally 'Meeting' or 'Assembly'), the Israeli parliament, takes its name from an ancient Jewish assembly which functioned in Jerusalem in the 5th century BC. Now, as then, there are 120 seats. Proportional representation ensures that any party with at least 1.3 per cent of the vote gains a seat. The result is a bewildering number of political parties. The advantage of the system is that it accurately reflects the diversity of viewpoints in Israeli society. The clear disadvantage is that the need to build coalitions results in the virtual dictatorship of minorities. Elections are held every four years and the leader of the majority party becomes prime minister. Israel also has a president, elected by Knesset members, whose term lasts five years.

Party players Nothing is quite as it seems in Israeli politics. Foreign journalists generally brand the Labour party as left wing and Likud as right. In fact, both are broadly in favour of free enterprise, and both wish to

protect the country's socialist and egalitarian infrastructure. Labour arose from the mainstream, dominant, collectivist forces in the pre-State Zionist movement. Likud was born of the hardline Zionists of the Revisionist breakaway, which considered the mainstream too soft towards the Arabs and the British (see page 44).

Historically Labour is the party of the affluent. Its 'constituency' is the intellectual east-European section of society. Likud garners support from the poorer people, especially of North African and Gulf States communities. Smaller parties cover every religious and philosophical hue – from Communist to far right.

No Israeli government has ever won a full majority. Therefore a succession of coalition deals and mergers has had to be struck between the most unlikely of bedfellows. In the pursuit of peace, Labour can count on the support of a far-right religious party if they ban non-kosher shrimp and lobster imports; a far-left party

Begin, Carter and Sadat at the Camp David peace summit, September 1978

❑ Israel's Arabs have the same voting rights as all other Israelis. Many support the Democratic Arabic Party, which gains about half the Arab votes cast. Hadash (the Communist party) also picks up considerable Arab support. There are around six Arab members of the Knesset. Judaea and Samaria (the West Bank), where most Palestinian Arabs live, are not part of Israel, and its Arab residents vote in Palestinian Authority elections. ❑

❏ Almost all political parties in Israel, including the far left and the peace lobby, are Zionist (that is, they believe Israel should be maintained as a homeland for the Jews). There are also non-Zionist parties and organisations in Israel, some Arab, some religious. They oppose Israel's existence as a Jewish state. ❏

will drop demands for buses to run on the sabbath in order to keep the far right within the peace camp.

Politics and peace Since the birth of modern Israel in 1948, politics has been dominated by the Arab/Israeli conflict. Enormous amounts of energy, and vast sums of money, have been spent on defence, slimming down the budget for everything else. Now, the peace process has freed some of that budget for investment in health, education and industry.

It was so-called 'right-wing' Menachem Begin and Likud who shook hands with President Sadat of Egypt in 1979 and made the first lasting peace treaty. In 1994 Prime Minister Rabin and Labour achieved

Israeli coalition governments involve unlikely alliances

the same with Jordan and instituted limited self-rule for the Palestinians. The bloody fatigue of war has made peace more desirable than ever and trading land for that vision seems to offer a tentative way forward. No-one in Israel expects such cordial arrangements with their Arab neighbours as exist between some European countries. But even if peace simply means 'no war', it would be priceless to almost all Israelis – whatever their political views.

A unique position As the only democracy in an undemocratic and anti-western region, Israel has long been seen by the United States as their 'ally in the desert' (the UK and Europe have tended to see their best interests being served through support for the Arab states). America's 'special relationship' has provided Israel with billions of dollars as a buffer against biting economic sanctions in the form of trade boycotts, arms embargos and diplomatic cold shoulders. The stumbling block to Israel's acceptance has been the Palestinian question. But since the start of Palestinian self-rule, and mutual interests expressed between the west and the Arab Gulf War allies, the possibilities for international *entente* now look more promising.

■ It was a tough battle to bring the nation of Israel into being, and it is a tough battle to prevent it from being destroyed. That is why you will notice that security is tight at all entry points into the country, and that soldiers, both men and women, are a distinct part of everyday life in Israel. Of course, soldiers are inseparable from the very existence of this constantly threatened country. ■

On permanent standby On and off duty, conscripts or professionals, members of the armed forces – the Israel Defence Forces (IDF) – carry their weapons at all times. This can be startling for unsuspecting tourists who have never seen anything like it before. Out of uniform, most of the

Israeli armed forces maintain a watchful but unobtrusive role

conscripts wear jeans, T-shirts and trainers, with an Uzi submachine gun hanging from one shoulder. In uniform, it has been normal for gun-carrying soldiers to travel the country by hitch-hiking (though now, they enjoy free bus travel).

Soldiers are treated with enormous respect and affection by the public. For one thing, and unlike the situation in many other countries, Israelis feel that the army is on their side. In fact, Israel is in one sense just one big army. All boys and all girls join the IDF at the age of 18, complete their term (3 years for men, 2 for women) and effectively remain in the army as reservists until the age of 51 (men) or 24 (women). Reservists have to serve around 30 days a year minimum. Certain occupations are entitled to exemption, and women do not serve if they have children.

The IDF is one of the most highly trained and battle-experienced armies in the world, having endured five wars since 1948. As a spin-off, Israel has become a major weapons manufacturer, a process started when the US imposed an arms embargo on Israel. As a result, Israel started its own arms manufacture and was so successful that it now even sells weapons to the US.

The terror threat High standards of vigilance have kept terrorist incidents down to levels comparable to any other nation, despite the well-publicised intention of certain Arab states (notably Iran and Iraq), guerrilla groups (Islamic Jihad and Hamas) and militias (Hezbullah) to destroy the Israeli state. Another terror threat which

24

Israel has to guard against is that posed by some of its own citizens bent on retaliation: the consequences of an attack by tough-minded settlers on West Bank Arabs could be disastrous. The assassination of Prime Minister Rabin in November 1995 by Yigal Amir, a student opposed to peace with the Palestinians, may herald anti-state terrorism from the unexpected quarter of right-wing Jews.

Security is light throughout the country. The ubiquitous groups of schoolchildren are always accompanied by an armed guard, usually an army reservist and generally a parent of a child in the group. In the past, children were a favourite target for Arab terrorists, but since the armed guards were introduced in the 1970s, there has only been one attack on a school group.

A Jewish army Israeli soldiers are sworn in at Masada (see pages 35 and 242–3), where they vow that 'Masada shall not fall again'. Back in 1973, Golda Meir was asked by a reporter whether Israelis did not have some sort of Masada complex. 'Yes', she said, 'we do. And a pogrom complex, and a Hitler complex'. The point was that Israelis see themselves as having a duty to protect the Jewish people and ensure their survival. The name Israel Defence Force is intended to be taken literally: the military grew out of brigades which stood guard at agricultural settlements, and continues to see itself in that defensive light. Memories of the Holocaust, of the powerlessness of Jews before the creation of the state of Israel, add extra force to the idea of Jews being

armed and able to defend themselves. Even so, there remains, for Israelis and other Jews, something remarkable about the idea of an army of Jews. Despite the ferocity of the Biblical Israelites, Jews came to be regarded, and to regard themselves, as vulnerable and open to attack. Israel, by changing that, has had a profound effect on Jewish psychology.

Jerusalem's Damascus Gate, the main entrance to the Old City

■ Israel has always held an uneasy place in the world community. Many countries were slow to recognise the state of Israel and quick to condemn its handling of the Intifada. It returned to favour after the collapse of the Soviet Union, which had bolstered many anti-Israeli states. Now that peace has been made with old enemies, Israel is on the way to acceptance. ■

The West Bank In the 1980s and early 1990s, Israel was routinely portrayed on news programmes as harrassing, hounding and harming the Palestinians. World media perceptions of Israel using violence against Arab civilians were based on a reality: since 1987, Israeli security forces sought to contain armed and organised resistance to their presence in the West Bank. They also tried to police a chaotic and menacing state of unrest where activists – often hooded teenagers and rock-throwing children – frequently attacked and killed fellow Palestinians.

Serious attacks, including murders, remain commonplace in the West Bank. News stories covering the disturbances tend to dwell on the police or army response, depicting rioters as victims, and shy away from the complex background to these events. On the other hand, it is not just outsiders who find the situation disturbing – most Israelis do too. The latest, risky, approach is to strengthen Fatah, the most moderate power-seeking faction within the PLO – and let them

War relics – abandoned Egyptian tanks in the Negev desert

deal with the unrest, whose root cause is not the occupation of the West Bank, but, as Palestinians put it, 'the occupation of Akko, Haifa and Jaffa'.

Israel and the Arabs Israel came into being in a region which did not want it. Palestine's Arabs fought tooth and nail to prevent the state of Israel being established. The surrounding Arab regimes pledged to destroy the 'Zionist entity', which they have seen as an outpost of western imperialism. From its inception in 1948, right up to 1994 when treaties were signed with former adversaries, the Jewish state has been officially 'at war' with most of the other nations in the Middle East.

Israel was not only threatened with military action, but faced economic war too. The Arab Boycott office in Damascus spent decades co-ordinating a worldwide campaign to pressurise all companies to cease trading with Israel, and to cease trading with any other company which has dealt with Israel. Such boycotts have nevertheless failed to prevent Israel becoming the most economically active country in the Middle East. That fact, and the loss of

U N VW TRANSPORTER

UNDOF-6070

their Soviet support, has tempted Arab states away from their traditional party line, to look instead at ways of making peace with their new, unstoppable neighbour.

Israel and the west In the US, there is a certain amount of warmth towards Israel. For tactical reasons, weighing Israel's presence as a pro western state in a hostile region, and also the electoral and economic importance of the ardently Zionist Jewish lobby, the United States has greatly assisted Israel in holding its ground. Without American support, Israel might well have been destroyed by now.

The European Union has over the years shown favour to the Arab cause – both Britain and France have long-standing links in the Arab world which they think it is in their interest to preserve. The treaty with the PLO, and growing Israeli economic strength, have given the EU countries an excuse to look for ways to make closer ties with Israel, which

The famous handshake: Israeli Prime Minister Rabin and PLO Chairman Arafat make peace in 1993, watched by President Clinton

already does a huge proportion of its trade with European Union countries.

Israel and the Third World Not all Third World and non-aligned states joined the anti-Israel bloc. Latin America, for example, has long had friendly relations with Israel. With the changing political scene, dozens more countries have struck up ties with the Jewish state. For some, there is a chance of tangible benefits. The states in the Organisation of African Unity managed to maintain amicable relations and close contacts with Israel while openly admitting that Russian and Arab pressure had forced them to cut off diplomatic relations. As a result, Israel has given a lot of commercial, cultural and technical assistance to these countries, including aid in the form of freshwater wells, hospitals and medical staff.

■ **Israel looks to be on the verge of another new beginning. With peace accords being put in place, the way may be open at last for the hostilities of the last decades to be swept aside. Freed from preoccupation with self-defence, Israel has boundless plans and potential that could make it an influence for good in the world out of all proportion to its size.** ■

The age of economic miracles Israel is booming. It has one of the fastest-growing economies in the world. Tel Aviv's stock exchange is becoming a focal point for the Middle East sector of the globe. Peace is good for Israel's economy, as is clear from the jump in share prices that followed each treaty-signing. Israel has a silicon valley, a rural heartland, industrial zones, and, out at sea, new sources of oil to explore. Its fashion companies have gained international recognition. The building trade is busy and banking is buzzing. Its medical and scientific research puts it among the world's leaders in those fields. If improving relations with the Arabs attracted massive investment in the early years of the decade, it's also notable that the heightened tensions of the late '90s have not seriously dampened the world's economic hopes in Israel.

Such growth has revolutionised Israeli lifestyles. Where 400 per cent inflation was once the norm, there is now aspirational living – new cars, new homes and two foreign holidays

Eilat and Tel Aviv are developing into major leisure resorts

a year. People still have to work hard six days a week, but the 'can do' attitude, characteristic of the Israelis, is ready to perform.

Israel's expertise Israel has already made its mark as a centre of medical research. It seems that this trend will continue, perhaps enabling Israel to contribute to the well-being of the entire region, including northeast Africa, as well as enhancing medical knowledge throughout the world. On a quite different front, Eilat and Tel Aviv are already world-class centres of entertainment and leisure.

Problems to solve With Arab help, regional problems, such as water shortage, can be tackled. Israel, already building a string of reservoirs to catch rain run-off, has ambitious plans involving the Mediterranean, the Red Sea and the Dead Sea. Peace and co-operation have the power to bring such schemes to fruition and Israelis believe that their neighbours – when they see the benefits that Israel can bring to the region – will drop their opposition and join with them in a better future.

■ The Bible – the world's best-selling book – is essentially the history, cosmology and ethics of the land and people of Israel. Whether you think the main characters are real, symbolic or imaginary – God, Adam and Eve, Noah, Abraham and Moses, right through to Jesus – the basic historical story line is broadly accurate: archaeologists are constantly digging up the evidence. ■

30

The countryside of this tiny nation is sprinkled with the scenes and sites of great events which have made their mark on humanity. And as you travel from place to place, the Bible deserves to be ranked as one of Israel's best guidebooks.

In the beginning The Torah (the Jewish name for the Pentateuch, or the first five books of the Bible) tells the story of the world from Creation up to the Israelite conquest of Canaan, roughly spanning the 20th to the 12th centuries BC. Each part of the narrative is full of information about the peoples of this country, then called Canaan, their beliefs, customs, conflicts and ambitions. As a record of early habitation in the

Pharaoh's army drowns chasing the Israelites through the Red Sea

Middle East, it is an incomparably valuable document the like of which hardly any other nation possesses: the pre-Israelite tribes which lived here in the Late Stone Age and Bronze Age – before and during Abraham's time – are named, and their territories delineated.

The lifestyle and relationships, world view and codes of behaviour of wandering pastoralists in the period at the origins of urbanisation are described in detail. The places where Abraham and the patriarchs and their families pitched their tents are named (and still called by the same names today). The places where they built shrines to the invisible God that Abraham believed in, and the cave which he purchased to bury his wife, are named, their locations described, and their significance known ever since.

The Promised Land
Around 1700 BC, many of the Israelites (more correctly called Hebrews in this pre-Judaic era) made their way to Egypt. The Sinai and Negev are thoroughly described, and their landmarks identified, in the Biblical account of the Exodus, the return from Egypt that took place in about 1250 BC. That adventure is celebrated in the festival of Pessah (Passover). On the way, the Israelites paused at Mount Sinai, where Jewish Law was born,

Top: the Israelites marching in the wilderness. Above: Moses receives the Ten Commandments, the basis of Jewish law

Defending the land In the time of the Book of Judges (the 10th and 11th centuries BC) the Israelites were often at war, notably with the Philistines, who established 'the five cities' on the Israelite shore (later six). These subsequently became known as Philistia: Gaza, Ashkelon, Ashdod, Ekron, Gath and Jaffa. From here they extended their territory across Judah and Galilee, the Israelites unable to defeat them until the era of the Book of Kings (from 1025 BC).

In the reign of King Saul, the shepherd boy David of Bethlehem considerably weakened the Philistines by killing their 'giant' Goliath. In 1006 BC, King Saul was killed fighting the Philistines. He had already chosen David to be his successor.

an event remembered at the festival of Shavuot.

In 1200 BC, Joshua led the Israelites across the Jordan to defeat one local king after another. In places the Israelites failed to secure a victory, but, by and large, the land of Canaan was won. These Children of Israel had only a weak grasp of their forefathers' religion, and frequently took up the local cults of Ba'al and Astarte, which required human sacrifice. Much of the Torah deals with the consolidation of power among the Israelite tribes, and the growing hold of the Jewish ethical code.

The First Temple David's outstanding achievement was to complete the Israelite conquest and bind together the Jewish people. Under him, the Land of Israel stretched from Damascus to the Red Sea. Conquering Jerusalem, the city of the Jebusites, he built a shrine there for the Ark of the Covenant – the gold-encrusted wooden chest containing Moses' tablets of stone, inscribed with the Law, which the Israelites had been carrying around with them for several centuries. Deeming himself, or being deemed by God, unfitted for the task of constructing the Holy Temple as a permanent sanctuary for the Ark, he left this to his son Solomon. In 953 BC King Solomon built the awesome, magnificent Temple on what was to be called Temple Mount, around which much subsequent political and religious history was to revolve.

■ **A new era started under Solomon. The Temple became the focal point of the nation and Jerusalem extended its political authority throughout the country. But it was a land caught between empires, crossed by trade routes, a land coveted by others. That was its strength, in forming the wealth and character of the nation, but its weakness, too, as one great regional power after another laid claim to the Land of Israel. ■**

Fighting for survival Solomon's unified nation did not survive long after his death in 928 BC. A split resulted in two Jewish kingdoms: Israel in the north and Judah in the south. Jerusalem remained the spiritual centre for both until, in the 8th century BC, the northern kingdom came more and more under the influence of Phoenicians, Assyrians and others. The 7th century BC saw a similar trend in Judah, but, in 727 BC, King Hezekiah purified the Temple and vigorously revived Jewish practice. Despite today's Orthodox belief that the Torah (the first five books of the Bible) was given to Moses at Sinai, the text makes plain that it was written in Jerusalem at this time.

Meanwhile, Assyrians conquered the northern kingdom; the mixing of the local Jews (many of whom were taken into slavery) with their colonists created the Samaritan people. Assyria moved on to re-create Philistia, virtually surrounding Judah. However, the Babylonians were also at war with the Assyrians. When they crushed the Assyrians in 630 BC, King Josiah of Judah quickly retook the north. He closed down all places of worship, except for the Temple at Jerusalem, which he purified.

A new Temple The whole of Israel was then conquered by the Babylonians, under Nebuchadnezzar II. In 597 BC, the Jews rebelled against Babylonian rule, but soon lost ground. The Jewish élite and priesthood were exiled to Babylon and, in 587 BC, the Temple was demolished. However, though significant in

religious terms, the Babylonian Exile only lasted 46 years. In 539 BC, the Persians conquered the Babylonian empire and permitted the exiles to return to Jerusalem. They marched back in two stages, one of them under Ezra, who revitalised Judaism and inspired the building of the Second Temple, dedicated in 519 BC. It is likely that the last part of the Torah was written at this time. Jerusalem then enjoyed a renaissance, and was enclosed by new ramparts. However, a new influence was being felt throughout the land: Greek culture.

Hellenisation During the 5th and 4th centuries BC, Hellenistic Greek culture, ideas, gastronomy, religion, architecture and art swept through the Mediterranean and the Middle East. In 333 BC, Alexander the Great, the king of Macedonia, northern Greece, set out to conquer the world. He began by defeating the Persians and setting up the Seleucid dynasty in Damascus to rule the whole region. The Seleucids often had to go to war to defend their territory, and from 312 BC to 198 BC, much of Judaea, including Jerusalem, fell to the rival Egyptian Ptolemaic dynasty.

As soon as the Seleucids had regained their losses in 198 BC, they started to come under pressure from the growing might of a new rival empire – that of Rome. In 175 BC the new Seleucid king, Antiochus IV, set out to replace Temple Judaism with worship of the Greek gods, and he sold off the Temple treasures to pay the debts of his army. An altar to the

33

Top: Babylon conquers Israel
Above: Mattathias slays the priest

wine god Dionysus (also known as Bacchus) was erected in the Temple in their place.

The Maccabees This was too much of a sacrilege for the Hasmoneans, one family of the priestly line, to bear. In 166 BC, the father (Mattathias) and his five sons (including Judah, known as the Maccabee, probably meaning 'the Hammer') killed a Seleucid official and a pagan priest, sparking off war between the Jews and the Seleucids. Mattathias was killed, but Judah continued with the rebellion, which resulted in complete independence for Judaea under Hasmonean rule. The Maccabees purified and rededicated the Temple (an act commemorated by the festival of Hanukka), and Judah's brother, Jonathan, became High Priest, later replaced by his brother Simeon. Yet the power-hungry Hasmonean dynasty proved a disaster for Israel. From 103 to 63 BC, religious traditionalists and their Hellenised neighbours were in open conflict with their Hasmonean rulers. Taking advantage of the chaos, the Romans simply moved in and conquered Judaea.

■ **Five centuries of Roman rule brought dramatic changes of lasting consequence. It was a Messianic age, marked by turmoil, violence and desperation. The Jews were in conflict with their imperial masters, whose repression proved inadequate to break the will of this 'stiff-necked people' (in the words of the Torah). Among the several messiahs who attracted a following, the influence of one was to stand far above the rest: Jesus of Nazareth. By the end, Israel was no longer a Jewish land. ■**

34

Herod In 37 BC, an ambitious, tough-minded half-Jewish friend of Rome, the notorious governor of Galilee, took control of the country. This was Herod, who arrived in Jerusalem at the head of a Roman force to execute the Hasmonean king, Antigonus. Brooking no opposition to his egomaniac rule, he murdered anyone who might stand in his way, including his wife, two of his younger sons, his brother-in-law (Aristobulus III, the last Hasmonean high priest), and, finally, his faithful oldest son, Antipater.

Herod's grandiose building schemes took in palaces and forts, such as Masada and Herodion, whole towns, such as Caesarea, and the reconstruction of the Temple along more Hellenistic lines. There was widespread discontent, murmurings of political rebellion and mass longing for the coming of a 'messiah' (the

Top: Romans at war
Below: Roman Jerusalem's main street, the Cardo

Jewish name for a great liberator or leader). Towards the end of his reign (perhaps in 5 BC, though the exact year is not known), Jesus was born.

Jesus Herod's death, in 4 BC, brought the disintegration of his kingdom, which was divided among his three remaining sons: Herod Antipas, Archelaus and Philip. All faced a popular mood of seething insurrection. According to Matthew's gospel, the family of Jesus fled to Egypt to escape the unrest, later settling in relatively safe Galilee. A messianic teacher, John the Baptist, attracted a big following; Herod Antipas had him executed. Jesus emerged as another possible messiah, urging Jews to remain faithful to Jewish law, while stressing its ethical content and new egalitarian ideas. After three years, he, too, was executed, but his following continued. Meanwhile the Zealots, an underground rebel movement whose members combined religious with political fervour, were preparing for all-out war.

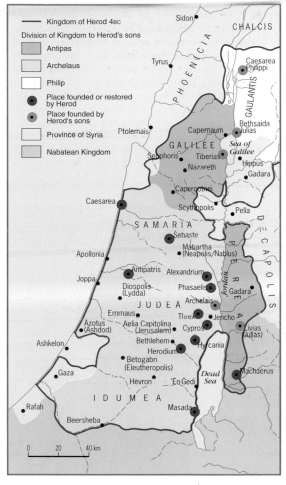

Map legend:

Kingdom of Herod 4BC
Division of Kingdom to Herod's sons
- Antipas
- Archelaus
- Philip
- Place founded or restored by Herod
- Place founded by Herod's sons
- Province of Syria
- Nabatean Kingdom

0   20   40 km

such as Gamla and Jericho. Eventually, in AD 70, Roman troops retook Jerusalem and destroyed the Temple itself. Only the Western Wall survived. Diehard Zealots gathered at Masada, but, facing defeat, they committed mass suicide in AD 73.

The Second Revolt
Roman troops were poured into Palestine, with large new military colonies created on the sites of destroyed towns, such as Nablus, Caesaria and Jerusalem. Yet Jewish life and law continued, even thrived, away from Jerusalem, with Galilee the principal centre. Christianity too was on the rise as St Paul's new universal vision of Christ's message gathered force among the Gentiles, including the Romans.

The First Revolt From AD 44, a succession of brutal Roman procurators were sent to administer the troublesome province, which they named Palaestina, or Palestine. In AD 66, the Zealots made their first attack on a Roman garrison: the soldiers surrendered but were killed anyway.

This was the trigger for a nationwide uprising. In one incident, Roman reinforcements numbering 6,000 soldiers, trapped by Jewish insurgents at Beit Horon, were slaughtered. A number of cities came into the hands of the rebels. Eventually, Rome began to master the situation. Town after town was destroyed, including major centres,

Hadrian became emperor in 117. He prohibited Torah study, circumcision and other Jewish practices. In 132, the Second Revolt erupted. Its leader, known as Bar Kochba (Son of the Star), was acclaimed as a messiah and scored 'miraculous' victories. The Roman response was ferocious. Almost a thousand Jewish towns and villages were wiped out. The Revolt was smashed by 135. Jerusalem was totally reconstructed, and a statue of Hadrian placed on Temple Mount; entry to the city was forbidden to Jews except on just one day a year. The Diaspora began – and would not end until the 20th century.

35

The decline of Jewish Israel was soon matched by the rise of Christian Israel. The new religion had quit its Jewish roots and was spreading fast through the Roman empire, its ideas and credo evolving in the Near East. When the Emperor Constantine granted tolerance to Christianity, huge numbers embraced the faith. The land of Jesus became the Holy Land. It was the start of the Byzantine period – three centuries of piety and pilgrimage, church-building and colonisation. ■

From Rome to Byzantium

Following the Revolts, the Romans allowed the decimated Jews freedom to practise their religion and live by their own laws, but they were only allowed to enter Jerusalem on one day a year – Tisha b'Av, the supposed anniversary of the Temple's destruction; the Jews marked this day by chanting mournful lamentations at the Western Wall (hence the name Wailing Wall). Palestine became increasingly Romanised and Christianised, and when the Emperor Constantine decreed official tolerance for Christianity in AD 313, tens of thousands joined the new creed. In 323, Constantine became sole ruler of the Eastern and Western Empires and made Christianity, in effect, into the state religion. Later the Roman empire split again into eastern and western spheres, and in 379, Byzantium, or Constantinopolis (today's Istanbul), became the capital from which Palestine was ruled.

To be a pilgrim Constantine's own mother, the Empress Helena, came to the Holy Land in 326 to search out relics of Jesus. She found them with surprising ease. As soon as she arrived in the Holy City, the Bishop of Jerusalem showed her the exact spot where, he said, Jesus had been crucified. The burial tomb was immediately at hand, and, close by, some old crucifixes, one of which she clearly identified as the True Cross. Over the site, Helena ordered the vast, splendid Church of the Holy Sepulchre to be built, still the focal

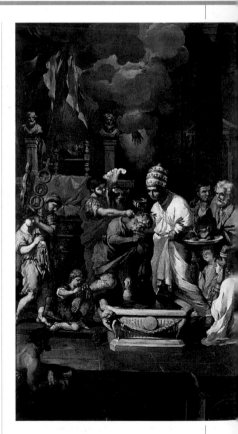

Top: Constantine carries the Cross in battle. Above: his baptism

point of Christian devotion in the city. On the Mount of Olives, she made more discoveries, such as the Garden of Gethsemane, and the place from which Jesus had

ascended into heaven, where another fine church was erected.

Moving on to Bethlehem, Helena at once identified the place where Jesus had been born, and enclosed it within the Church of the Nativity. Travelling through the Holy Land, she located scores more sites which she believed were associated with Jesus. Most were of doubtful authenticity, but that did not deter her from ordering churches to be built or Christians from flocking to see them. Relics of saints' bodies were eagerly sought out and found everywhere. Numerous non-Biblical legends date from this time: that Mary drew water from this well, for example, or that the Archangel Gabriel appeared in that cave.

The beginnings of schism In this early stage, churches became a feature of the land. Christian communities grew around holy places. Jerusalem again grew to be as large as in Herodian times. By the year 450, most people in Palestine were Christian. But the division of empire into east and west mirrored a cultural gulf. Arguments about doctrine and practice shattered the unity of the church.

In 451, the Roman and Eastern churches agreed to differ, and the Patriarchate of Jerusalem became

Constantine made Christianity the Roman state religion

part of the Eastern, or Orthodox, church. In 456, the Monophysite doctrine, that Jesus had a single nature, part human, part divine, was condemned as heresy, the Orthodox view being that Christ had two natures. But large numbers of Christians in Palestine were Monophysite, and this rather academic matter threatened the unity of the Byzantine empire. The Copts and other eastern churches remained Monophysite.

The end of the dream Along with growing discord in the church, there was sporadic unrest among the Jewish population from 484 onwards. When the Persians invaded Palestine in 614, they were aided and advised by disaffected Jews whose complaints had been ignored by the Byzantines. The empire proved too weak to defend Palestine's holy places, and even the True Cross was carried off as booty. Fourteen years later, the Byzantines took on the Persians, this time defeating them and restoring the Cross to the Church of the Holy Sepulchre. But already the end was in sight for the Byzantine Christians. Islam was on the march from Arabia.

■ Islam rose like a whirlwind from the Arabian desert, taking the whole of the Middle East by storm. Islam (literally meaning 'submission') prescribed forcible conversion for pagans. To the Christians and the Jews – 'Peoples of the Book' – Muhammad promised mercy, while replacing their spent, outdated religions with the teachings of the Koran. ■

Muhammad's vision Muhammad, born in Mecca in AD 570, married a wealthy widow and became an influential figure. He took other wives, one of them Jewish, and became interested in religion and ethics. The defeat of the Jews was seen as a lesson; he felt the time was right for a creed that could not be conquered. In 610 he had the first of the 'revelations', which were to be recorded in the Koran. He argued that Arabs, like Jews, were descendants of Abraham, and claimed that his new religion had been revealed to supersede both Judaism and Christianity. Arming his supporters, he compelled the inhabitants of Mecca to adopt his faith in 630. When Muhammad died in 632, his followers set about fulfilling his dreams.

Islam's triumph Islamic forces reached Palestine just two years after the Prophet's death, and they defeated the Byzantines in 638.

Top: Dome of the Rock
Below: Nimrod, the 12th-century Crusader castle

The region was then ruled from Damascus by the Omayyad dynasty, whose leaders bore the title Caliph (literally, successor – ie successor to Muhammad). In Jerusalem (which the Arabs called Aelia, the Roman name) Caliph Omar went to Temple Mount to pray at the rock where Abraham had supposedly placed his son for sacrifice. He toured the Holy Land, his followers claiming for Islam each place where he prayed. He refused to pray at the Church of the Holy Sepulchre, so that it would remain a Christian shrine. The next caliph, Abd el-Malik, wanted to establish a place of pilgrimage within his own domain. He declared Temple Mount was 'the far distant place of worship' to which Muhammad flew in a dream, according to the Koran, and he built the Dome of the Rock on top of the Mount in around AD 700. Aelia was then renamed Beit al-Makds (from Beit HaMikdash, the Hebrew name of the Temple), later abbreviated to Al-Kds. Abd el-Malik's son, Al-Walid, converted another church on the Temple Mount site into the El-Aksa mosque.

Violence and chaos In 750 the Abbasids succeeded the Omayyads and gradually lost control of Palestine, which they ruled from distant Baghdad. For a century Turkish warlords vied for mastery of the region. Christians were attacked, and the Holy Sepulchre set on fire, but later repaired. Around AD 977, the brutal Fatimid dynasty, based in Egypt, took over. Between 1004 and 1021, their caliph Al-Hakim (the Mad) destroyed almost all Palestine's churches. In 1055 the Fatimids were overrun by the equally savage Seljuk Turks. Christian pilgrims were murdered when visiting holy sites.

The Crusades Full of naïve zeal, thousands of Christian soldiers (mainly young noblemen) set off in waves from western Europe to 'save' Palestine's holy places. The First Crusade of 20,000 men entered Jerusalem on 15 July 1099 and massacred the entire population. On Christmas Day, 1100, Baldwin I was crowned King of Jerusalem. Meeting no resistance, they conquered more of Palestine, built fortified churches and castles, and discovered countless dubious saintly relics and holy places. Military monastic orders came into being, notably the Knights Hospitallers and the Templars.

The Second Crusade arrived in 1147. Now a powerful Muslim opponent emerged: Salah ed-Din, the Egyptian sultan. In 1187, at the Horns of Hittim, Salah ed-Din and his army encountered a vast force of Crusaders and slaughtered them. Almost at once, the Crusader kingdom collapsed, though Soldiers of the Cross continued to arrive (with

Christian captives suffer the vengeance of the mighty sultan Salah ed-Din

the Third Crusade of 1189, the Fourth of 1202, the Fifth of 1228 and the Sixth of 1248), achieving brief victories and making a new 'capital' at Akko (Acre). In 1261, the Mamelukes, under Sultan Baibars, rode in. These terrifying master horsemen and swordsmen, blood-thirsty former slaves, were to rule for two centuries. They made brisk work of the Europeans. In 1270 the final Crusade arrived and was massacred.

■ **The Mamelukes ruled Palestine for two centuries, and the Ottomans for four. This lengthy period was marked chiefly by the absence of any progress. While the Mamelukes were noted for anarchy and turbulence, the Ottomans imposed a regime of suffocating stability. As an obscure Ottoman province, Palestine went into steady decline.** ■

40

Mamelukes The Mamelukes were freed slaves of the Egyptians, mostly of Circassian origin, and they failed to establish any cohesive government in Palestine. Nevertheless, they constructed fine buildings, some of which still stand to this day. At the end of their period of rule, an Islamic defeat on the other side of the Mediterranean began to send out ripples that would last for centuries: tens of thousands of Jews, expelled from Spain by the Christian conquerors in 1492, began making their way back to Palestine.

Turkish rule The Crusader period was a disaster for the Holy Land and for Christendom. The Crusader attack on Constantinople so weakened it that Sultan Osman would soon be able to add this remnant of the Byzantine empire to his own massive Ottoman empire. The Ottoman Sultan Selim next defeated the Mamelukes in 1517 to gain the Holy Land, and Palestine was once again ruled from Constantinople, now renamed Istanbul. The famous flowering of the Ottoman period all took place at the start. Selim's son, Suleiman (the Magnificent) did much to improve Jerusalem, in particular repairing and restoring its ramparts. The majestic city walls that stand today are principally his work.

Top: Akko, the once-mighty fortress town revived under Ottoman rule
Above: Suleiman the Magnificent

Thereafter, Ottoman rule was characterised by benign neglect. The population divided into small local clans and fiefdoms, often caught up in insoluble feuds. Exceptions to the general decline were the rebuilding of Galilean towns (notably Akko) by the Druze Emir ed-Din in the mid-17th century, the late-18th-century rise to power of Ahmed el-Jazzar (the Butcher) in Galilee, and the brief early-19th-century takeover of Palestine by Egyptian pashas. Then, in the 1870s, to the surprise of all, large numbers of East European Jews started to arrive.

ISRAEL WAS *Zionist*

■ In the 1880s, the destiny of Palestine was being decided by events in Poland and Russia. The reigns of Tsar Alexander III (1881–94) and his son Tsar Nicholas II (1894–1917) were marked by repressive anti-Jewish legislation and a succession of vicious pogroms. These added fuel to the new Zionist movement, which was calling for a return to the Jewish homeland. ■

The First Aliyah Aliyah means 'ascent', and that is how Jews speak of going to live in Israel. From 1850 to 1880, some 20,000 had come to live in Palestine. This was followed in 1882 to 1903, by the first organised mass immigration, driven by religious and political ideals. It brought 25,000 settlers, almost all fleeing Russian pogroms. The settlers' enthusiastic desire to farm and 'redeem' the land often petered out as they ran into serious difficulties, many reaching starvation point or dying of disease. Several settlements were bailed out by well-to-do western Jews, who also contributed large sums for the purchase of land.

The Second Aliyah In Europe, Theodor Herzl's influential book *The Jewish State* was published in 1896, and the First Zionist Conference, held the following year, announced plans to create a Jewish home in Palestine. The Jewish National Fund was founded to buy land for settlements.

A new type of immigrant also began to appear on the scene. Many Russian Jews had been involved in the attempted revolution of 1905; with its failure, and the subsequent pogroms, these hard-headed socialists embraced the dream of creating a Jewish nation in the ancient homeland. From 1904 to 1914, some 40,000 of them settled in Palestine, founding farm collectives and small towns. Arab opposition numbered among the problems they faced, but these Halutzim (pioneers), as they are still known, seemed undeterred by any obstacle. To rousing songs in Hebrew, they took on the Hula swamp, Judaean desert and coastal dunes. They founded the city of Tel Aviv and set up a network of armed groups (Hashomer) to protect themselves.

Above and below:
Zionist pioneers

■ **As the Second Aliyah ended, the Turks were drawn into World War I – on the losing side. It was to cost them Palestine. The arrival of endless streams of Jewish refugees seemed, perhaps, the least important of anyone's concerns. From the end of the World War I to the end of World War II, Palestine was in British hands. They were to discover that the Jewish return to Israel was unstoppable. ■**

Diplomacy and deception In 1914, the Turks joined the war on Germany's side, a decision that was later to give the Allies, in victory, an opportunity to exert greater influence in the Near East. Britain was eager for a role in the Arab world. Behind the scenes, a leading Zionist, Chaim Weizmann, a persuasive diplomat as well as a distinguished scientist, was visiting people of influence in the western world to win international support for a Jewish homeland in Palestine.

Thanks to his efforts, the British foreign secretary, A J Balfour, wrote a letter (the famous Balfour Declaration of 1917) guaranteeing British sup-

General Allenby, head of the British forces

port – against the wishes of many other British politicians. In the very same year, British forces moved into Palestine, seizing it with ease from the Turks. A dignified and emotional General Allenby entered the Old City of Jerusalem on foot and announced the start of British rule.

Zionism on the march 1920 was a busy year. In the aftermath of the war, Palestine (on both sides of the Jordan) came under British Mandate on behalf of the League of Nations. At the same moment the Third Aliyah (1919–23) began, bringing 40,000 youthful Zionist activists from eastern Europe (this Aliyah, the first to be given advance training, had a dramatic effect on farming). Within weeks, the Hashomer defence volunteers regrouped to form Haganah, an underground army whose aim was to protect the Jews of Palestine. In the same year, the first collectives of the new kibbutz and moshav movements (see page 174) were established, the

Palestinian rebels

labour union Histadrut was founded (and remains part of the bedrock of Israeli society), and Hebrew was declared the official language of the Yishuv (Jews living in Palestine). Suddenly, the country's 700,000 Arabs realised the possible consequences of Zionism.

Attack and defence 1920 was also the year of the first big anti-Jewish riots. Worse followed in 1921, in two outbreaks which left 79 Jews and 48 Arabs dead. 1924 brought the Fourth Aliyah (1924–26) and another 80,000 Jews arrived, mainly Polish artisans and small businessmen, quickening the pace of urban development. The ports grew, Tel Aviv expanded, Haifa's Technion research institute opened in 1924 and the Hebrew University at Jerusalem in 1925. Arab fury erupted again in 1929 and left 133 Jews dead, with the destruction of the ancient Hebron community

The decade of the Fifth Aliyah (1931–40) – the flight from Nazism –

Top : Yad Vashem Holocaust memorial. Below: British law enforcement

brought 180,000 newcomers. The 1929 massacres had led to a split in Haganah, which had failed in its aim of protecting the Jews. The more hardline Irgun was born – its objective to meet opponents head on. 1936 saw a change in the Arab side too with the start of the Arab Revolt against both the Jews and the British. Within two years, 415 Jews had been murdered. To appease the Arabs, the British agreed to curtail Jewish immigration. At the same time, they were attempting to appease Hitler. Both proved to be blind alleys.

Holocaust The Fifth Aliyah ended with two years of 'restricted immigration' (1939–40), when 15,000 arrived clandestinely, aided by the secret Aliyah Bet group. In Europe the Nazi conquest had begun, and the Jewish extermination plan was ready to start. Some Jews could see what was coming. The Sixth Aliyah (1941–47) brought those frantic to escape the Holocaust and the few who survived.

Throughout the war, the British held the doors of Palestine firmly closed to 'unauthorised immigrants'. They came anyway: 20,000 were detained as they set foot in Palestine. Most were returned to Europe, via detention centres. In a notorious incident in 1947, the ship *Exodus*, with 4,554 camp survivors crammed on board, reached the coast of Israel. British ships took them all back to Europe, forcibly disembarking them at Hamburg. This was the last year of British rule in Palestine.

■ **Zionist emotion ran high before World War II, due to the trauma of Nazism. The movement split on whether or not to help the British war effort against the Germans. Both viewpoints had their day. When World War II was won, the Zionists reunited for a last push against the British, who packed their bags and quit Palestine in 1948. After just 50 years of determination, Israel was reborn.** ■

44

Friends and enemies Palestine's Jews were incensed by the British White Paper of May 1939 proposing that the Balfour Declaration be ditched and Jewish immigration halted. The Irgun decided that the time had come to use guerrilla tactics against the British. But the outbreak of war with Germany changed all that. The Arabs threw in their lot with the Nazis. David Ben-Gurion spoke for both Haganah and Irgun when he said: 'We shall fight the White Paper as if there were no War, and we shall fight the War as if there were no White Paper'. Not all agreed, however. The Irgun breakaway group, Lehi (the Stern Gang), vowed to fight the British even during the war.

Fighting the British With Germany's defeat in 1945, Irgun rejoined Lehi in its battle. The British headquarters, at the King David Hotel, was blown up. Irgun prisoners were daringly freed from Akko's fortress prison. The British took the Jewish homeland issue to the United Nations (UN), and on 29 November 1947, the UN voted to partition Palestine (west of the Jordan) into Jewish and Arab areas. Jews would have small unconnected zones in Galilee, on the coast and in the Negev. It looked unworkable even on paper. The Zionists agreed, since

David Ben-Gurion declares the founding of Israel

anything was better than nothing. The Arabs rejected it. Their intransigence worked to the Jews' advantage.

Proclaiming a state The day after the UN vote, the Arabs began a rampage of violence which flared into full-scale civil war. By April 1948 Haganah held territory that included the coast, western Jerusalem, the Negev and Galilee. On 14 May 1948, at Tel Aviv, David Ben-Gurion, Israel's first prime minister, proclaimed the founding of the State of Israel with the words: 'In the Land of Israel the Jewish people came into being'. Behind him hung Herzl's portrait. Chaim Weizmann became president. It seemed a triumphant moment, but the Jews fearfully awaited the Arab world's response.

War and peace On 15 May 1948, the massed military might of Jordan, Egypt, Iraq, Syria and Lebanon rolled to crush the newborn 'Zionist entity'. Israel emerged the victor, as it did in 1956 (when Egypt closed the Red Sea to Israeli ships), 1967 (when, repulsing an attack by Syria, Jordan and Egypt, Israel gained Sinai, Judaea and Samaria, Golan, Gaza and east Jerusalem over a six-day period) and 1973 (Yom Kippur, when Syria and Egypt attacked Israel on its principal day of prayer and fasting).

Egypt decided to make peace, signing the Camp David Treaty in 1978. Harder to deal with was terrorism. The

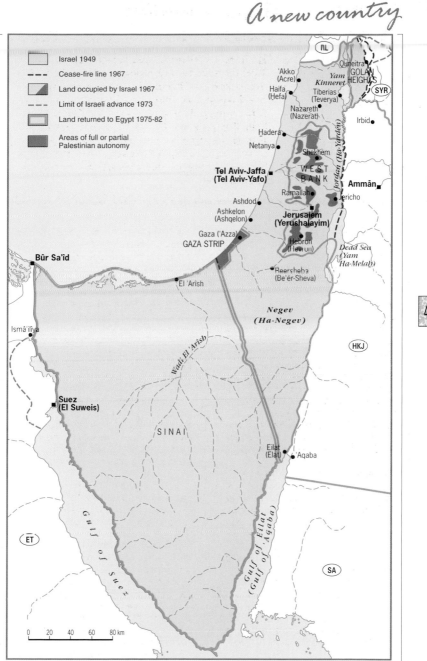

Israel 1949

Cease-fire line 1967

Land occupied by Israel 1967

Limit of Israeli advance 1973

Land returned to Egypt 1975-82

Areas of full or partial Palestinian autonomy

'Akko (Acre)
Haifa (Hefa)
Nazareth (Nazerat)
Hadera
Netanya
Tel Aviv-Jaffa (Tel Aviv-Yafo)
Ashdod
Ashkelon (Ashqelon)
Gaza ('Azza)
GAZA STRIP
Shekhem
WEST BANK
Ramallah
Jerusalem (Yerushalayim)
Hebron (Hevron)
Beersheba (Be'er-Sheva)
Jericho
Ammân
Irbid
Yam Kinneret
Tiberias (Teverya)
Quneitra
GOLAN HEIGHTS
Jordan (Ha-Yarden)
Dead Sea (Yam Ha-Melah)

Bûr Sa'id
El 'Arish
Ismâ'iliya
Suez (El Suweis)
SINAI
Wadi El 'Arish
Negev (Ha-Negev)
Eilat (Elat)
Aqaba
Gulf of Suez
Gulf of Eilat (Gulf of Aqaba)

NL
SYR
HKJ
ET
SA

45

0   20   40   60   80 km

Palestine Liberation Organisation (PLO), founded in 1964, scored demoralising blows, such as the murder of Israelis at the 1972 Munich Olympics. Similarly, the Intifada (popular uprising), in 1987, proved indomitable. Then, in 1993, Israel signed a peace treaty with the PLO, sealed with Rabin and Arafat's famous handshake on the White House lawn. In 1994, Jordan also made peace with Israel. Other former enemies of Israel signalled that they too would at last like to sign away the bitter past.

JERUSALEM

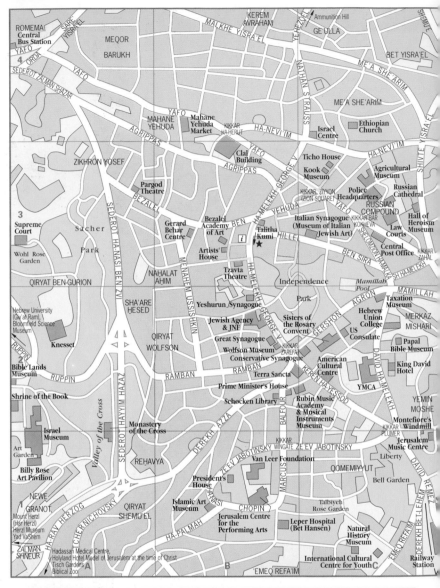

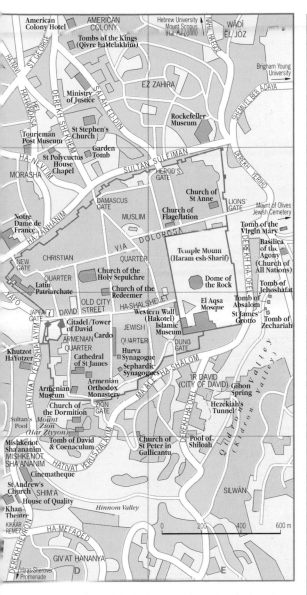

Jerusalem (Hebrew: Yerushalayim; Arabic: El-Kuds)
Highway 1 climbs gradually into the hills of Judaea and up to the city of Jerusalem. This is the way that most people arrive, in a taxi or a hire car. When, at last, the city-entrance sign is reached, it makes the town look just like any other. No brilliant light radiates from the earth at this point. The sign is not encrusted with gold or jewels. Yet there is, without doubt, something magical about the name of Jerusalem. The fact that so many people, through the centuries, have yearned for this city – the fact that it became a metaphor for heaven, for the kingdom of God on earth, for a return to the Promised Land – this cannot fail to affect anyone who arrives here today.

JERUSALEM

48

*The Old City from the
Mount of Olives*

Culture collision In Jerusalem, Israel meets Arabia;
West meets East. Behind the scenes, battles rage on
diplomatic, economic and political fronts for full legal title
to the city. However, the conflict of interests is barely
apparent to outsiders, and visitors are warmly welcomed
nearly everywhere. The intensely Arab character of parts
of the city creates an exotic atmosphere that adds another dimension to Israel's otherwise overwhelmingly
Jewish capital. In the Muslim and Christian quarters of
the walled Old City, and in East Jerusalem just outside
the walls, Arab culture powerfully predominates. To wander through the *souks*, assailed by spicy aromas and
numerous invitations to buy – or at least to look at the
merchandise – is to plunge straight into the midst of the
Orient. It's a reminder, perhaps, that Abraham himself
was father of both the Jews and the Arabs and arrived
here from the east.

Ancient capital Archaeology and the Bible concur in saying that Jerusalem, as capital of the Jews, was built by
King David about 1004 BC. His original city covered a ridge
of land encircled to the south by the valleys of the Kidron
and Hinnom rivers, an area now outside the city walls.
This was not virgin land, however, and a Jebusite city-
state already existed here, on a site that had been inhabited since 3500 BC. Egyptian texts of 1900 BC call it

Urushamem. In the Book of Genesis (chapter 14) it is called Salem, the place where (in about 1900 BC) Abraham visited Melchizedek. Centuries later the Jews returned to the city, led by David (II Samuel 4), who purchased a threshing floor (II Samuel 24) as the site on which his son, King Solomon, was to erect the Temple.

A time of war Although the Israelites were to become divided, Jerusalem, with its Temple, was to remain their capital ever afterwards. Over the millennia, the city walls were built, knocked down and rebuilt again, sometimes along a different course. The city suffered conquest, destruction and oppression (with episodes of Jewish independence in between) at the hands of half a dozen imperial powers and over a period of history that stretched from the Babylonians to the British (see side panel). Most of these conquering civilisations have waxed and waned; their day is over. Despite their efforts to take and hold Jerusalem, despite competing claims upon the city's holy sites, despite being divided in two (from 1948 to 1967), the city's identity as an 'Eternal City', and capital of the people of Israel, has survived.

City of faith Yet Jerusalem is a city of other peoples, too. The city witnessed events that lie near the heart of millions of believers worldwide – Jewish, Christian and Muslim. The finest landmark in the Old City is an Islamic mosque, the glorious Dome of the Rock, covering the Holy Rock – the very same rock that marks the site of the Jewish Temple's Holy of Holies (the sanctuary containing the Ark of the Covenant) – and from which, some Muslims believe, Muhammad flew to meet God on a winged horse. The spires and domes of scores of churches pierce the skyline, chief among them being the Holy Sepulchre, enshrining the place where, Christians believe, Jesus died on the cross and then rose again.

New and old There is more to Jerusalem than the Old City at its centre. The East and West Jerusalem neighbourhoods have, for the most part, sprung up in the last 100 years. West Jerusalem is dynamic and teeming with energy. For most residents, and for many visitors, this is the 'real' Jerusalem, the Jerusalem of today, while the Old City, within its magnificent cordon of ramparts, serves as an evocative reminder of the city's origins in the unfathomable past.

Orientation The walled Old City, focal point for most visitors, lies close to Jerusalem's eastern edge. The Old City is informally divided into four quarters – Muslim, Christian, Armenian and Jewish. To the east of it rises the Mount of Olives. Just north of the Old City walls lies the mainly Arab neighbourhood known as East Jerusalem, though further north are extensive Jewish residential areas which technically are also part of the eastern section. The majority of the city, extending westward, is known as West Jerusalem or New Jerusalem. Consisting of dozens of more or less modern neighbourhoods, this part is almost entirely Jewish. Jerusalem's city centre is around Zion Square, a short distance west of the Old City.

Occupied territory
Though the people of Israel have regarded Jerusalem as their capital since 1004 BC, the city has been under foreign occupation for much of history. Despite the ferocious attacks made upon it, the city has shown remarkable powers of survival. The foreign conquerors of Jerusalem were the Babylonians (587 BC), the Egyptians (320–198 BC), the Seleucids (198–167 BC), the Romans and Byzantines (37 BC–AD 638), the Arabs (638–1099), the Crusaders (1099–1187), the Mamelukes (1260–1517), the Turks (1517–1917), the British (1917–48), and the Jordanians (1948–67).

49

Littered highway
Alongside Highway 1, on both sides of the road, are the burned out wrecks of cars and trucks that once plied from Tel Aviv and Jerusalem, keeping the route open and bringing supplies to the besieged Jews of Jerusalem during the 1948 War of Independence. To reach the city, they had to cross Arab-held territory, and were bombarded all the way. Vehicles that didn't make it were never cleared away – just pushed to the side of the road as a memorial.

Walk On the City Walls

Turreted ramparts of golden stone enclose the Old City. Built by Suleiman the Magnificent in the 16th century, they stand on top of 2,000-year-old ruins. Part of the walkway, from the Damascus Gate to the Dung Gate (the Muslim quarter), is presently closed for security reasons. The rest is reached in two sections, both starting at the Jaffa Gate (entrance fee). *Allow 3 hours.*

The towers of the Citadel dominate the west of the city

Jerusalem's walls are the legacy of Suleiman the Magnificent

Jaffa Gate to Damascus Gate (note: women should not do this walk unaccompanied). A wide stone walkway, skirting the Christian quarter, at first passes by the battlements that peep on to busy West Jerusalem. It then turns a series of corners into the Arab side of town. Below, on the city side, gardens, a school and the dome of a mosque are passed. The tall spire of the **Franciscan church of St Saviour**

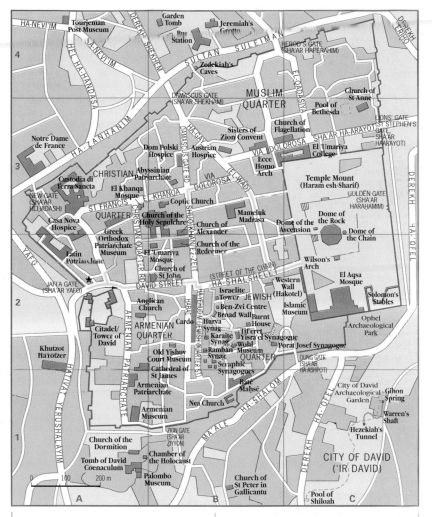

stays in view. Steps take the path up and down, and over the 19th-century **New Gate** (possible exit here). The path then narrows. Suddenly, ahead, the golden **Dome of the Rock** (see page 72) rises spectacularly above the grey roofs. The path then enters the chambers over the fortified **Damascus Gate,** built in the 16th century. Below, the streets throng with Arab crowds and a wonderful view sweeps over the Old City. Take the same route back.

Jaffa Gate to Dung Gate The footway, reached by metal steps beside the Citadel, goes between high walls, with views into the **Armenian quarter,** where no housing abuts the wall.

At the **southwest tower,** the view extends over stony Judaean hills to the south. Turning here, the wall passes a few dwellings and lush gardens belonging to the Armenian Patriarchate. The Dome of the Rock comes into view. The walk now crosses the splendid 16th-century **Zion Gate,** and reaches the **Jewish quarter.** Narrow steps go down to a wider path looking onto a little Old City **archaeological park.** Here the ramparts run along the side of a hill looking over a poor Arab district to barren hills beyond, with a good view to Temple Mount and the Mount of Olives. The path now descends to the road, with no further access to the rampart walk.

■ **The gateways which enter the Old City tell as much of Jerusalem's story as the walls themselves. From the simple New Gate to the imposing fortifications of Zion Gate, from the sealed and silent Golden Gate to the thronging Jaffa or Damascus Gates, the city's complex character is reflected in its handsome, historic entrances. ■**

Hole in the wall
The hole that was knocked through the fortifications beside the Jaffa Gate was made by the Ottomans in 1898 to allow Kaiser Wilhelm II to drive through without having to leave his carriage. Contrast the Kaiser with the more respectful General Allenby, who, when taking the city for the British, dismounted from his horse and came through on foot, pausing at the gate to say 'We return to you'.

Jaffa Gate Forming the main entrance to the Old City from West Jerusalem, this magnificently fortified gateway (built in 1588) is the best known to visitors and the most used by residents. Unfortunately, the Ottomans knocked a road through the fortifications beside the gate (see side panel). The original pedestrian entrance turns a couple of sharp corners within the gateway to deter attackers. Jaffa is one of the oldest of the city gates, protected by the might of Herod's citadel (or David's Tower) rising beside it. The gate opens directly on to David Street, which leads to the Street of the Chain – the Old City's colourful main thoroughfare – marking the boundary between the Armenian and Christian quarters.

Zion Gate This superb fortification of 1540 marks the line between the Armenian and Jewish quarters. The road passing through it forms the main access to West Jerusalem on the south side of the city walls, and is much used by residents of the Jewish quarter. It was through this gate that the quarter's residents were driven out of the city by the Jordanians in 1948. The gateway was then sealed, and remained so until 1967, when the Jews returned.

Dung Gate This historic gateway, close to the Western Walls, built in 1540 on the site of an older gateway mentioned in the Bible, is the closest to the Western Wall and originally gave access to the Temple. It stands between the Jewish quarter and an Arab district outside the walls, and is therefore subject to security measures, though it is much used by buses, whose terminus is just inside the gate.

Jaffa Gate, most splendid of the entrances into The Old City

Golden Gate Blocked up by the Muslims in 1530 to protect their holy sites, this gateway gives access to the Temple Mount from the Mount of Olives and the Kidron Valley. Christians say that this is the gateway through which Jesus rode on a donkey on Palm Sunday. Some Jews assert that a messiah will one day enter the city through this gate, or that it will be reopened on Judgement Day. Both groups attach much significance to the enigmatic passage in Ezekiel which says that the gate will be shut because God has passed through it, and will in future only be used by the prince.

Lions', or St Stephen's, Gate The only gateway on the eastern wall (apart from the Golden Gate, see opposite), this guards the main route from the Old City to the Mount of Olives, and forms the principal connection between the Muslim quarter and the Arab neighbourhoods to the east and southeast. The gate was built in 1538 on the site of a Roman gateway, and various Christian legends attach to it, including one that says that St Stephen was led through this gate, to be stoned to death (however, this story, and the name St Stephen's Gate, were originally attached to the Damascus Gate). Another claims that the Virgin Mary was both born and buried beside it. The name comes from the charming stone lions on the walls to either side of the entrance.

Herod's Gate or Gate of Flowers Having nothing at all to do with either Herod or flowers, this 16th-century gate opens from the Muslim quarter into the heart of East Jerusalem

Damascus, or Shechem, Gate Superbly fortified, the turreted main entrance to the Old City from East Jerusalem is exotic and fascinating. On the plaza in front, vendors hawk their wares to a bustling Arab crowd. Constructed by Suleiman the Magnificent in 1530, the gateway separates the Muslim and Christian quarters. The present gate was built in 1537, and the Crusader-period and Roman remains upon which it stands are still visible. There is also a Roman courtyard just within the gateway.

New Gate Correctly named, this simple opening into the Christian quarter at the northwestern corner of the ramparts was made in 1887, closed during the Jordanian occupation and reopened in 1967.

Divine writing
Pious Orthodox Jews claim to believe that a *mezuzah* (doorpost scroll) hidden within the Jaffa Gate masonry was written by God himself.

Above: Herod's Gate
Below: the Lions' Gate

■ The square kilometre of land which makes up the Old City of Jerusalem is packed with 20,000 residents of varied faiths and backgrounds. As is normal in the Middle and Near East, different communities live in different areas. Although there are no physical barriers between the Old City's four quarters (and at times their borders do change), in atmosphere and culture the dividing lines between them could hardly be plainer. ■

Armenian memories
The Armenian Museum, in Armenian Patriarchate Street (*open* Mon to Sat, 10–5) contains displays of Armenian art and artefacts, and documents relating to the destruction of the Armenian people. 24 April is the Armenians' Remembrance Day, in honour of the 1.5 million Armenians killed by the Turks during their campaign of genocide, which was carried out between 1894 and 1920.

Intimate moments in the Jewish quarter

The Christian quarter The calm, quiet streets and lanes of the northwestern sector are home to thousands of Arab and European Christians. The area contains many hospices and the large, grandiose buildings of the offices, churches and patriarchates of several sects, clustered around the Holy Sepulchre.

The Armenian quarter Although Armenians are Christians, they have their own separate quarter in the southwestern corner of the Old City. The atmosphere is extremely tranquil, with an almost secretive air, the area's institutions and dwellings concealed behind high walls. Although the place seems virtually uninhabited, thousands of Armenians live here, over 1,000 of them in a single converted hostel. Apart from the Zion Gate, which it shares with the Jewish quarter, the Armenian district has no city gate of its own. On the city walls as they pass around the Armenian quarter, maps and notices recall massacres of the Armenians at the hands of the Turks in the 25 years leading up to 1920, giving details of locations, dates and the number of dead. Armenians feel bitter that the world has taken no interest in these events.

The Jewish quarter The Jewish quarter, lying south of the Street of the Chain, is the smallest and most attractive of the city's districts, and it has a distinctively sedate atmosphere. There are even signs requesting visitors not

מוזיאון חצר הישוב הישן
OLD YISHUV COURT MUSEUM

شارع القديس يعقوب
ST. JAMES RD.

to make too much noise. It is clean and new-looking, partly because the entire district had to be rebuilt from scratch after 1967: during their occupation of the Old City (1948–67), the Jordanians destroyed this neighbourhood and attempted to erase all traces of Jewishness. Most of the quarter's ancient buildings were reduced to rubble, though often the ground floors escaped, and some of the ruins have since been beautifully restored. Behaviour in these streets is decorous, and the children playing are not in the least menacing – as they sometimes can be in other parts of town. Although densely populated, the narrow winding lanes often seem deserted. The quarter's centre is the pleasant Hurva Square plaza.

The Muslim quarter By far the largest district, and the most characterful of the Old City, the Muslim area embraces the north and centre of the walled city. It is a confusing and densely populated warren of sometimes squalid lanes and bustling *souks* (markets), exotic and colourful. Arab crowds in flowing traditional dress throng the narrow streets and oriental music fills the air.

What's in a name?
The name Jerusalem comes from the Hebrew Biblical name of the city, Yerushalayim. It is often said that the name means City of Peace *(shalayim* resembling *shalom,* peace), but it is more likely to derive from Salem, the name of the Jebusite settlement that was here before the Israelites arrived. David called his fortress Zion, and this became an alternative poetic name for the city. The Romans called it Aelia Capitolina. Islamic conquerors turned this into Ilya. Muslim Jerusalem became El-Kuds (the Holy). Throughout, Jews continued to call the city Yerushalayim (the name is used in the Old Testament over 700 times), and this again became the official name of the city in 1948.

55

Left: Muslim-quarter souk (market). Below: quiet lanes thread the Jewish quarter

Walk The Old City (*for map see page 51*)

Within the walls, Jerusalem assails the mind with a dizzying blend of sights, sounds and historic sites. Along busy lanes, shops hawk anything from souvenirs to spices, sandals to silver. East and West mingle freely, natives and tourists together, imams and rabbis and priests, until you are no longer sure which is which. *Allow a full day.*

Start at the **Jaffa Gate**►►► (see page 52), the superb fortified entrance to the Old City (tourist office here). Beside it is Herod's vast Citadel, or the **Tower of David**►►► (see page 66). Go straight ahead on David Street, a narrow hectic Arab and Jewish *souk* (market). At a T-junction, turn right (Jewish Quarter Street) for the **Cardo**►► (see page 58), the Byzantine city's main street. At the end, turn left (Beit El Street) to enter the Jewish quarter's quiet lanes. Pass the **Four Sephardic Synagogues**►► (see page 63) and come to **Hurva Square**►► (see page 68). Around it are many things worth seeing – the **Ramban**► (see page 69), **Hurva**►► (see page 68) and **Karaite**► synagogues, and the **Wohl Museum**►► (see page 80).

Across the square, take Tifret Yisrael Street and Plugat HaKotel Street, following the city limits of 2,000 years ago, and pass the **Broad Wall**► (see page 57), remnant of former ramparts. Turn right along the hectic, covered Street of the Chain. Walk to the entrance of **Temple Mount**►►► (see page 72). If it is before 3pm, go in and visit the **Dome of the Rock**►►► and El

Through Jaffa Gate, the main entrance to the Old City

Aksa Mosque►►► (for both see page 72). A few paces back along the Street of the Chain, steps (on the left) twist down to the tunnel which leads to the **Western Wall**►►► (see page 78).

Return via the tunnel to El-Wad Street. At a turning on the left, join the **Via Dolorosa**►►► (see page 76), which climbs in steps back into the *souk* district, passing the Stations of the Cross emblazoned on the walls in Roman numerals. These lead to the **Holy Sepulchre**►►► (see page 60). From here, continue up Souk ed-Dabbagha, cross into St George Street and return to the Jaffa Gate.

Strolling in the souk (market)

The Old City

▶ **Batei Mahaseh (Shelter Houses) Square** _51B1_

Entered through a gate, this attractive little plaza was a main square of the Jewish quarter in the 19th century. It is enclosed on one side by the Rothschilds' almshouse-like dwellings known as Batei Mahaseh, which provided shelter and temporary accommodation for newly arrived Jews from Europe. A memorial reminds visitors that it was in this square that the Jews of Jerusalem were gathered with their possessions in 1948 when the Jordanians captured the city. The square was then largely destroyed. Beside the Rothschild building, steps lead down, through a door, to the ruined subterranean apse of the Nea Church, built in AD 543 and once among the most splendid and best-known churches in Christendom.

▶ **Broad Wall** _51B2_

Plugat HaKotel Street

Just off the Cardo, this is a length of massive, ancient stonework exposed to view. It was constructed about 800 BC to protect Jerusalem from a Syrian attack, as referred to in Isaiah 22: 10–11, Nehemiah 3: 8 and 12: 38, thus becoming part of the city walls of the period. In total the Broad Wall was 65m long (45m are now visible) and a full 7m thick. The biblical account describes dwellings having to be demolished to make way for the wall, which quite clearly does run across the ruins of ancient houses.

▶ **Burnt House** _51B2_

Misgave Ladach Street

This is the basement of a grand private dwelling of the 1st century AD, burnt down during the Roman destruction of Jerusalem. Inscriptions inside suggest it was the home of Kathros, a High Priest mentioned in the Talmud. An audio-visual on the house and its historical background is shown in the midst of the excavations every 30 minutes.

Exile's lament

'By the waters of Babylon we sat down and wept When we remembered thee, O Zion.
If I forget thee,
O Jerusalem, let my right hand forget her cunning;
If I do not remember thee, let my tongue cleave to the roof of my mouth; yea if I prefer not Jerusalem in my mirth."
– from 'The Babylonian Exile' (Psalm 137)

57

Discover Roman Jerusalem in the Burnt House

Souvenirs galore in the Cardo district

▶▶   **The Cardo**   51B2

Off the Street of the Chain, and beside Jewish Quarter Street, can be seen one of the most remarkable archaeological accomplishments in Jerusalem: the uncovering (between 1976 and 1985) of a 200m-length of the city's Roman and Byzantine main street, most of which lies about 6m below present-day ground level. Steps lead down to the Byzantine paving, and signboards give information about the street. Take a look at the 6th-century mosaic **Madaba Map**, taken from a church in Jordan, which shows the street plan of Jerusalem at that time. From it, much can be learned about the Cardo. A fine arcaded avenue lined with 5m-high columns (supporting the roof), the original thoroughfare was more than 20m wide and handsomely paved. The Crusaders tried to revive the Cardo, restored part of it and lined it with vaulted **traders' and craftsmen's shops**. Almost as impressive is the modern attempt, partially successful, to revive the Crusader section of the street by turning it into an arty, stylish shopping area.

A new city After the crushing of the First Jewish Revolt in AD 70, most of Jerusalem was laid waste by the Romans, the population driven out and their houses demolished. With the defeat of the Second Jewish Revolt, in AD 135, old Jerusalem was entirely razed and the Romans set about constructing a completely new city on the site – Aelia Capitolina. The street plan of today originates from that new Roman city.

The main street The main street of Aelia Capitolina was Cardo Maximus. It ran due south from today's Damascus Gate, along the course of what is now Souk Khan ez-Zeit, as far as David Street. After the Emperor Constantine had legalised Christianity in AD 313, churches sprang up and Christians flocked into the town. It was the start of the Byzantine period. The Holy Sepulchre was built; the town grew and flourished. In the 6th century, the Cardo, its lively central promenade, was extended southwards along what is now Jewish Quarter Street. It is that section of the Cardo which can be seen today.

▶   **The Cathedral of St James**   51A2
St James Street
Open: for services only (around 3pm daily)
Part of a complex of ecclesiastical and theological buildings at the heart of the Armenian quarter, this 12th-century

Opening times
Most of the city's sights, museums and attractions are open at the following times:
Sun to Thu: 8:30 or 9am to 5:30 or 6pm
Fri: early closing, usually 1pm
Sat: closed all day.
Exceptions are shown in the text for each entry.

Jordanian occupation
On the Cardo, the One Last Day Museum records details of the events and consequences of 28 May 1948, the day when the Jewish quarter fell into the hands of the Jordanians.

Crusader-era cathedral has an elaborate interior heavy with ornament. Note especially the carvings and painted tiles. It honours both the disciple James, stoned to death, whose body is beneath the altar, and the beheaded James the Apostle, whose head is in a side chapel.

► Church of the Holy Sepulchre

See pages 60–2.

► Church of the Redeemer 51B2

Muristan Road

This handsome Lutheran church, just outside the Church of the Holy Sepulchre, is all in bare pale stone and almost entirely without adornment, inside or out. There is an excellent view from the top of the tall tower. The ground on which it stands was presented as a gift to Charlemagne by the Caliph Haroun el-Rashid and remained in the hands of western religious orders until 1868, when Crown Prince Frederic Wilhelm of Prussia made an official visit to Jerusalem. The Ottomans (with debatable legality) gave him this land and he ordered the building of this church, which was consecrated in 1898.

► Church of St Anne 51C3

Via Dolorosa

By Lions' Gate, beyond a courtyard, this Crusader-era church, with its shallow dome and triangular apse, is striking for its stark dignity. It is said to stand on the site of the home of the Virgin Mary's parents; a chapel beneath purports to be Mary's birthplace. The adjacent **Pool of Bethesda** is described in the gospels (see side panel).

► The Church of St John 51B2

Muristan Road

An 11th-century Greek Orthodox church standing on 5th-century Byzantine ruins (which now form the crypt), this intriguing old building incorporates some Roman masonry in the façade.

Curing on the sabbath
In Roman times the Pool of Bethesda was thought to have restorative powers. Here, according to the gospels (John 5: 1–16), Jesus healed a man on the sabbath simply by saying 'Take up thy bed and walk.' For this, he incurred the wrath of 'the Jews', as the gospel writer puts it (John often uses this device apparently to create an impression that only the villains of his tale were Jews; Jesus and the sick man were also Jews). The gospel appears to suggest that 'the Jews' objected to Jesus healing on the sabbath. In fact, Jewish law permits medical treatment on the sabbath. It does not, however, permit carrying, considered a serious breach in those days. The objection was that Jesus had told the man to carry his bed.

59

Sphinx-shaped handle (above) and palm-shaded cloister (left) in the Church of the Redeemer

Differences of opinion
The Church of the Holy Sepulchre and its holy relics are officially recognised by the Catholic and Orthodox churches. The Protestant churches do not all acknowledge the veracity of the sites, some preferring the Garden Tomb, north of the city walls in East Jerusalem. Non-conformist churches take the same view as the early Christians, that revering such sites is a departure from Christ's teaching and tantamount to paganism.

The simple truth
'When one stands where the Saviour was crucified, he finds it all he can do to keep it strictly before his mind that Christ was not crucified in a Catholic Church. He must remind himself that the great event transpired in the open air, and not in a gloomy candle-lighted cell, upstairs, all bejewelled and bespangled with flashy ornamentation, in execrable taste.'
– Mark Twain, on the Church of the Holy Sepulchre, in *The Innocents Abroad* (1869)

Right and below: focus of Christian devotion, the Holy Sepulchre church is believed to contain Christ's tomb

▶▶▶ Church of the Holy Sepulchre 51B3
Souk ed-Dabagha and Christian Quarter Road
Open: summer 5am–8pm; winter 4am–7pm daily

This striking edifice, an Old City landmark with the larger of its two domes topped by a gilded cross, is physically and spiritually the heart of the Christian quarter. It has been revered and fought over for centuries. Entered across a paved courtyard, through a large arched doorway within a low, narrow façade of pale Jerusalem stone, this complex of shrines, tombs, relics and churches under a single roof – there is even an Ethiopian monastery *on* the roof – encloses the area in which, according to the mother of Constantine, the 4th-century empress Helena, Christ was crucified, lain in his tomb, and resurrected. The existing structure dates mainly from the Crusader period.

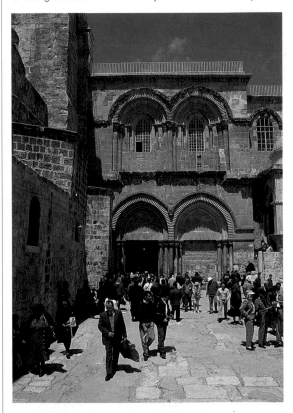

Within the building – main sights To follow the last of the Stations of the Cross marking Jesus's route to the Crucifixion, you can, immediately upon entering the dark, labyrinthine interior, turn right on to a short staircase. This leads up 5m to the top of a rock reputed to be the summit of Golgotha. Here you will find the highly ornate chapels, decorated with mosaics, dedicated to the **Nailing to the Cross** (Station X, at the door – *Jesus Stripped*; Station XI, at the altar – *Jesus Nailed to the Cross*) and the **Crucifixion** (Station XII – *The Cross is Raised and Jesus Dies*). In the latter is a lifesize model of Christ and (behind glass) a slab of rock which is claimed to be the very one on which the cross stood. Between the two chapels is a statue of the Virgin Mary (Station XIII – *Jesus Removed from the Cross*).

Descend the stairs from the second chapel to the **Stone of Unction**, a red slab supposedly on the spot where Jesus's body was anointed prior to entombment. Behind this stone (under Golgotha) is the atmospheric **Chapel of Adam**, which houses a skull found during 12th-century excavations and, rather unscientifically, declared on the spot to be the skull of Adam. Tombs of two Crusader kings that used to lie here were subsequently destroyed by Greek monks.

To the left of the Stone of Unction, you enter the extravagantly ornate **Rotunda**, probably the only part of the present church resembling the Empress Helena's original. At the centre is the **Holy Sepulchre** (Station XIV – *Jesus is Entombed and Returns to Life*). Enter the low doorway into the narrow marble-clad burial chamber; a marble slab along the side is supposed to suggest the place where the body of Jesus lay. Also within the Rotunda, the **Jacobite Chapel** has its own bare and unclad rock-cut tomb, improbably claimed to be that of Joseph of Arimathaea. North and east of the Rotunda are chapels dedicated to events – some biblical, others entirely legendary – associated with the death and resurrection of Christ, such as the so-called **Prison of Christ**.

Pulling the emotions Reactions to this astonishing church vary across the entire spectrum of human emotion. Awe and reverence it certainly does inspire in the most pious: one may even see pilgrims entering on their knees, and weeping in their fervour. But for others, there is disappointment and disbelief, even despair. Some have come with unreasonable expectations: this is, after all, just a building, standing on ordinary ground. Sometimes, though, the expectation that has been dashed is simply that this would be a splendid edifice, worthy of its sanctity, and that the sites within it would at least seem credible. Instead visitors find a chaotic, confusing structure containing a jumble of implausible holy places and relics. People may be shocked by the uncouth, unseemly behaviour of the custodian monks, of a variety of sects, who are permanently in dispute with one another. In some visitors, to the dismay of others, the church inspires overt ridicule and disrespect. In addition, there are plenty of tourists who wander in aimlessly without knowing, or caring much, about its status.

History The Empress Helena, mother of the Emperor Constantine, ordered the building of the original church in AD 326. It was completed in 335, but destroyed by the Persians in 614. When the Emperor

LOVE one another
The ownership of the Church of the Holy Sepulchre is divided among six Christian denominations, each with responsibility for its own shrines and areas of the building. They are the Roman Catholics, the Greek Orthodox and the Armenian, Syrian, Coptic and Abyssinian churches. Disputes between the factions are so fierce that maintenance of the building cannot be carried out, and they even try to disrupt each other's religious services. Visitors will sometimes see monks come to blows for entering each other's territories. After discussions that lasted from 1927 to 1959, the factions finally agreed to have some building work done at the church. This remains incomplete owing to further disagreements.

Sacristy lamp, symbol of the living Christ, Holy Sepulchre

Faithful pilgrim

A visitor with faith
'Tradition could not err in the identity of so famous a spot, and the smallest scepticism would deprive it of all its powerful charm.' – John Carne, on the Church of the Holy Sepulchre, in *Letters from the East* (1830)

Handsome buildings of golden stone

Heraclius took Jerusalem again for the Byzantines about 15 years later, the church was rebuilt; the Persians returned Christ's Crucifix, which they had removed. However, in 1009, Caliph el-Hakim demolished the whole church and the Crucifix. In 1048, another smaller church was built on the site by the Byzantine Emperor Constantine IX, which the Crusaders enlarged in 1149. After the 1927 earthquake, discussions began between the part-owners of the church about renovations. These began in 1959 and have continued intermittently.

Authenticity Most of the sites associated with Christ's early years and ministry are legendary and mythical. But the hill on which he was executed was, and remained, visible for all to see. In AD 70 Jerusalem was destroyed, but, in AD 135, when Hadrian built Aelia Capitolina on its ruins, the place of the Crucifixion was so well known that the emperor erected a temple to Venus on the site to discourage Christian worship.

Constantine the Great legalised Christianity in 313 at the instigation of his convert mother, Helena. She was taken in 326 by Jerusalem's Bishop Macarius, to Golgotha, where Hadrian's shrine to Venus still stood – outside the city walls and on the site of a former quarry, exactly as described in the gospels. In the base of the hill were caverns dug out of rock, one of which Helena declared was the sepulchre of Jesus. In fact, we know from the Gospels that the tomb in which Jesus lay was that of Joseph, 'a rich man of Arimathaea' (Matthew 27: 57) and that it was a new one, set in a garden (John 19: 41). As a rich and pious man, Joseph is not likely to have made his tomb beside a place of public execution. The preferred burial places were on the Mount of Olives or a little north of the city. However, his tomb was also described as 'hewn out of the rock' (Matthew 27: 61 and Mark 15: 42–7) and 'nigh at hand' (John 19: 42).

Close by, Helena was shown some old wooden crucifixes in a disused cistern. Having selected one of these as the cross upon which Christ had died, she ordered it erected on the top of Golgotha, and a church built over the whole site. In the construction, much of the hill was removed. Other holy sites in the church, such as the Stone of Unction and the place where Adam's skull is buried, have no Biblical or historical foundation.

▶▶▶ **Citadel** 51A2
See History of Jerusalem Museum, pages 66–7.

▶▶▶ **Dome of the Rock and El-Aksa Mosque** 51C3
See Temple Mount, pages 72–3.

▶▶ **Four Sephardic Synagogues** 51B2
Off Beit El Street
At the end of a little alley in the heart of the Jewish Quarter, these four small connecting synagogues are set within a courtyard enclosed behind a beautifully carved door and decorated archway. With the closing of the Ramban Synagogue in 1588, the Sephardim made their centre here for 300 years. The oldest of the four synagogues is the Kahal Kadosh Talmud Torah, which became the Eliahu HaNavi Synagogue in 1588 – supposedly because Elijah (Eliahu) appeared here during a High Holy Days service to make up a *minyan* (10 men, the minimum worshippers required for a service); ever since, a chair has been reserved for his next appearance in a room at the back.

The age of the Kahal Kadosh Gadol, or Rabbi Yohanan ben Zakkai Synagogue, is uncertain but it certainly dates to before 1615, and could be much earlier – indeed this may be the oldest of the four. The Middle Synagogue, opened about 1750, was previously the site of a women's courtyard attached to the Yohanan ben Zakkai. The Istambuli Synagogue, of 1764, was erected by refugees from Turkey.

During the 1948 War of Independence, 800 Jewish residents of the Old City hid here for 14 days. Taken by the Jordanians, the synagogues were partially destroyed and looted. After the recapture of the area by Israel, they were painstakingly reconstructed, and rededicated in 1972. Since then the synagogues have been in regular use, though no longer just by Sephardi Jews. When there are no services, entrance hours can be unpredictable.

▶ **Greek Orthodox Patriarchate Museum** 51A3
Greek Patriarchate Street
Many treasures of the Greek Patriarchate are displayed in a restored Crusader setting. There is an attractive garden.

Four beautiful little synagogues, the city's centre of Sephardi worship since the 16th century

City of synagogues
During and after the Jordanian capture of the Jewish quarter in May 1948, a total of 58 synagogues were destroyed or badly damaged – almost all the synagogues in the city at the time. While many of the ruins have been preserved or partly restored since 1967, few have been as completely reconstructed as the four Sephardic synagogues. However, there are now 450 synagogues in Jerusalem, most of them outside the Old City walls.

■ **The Jews of modern Israel have come from 80 countries. But the population is mainly divided into two major groups: the Ashkenazim, whose background is in Christian Northern Europe, and the Sephardim, whose culture evolved in the Islamic Mediterranean. Other Israelis include the Mizrahim of Eastern origin, the Ethiopians, the Cochin Jews of India and others.** ■

64

The language of the Jews
A century ago almost no one spoke Hebrew. Yiddish, based on medieval German mixed with Hebrew, was the everyday language of Ashkenazi Jews. Hitler's 'Final Solution' finished off the Yiddish-speaking world – its culture, its people and their language. Those who fled to America and the British Commonwealth became fluent in English, which now stands alongside Hebrew as a new language for the Jews. Many Sephardi Jews, especially the elderly, speak Ladino, a mix of old Spanish, Arabic and Hebrew created in the Middle Ages.

Top: skull caps
Below: Hasidic sidelocks
Right: young Crusaders

The cross and the swastika Modern Israel's Ashkenazim did not all come here from eastern Europe – though their parents or grandparents probably did, even if they themselves were born in Israel, England or America. Their culture absorbed violent anti-semitism, as well as the Enlightenment, the French Revolution, the rise of secularism and socialism – and Zionism.

Ashkenaz is a Biblical place-name that came to mean Germany. As far back as Roman times, Jews settled along the Rhine valley and from there spread across Germany. The Crusades forced them east into Poland and Russia. For centuries eastern Europe was the focal point of Jewish culture and religion. In Russia there were thousands of *shtetls* – Jewish towns and villages – within the Pale of Settlement (the permitted area of Jewish settlement under the Tsars) and millions of people lived in the Jewish ghettos of the larger cities. Russian pogroms in the 1880s caused an exodus to Palestine, America and the British Commonwealth. The rise of the Nazis in the 1930s caused another rush to escape. The 6 million or more Ashkenazim who remained behind died in the Holocaust: a culture and a language died with them, and eastern Europe was emptied of Jews.

Under the crescent Some visitors assume at first that Sephardim are Arabs, something to which they would not take kindly, as most are refugees from Arab countries. The Sephardim, after a long medieval Golden Age during the Arab occupation of Spain, remained little affected by Europe's intellectual developments until they arrived in Israel in the late 15th century. A more cohesive, more traditional society, the Sephardim brought to Israel a resistance to secularism allied to a more easy-going and accepting approach to Jewish observance and custom. They have also given Israel its best food. They remain largely on the lower rungs of society, but that is changing.

Sefarad means Spain, a place where Jews have lived from Biblical times and where Sephardic culture evolved during 680 years of Muslim domination (711–1391). When Christians completed the conquest of Spain in 1492, all Jews were forced to renounce their religion or face expulsion. Most followed the Muslims to North Africa and to other areas of the Mediterranean, such as Turkey, Greece, the Balkans and Palestine. Under Islam, Jews suffered discrimination but rarely outright persecution. They lived in their own districts with the official status of *dhimmis* (second-class citizens). Persecution increased during the 20th century, however, and when the State of Israel was created, most were forced to leave their homes.

The other Jews Most other Israelis fall into one of two conspicuous groups, both of which arrived *en masse* in big rescue operations. Mizrahim (though they too are often called Sephardim) also come from Muslim countries, but further to the east, especially from the Yemen. They have brought ancient tradition, ethnic colour and superb oriental cuisine. The black Jews of Ethiopia (no longer called 'Falashas', strangers, the name they hated in Ethiopia) add yet another dimension to Israel's extraordinary cultural and ethnic diversity.

Children of Israel Half the population of Israel was born in the country, and one-third of its children now have mixed Ashkenazi/Sephardi parentage. The effect has been dramatic in creating a new culture. It is also remarkable how alike Ashkenazi and Sephardi children have become in appearance, mannerisms and outlook after growing up in the sunshine of Israel, without the pressures of being a minority population, after going through school in Hebrew and doing army service together. They emerge as young adults who are neither Ashkenazi nor Sephardi, but truly Israeli.

Ashkenazim dominant
Modern Israel was created by Ashkenazim. They still dominate government and institutions in Israel, and they have been credited with giving the country not just its idealism, secularism, democracy and know-how, but also its red tape and bureaucracy.
However, their role has given way to the increasing influence and numbers of the Sephardim – Jews of the Mediterranean, whose cultural roots pass through the Islamic world.

World populations
In 1933, there were 16.5 million Jews in the world, 90 per cent of them in eastern Europe. Today there are about 12 million Jews in the world, only 2 million of whom live in Europe. Over 4 million live in Israel and 6 million in the USA.

Happier here than in Ethiopia

The Tower of David bears the name of Jerusalem's founder

►►► History of Jerusalem Museum (Citadel, or Tower of David) *51A2*

Beside Jaffa Gate

The History of Jerusalem Museum is housed in the city's ancient Citadel. The entry charge for the museum includes a 1½-hour guided tour (in English) each morning, except Saturday, at 11am. The museum and tour provide a uniquely informative, entertaining and accessible overview of Jerusalem and its history.

Herod's Citadel One of the most imposing and evocative landmarks of the Old City is the high, slender Tower of David, rising from within the massive defences of the superb medieval fortress, known as the Citadel. This stands alongside the powerful stonework of Jaffa Gate. Despite the name, nothing but myth connects this magnificent structure with King David, the city's founder. The Citadel, standing on the Old City's highest point, was, in fact, constructed much later by King Herod in the 1st century BC, though archaeological exploration points to the presence of major fortified structures here since the First Temple period (950–538 BC). Herod's fortress was even more imposing than today's, mainly medieval building; his had three monumental square towers, one 40m high, named after his brother, his close friend, and his wife – Phasael, Hippicus and Miriam.

Through the centuries After the crushing of the Second Jewish Revolt (AD 132–135), the Romans ordered that Jerusalem be levelled to the ground. Only the Citadel and its tallest tower, Phasael's (the bulky square tower beside Jaffa Gate), were to be left standing. Roman troops were stationed inside the fort, and in later centuries it served as a garrison for Arabs (who built a smaller – now ruined – fortress within the Citadel), Crusaders, Mamelukes and Ottomans. It was the ferocious Mamelukes who, in 1310, restored the Citadel and rebuilt the walls which stand today. Under the Ottomans it was similarly reconstructed in 1610, and it was they who erected a mosque within the fortress, with the slender stone minaret which became known romantically to many a 19th-century visitor as the Tower of David.

In 1917, under British rule, the fortress retained a nominal military function, but, for the most part, it was transformed into a cultural and historical site, with performances and exhibitions, a role which it has maintained under the Israelis (during the Jordanian occupation, it was again an army post).

On the roof From the flat roof of the Phasael Tower, restored in 1987, there is an immense panorama over the Old City. The dominant position of Temple Mount, a huge lofty plateau elevated above the town's warren of crowded alleys and streets, gives a powerful impression of its importance in Temple times. Today, the beautiful blue-walled and gold-crowned Dome of the Rock occupies the site, and from this vantage point the building can be appreciated in all its glory. The Mount of Olives rises magnificently behind. Within the city, a surprising number of buildings have black and white stripes, a Mameluke style, and the astonishing number of fine churches testifies to centuries of Christian devotion in Jerusalem.

Inside the museum The Citadel's ancient halls, rooms, cellars and outdoor terraces today house a superb and extensive museum of Jerusalem's history. The structure forms a five-sided enclosure around a large central open-air archaeological site. Using films, maps, attention-grabbing pictures, dioramas, holograms, life-size fibreglass statuary, superbly detailed models and numerous other types of displays, as well as thousands of the historic objects found here, the museum leads room-by-room, age-by-age, through the long and intricate Jerusalem story, allowing even the most casual visitor to grasp something of its scale and scope. The final stages are presented with genuine film footage and modern artefacts. Four possible quick itineraries through the museum are indicated at the entrance: the Exhibit Route (2 hours), the Excavation Route (1½ hours), the Observation Route (1 hour), and the Short Route (40 minutes).

Museum opening hours and events:
Open daily except Yom Kippur (late Sep or early Oct): Sun–Thu 9–4 in summer, 10–5 in winter, Fri and Sat (and the day before public holidays) 9–2 in summer, 10–2 in winter.

On summer evenings an entertaining *son et lumière* is put on in the Citadel courtyard. Under the stars in the dramatic setting of the fortress, it tells the story of the city and its citadel. Shows in English take place at 9.30 on Mon and Wed, and on Sat at 10.30pm.

City centre
In Jewish prayer, the name 'Jerusalem' is still synonymous with the Temple, the vast gilded palace of sacrifice and worship which dominated the life of the city for over 1000 years (950 BC to 70 AD). Even though the Temple has been destroyed, it remains the theoretical centre of Judaism: at morning services in synagogues throughout the world, Temple sacrifice instructions are read aloud as part of the prayers.

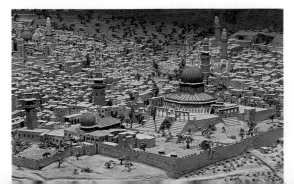

As it was: Stefan Illes's 1872 model of the Old City

Jerusalem redeemed
'Break forth into joy, sing together, ye waste places of Jerusalem: for the Lord hath comforted his people, he hath redeemed Jerusalem.'
– Isaiah 52: 8

►► Hurva Square 51B2

This pleasant, paved plaza lies at the heart of today's Jewish quarter. A calm, peaceful atmosphere prevails, with children playing and parents quietly chatting. The square is enclosed by interesting historical sights: on one side soars the memorial arch over the **Ramban Synagogue** and the ruined **Hurva Synagogue** (see below and opposite); on the other, the square is overlooked by the attractive **Wohl Archaeological Museum►►** (see page 80). Several streets lead off, including HaKaraim St, named for the Karaites, whose **Anan ben-David Synagogue** (built 1400), damaged and looted during the Jordanian occupation, has been repaired and rededicated. Facing it are handsome remnants of the **Tefillat Israel Synagogue**, a grand 19th-century edifice and former Old City landmark completely destroyed in 1948.

►► Hurva Synagogue 51B2

Hurva Square
During the 19th century this was the principal synagogue in Jerusalem. Its ruins can be reached by descending

Relics of Hurva Synagogue's former glory

steep steps from the roof terrace of the Ramban Synagogue in front. Construction began in the early 10th century on Crusader ruins, but the building remained incomplete and fell into disrepair – hence the name *hurva*, or ruin. In 1856 the Jewish community received permission to complete the building. The result was, by all accounts, a splendid edifice, but this was completely destroyed in 1948. In 1977 sensitive restoration work preserved the ruins while making the site delightful, with a paved marble floor and walls of massive stone blocks and some arched windows. The blue sky makes a lovely roof. A delicate high arch constructed on the site symbolises its former grandeur. Diagrams and pictures on display show what a fine structure the Hurva once was.

▶ **Israelite Tower** 51B2
Plugat HaKotel Street
This remnant of a tower of the First Temple period was once part of the city walls. Inside is a small museum. Beside it stand remains of another tower, dating from the 2nd century DC.

▶ **Old Yishuv Court Museum** 51B2
6 Or HaHaim Street
Yishuv refers to the Jewish community living in Palestine before the creation of the modern State of Israel. When Jordan invaded the Old City in 1948, Rivka Weingarten had the foresight to gather together all kinds of objects that would give an impression of what life was like in the Jewish quarter. Subsequently returning to restore her home, a courtyard with simple family dwellings built around it, she created a museum, with each room dedicated to a particular theme, illustrating the trades, the crafts and the different lifestyles of Sephardim and Ashkenazim.

▶ **Rachel Yanait Ben Zvi Centre** 51B2
Plugat HaKotel Street
This educational and research centre has a museum and a permanent exhibition on Jerusalem in the First Temple period (950–538 BC), with a model of the city as it was at that time.

▶ **Ramban Synagogue** 51B2
Hurva Square
Alongside Hurva Square, and beneath the slender Hurva Arch, can be found this attractive little synagogue, probably the oldest in Jerusalem, founded in 1267 by Ramban (an acronym based on the name of the respected medieval Rabbi Moshe ben Nahman, also known as Nahmanides) and built on top of Crusader-era ruins. The city's Muslims destroyed the building in 1474, but it was rebuilt to became Jerusalem's main synagogue. Muslim opposition to its presence continued; a mosque was built alongside (there is still one there today) and, in 1588, Jewish prayer was prohibited in the area. Abandoned, the synagogue became a workshop, remaining so until 1967. It was then fully restored and rededicated as a synagogue. On top of the building is a roof terrace from where visitors can enjoy a view directly on to the Hurva Synagogue ruins (see opposite).

Nahmanides
Rabbi Moshe ben Nahman, better known as Nahmanides or Ramban, was born in 1194 in Spain, and is acknowledged as one of the greatest Talmudic scholars of his era. Like Maimonides (see page 204), who died when Nahmanides was 10 years old, he wished to simplify and interpret the scriptures and formalise a Jewish 'creed' to stand against those of Christianity and Islam. As Rabbi of Gerona, he took part in a public debate (almost a trial) with the noted Jewish convert to Christianity Pablo Christiani, in the presence of King James I of England at Barcelona in 1263. Accused of blasphemy during the debate, Nahmanides had to flee from Spain, making his way to Jerusalem, where he founded the Ramban Synagogue before meeting his death in about 1270.

Holy Rock and Wailing Wall
'Until 688 AD Jews met yearly, to mourn over and anoint the 'Stone of Foundation', on which the Holy of Holies once was raised, and which is now covered by the old Arab Dome of the Rock which was erected in 688 AD. In later times they were only able to wail at the outer wall of Herod's great temple enclosure, and they have continued to do so down to our own times.'

Palestine Exploration Fund Lectures, 1892.

The Temple

■ 'And it came to pass in the four hundred and eightieth year after the children of Israel were come out of the land of Egypt, in the fourth year of Solomon's reign over Israel, in the month Zif, which is the second month, that he began to build the house of the Lord' (I Kings 6: 1). Though the Temple has now gone, it remains at the very heart of Judaism. ■

God as a cloud
According to II Chronicles 6: 13–14, when Solomon's Temple was complete it was dedicated by placing the Ark in the Holy of Holies. During the ceremony, hundreds of men in white linen played trumpets, cymbals and other instruments. As they did this a cloud filled the building 'so that the priests could not stand to minister by reason of the cloud: for the glory of God had filled the house of God'.

*Top: Holyland Hotel's model of the Second Temple
Below: the building of the Temple*

The centre of a nation The First Temple was completed in 950 BC, the 11th year of his reign, by King Solomon, son of King David, the Israelite ruler who took Jerusalem from the Jebusites and proclaimed it the capital of Israel. In Solomon's Temple was placed the Ark of the Covenant – the gold-encrusted chest containing Moses' Tablets of the Law – and other sacred objects which the Jews had carried with them in their exile. The Temple became the focal point for the Jewish people, and, wherever they lived, adult males were obliged to come to it for three annual festivals: Pessah (Passover), Sukkot (Tabernacles) and Shavuot (Weeks or Pentecost). Destroyed in 586 BC by Nebuchadnezzar, it was rebuilt as the Second Temple between 538 and 515 BC, being enlarged and aggrandised on several occasions afterwards, especially under King Herod in the decades before his death in 4 BC. After the Jewish Revolt, this Second Temple was reduced to rubble by the Romans in AD 70. Jerusalem's most spectacular landmark, the Dome of the Rock, a Muslim holy place, now occupies the site. Part of the Temple Mount outer wall survives as the Western Wall, the holiest place of prayer for Jews.

History and myth Tradition has it that Mount Moriah was the place where Abraham bound Isaac and prepared to sacrifice him (Genesis 22: 2 and 14; Sura 37, Koran), though there is no mention of this event in II Samuel 24: 16–25, describing David's purchase of the threshing floor on which the Temple would stand, nor in II Chronicles 3: 1, describing the Temple's construction. In 167 BC, the Maccabees drove the Syrians out of Israel and had to rededicate the Temple: the festival of Hanukka commemorates their victory and the miracle of a single day's lamp oil being sufficient to light the Temple *menorah* (candelabrum) for eight days, as required for the rededication. The Temple featured several times in the life of Jesus: when he remained for three days in learned discussion with the elders at the age of 12 (Luke 2: 41); when he overturned the moneychangers' tables (Matthew 21: 12); when he predicted the Temple's total destruction (Matthew 24: 1) and when the Temple veil was torn in two at the moment of his death (Matthew 27: 52).

Lamentation and longing The destruction of both the First and Second Temples is commemorated on the 9th day of the Hebrew month of Av. By coincidence, the Jews were expelled from Spain the same day. When the

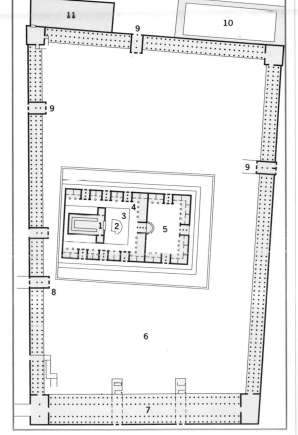

The Second Temple – key to plan

1 Temple
2 Altar
3 Court of Priests
4 Court of Israel
5 Court of Women
6 Court of the Gentiles
7 Royal Portico
8 Bridge and gate
9 Gate
10 Pool of Isra' il
11 Antonia

All that now remains: the Western Wall below the El-Aksa mosque

Arabs conquered Jerusalem, they allowed Jews to visit Temple Mount for just one day in the year to mourn their lost Temple. That day, too, was the 9th of Av (Tisha b'Av in Hebrew). Today there is a special procedure for prayer on that day; it is also a day of fasting, of not wearing leather and for reciting, in a wailing tone, the Book of Lamentations. In later centuries the Jews were permitted only to come as far as the Western Wall, and only on that day. Thus the Western Wall became known as the 'wailing wall' because of the Jewish practice for that day This ceremony can still be seen every year on Tisha b'Av (around mid to late July).

The Third Temple Much of today's synagogue service takes the form of a temporary substitute for Temple practice. At every Orthodox service, prayers are said for the rebuilding of the Temple. But many Jews have doubts about the wisdom of this; if it were rebuilt, Temple practices like animal sacrifice would have to be resumed. Some say it can only be rebuilt when the Messiah comes. There are those who wish to begin at once. For others, it will be rebuilt when the time is politically right, which it isn't yet. Some Israeli parliamentarians have referred to the State of Israel itself as the Third Temple.

Muslim gates

Non-Muslims may only enter Temple Mount through Bab el-Maghrebeh (the Moors' Gate) and Bab el-Silsileh (the Chain Gate), both of which pass into the enclosure on either side of the Western Wall. Muslims may enter or leave by any of the other gateways. The other Temple Mount gates are (on the western side) Bab el-Masatarak, Bab el-Qatanin, Bab el-Hadid, Bab el-Nazir, Bab el-Ghawanima and (on the northern side) Bab el-Atim, Bab Hitta and Bab el-Asbat.

▶▶▶ Temple Mount (Arabic: Haram esh-Sharif)   51C3

The star of the Old City is the glorious Dome of the Rock on Temple Mount. It is just one of several fine Muslim Islamic constructions within the ancient Temple Mount enclosure (*open* Sat–Thu, 8–noon and 1.30–3) which is entered at the end of Street of the Chain (through the Chain Gate; Bab el-Silsileh in Arabic) or on the ramp from Western Wall Plaza (through the Moors' Gate; Bab el-Maghrebeh in Arabic). Inside, the enclosure is of grand dimensions and partly shaded by trees. Ahead rises the exquisite blue-tiled façade and golden dome of the Dome of the Rock. To either side stand arches and minarets and two attractive fountains where Muslims wash before prayers.

Claims to holiness Sura 17 of the Koran states: 'Glorified be He Who carried His servant by night from the Inviolable Place of Worship to the Far Distant Place of Worship, the neighbourhood whereof We have blessed, that We might show him of Our tokens!' Although Muhammad never visited Jerusalem, Muslims came to believe that Temple Mount was 'the far distant Place of Worship' referred to in this sura. The legend developed that he travelled on a winged horse with the Angel Gabriel, and that, on reaching the Temple Mount, he physically ascended through the seven heavens and met God, before waking to find himself back in Mecca. In addition, Sura 2 refers to Mecca as the *kiblah* (the place one should face while praying) instead of other places which had previously been used. From this, the tradition arose that Muhammad had previously allowed people to face Jerusalem – perhaps to encourage Jews to convert to Islam.

Principal sights The El-Aksa Mosque▶▶▶ was extensively restored in 1948. Jerusalem's main place of Islamic prayer is sumptuous with marble columns, fine carpets, stained-glass windows and an impressive gilded wooden ceiling. Adjacent is the Islamic Museum▶ containing a collection of artefacts from several mosques.

The Dome of the Rock▶▶▶ (Arabic: Qubbet el-Sakhra) is an awesomely beautiful, symmetrical, octagonal structure of blue tiles topped by a gleaming dome of bronze-aluminium alloy (not gold). The building is reached by broad flights of steps on each side over which are triple arches built by the Crusaders. Inside, the air is evocatively filled with echoing prayers and music. Mosaic covers the interior of the dome. The huge black stone beneath the dome, the impressive rock for which it is named, has an indentation which Muslims solemnly assert was made by Muhammad's flying horse as it leapt to the sky.

Gilded magnificence: inside the Dome of the Rock

*Burnished bronze
and azure blue*

Night ride
In real life, Muhammad did
not visit Haram esh-Sharif
(Temple Mount), and the
Koran's reference to his
'being carried by night'
makes no mention of
angels, or flying horses, or
of leaping to heaven. The
importance of the legend
lies in its metaphorical
meaning: that Muhammad,
as the last of the prophets,
with a mission to take the
word and laws of God (or
Allah) to the entire world,
had taken over Judaism
and replaced it. Judaism at
the time had suffered dis-
persion and defeat. It was
almost logical for Muslims
to view the sanctity of the
Jewish holy site as
subsumed into the newer,
conquering sanctity of the
Prophet.

Smaller, attractive structures within the enclosure include the **Dome of the Chain►**, the **Dome of the Ascension►**, and the **Islamic schools►**, as well as the sealed **Golden Gate►** and the other **gates►** into the Muslim quarter (see panel opposite).

History and politics Having destroyed the Temple, the Romans erected their own temple on the site. In the 6th century this was replaced by a church. After the Arab conquest in 638, Caliph Omar visited Temple Mount to pray at the black rock supposed to be the one on which Abraham laid his son, Isaac, for sacrifice. The present Dome of the Rock was built under Omayyad rule in 691, when the claim was first made that Temple Mount was 'the far distant Place of Worship' to which Muhammad flew in his night-time vision. The church was converted into the El-Aksa mosque in 715.

Crusaders took Jerusalem in 1000 and made El-Aksa into a residence which became the headquarters of the Knights Templar (who took their name from the site). The Templars renamed El-Aksa the Temple of Solomon, and the Dome of the Rock as the Temple of the Lord. The sites were taken by Islam in 1187 and the Mamelukes built new structures on the site.

Following the 1948 war, Arab states took great interest in Temple Mount, and the Dome of the Rock was restored jointly by Jordan, Egypt and Saudi Arabia. After reconquering Jerusalem in 1967, the Israelis allowed Temple Mount to remain under Islamic administration. Since that time the legend of Muhammad's night journey has led the Arab world to lay claim not just to Temple Mount, but to the whole city of Jerusalem, adding yet another source of friction between the Jewish and Arab communities.

Contemplation

■ Israel's population of 5.3 million includes over 750,000 Arabs. Arabic is one of Israel's two official languages. Arabs have full citizenship, send their children to Arab-speaking state schools and elect Arab members of Parliament (who address the Knesset in Arabic). ■

The population of Israel
81.6 per cent Jewish
14.0 per cent Muslim
2.7 per cent Christian
1.7 per cent Druze and others.

The non-Jews of Israel The Israelite conquest of Canaan was never total and – despite a biblical injunction – the non-Jews (Gentiles) were not wiped out. Numerous biblical references show that the land of the Jews always had its minority of Gentiles. Big population changes followed each subsequent conquest. It was Roman policy to dilute difficult peoples: after the Jewish Revolts of AD 70 and 135, non-Jewish settlers were brought into the area around Jerusalem and the coastal towns. Subsequently, the legalisation of Christianity encouraged its followers in the Near East to move to the Holy Land.

New religion, new empire In 630 Muhammad and his followers forcibly converted Mecca to the new Islamic religion. Forced conversion (except of Christians and Jews) was part of Islam's creed and just six years later Muslim forces swept up the Arabian peninsula and into Palestine. Some settled, and the non-Jews of Israel were converted by the sword. By the middle of the 8th century a vast region – extending from Spain, across North Africa and the entire Middle East to the Indus valley – had been brought under Islam's yoke. The whole empire was ruled from Mecca by the Umayyad dynasty. The administration of Palestine was centred on Damascus, in Syria. People then moved freely over the border, and Israel's Arabs still speak the Syrian dialect.

A Muslim Israel The defeat of the Umayyads by the Abbasids meant a transfer of power from Damascus to distant Baghdad. Apart from the brief Crusader kingdom, Israel was to remain under Muslim rule for many centuries – under the Egyptians, Persians, Mamelukes, and, for 400 years, as part of the Ottoman Empire. Each ruler brought changes, to the cost of Palestine. When the British took over in 1917, the land was largely uncultivated, with inadequate water and extensive areas of desert, rock, dunes and swamp. The population stood well under one million.

Face of Palestine, citizen of Israel

The fight against Zionism British rule was benign, created work and improved the country. Arab workers drifted in from surrounding lands to take advantage. From the 1880s onwards, Jews also flocked to Palestine, but for a different reason. By 1936, the population of Palestine had risen to 1,367,000 – of whom 384,000 were Jews. The Arabs were uneasy: Jews traditionally held low status in Muslim society. Muhammad had said that their time was over, their religion supplanted. Yet the Jews were purchasing land, displacing Arab tenants, forming settlements and draining swamps, all in pursuit of their avowed aim of creating a Jewish state. During the 1920s and 1930s, riots and attacks against the newcomers were frequent. When the State of Israel was declared in 1948, the Arab nations joined with the Arabs of Israel to crush the new country. To their surprise, they failed; many then fled across Israel's borders into Gaza and the West Bank, joining those who had left in advance of the war. Jews call this the War of Independence. Arabs call it the Catastrophe. Some 700,000 Arabs fled, leaving about 200,000 who stayed to become Israeli citizens.

Israeli Arabs Not all Arabs opposed Israel, and in particular not the Christians or the Druze. Many who fought against Israel also stayed. Israel's largest Arab town is Nazareth. Other main centres of Arab population are Jerusalem, Haifa and Akko, with communities in Ramla, Jaffa and several small towns in Galilee. At first sight, they appear to have come out on the winning side. Under no Arab regime do citizens have anything like the rights and freedoms of Israelis: all religions and sects enjoy full freedom of worship and Arabs are exempt from military service (though some, the Druze in particular, have chosen to accept conscription). Yet there is discontent, as Israeli Arabs compare themselves not with the Arabs who fled, but with their Jewish fellow citizens. On the whole, Israeli Arabs are held in low esteem, and undoubtedly there is discrimination against them – as against non-Jews generally (though most Israelis deplore this). And of course, they will forever be seen as a minority: gentile citizens in a Jewish land.

In the eye of the beholder
'Palestine, a country scarcely superior to Wales either in fertility or extent.'
– Edward Gibbon, *Decline and Fall of the Roman Empire* (1776)

'A bare limestone country of little natural beauty.'
– Charles Doughty, *Travels in Arabia Deserta* (1888)

'A good land and a large, flowing with milk and honey.'
– Exodus 3: 8

75

Arab schoolchildren in the souk

Top right: Jesus meets his mother (Station IV) Below: the Via Dolorosa, the Sorrowful Road

▶▶▶ **Via Dolorosa** 51B3

The 'Sorrowful Road' passes through the Muslim quarter to the Church of the Holy Sepulchre and is honoured as the route taken by Christ as he carried his cross to Golgotha, where he was crucified. Along the way, the Stations of the Cross – stages on his journey to death – are marked.

History The idea of the Stations of the Cross arose in the Middle Ages. Popular notions of what had happened to Jesus on the way to Calvary, unconnected with the gospel accounts, passed into folklore and church tradition. In response to the demands of pilgrims, sites for the Stations of the Cross were first chosen in the mid-18th century by the Franciscans. In the 19th century the route of the Via Dolorosa was altered to its present course.

Spiritual journey Most Christian communities take the view that Christ's suffering was spiritual and symbolic, and that it is not important where the Via Dolorosa actually runs. However, these views make little impression on the tens of thousands of pilgrims of all denominations who walk the Via Dolorosa each year in the belief that they are stepping in Christ's footsteps.

The route *I – Condemnation*: the first part of the way is relatively wide and quiet. The first Station is the courtyard of the **Omariye Islamic College▶**, which some claim as the site of the Praetorium where Jesus was sentenced. A minaret has been fancifully named Antonia Tower, after Herod's Antonia Fortress which stood here. Historically, it is more likely that Jesus was sentenced at the Citadel, and (despite the gospel version) it is most unlikely that Temple priests were involved, the day of his trial being the first day of Passover.

II – Taking up the Cross: across the street the ancient paving or **Lithostratos▶** in the Franciscan Churches of the Condemnation and the Flagellation is supposedly where Jesus was scourged, mocked, crowned with

thorns and given his cross to carry. A stone archway or buttress spanning the street here is called Ecce Homo Arch▶ and is traditionally held to mark the spot where Pilate said of Jesus: 'Behold the Man' ('Ecce Homo'). In fact the arch was erected in AD 135 as a support for Herod's fortress.

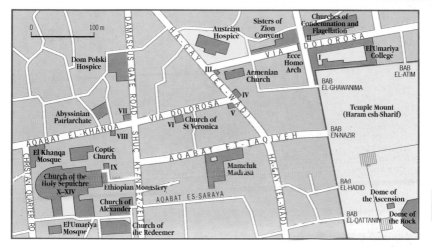

III – Jesus falls: continue to the Austrian Hospice and turn left into busier El-Wad Street. Here a plaque shows where Jesus supposedly fell under the weight of the cross. The route passes Arab shops and teashops.

IV – Meeting Mary: on the left (opposite a right turn), a shrine marks the place where tradition claims that Jesus saw his mother. Turning right, the street is again called Via Dolorosa.

V – Simon helps Jesus: take the turning, and straight away on the corner is where Simon the Cyrenian is said to have taken the cross from Jesus to help him (see panel opposite). Narrower and climbing, frequently in steps, the route passes souvenir shops.

VI – Veronica wipes the face of Jesus: a door leads down to **St Veronica's Church**▶▶ in Crusader vaults. The story that a woman called Veronica (whose name simply means 'true image') wiped the face of Jesus arose in the 7th century. A cloth, said to have belonged to Veronica and marked with the image of a man's face, is preserved in Rome.

VII – Jesus falls again: the route reaches a T-junction in the midst of the crowded shopping streets of the Arab souk (market). Just here, believers say, Jesus fell.

VIII – Speaking to the women: the site (marked by a Latin cross on the wall of a Greek monastery) lies a few paces ahead. Here Jesus urged the women of Jerusalem to weep not for him but for themselves and their children.

IX – Jesus falls again: return to the junction, turn right along the covered Souk Khan ez-Zeit. A right turn leads off the souk to a Roman column at the back of the Holy Sepulchre. Here the faithful say Jesus fell for a third time.

X–XIV – Golgotha: return to the souk. Via Dolorosa turns right, passes the Lutheran Church of the Redeemer and reaches the Holy Sepulchre. The remainder of the Stations are inside the church (see page 60).

Via Dolorosa – key to plan

I	Condemnation
II	Taking up the Cross
III	Jesus falls
IV	Meeting Mary
V	Simon helps Jesus
VI	Veronica wipes the face of Jesus
VII	Jesus falls again
VIII	Speaking to the women
IX	Jesus falls again
X	Disrobing
XI	Crucifixion
XII	Death
XIII	Descent from the Cross
XIV	Laid in the tomb

The Way of the Cross

'They took the robe off from him, and put his own raiment on him, and led him away to crucify him. And as they came out, they found a man of Cyrene, Simon by name: and him they compelled to bear his cross. And when they had come unto a place called Golgotha, that is to say, a place of a skull, they gave him vinegar to drink mingled with gall: and when he had tasted thereof, he would not drink. And they crucified him.'
– Matthew 27: 31–35

Temple remnant: the
Western Wall

**Western Wall (or
Hasmonean) tunnels**
'The Western Wall epito-
mises recollections of the
Jewish past and the
hopes and aspirations of
the Jewish future' (sign
in Western Wall Tunnels).
The tunnel tour starts in
the medieval basement
from which archaeologist
Charles Warren set out in
1867 to make the first
exploration of the under-
ground remains of the
Temple Mount. Further
excavations since 1967
have exposed a 448m
stretch of the Wall (one of
the stones alone weighs
40 tonnes). You enter the
area through a secret
passage, come to stairs
that date from the time of
the Second Temple and
enter a large hall behind
Wilson's Arch. A long
stroll through a tunnel
beside the Wall reveals
part of a Herodian street,
a quarry, an ancient
aqueduct and a pool. The
final section, opened in
1996, emerges onto the Via
Dolorosa.

▶▶▶ **The Western Wall (also known as Kotel,
HaKotel, Kotel Ma'aravi or Wailing Wall)** *51C2*
The Western Wall is not itself sacred to the Jews. It is
revered because it is the last remnant of the only sacred
place in the world: the Temple. Two millennia of prayer
and tradition have sanctified this link with Temple times,
making it the holiest place of prayer in the Jewish world.
In addition, its relative proximity to the Holy of Holies
(which was at the western end of the Temple) confers an
additional claim to reverence. Today, as always, every
Jew in prayer, anywhere in the world, faces the Holy of
Holies inside the Temple on Temple Mount in Jerusalem
– even though it physically no longer exists.

The stonework The Western Wall is the western section
of the outer retaining wall of the Temple compound
which, until 1,900 years ago, entirely covered Mount
Moriah, or the Temple Mount. The Wall was not part of
the Temple building itself. The Second Temple, completed in 513 BC, was reconstructed by Herod in about
30 BC; that is when the Wall's massive blocks of dressed
golden limestone were put in place. The visible part of the
Wall reaches 18m in height, while a further 18m extends
below the present-day ground level.

Visiting the Wall A visit to the Western Wall can be one
of the most thought-provoking, interesting and satisfying
experiences in the schedule of Old City sightseeing. After
Israel recaptured the Wall in 1967, the squalid shacks and
slum which abutted it were swept away and a vast open
plaza constructed, enabling thousands of people to gather
at the Wall for festivals or special occasions. The exposed
length of the Wall has been cordoned into two sections,
one for men and the other for women, in keeping with
Orthodox practice.
  A low barrier a few paces from the Wall keeps sight-
seers apart from the area reserved for prayer and religious
ritual, which is carried out in the open under the gaze of
tourists. Any man, Jew or non-Jew, may enter the men's

enclosure so long as he is wearing a head covering (even a baseball cap will do), just as any woman may enter the women's section. Most who do, come to recite prayers, visit the adjoining rooms or simply to take a closer look at the Wall.

Beside the Wall Off the men's section (so there is no access for women), the Wall continues into the structures abutting it. These consist of **two rooms►** beneath the arches which support the Street of the Chain. These are in effect, synagogues, with shelves of prayer books and, attached to the Wall, arks containing Torah scrolls which are constantly being taken out and read by groups of men, while crowds of visitors file in simply to have a good look round. The first narrow chamber has a glass-covered opening in the floor that provides a view to the lower levels of the Wall. Beyond, in a larger room which has probably existed here since 100 BC, is **Wilson's arch►**, the ancient vaulted structure which used to support the original access road to the Second Temple. At the foot of the arch, illuminated openings give a view to the Wall's lower levels.

Off the plaza On the north side of the plaza, below the words 'Under the auspices of Chief Rabbi Shlomo Goren', an inconspicuous door leads into the labyrinth of the **Western Wall Tunnels►►** (Kotel Haldra). These can only be visited by booking three days in advance (fee payable) and joining a fascinating 1½-hour guided tour. This passes along the underground passages that run alongside the excavated Wall for several hundred metres.

At the back (western side) of the plaza, the **northern passage►** runs beneath the Street of the Chain and links the plaza with El Wad (or Hagai) Street. Its roof is made by an arch of massive stones, dating from the 8th to the 11th centuries. On one side of the floor, openings reveal Roman paving below today's ground level. At the far end of the passage, steps climb to the Street of the Chain close to the Temple Mount entrance.

Wall etiquette

Be prepared for hassle at the Wall. The enclosure is technically a synagogue, so modest dress and behaviour are required and it is technically forbidden to eat or smoke there, or take photographs. Despite these regulations, it is not unusual to see Hasidim snacking or smoking within the enclosure, while photographers offering to take 'souvenir' pictures tout with impunity. Religious beggars harass visitors constantly (sometimes while they are praying), asking for 'donations'.

Jewish visitors can seek assistance at one of the stands within the men's section where volunteers will help you to put on the *tefillin* and say the blessings (there is no charge).

79

Praying at the holiest place in the Jewish world

The uniform of the ultra-Orthodox Hasidic Jews

Jewish baths

Mikvahs, or, more correctly, *mikvaot*, are ritual baths, which are filled with rainwater. Religious law requires immersion in the *mikva* for men before a number of Temple rituals, but since the destruction of the Temple, these are no longer required. Women have to immerse themselves at the end of their menstruation. Before marriage, both bride and groom enter (separately!). Converts to Judaism immerse themselves to complete the conversion process. Some *mikvaot* in the Herodian Houses have separate entrances and exits (unusual today), allowing the person to enter impure on one side and leave purified on the other. Immersion is total with the body upright, entirely clean and naked and without any jewellery.

▶▶ **Wohl Archaeological Museum (Herodian Houses)** 51B2

HaKaraim Street off Hurva Square

The Wohl Archaeological Museum preserves *in situ* the extraordinary discoveries made when this handsome religious institution, built in pale Jerusalem stone, was being constructed. From the small, unostentatious museum entrance, steps lead down to the preserved area, which lies 3m below the street level, or 2,000 years back in time. Here the floor-level rooms of ruined houses of the period are displayed in a remarkable state of preservation.

History The Jewish quarter of today covers the remains of the Upper City of 37 BC–AD 70. In AD 70, during the crushing of the First Jewish Revolt, the Romans totally destroyed the Temple and the area around it, and drove the population, including the priestly class, out of the city. The whole area was set alight in a vast fire, which was described by the 1st-century historian, Josephus Flavius. Seventy years later the city was transformed and given new buildings, new ramparts and a new, non-Jewish name – Aelia Capitolina. On the site of ruined Jewish homes new houses were erected.

The museum The Wohl museum stands on an archaeological site where part of a prosperous residential district of the Herodian period has been exposed. Here wealthy families of the Jerusalem aristocracy and priesthood used to live, in fine homes overlooking Temple Mount. A wide low-ceilinged room has been built around the ruins of six of these 1st-century houses, including the largest ever found in the Upper City, the 600sq m 'Mansion'. Their state of preservation varies; what can be seen are ground floors and basements, with sections of the ground floor walls standing as much as 2.5m high in parts. In some cases, original mosaic floors and wall decorations survive in good condition. In one house, a mosaic of the Herodian period was cut right through when drains were installed for later Byzantine dwellings.

Steps lead down to the next level following the ancient walls as they descend the hill. Walkways enclose the house ruins, giving an excellent view into the rooms, and explanatory diagrams indicate the significance of everything that can be seen. A great many artefacts were discovered among the ruins, and it has been possible to give some idea of the furnishing and décor of the houses. In the museum there are displays of the numerous luxury and household items found, as well as a detailed model of the 'Mansion'.

The houses Built close together on the hillside facing Temple Mount, the houses are constructed of large pale blocks of the local Jerusalem stone still used today. The interior of the homes bears a startling resemblance to modern well-to-do interiors in today's eastern Mediterranean countries (the similarity to Greek houses gives an insight into the Hellenism that influenced life before and during Herod's reign). The impression is of uncluttered elegance and plenty of cool stone and plasterwork. Houses are divided into large and small rooms, some with attractive mosaic floors. Patterned mosaic often features in the middle of the room, with an undecorated area around the edges. Walls are decorated with paintings and stucco.

The occupants The wealth of the inhabitants is shown by the spaciousness of their homes, the fine quality of the stucco and the excellence of the mosaic work. Inside, they have private bathrooms and their own *mikvahs* (ritual baths), an indication that they were highly observant Jews. It is clear that rooms were often redecorated, old frescos being painted over with new.

Step down 3 metres and back 2,000 years at the Wohl Archaeological Museum

City of David opening times
Note that a visit involves a lot of steep walking out of doors in the sun. All parts of the site are open Sun to Thu, 9–4, and Fri 9–2.

Computer control
An enjoyable feature of the Bible Lands Museum is the interactive computer system, which provides information through touch-sensitive screens. The museum's gift shop offers a good range of reproductions of the ancient artefacts displayed in the museum.

Right: Roman mosaic in the Bible Lands Museum

The New City

Outside the Old City walls New Jerusalem spreads in every direction except east, a fact that is critically confusing given that Jerusalem has a large Arab district known as East Jerusalem. In fact, East Jerusalem lies to the north of the Old City walls, while to the geographical east of Jerusalem is the steep hillside of the Mount of Olives. There is another Arabic district just to the south of the City Walls, but the rest of the city, including the modern city centre, consists of Jewish districts.

Despite Jerusalem's 3,000-year-old pedigree, almost all of the city outside the walls is less than 100 years old – and most is under 50. No matter how modern, all buildings in New Jerusalem have to be clad in the attractive traditional golden sandstone called Jerusalem stone.

► **Ammunition Hill**   *46C4*
Eshkol Boulevard (northeastern edge of the city)
On the site of a Jordanian army position captured after a long battle, this is the city's principal memorial to the liberation of Jerusalem in 1967. Now an outdoor museum, the preserved battleground is dedicated to the 183 Israelis who died. Beneath it, the underground Jordanian command post has also been preserved as a museum. There are gardens and a picnic area at the site.

► **Bethany** See page 209.

► **Bible Lands Museum**   *46A2*
Museum Row (between the Knesset and the Shrine of the Book)
With remarkable displays of thousands of superb archaeological finds, this light, attractive museum explores Near East ritual and religion throughout the 6,600-year period from Abraham to the Byzantines.

► **Bloomfield Science Museum**   *46A2*
Museum Boulevard, at the Hebrew University, Givat Ram campus
This is an imaginative and highly entertaining hands-on science museum with fascinating displays, talks, exhibitions and workshops geared for different age groups.

▶▶ **City of David**   *47E2*

Between the Old City's southern wall and the Kidron Valley lies this extensive archaeological site where the original Jerusalem, the city built by King David in 1004 BC has been revealed. Some features have long been open to the public, while other parts continue to be excavated.

Historical background The Jebusite settlement conquered by David lay along the Ofel ridge. Here he constructed the Jewish capital, later acquiring a threshing floor on Mount Moriah as a site for the Temple. Under Solomon the city grew north to encompass the Temple area. In 1978 a project was established to bring together all the finds from the area and to create a single Ancient Jerusalem Archaeological Park. So far, 25 layers of civilisation have been discovered, dating back to 4000 BC. Work is still in progress.

What to see Outside Dung Gate, take Ofel Boulevard (eastward) for a view of the excavations at **Ofel Archaeological Garden▶**, abutting Herod's Temple wall and the city's south wall and lying below El-Aksa mosque. Turn right down the Observation Point Path to reach the **City of David Archaeological Garden▶▶**, where impressive ruins include some Israelite houses destroyed by Babylonians in 586 BC, the Canaanite citadel walls and the foundations of David's fortress. Continue 100m downhill to **Warren's Shaft▶▶**, the ancient city's underground water system. This tunnel and well shaft were used to pull water up to the city from the sporadic gushing **Gihon spring▶** inside a cave. David's men managed to breach the Jebusite town by climbing up the interior of the shaft (British soldiers did the same thing in 1910).

Carry on to **Hezekiah's Tunnel▶**, built 700 BC. Dug from both ends at once, it is about 550m long, and was used to channel water from the Gihon spring to the **Siloam Pool▶**, which acted as a reservoir within the city walls. Jesus healed a blind man here by rinsing his eyes. The water still flows, and visitors are welcome to wade in the dark from one end to the other! This is quite an adventure, takes half an hour and requires suitable clothing and footwear as well as a torch.

Ofel Archaeological Garden
Part of this interesting excavation area at the foot of Temple Mount lies within the city walls. Just south of the Western Wall can be seen Robinson's Arch, a broken stump which is all that survives of an arch that once supported a flight of steps up to the Temple platform. The main attraction along the south wall is the remaining stairway which gave direct access to the Temple via Hulda's Gate: tens of thousands of people coming here in Second Temple days would have climbed these steps, including Jesus. A two-storey palace discovered on the site was that of the 1st-century AD queen of Adiabene who converted to Judaism (see page 85).

David's City in ruins

Outdated definitions
In 1967, after Israel had recaptured East Jerusalem from the Jordanians, the total population of the city was about 267,000, made up of some 70,000 Arabs east of the former border and 197,000 Jews to its west. Today, those sharp divisions have been blurred. Owing to the influx of population from both sides, new housing developments, people moving around within the city and a redefinition of the city limits, Jerusalem's total population has more than doubled to about 570,000, and the districts east of the 1948 border now have just as many Jewish residents as Arab – about 150,000 of each.

►► **East Jerusalem**   47D4

In fact lying to the north, rather than east, of the Old City walls, this mainly 19th-century area is Jerusalem's principal Arab district. The neighbourhood is bounded by Hatzanhanim and Suleiman boulevards, beside the Old City wall, Shivtei Israel and St George boulevards, curving northeastwards to the American Colony, and the slopes of Mount Scopus to the east. The busiest thoroughfares are Sultan Suleiman and Salah ed-Din, both just outside the Old City's Herod's Gate, and the whole densely populated area has a fascinating oriental atmosphere.

Archaeology and caves In the eastern part of the district is the **Rockefeller Museum►►►**, a substantial building beneath a large tower at the end of Suleiman Street, housing one of Jerusalem's leading archaeological collections. In a sequence of well-laid out rooms, set around a central courtyard, its displays cover the full range of human history, from its origins almost to the present day. Among the most interesting and impressive items are the Galilee skull (dated 200,000 BC) and other very early human remains found in Israel, ancient jewellery (some over 4,000 years old), a board game (of about 1600 BC), and ancient Egyptian and Mesopotamian items found in Israel. There are especially interesting reconstructions of a 7th-century Islamic palace and baths. The free guided tours by qualified volunteers are an additional attraction for visitors.

The Old City wall leads to **Zedekiah's Caves►**, a group of subterranean tunnels, probably former quarries, that run for some 200m beneath the streets. Among various stories about the caves, it is said that Zedekiah, together with hundreds of other Jerusalemites, hid here at the time of the Babylonian conquest.

If you continue beside the wall, you will reach the lively area in front of **Damascus Gate►►►** (see page 53). Cross the road and head up the busy Nablus (or Shehem) Road, turning right for the **Garden Tomb►►** (see page 86), the calm and attractive spot which many Protestants believe to be the true place of Christ's Crucifixion and Resurrection.

Heading to the western edge of the district, a left turn along Nablus Road leads to the interesting **Tourjeman Post Museum►**, located at the junction of narrow Hayil Handassa Street and wider Antara ben Shadad and HaNevi'im streets. The museum building stands beside the old Mandelbaum Gate (named after the Mandelbaum family whose house once stood alongside), which was the only crossing point between the eastern and western sectors of Jerusalem during the Jordanian occupation of 1948 to 1967. Further down HaNevi'im Street, the **St Polyeuctus House Chapel►** is an Armenian establishment with an exceptionally beautiful 5th-century mosaic floor.

On the north side of the Arab district, the interesting **Tombs of the Kings►**, at the top of Salah ed-Din Street (close to the junction with Nablus Road), form a majestic complex of catacombs now known to be the 1st-century AD

Ancient art, the Rockefeller Museum

American colony
This district, part of east
Jerusalem, was founded
by American Christians in
the 1880s. It still has a
strong western and
Christian presence and its
buildings include the US
consulate, a YMCA, the
American Colony Hotel and
St George's Anglican
Cathedral of 1898.

*Understated
elegance, the
American Colony
Hotel*

85

Burial place of two unlikely converts to Judaism – Helena,
queen of Adiabene (present-day Kırkuk, near Baghdad),
and her son Izates. The queen took the name Sarah and
became a distinguished benefactor of the Jewish people.
She actually died in her homeland, but wished her
remains to lie in Jerusalem. The sarcophagi from the
tombs are in the Louvre, in Paris.

Just behind the tombs is the **American Colony** district,
built in the 1880s. The **American Colony Hotel**▶▶ is one
of Jerusalem's best-known hotels. Formerly the grand,
opulent palace of a Turkish pasha, handsomely restored,
it is now the favourite haunt of the many foreign correspondents based in the city, and deserves a visit for a
drink, a snack or a meal.

*Trade flourishes
before the Damascus
Gate*

Chagall masterpieces
The artist Marc Chagall (who was Jewish) created a great deal of work for Israeli institutions. Particularly fine are his 12 stained-glass windows in the synagogue of the Hadassah University Hospital, just south of En Kerem. They show, in his typically vivid, other-worldly style, Jacob blessing his sons, the founders of the 12 tribes of Israel.

Above: En Kerem, birthplace of John the Baptist. Below: the Garden Tomb

▶ **En Kerem** *206B2*

This picturesque village on the city's western edge is traditionally believed to be the birthplace of John the Baptist, as well as the place where the Virgin Mary visited John's mother Elizabeth. The reverence attached to the village dates mainly from the Crusader period. Barluzzi's modern **Sanctuary and Church of the Visitation▶▶** and the 17th-century **Church of John the Baptist▶▶** are two attractive buildings honouring these events.

▶▶ **Garden Tomb** *47D3*

Access from Nablus (Shehem) Road

This supposed site of the burial and Resurrection of Jesus was chosen by General Gordon in 1883 and has been acknowledged by several Protestant denominations. Gordon was concerned that the accepted site, inside the Church of the Holy Sepulchre (see page 60), stood within the city walls, in contradiction to the gospels. In fact, the city walls at the time of Christ took a different course, and Holy Sepulchre does lie outside those walls. For all that, this hill looks like a skull (the Gospel description of Golgotha), has a fine rock-hewn burial tomb adjacent, and is in a garden location, all of which makes it just as likely a candidate as the Holy Sepulchre site chosen by Helena in the 4th century. Other high-quality rock-cut tombs found nearby, for example the Tombs of the Kings (see page 84–5), suggests that this was a burial area preferred by the wealthy (Christ was laid in the tomb of Joseph, a rich man of Arimathaea).

▶ **Holyland Hotel Model** *46A1*

Off David Nezer Street, Ramat Sharett (southwest of the city centre)

This superb miniature model of Jerusalem at the time of Christ, built on a scale of 1:50 and covering one hectare in area, has been laid out in the grounds of this hotel.

▶▶▶ **Israel Museum** *46A1*

Ruppin Road (near the Knesset)

This large modern museum is the nation's leading show-case for history, anthropology, art and cultural heritage, placing Israel within its regional and global context. A full appreciation of its exhibits would take several days; in a short visit it is better to concentrate on highlights, and the museum itself provides leaflets enabling visitors to

concentrate on these, as well as daily **guided tours in English** of the most important and interesting exhibits. Perhaps the Museum's most famous exhibits, the Dead Sea Scrolls are housed in the **Shrine of the Book►►►** (see page 98), a striking, purpose-built structure separate from the rest, which itself takes some time to visit.

Permanent displays Outside the main complex there are 55 modern sculptures set in the **Art Garden►**, including work by Henry Moore. The main part of the museum is a huge arrangement of rooms and halls. Of special interest are the **Ethnography and Judaica Wing►►**; the **20th-century Art Pavilion►►**, with work by Picasso and other seminal modern artists; the **Israel Art Pavilion►►**, where artists such as Reuven Rubin are displayed; and the **Archaeological Galleries►►**, where the main discoveries made in Israel are exhibited.

Exhibitions, concerts and talks There are always several special exhibitions in progress at the museum, on a wide variety of themes in fields such as design, photography, or the art of Asia or Africa. Often these are on loan from other leading museums. The **Youth Wing** offers activities and special exhibitions for children. Concerts, mainly of classical music but also sometimes of jazz or Jewish genres, are given during the day and in the evening. Frequent lectures and talks cover a wide range of subjects of academic, Jewish or general interest.

Judaica
The Israel Museum's Judaica section has the world's most complete collection of Jewish ceremonial art and ritual objects, gathered together from every part of the world in which there have ever been Jewish communities. The Ethnography section includes among the varied displays, the costumes of Jewish brides in Yemen, Bukhara, Morocco and other Islamic countries.

The Art Garden, Israel Museum

■ **An Israeli meal is served from a melting-pot of cultures. Menus reflect cooking styles from around the world. The robust, filling Ashkenazi (East European) and more delicate, tastier Sephardi (Mediterranean and Middle Eastern) cuisine are both well represented, together with American (or international) dishes, and more exotic options like the exquisite spicy food of the Yemenite Jews.** ■

How to eat falafel in pitta
The easiest way to spot a tourist is by the amount of mess they make when trying to eat this awkward, overflowing hand-held snack. The trick is to nibble from the top, not the sides. Use the wrap-around paper to hold the whole snack together as you gradually eat downwards. Israelis can eat this without dropping even a shred of lettuce. After a couple of weeks' practice you will be almost as good as them.

Falafel is often served with salad in pitta bread

Salad days Israelis may be the only people in the world who start the day with a salad – not just as a little accompaniment to something else, and not just a slice of tomato and a leaf of lettuce, but a huge pile of chopped green peppers, radishes and grated carrot, topped by a generous helping of yoghurt-like cheese. In fact salad appears at every meal, and in huge quantities. It can vary from something roughly cut and thrown together, to a superb mix of finely cut vegetables, all at the peak of freshness, ripeness and colour, in a delicious olive oil dressing. Then there is houmous (chickpea purée), served in vast amounts with a big splash of olive oil and a delicious condiment called *za'atar* (hyssop and sesame). Similar dishes include avocado purée and *salat khatzilim* (aubergine purée with tomatoes, lemon juice and onion). They are mostly eaten with pitta bread.

Milk and honey Milk, it seems, can be made into more variations on the theme of cottage cheese, cream cheese, soured cream and yoghurt than most of us ever dreamed of. A breakfast or lunch buffet can include half-a-dozen soft or semi-liquid white cheeses, some bland, some flavoured with herbs and spices, some mouthwatering, some more of an acquired taste! Generically they are known just as *leben*, literally 'white'. One particular plain white cheese, moist, with a cuttable consistency, could be regarded as one of the country's staple foods; it is called simply *gvina lavana*, white cheese. Of course, thanks to Jewish dietary laws, milk products are never eaten at the same meal as meat in kosher restaurants.

One falafel or six The basic snack meal is falafel in pitta. Flexible enough to be either a quick bite or a full sit-down meal, it is also utterly delicious and so healthy you could live on it and nothing else. The falafel is a deep-fried ball of seasoned chickpea paste (plus wheatflour, onions and garlic). Usually four or five of them are crammed into the bottom of a cut-open pitta with as much diced salad and chopped vegetables as will fit. All this is then smothered with houmous and tahina (sauces made of chickpeas and sesame seeds with olive oil) and, optionally,

Food

Lebanese delicacy: a honey-soaked dessert

either sweet mango sauce, or the oily, spicy chilli pepper sauce called *zehoug*. Falafel in pitta is available everywhere, and in the cheaper places where you serve yourself you can top up as often as you like.

Meat dishes Plain grilled meats and fish, served with French fries, *hamutzim* (pickles) and (of course) fresh salads make a good, typical meal. Succulent stews with plenty of beans and pulses, especially *ful* beans, are widely seen. *Shwarma* (slices cut from pressed mutton roasted on a vertical spit) is ubiquitous, popular and (when stuffed into a pitta with salad) provides a mobile carnivorous alternative to falafel. Menus often feature *schnitzel*, but in Israel it is usually made of turkey or chicken, not veal. *Blintzes* (stuffed rolled pancakes) can be filled with meat or cheese, sweet or savoury, and can make a good snack, meal or (especially a cheese *blintz* sprinkled with sugar) a gorgeous dessert. Chunky little wedges of *baklava*, the super-sweet honey, nut and filo pastry pudding, also make a good finish. Israeli ice cream and yoghurt desserts are great too.

So eat! Portions are huge. You will probably never feel hungry in Israel. Cooking reaches a decent level almost everywhere, though rarely exceeding it (despite the overworked 'gourmet' label). Most Israeli restaurants lack finesse and imagination, but the ingredients are good and everything is so fresh and tasty that eating out is a real pleasure. There is also an admiration in Israel for the rough-and-ready, the down-to-earth, that works against refinement. Diners are not especially discerning, and generally care little about the finer points of cuisine. They just want good, fresh food, properly prepared, and plenty of it – and that is what they get. For the visitor this can come as a refreshing, tasty change from the more usual over-priced fare.

Vegetarian treats
Vegetarians will be in their element in Israel. Salads and delicious vegetable dishes are the norm everywhere and the numerous meat-free 'dairy' restaurants (they do also serve fish) supply a wealth of interesting choice. In meat restaurants though, despite excellent salads, you might get tired of the factory-made vegetarian *schnitzel* – the automatic response to a request for a vegetarian hot dish.

Bagels, a Jewish staple food

Waiting for Judgement Day: tombs in the Kidron Valley

Herod's family tomb
Behind the King David Hotel is a tomb of the Second Temple period, now known to contain the graves of members of Herod's family – many of whom he murdered. The opening still possesses its rolling stone 'door'.

YMCA
The wonderfully grand building opposite the King David, which seems even to outclass the famous hotel, is a YMCA. It was designed in 1933 by Arthur Louis Harmon, architect of the Empire State Building in New York.

▶ **Kidron Valley** 47E2

The dry valley of Nahal Kidron (a *nahal* is a natural watercourse that only runs after heavy rain), accompanied by a dusty road, runs past the Old City on the east, between the city wall and the Mount of Olives. It forms the eastern limit of the original City of David. Pious Jews and Muslims both believe that the Last Judgement will take place below the Mount of Olives (see page 94). For that reason, this part of the valley is also known as Jehoshaphat Valley (literally, 'valley of God's judgement'), a name used metaphorically in the scriptures for the place of judgement. Various superstitions attach to the area: one is that the dead will physically revive and, if they are righteous, immediately enter Temple Mount. In addition, certain remarkably elaborate **Kidron valley tombs▶**, set on the lower slopes of the Mount of Olives, are popularly thought to be those of early biblical characters. These are in fact the tombs of wealthy Jews of the 1st century BC and are constructed in typical Judaeo-Hellenised Roman style of that period. One with a curious conical roof is referred to as the **Tomb of Absalom▶**, the son of King David, while another is said to be the **Tomb of Zacharia▶** and a third is called **St James's Grotto▶**, supposedly where James the Less hid when Jesus was arrested.

▶ **King David Hotel** 46C2
King David Street

This grand 1930s hotel, now equipped with every modern amenity, remains the venue for state banquets and receptions. It is the flagship of the Dan chain, Israel's most prestigious hotel group. The King David entered the pages of Israel's history when the front of its right wing, being used as the military headquarters of the British in Palestine, was blown apart by the Irgun guerrilla group in July 1946. Ninety-one people died in the incident, one of several at that time which were aimed at persuading the British to withdraw from Palestine.

Historic hotel: the King David, former headquarters of the British in Palestine

▶▶ The Knesset 46A2

Eliezer Kaplan Street (HaKyria district)

The Israeli parliament building of 1966 is a bleak fortress surrounded by a large open space, located on a hill west of the city centre. This is the focal point of modern Israel. It was necessarily constructed with defence very much in mind: it looks like a bunker and a good deal of the structure lies below ground level. Here, in debates, the nation's divisions are starkly revealed, as is its essential unity. Religious and secular forces, left and right-wing ideologues, Zionists and anti-Zionists, meet, clash, and form pragmatic alliances. Few countries in the world are as wholeheartedly democratic, with a system of proportional representation that permits almost any and every voice to be heard under this roof. The name itself – *knesset* means assembly – reflects this role too, and the name contains an echo of Beit Knesset, the Hebrew for synagogue. The 5m-tall bronze *menorah* outside, a gift from Britain, depicts landmarks in Israeli history and symbolises the central place of the Knesset in the Jewish homeland. Tapestries in the entrance hall, depicting scenes from Genesis and Exodus and the Entry into Jerusalem, are the work of Marc Chagall.

Debate in the chamber (in Hebrew or Arabic) is fast and lively, with startling displays of real temper. Parliamentary sessions are open to the public (*open* Mon–Wed 4–7pm, or Sun and Thu 11am–7pm. Guided tours take place on Sun and Thu 8.30–2.30 when Parliament is not sitting). Take your passport.

Knesset roses

The beautiful Knesset Rose Garden, open to the public (who come here from time to time with placards to voice their concerns), contains hundreds of different varieties of roses.

91

Heart of Israeli democracy: the Knesset in its hilltop setting

*In this neighbour-
hood, strict rules
hold sway: Hasidic
Jews uphold the
Orthodox view*

Hasidism
The Hasidic movement
was founded by Israel ben
Eliezer (known as Baal
Shem Tov, meaning
'Master of the Good
Name') during the mid-17th
century in the Ukraine. At
the time, following savage
persecution by the Church,
Jewish life in eastern
Europe was at a low ebb.
He taught that communica-
tion with God could only be
attained through real fervour, whether in study or
observance. The dress of
the Hasidim (varied
according to sub-sects to
which they belong) reflects
devotion to their 17th-cen-
tury roots, as does their
ostentatious observance.
Sadly, many of Baal Shem
Tov's ideals seem to have
been lost, including love of
nature and of all one's fellow Jews, irrespective of
their level of learning.

▶▶ **Mea She'arim** 46C4

This city-centre district north of Zion Square is a strictly
Orthodox Jewish area where *Hasidim* (see panel) can be
seen at leisure. Here they are on home ground, and
children play in the streets (boys making sure never to
lose their *kippot*, or skullcaps) watched by the men in
their *tsitsit* (fringed garments) and the very demurely clad
women who chat, stroll, work or hurry home with bags of
shopping. Understandably, the residents object to being a
tourist attraction, and many streets have been closed off
with barriers and signs erected bearing this message:
'Entrance for women immodestly dressed, tourists and
groups, STRICTLY FORBIDDEN!!! This is a residence
area, not a tourist site; please do not irritate our feelings.
Neighbourhood Council.' It is wise to heed this warning,
as Hasidim have a daunting reputation for acting violently
against those they regard as transgressors. Men or
women in shorts will be spat upon, maybe even stoned.

Certain other streets have no such barriers, and it is
even possible to go on an organised synagogue tour (ask
at the tourist office). The usual guidebook descriptions of
this neighbourhood as being like an East European *shtetl*
(Jewish township) are quite misleading – there is almost
no resemblance at all. Mea She'arim's housing, narrow
lanes and overhanging balconies seem as much Middle
Eastern as East European. The European *shtetls* were
simple, rustic and long predated the Hasidic movement.
Many residents were not especially religious. Nor were
there any cars, metalled streets, electricity ... or signs
warning visitors to keep away.

▶ **Monastery of the Cross** 46A2
Háyim Hazar Boulevard
Built in the 11th century on 5th-century ruins, this stoutly
fortified Greek Orthodox monastery looks incongruous
among the modern architecture of the HaKyria district,
with its government offices and big museums. Much
superstition and legend surrounds the site. Hundreds of
monks used to live in the monastery, and its library of
precious manuscripts (now kept elsewhere) had a

considerable reputation. Today it is a college for Orthodox priests. Tradition has it that it was from among the olive groves in front of the building that Christ's Cross was made, hence the monastery's name.

▶▶ Mount Herzl 46A1

Herzl Boulevard winds through western Jerusalem to reach this hill, which has been turned into a magnificent shrine to the creation of the State of Israel. At its summit rests a massive plain black stone sarcophagus inscribed with no sentiments of praise or pathos but one simple word: Herzl. Around the tomb, a lovely, serene garden honours the memory of the founder of the Zionist movement, Theodor Herzl.

Without this cosmopolitan, secular Jew from Hungary, who was born in 1860, it is unlikely that the State of Israel would exist. Herzl was suddenly fired into activity when he witnessed the public parade-ground humiliation of the Jewish officer Alfred Dreyfus in France. He decided to throw himself, body and soul, into the creation of a world-wide Zionist movement that would work on all fronts – especially through politics and diplomacy – to win a homeland for the Jews. He convened the First Zionist Congress in 1897, and by the time of his death in 1904, his dream had gone a long way to becoming reality. When the State was proclaimed by David Ben-Gurion in 1948, a picture of Theodor Herzl hung on the wall behind him. In 1949, his remains were brought to Israel and laid to rest here.

The tombs of Herzl's parents and many prominent Israeli figures also lie here, including Vladimir 'Zeev' Jabotinsky (1880–1940: head of the Irgun guerrilla organisation), Levi Eshkol (1895–1969: Israel's third prime minister) and Golda Meir (1898–1978: Israel's fourth prime minister). The principal military cemetery is also on this hill, lower down. The **Herzl Museum▶▶▶**, the first building you reach on entering the site from Herzl Boulevard, tells the story of the man and his life, and preserves some original documents and other artefacts relating to him, in a reconstruction of his well-appointed study.

Bus 00
The easy way to see the sights of Jerusalem beyond the walls is to catch a number 99 bus. Running on a circuit right around the city, it calls at 36 stops, all of them places of interest. You can get off wherever you like, take a look round, and catch the next 99 bus to continue with your tour.

The tomb of Theodor Herzl, founder of Zionism, on the summit of the hill which bears his name

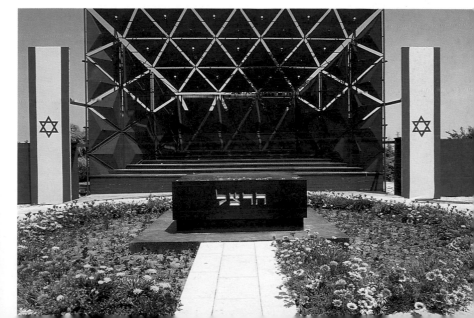

Ancient tombs on the Mount of Olives

The end of days

'And the Mount of Olives shall cleave in the midst thereof towards the east and towards the west, and there shall be a very great valley; and half of the mountain shall remove toward the north, and half of it toward the south – Zechariah 14

'The sun shall be turned into darkness, and the moon into blood, before the great and the terrible day of the Lord come. And it shall come to pass, that whosoever shall call upon the name of the Lord shall be delivered; for in Mount Zion and in Jerusalem shall be deliverance.' – Joel 2: 31–32

'Beat your ploughshares into swords, and your pruning hooks into spears: let the weak say, I am strong. Assemble yourselves, and come, all ye heathen ... Let the heathen be wakened, and come up to the valley of Jehoshaphat: for there will I sit to judge all the heathen round about.' – Joel 3: 9–12

The Russian church of Mary Magdalene, built by Tsar Alexander III

▶▶▶ **Mount of Olives**   *47E3*

White tombs, not olives, cover the steep hillside rising beyond the city wall east of Temple Mount. This slope has long been wreathed in myth and legend.

Fact, fiction, and faith Almost the only time the hill is mentioned by name in Jewish scripture comes after the revolt of Absalom, when his father, King David, is described as weeping while he walks barefoot up the Mount of Olives to pray (II Samuel 15: 30). However, the apocalyptic predictions of Joel 3, that the nations shall be judged in the valley of Jehoshaphat (meaning 'God's Judgement') has been taken by some to refer to the nearby Kidron valley. Zechariah's hallucinatory vision (14: 4) of the Mount of Olives being torn into two, and the whole world coming to Jerusalem for the festival of Sukkot has also led pious Jews to believe that the 'Last Judgement' will be held here. The notion that the dead will physically rise on the Day of Judgement has caused Jews to attach special value to being buried on this slope above the Kidron.

Christians know this as the place to which Jesus and the disciples came on the night before his arrest and trial. The 'place called Gethsemane' (Matthew 26: 36) is assumed to be on the slope. Fine buildings on the Mount of Olives commemorate these events, although, almost without exception, they are based on Byzantine fervour rather than biblical or historical evidence.

Down the mountain There is direct access to the Mount from the Old City, via Lions' Gate, but an easier way to visit the shrines and churches is from the top of the hill. Take a bus or taxi to **Et-Tur**▶ (literally, Olive Mount), the Arab village at its summit, and walk past the Church of the Ascension (no entry) to the **Chapel of the Ascension**▶, a simple domed structure within the grounds of a mosque converted from a Crusader church. This is claimed to be the place from which Christ ascended into heaven (despite Luke 24: 50, which clearly states that this event occurred at Bethany, present day Eizaria). Inside, a mark in the floor is said to be the footprint of Christ. **Paternoster Church►**, belonging to Carmelite nuns, recalls Christ's teaching of the Lord's Prayer, supposedly at a grotto which now forms part of a lovely cloister. Beyond, on the left, rises the unsightly Hotel InterContinental. Just below, an **observation point►►►** gives one of Jerusalem's best views.

Another road from the Carmelite church leads down past the so-called **Tombs of the Prophets►** (Haggai, Zacharia and Malachi), in reality a much later complex of catacombs, to the entrance of the **Jewish cemetery►►**, the oldest, as well as the largest, continuously used Jewish cemetery in the world. Tragically it was badly damaged during the Jordanian occupation, when graves were smashed or removed for use as building stone.

The curious **Dominus Flevit Church►►** (meaning 'the Lord wept'), was built in 1953 and incorporates 5th-century ruins. It has a glass wall and is shaped as a teardrop in memory of Jesus weeping for Jerusalem. The 19th-century Russian **Church of Mary Magdalene►►**, with its elaborate coloured façade and cluster of onion domes topped with prominent Orthodox crosses, is one of the city's more distinctive landmarks. Ironically, it was built by Tsar Alexander III, whose savage pogroms in the 1880s inspired the first great influx of Zionists into Palestine.

At the bottom of the hill, a putative **Garden of Gethsemane►** with a few olive trees, recalls Christ's last hours, as does the **Cave of Gethsemane►**, said to be where the disciples slept while Jesus prayed. The **Basilica of the Agony►**, an attractive modern building on a Byzantine and Crusader site, is decorated inside and out with mosaics and murals.

The **Tomb of the Virgin Mary►►**, a mainly Byzantine and Crusader structure, is reached through a fine door-way which leads to an underground shrine containing various tombs. They are medieval but said to be those of Mary's parents, Joachim and Anne, her husband Joseph, and, at the end of a long chamber, Mary herself. This is one of many places, in Israel and in other countries, where the Virgin Mary is said to lie.

A beacon to the Jews
In Second Temple times, the Mount of Olives had, on its summit, the first in a chain of beacons that extended all over Israel and into Babylon, used to inform Jews of the timing of new moons and festivals.

Beneath here lies the Virgin's tomb

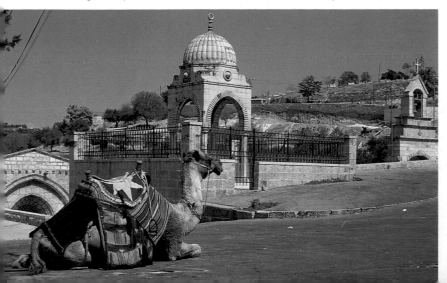

The Valley of the Shadow of Death

Encircling the foot of Mount Zion is the Hinnom Valley, called Gehenna, meaning Hell, in the Bible. Its evil associations can be traced back to Canaanite times when the valley was sacred to the cult of Moloch, whose followers sacrificed children by burning them alive. Fires were kept aflame here specifically for that purpose. Incredibly, such a religion had a strong appeal, and was widely practised throughout the region. Even the Israelites sometimes succumbed to it, perhaps because the followers of Moloch also had intercourse with temple prostitutes. The Haceldama Monastery along here, in another link with evil, is believed to stand on the Field of Blood purchased with the 30 pieces of silver given to Judas for betraying Jesus.

▶ **Mount Scopus**
(Hebrew: Har HaTsofim)   47E4

The Hebrew name for Mount Scopus means, 'Looking Over', as does the Greek translation, Scopus. As a viewpoint over the Old City and the hills beyond, it is hard to beat. Roman legions camped here in AD 70 before moving to crush the Jewish rebels. The Crusaders, too, camped at the summit on the eve of their attack on Jerusalem. In 1917, British forces rallied on Mount Scopus before their descent on to the city. In 1948, however, when the Arab Legion assembled here for the advance on west Jerusalem, they were defeated and driven off the peak. The Israelis then held it as a besieged island of Jewish territory east of the ceasefire line until 1967, when normal life resumed.

Much of Mount Scopus was purchased in the 1920s by Jewish organisations. High on the hill, the impressive **Hebrew University**▶▶, opened in 1925, was rebuilt on dramatic lines (tours daily at 9 and 11am). Near by stands the **Hadassah Hospital**▶, also opened in 1925. Just below is the **Commonwealth Cemetery**▶, containing the graves of British soldiers who fell fighting in Palestine during World War I.

▶▶ **Mount Zion**
(Hebrew: Har Tsion)   47D2

The name Zion, as a synonym for Jerusalem and even for Israel, conjures much passion. The hill called Zion today is the westerly of two small peaks lying south of the Old City. Apart from the Armenian quarter, which climbs the northern slope, Mount Zion lies outside the city wall. It is dominated by churches built over revered religious sites, yet these, more than most, are without biblical or historical provenance.

A place of history In earlier times, Zion was the name given to the most easterly of the two hills – the one on which stood the Jerusalem of King David and King Solomon. Nowadays that is called Mount Ofel. Under Hezekiah, the city grew to cover Ofel, Zion and Mount Moriah (Temple Mount): his city limits remained right up to the time of Herod, when Jerusalem expanded into the area of today's Old City (except for the northeastern and northwestern corners). By Byzantine times it filled the whole of the present Old City, plus the Zion and Ofel peaks, and so it stayed until Crusader times, when the Soldiers of the Cross erected new defences, roughly following the city walls as we see them now – this time leaving the Ofel and Zion hills outside their defensive circle.

A place of piety Half the hill is taken up by Christian cemeteries. The pretty **Church of St Peter in Galicantu**▶ (meaning, 'at the cock-crow'), was built in 1931 by Barluzzi on 1st-century ruins and recalls St Peter's three denials of Christ before cock-crow. It is also claimed as the site of the **House of Caiaphas**▶, the high priest before whom Jesus

Mount Scopus is now dominated by the Hebrew University

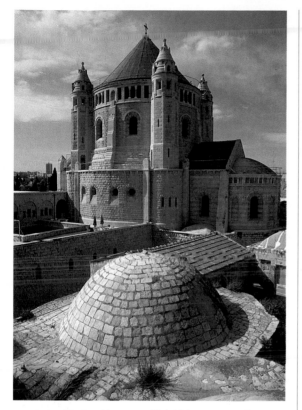

Schindler's grave
Jews and Catholics alike
make their way through
the Catholic cemetery on
Mount Zion to pay their
respects to a notorious
womaniser, drinker and
wheeler-dealer who joined
the Nazi party and played
the Nazi era for all he
could make out of it. Oskar
Schindler, immortalised in
Spielberg's 1994
blockbuster, *Schindler's
List*, lies buried here. Like
many other German busi-
nessmen, Schindler used
Jewish slave labour in his
Polish factory but, while
other manufacturers
worked their slaves to
death, Schindler found
ways of helping them
escape to Palestine. Some
1,200 owed their lives to
him. Schindler died in
Germany in 1974 and, at
his own request, was
buried on Mount Zion.

97

*The fairy-tale church
of the sleepy Virgin*

was brought after his arrest. The 19th-century pale stone
Church of the Dormition▶ under its conical roof, stands
where, according to Byzantine legend, Mary fell into eternal
sleep. Lavish gold mosaic work decorates the interior.

Just beyond is a building that contains **David's Tomb▶**,
revered by Orthodox Jews as well as Christians, even
though its location is incorrect: David was buried in the
City of David (I Kings 2: 10). This present 'tomb' is a 4th-
century invention within the remnant of a synagogue later
incorporated into a Crusader church. It is richly adorned,
with an embroidered cloth cover. The room itself contains
Torah scrolls and is used as a synagogue. Many Jews
pray here on Shavuot, traditionally the day of King David's
death. Upstairs is the vaulted **Cenacle▶**, or Coenaculum,
the so-called Room of the Last Supper, whose location
was chosen in the 12th century. Inside, a slab of stone
shows exactly where Jesus sat during the meal! Facing
it is a Muslim prayer niche. This room is also revered
as the place where the Holy Spirit descended
upon the disciples as they gathered for Shavuot
(Pentecost in the Christian church), seven
weeks later.

Opposite David's Tomb, the **Chamber of the
Holocaust▶▶▶** may lack Yad Vashem's awesome memorial (see page 102), but this small
museum is just as heart-wrenching. A particularly horrifying feature is the display of anti-
Jewish material published since the Holocaust.

*Sun symbol carved
on the façade of the
Room of the Last
Supper*

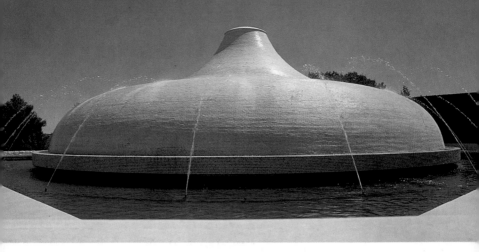

*The lid-shaped
Shrine of the Book*

Bedouin scroll hunters
The first of the Dead Sea
Scrolls was found in 1947
by a young Bedouin
shepherd. He sold it a
few months later to Arab
traders who, to maximise
their profits, divided the
scroll up and offered the
parts for sale separately to
academics and institutions.
In 1949, archaeologists and
researchers moved in to
look for more scrolls. Even
while they were conducting
their research unsuccess-
fully, new finds were being
made by Bedouins. Of the
10 new caves containing
scrolls, most were dis-
covered by Bedouin
shepherds, including the
two caves that contained
the most important of the
documents.

►►► **Shrine of the Book**   46A2

Ruppin Street

This is the permanent home of the Dead Sea Scrolls (see
pages 222–3) and other ancient manuscripts, including
original biblical texts. The strange white shape of the
Shrine of the Book represents the lids of the earthenware
jars in which the scrolls were found. The Shrine forms
part of the Israel Museum, and stands alongside the main
museum complex.

Inside, the unusual roof covers a vast circular room
around which is displayed an unrolled scroll containing a
large part of the Book of Isaiah, written in 100 BC. Almost
identical in every detail to the Book of Isaiah contained in
later and modern Bibles, it is used as evidence that the
Jewish scriptures remained unchanged as they were
copied faithfully by one generation of scribes and passed
down to the next.

Other rooms downstairs display a range of letters and
scripts from the Second Temple period, as well as documents from Masada (AD 70) and others written during the
Second Revolt (AD 135), all of which have been of vital
importance in enabling scholars to reconstruct the events
of this troubled period. The low lighting of the room has a
perfectly scientific rationale, yet it inspires a fitting sense
of awe and an almost reverential atmosphere. The official
guides seem infected, too, speaking with quiet urgency
and passion about the 2,000-year-old writings.

►   **Supreme Court**   46A3

Guided tours (in English) Sun–Thu at noon

Israeli architecture has won few accolades. From 1948 to
the 1990s, it can be characterised as bland and functional.
A breakthrough came with the opening in 1992 of the
new Supreme Court building on a hilltop near the
Knesset, to which it is linked by a walkway. Since then
several often inspired, imaginative and satisfying designs
have been brought to fruition. Brother and sister archi-
tects Ram and Ada Karmi were responsible for the
Supreme Court, a triumph of elegant traditional simplicity
in pale Jerusalem stone which proves that it is possible
for the modern, functional and unpretentious to be beautiful as well. The building was entirely paid for by the
Rothschild family and estate.

■ **Non-Jews often think that all Jewish men wear a *kippah* (*kappel* or *yarmulke* in Yiddish), a small skullcap. In fact, most do not, unless they are in a synagogue. Misconceptions about the Jewish religion are rife among outsiders, and that has led to wild accusations and murderous hatred in the past. But the Jews are not very forthcoming about their beliefs, and even on a visit to Israel it is possible to spend time among observant Jews and yet come away with no idea what they believe or how they practise their religion.** ■

An open book 'People of the Book' is an apt description for the Jews. Jewish prayer is formalised and traditional, with set words being read in a set order from an authorised prayer book. Synagogue services are relaxed, amiable and not especially reverent. At morning prayers men wear a *tallit* (prayer shawl), *tefillin* (two small leather boxes containing scriptural texts, worn every day except the Sabbath), and *kippah* as a head covering; at least 10 men (or women, in non-Orthodox congregations) must be present for key prayers to be said. At Monday, Thursday and Saturday (sabbath) services, the week's 'portion' of the Torah (the first five biblical books) is read aloud by selected congregants from a handwritten scroll; other members of the congregation follow the text in a book (the *Humash*). Much daily ritual, blessing and prayer, again from the prayer book, takes place at home.

Time and ritual The weeks, months and years are marked by their own prayers and rituals. High point of the week is sabbath, welcomed on Friday night with blessings, candle-lighting, wine and *hallah* (sabbath bread), and followed by a family meal. Annual festivals recall historical events, in accord with biblical precepts and seasonal customs. Pessah (Passover), for example, is a spring festival, decreed in the Torah as a memorial to the Jewish exodus from their enslavement in Egypt.

Getting it right The essence of Judaism is not belief, but behaviour. The important thing is to observe the *mitzvot* (commandments) laid down in the scriptures. Numbering 613 altogether, these encompass every area of life from business to bedroom, childbirth to charity.

A la carte religion For most Israelis, though, the *mitzvot* are not really rules at all, but traditions. Some are considered part of 'being Jewish' – like having sons circumcised, keeping the festivals and not eating pig meat. Others are considered unnecessary – like going in the *mikveh* (ritual bath) after menstruation, saying a blessing over bread before every meal or having the hairstyle described in Leviticus. Even some 'observant' Jews don't obey all the rules, and those who do are in the minority.

For non-Jews visiting a synagogue ...
● Any room containing a Torah scroll may be a synagogue.
● Men should cover their heads whether or not a service is in progress. Paper skullcaps are usually provided for visitors.
● Formal dress is not required, but modesty is. Legs should be covered to the knee, but women should not wear trousers.
● Do not walk about while the congregation is standing or while the Torah is being read, and do not speak or distract anyone while the silent prayers are being read.
● In an Orthodox or Conservative synagogue, ensure that you remain in the men's or women's section as appropriate.
● There is no need to take part in the prayers.
● Do take a *Humash* (Torah text) and *siddur* (prayer book) from the shelves if you wish, but do not touch *tefillin* (leather scroll boxes), as these are sanctified ritual objects.

Top: Torah scrolls
Below: reading the Torah

After dark
After you have seen the Nahalat Shiv'a pedestrianised area during the day, come again in the evening. These traffic-free lanes, between Jaffa Street and King George V, are the city's favourite after-dark hangout, with a café every few metres, scores of crowded tables in the open air, bookshops, jewellery stores and snack take-aways open late into the night.

▶▶▶   **West Jerusalem**   *46B1 and 2/C1 and 2*

Sir Moses Montefiore built the first new Jewish district outside the Old City in 1860. Mishkenot Sha'ananim, as it is called, stands at the southern end of what is now the picturesque and appealing old **Yemin Moshe**▶ district (see page 104) beside the walls. Nowadays, almost all Jerusalem's residents (including the Arab minority) live, work and play outside the walled tourist heartland and the area to the west of the Old City has become the bustling city centre of today.

The second of the new Jewish districts was Nahalat Shiv'a. Part of it, a little tangle of renovated pedestrianised streets around **Ben Yehuda Street**▶▶▶ is now the favourite area of Jerusalemites for strolling, browsing, chatting in the open air and whiling away the hours at outdoor café tables. At the junctions of these traffic-free lanes, vendors hawk newspapers in a dozen languages and buskers sing or play the violin. The atmosphere thrillingly combines the Middle East with middle Europe.

In 1886 the city's big, busy food market was started at **Mahaneh Yehuda**▶▶, a few minutes' walk northwest from Ben Yehuda. Later, broad avenues with dignified names were laid out linking the new neighbourhoods. They have since become the city's traffic-filled main streets. **King George V**▶▶ (and its continuation Keren HaYesod) and **King David**▶ are lined with substantial civic and religious buildings, international offices and hotels. The two streets, meeting at Plumer Square, form the arms of a triangle whose third side is **Yafo (Jaffa) Street**▶▶, a hectic, crowded, fascinating thoroughfare.

Above and right: passing the time in the streets of Jerusalem

Walk West Jerusalem

Allow at least 3–4 hours for this quick tour of the modern city centre (for map see page 46B2/C2). Start from the **Tourist Office** at 24 King George V Street. Head along King George and turn right into Shatz Street, which reaches HaNagid Street: at No 12, see the **Jerusalem Artists' House►**, with galleries and a café, next to the **Bezalel Academy of Art►** founded at the start of the century. Turn back to King George and turn right, passing the **Tzavta Theatre**. At the **Jewish National Fund** office, you can arrange to plant a tree in one of the forests on the city's perimeter.

The large Orthodox **Great Synagogue►** is well worth a look inside. Beside it, the **Wolfson Museum of Art►**, specialising in Judaica, shares a building with the Chief Rabbi's office. You then come to **Kikkar Tsarfat►** (or France Square, also called Place de France), Jerusalem's central square, formed by the meeting of King George V, Keren Hayesod, Ramban, Aza (or Gaza), and Gershon Agron streets. On one corner stands the main Conservative Synagogue.

A few paces along Ramban Street, an old windmill has become the basis for a shopping centre full of fashion boutiques and eating places. Turn left along Gershon Agron Street and left again into pleasant **Independence Park►**. Stroll across to Hillel Street. At No 27 is the interesting **Museum of Italian Jewish Art►** and a restored 18th-century **Italian synagogue►** brought stone by stone from Italy and reconstructed.

Take Angelo Blanchini Street to reach the pedestrianised area. Walk along **Ben Yehuda Street►►►** to another focal point, **Kikkar Tsion►** (or Zion Square). Head up Harav Kook Street to **Ticho House►►**, once the home of artist Anna Ticho, now part of the Israel Museum, and full of her pictures. Walk along Jaffa Road and turn left into King George V. This busy section has many shops selling clothes, books, food and much else.

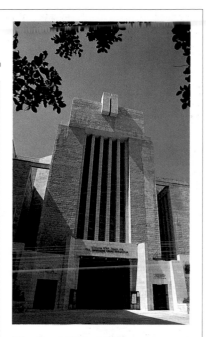

101

The Great Synagogue

Independence Park

Yad Vashem
The name, Yad v'Shem, means 'A Memorial and a Name' – that is, for every victim of the Holocaust. The opening times are Sunday to Thursday, 10–4.45 and Friday, 9–2.

The symbolic Pillar of Heroism

The Silent Cry, one of the sculptures making up Yad Vashem's Art Museum

The Holocaust
Holocaust *(shoah* in Hebrew) literally means 'burn whole'. Until the Nazi era, the word usually referred to religious sacrifices. The Nazi Holocaust burned deep scars in the contemporary Jewish psyche and the creation of the State of Israel received much of its impetus from the heightened desperation of Jews to find a safe haven, just as much of its international support is due to the moral legitimacy conferred by the tragedy.

▶▶▶   **Yad Vashem**   *46A1*

The world's leading Holocaust memorial, museum and documentation centre covers a ridge of high ground named Har HaZikaron – literally, the Hill of Memory – rising west of the Mount Herzl summit.

For anyone who has come to Israel for enjoyment and relaxation, a visit to Yad Vashem may seem a daunting prospect. Difficult though the experience can be, it will only heighten an appreciation of the country and its people. Once you have absorbed the awful facts of recent Jewish history, you will view the energy and determination of Israelis to enjoy life to the full with new eyes. As for anyone who has come to Israel in order to gain greater understanding of the Jews and their land, a morning at Yad Vashem is essential. Not always easy to find your way around, the site is sprawling, wooded in part, offers broad views westwards towards central Jerusalem and contains several different buildings.

Visiting the site Start by walking the length of the **Avenue of the Righteous among the Nations**▶, along the south side of the memorial area. This commemorates non-Jews who risked their own lives in order to save Jews during the Holocaust. They are named individually. The avenue is lined with trees planted by the Righteous themselves. This leads to the **Historical Museum**▶▶▶, containing the main permanent exhibition. Here documents and photographs chronologically trace the course of Hitler's 'final solution to the Jewish problem.' Many dry German government publications and posters are

displayed; this matter-of-fact material contrasts with the disturbing photographs of dead women piled in heaps like rag dolls, camp inmates pushing corpses into furnaces and of laughing German soldiers humiliating or arresting Jewish children. Immediately opposite, the massive, undecorated **Hall of Remembrance►** is a large, grim chamber containing little but a memorial flame in front of a vault full of victims' ashes. The names of the Nazi death camps are set into the floor.

Ahead is a plaza with a building on the far side. The entrance on the right leads into a synagogue. That on the left leads to the **Hall of Names►►**, where the names of all Holocaust victims are inscribed on plaques once the evidence has been verified. So far, over three million names have been written up, and more are being added constantly. Below is the access to the **Art Museum►►**, a remarkable collection of drawings and paintings made by concentration camp inmates. Further on is the **Partisan's Memorial►►** and, further still, the wooded, walled **Valley of the Communities►►**, recording the names of the communities entirely destroyed during the Holocaust.

In the Yad Vashem grounds, several **sculptures►►►** form an integral part of the memorial. Outside the Art Museum the disturbing collection includes *The Unknown Righteous Man among the Gentiles*, *Auschwitz*, *Job*, *Ultima* and, by the plaza, *Dry Bones*. Across the plaza stands the powerful *Silent Cry*. From here, walk towards the Children's Memorial, pausing at the heart-rending *Korczak and the Children of the Ghetto* Korczak was a teacher who voluntarily accompanied his pupils to death at Treblinka because he could not bear to see them taken away with no one to care for them.

The underground **Children's Memorial►►►** is in memory of the 1.5 million young children and babies killed in the death camps. Inside, it is dark except for myriad pinpoints of light like stars, each representing the life of a child taken away. A ceaseless, droning tape reads the list of their names, places of birth and ages. More sculpture, including *Hope*, can be seen on the way to the site exit.

The Hall of Names records all known victims of the Holocaust

Tips for a visit to Yad Vashem
● Don't take children to see Yad Vashem. Although groups of Israeli schoolchildren are taken around the site, most clearly either do not understand its importance or, in a few cases, are very deeply shocked by what they see. Noisy, laughing youngsters also diminish the impact of the memorial for others, dishonouring the Holocaust victims.
● Come in the morning, giving time to see the whole museum and memorial without haste.
● Avoid coming with a group if possible. Yad Vashem should be seen at your own speed, with the time and privacy to reflect on the exhibits.
● However long or short a time you spend here, do not miss the Children's Memorial on any account.

*Desirable residences
in the Yemin Moshe
district*

**Haas and Sherover
promenades**
The most spectacular view
of Jerusalem, Old and
New, is from the Walter
and Elise Haas Promenade,
a handsome paved walk-
way some 600m long , set
on a ridge of high ground
in the new southern neighbourhood of East Talpiot.
The more recent Gabriel
Sherover Promenade
(more usually called by the
Hebrew name Tayelet
Sherover), again with
superb Old City views,
descends through fine
landscaped gardens.

► **Yemin Moshe** 46C2

This charming, picturesque neighbourhood, constructed
by the philanthropist, Sir Moses Montefiore, in the 1860s,
rises from close to the southwestern tower of the Old City
walls. This was the first settlement to be built outside the
walls, and it has since attracted a number of artists whose
work is sold in the area's galleries. The whole district has a
quiet sense of well-being. Its pale stone paving and
buildings climb in stepped alleys and lanes, giving glorious
views, up to **Bloomfield Gardens►** and the famous
Jerusalem landmark, **Montefiore's Windmill►**. Intended
to provide a means of income for the first residents of
Yemin Moshe, the windmill has since been transformed
into a museum dedicated to the life and times of Sir
Moses Montefiore (1784–1885) who was a remarkable
early pioneer of Jewish rights. Born in Livorno, Italy, he
made a fortune as a stockbroker in London, becoming
sheriff of the city in 1824 before retiring to devote the rest
of his long life to founding schools and hospitals, both in
Britain and in Jerusalem.

► **Zoo** 46A1

At Manahat (also known as Malka), on the southwestern
outskirts of the city, the modern **Tisch Gardens Biblical
Zoo►►** consists of 26 hectares of landscaped parkland
with lakes, waterfalls and lawns, set against a backdrop of
desert hills. Animals wander at liberty, separated from
humans by moats or natural earth banks. Here you can
see the now-rare animals mentioned in the Old
Testament, all of which were once native to the region,
including lions and tigers.

■ **Israel adores its children. They are indulged, undisciplined, ill-mannered, and forgiven by everyone. Even dare to mention that they might be a nuisance, and eyebrows will be raised. Somehow, their exuberance and enthusiasm, their noisy boisterousness, their robust, tanned health and energy, all seem to symbolise the state itself. Israel, too, is young and new and vulnerable. But above all, the children of today are alive. Even now, when Israelis look at their children, they are reminded of a dark past, and an uncertain future.** ■

A precious generation Children seem to be everywhere. School groups, sometimes in neat lines, but more usually like a horde of Tartars, are taken to see every monument and memorial to Israel's creation, every museum of importance. They are always accompanied by an armed guard, sometimes a soldier but more often a parent who is an army reservist with full weapons training (the guns are not loaded – bullets are carried separately).

Those who died Before the policy of providing guards began in the 1970s, Palestinian attacks on children were common. School parties, school buses and children's houses in kibbutzim were considered legitimate targets by the PLO. Scores of children were murdered. But overshadowing even these tragedies looms the Holocaust. Common images of Holocaust victims are of adults. In reality, a quarter of all Jews killed in the gas chambers were children. For Israelis today, it is a joy to see Jewish children alive and enjoying their liberty.

Sabras The *sabra* is a prickly pear cactus, spiny outside, sweet within. That is how the new generation of Israelis looks to outsiders. A third of all Israeli children now have mixed Ashkenazi/Sephardic families. Chattering (or rather, shouting) in fluent secular Hebrew, a language that did not exist a century ago, taller, stronger, healthier than their mothers and fathers, bold and forthright, and with a country to call their own, they are being nurtured as a new type of Jew.

Israeli children enjoy a freedom their parents did not know

Innocent play

Accommodation

Bed and breakfast

'Good Morning Jerusalem' is the organisation that co-ordinates over 100 bed and breakfast guesthouses in the city and environs. Prices are relatively modest, guesthouses are graded by size and comfort, and all the host families speak English. For bookings or information, contact their reservations centre in Jaffa Road, opposite Jerusalem's central bus station, tel: 02 651 1270.

King David Hotel is the grandest in Israel, and full of historic importance

The Laromme, with innovative architecture and luxurious accommodation, is the modern style of Israeli hotel

The key to enjoying this sprawling city is to be in the right part of it. Top choice would be to stay near the attractions of the Old City, though not too near, as it can be noisy and crowded. The vivacious and agreeable city centre (west Jerusalem) has most of the best hotels in every price range, and is an easy walk from the Old City. The smallish Arab district (East Jerusalem) just north of the Old City walls is atmospheric but less modern. One or two of the further-flung districts are also surprisingly convenient and enjoyable. In most parts of town, there is a wide choice. Of some 8,000 hotel rooms in the city, over 3,000 are graded de-luxe, but there is a good range of budget-priced accommodation, as well.

Central Jerusalem On the top rung, the King David Hotel (King David Street, or Rehov David HaMelek), built in 1931 (see page 90), is legendary, although, thanks to

continuous updating and modernisation, it has left behind much of its pre-war grandeur. For all that, it is supremely comfortable, well located, with excellent food, facilities and service, and set in considerable grounds, which face the Old City. The King David is part of the top-level Dan chain, which also owns the atrium-style Dan Pearl, facing Mount Zion and not far from Jaffa Gate.

Most international names are on or near King David, Keren Hayesod and King George V streets: here you will find the Sheraton, Hyatt, Hilton, Laromme and Moriah Plaza. Plenty of good places fill the middle and lower price bands, such as the Windmill (off Keren Hayesod) and Tirat Batsheva (King George V Street). Lower down the scale, the inexpensive YMCA (opposite the King David) is almost absurdly grand looking, and the facilities (especially for sports) are very good. There are also several ultra-cheap hostels, such as the Jerusalem Inn (Histadrut Street, near the pedestrian streets) and the Bernstein Youth Hostel (1 Keren Hayesod Street) for card-carrying youth hostel members.

Neo-Byzantine splendour: the grand but inexpensive YMCA

The Old City and East Jerusalem There is a plethora of budget hotels, dorms, religious hospices and hostels in the Arab districts around Damascus and Jaffa Gates and in the Old City Christian and Muslim quarters. Most are rather down at heel. The best are in HaNeviim Street. Note that late-night music and noise, as well as early morning *muezzins* calling the faithful to prayer, can be a nuisance. Up Salah ed-Din (Saladin) Street there is a string of low-priced hotels. Carry on into the American Colony to find arguably the most interesting and atmospheric hotel in the whole city, the oriental-style American Colony Hotel. A former pasha's palace, it is now a favourite venue for foreign correspondents and Palestinian leaders.

On a limb The original Jerusalem Hilton, the Sonesta and the huge Ramada Renaissance hotels, all superbly equipped, stand out west on, or just off, Herzl Boulevard, not far from the Knesset and the major museums, and close to the bus station with its regular departures to points all over the country. Further out, to the southwest, the Holyland Hotel is the place with the superb model of biblical Jerusalem in its grounds (see page 86). In the other direction, the vast and luxurious Hyatt Regency (32 Lehi Street) sits on the slope of Mount Scopus, with a magnificent city view.

Kibbutz near the city One of the best choices on many counts is the hotel at Kibbutz Ramat Rahel (or Rachel). This is equal to any 4-star hotel, is quiet and civilised, has good food, extensive grounds, a pleasant atmosphere, offers full use of the good kibbutz recreational facilities, and enjoys glorious views out towards the Judaean hills. The kibbutz passed into both Jewish and Arab lore in the 1948 war when it was on the front line and focus of ferocious battles; a kibbutz museum (8–noon daily) tells the story. The kibbutz stands half way between central Jerusalem and Bethlehem, thus making a useful base for touring and sightseeing.

Jerusalem's annual festivals and events
Poetry Festival: March
Book Fair: mid-April
Arabic Arts and Crafts: early May
Fireworks: two nights in May
Yom Yerushalayim (Jerusalem Day): three nights of festivities in May
Israel Festival: three weeks in May and June
Film: early July
Arts and Crafts: July and August
Puppet Theatre: August
Artists' Week: August
Early Music: September/October
Jerusalem March: October
Marathon: October

Eating out

Fink's
Fink's Bar (corner of Histadrut and King George V Streets) is a high-quality bar and restaurant in the style of pre-War Eastern Europe, much favoured by journalists and politicians. Eat hearty Slavic or Ashkenazi favourites or sit with a drink at the bar.

Kosher
The majority of eating places in Jerusalem are kosher (although most in Arab districts are not). Most big hotels offer something special and traditional for the Friday night sabbath dinner. On sabbaths and festivals, many Jerusalem restaurants are closed, but nearly all hotel restaurants remain open.

Israeli restaurants are refreshingly informal

Bed and board Almost all hotels offer a magnificent self-service buffet breakfast of hot and cold dishes, salads, fresh breads and fruit juices. It makes a great start to the day, and can take the edge off lunchtime appetite; a short midday break is usually enough. Bed and breakfast is the most sensible option when booking your trip, giving the freedom to eat dinner in or out of the hotel.

On the hoof In the Old City, the many small, unpretentious café-restaurants are a pleasure to use. The format is generally the same: frontage open to the street, and, within, a display of salads, pastries, sweets and savouries, falafels frying, shwarma on the spit, and some wipe-clean tables. In the city centre (West Jerusalem) there are scores of small restaurants offering houmous, falafels, latkes (potato fritters), omelettes, grilled meats, shwarma or shishlik (lamb or turkey kebab), salads, pizzas, ice-cream, cakes, juices and coffee.

Some mouthwatering little bakeries can be found on Jaffa and King George V Streets near Ben Yehuda Street and on the other pedestrian lanes – Lunz, Rishonim, Ben Hillel and Nahalat Shiv'a – which are packed with open-air tables. Most are adequate rather than good, though some have more style and reach a higher standard. Well-established favourites include the Rimon and Alno cafés around Ben Yehuda.

Dinner time Most hotels in town have at least one restaurant, usually 'dairy' as well as 'meat' eating places. Try the King David and the American Colony. Away from the hotels, better restaurants aim for either a French-Italian or an Austro-Hungarian style, though Yemenite restaurants provide a more exotic experience as well as excellent food. Well established are Little Italy (38 Keren Hayesod Street) for home-made pasta, Mishkenot Sha'ananim (Yemin Moshe, below the windmill) for Moroccan and French dishes, El Gaucho (22 Rivlin Street) for grills and Oceanus (7 Rivlin Street) for fish. For more ideas, pick up *Jerusalem Menus* from the tourist office.

Shopping

Where to shop Wandering along David Street and Street of the Chain, in the Old City, is sheer delight if you enjoy being assailed by a cornucopia of shopping choice across the whole range from cheap souvenirs to antique silver. From small open-fronted premises, some fine workmanship can be found at moderate prices, though a little haggling may be in order. All the specialities of Israel can be bought here. Outside the walls, there is no need to stay in the central shopping district along and between Jaffa Street and King George V Street: almost every other neighbourhood has its well-stocked shopping malls and centres. Some are huge. Talpiot (in the southwest) has the big Canyon Israel Shopping Centre, and Manahat or Malka (in the west) has the Malka Mall, the largest shopping centre in Israel.

What to buy Jewellery and silverware are great specialities. Silver ornaments and modern Judaica are seen in numerous shops, large and small, throughout the city centre and in the Old City. Necklaces and other jewellery of silver, gold and precious stones are also widely available at specialist stores, including along the Cardo, in the Jewish quarter of the Old City.

Diamonds are a major Israeli product and a tour of the National Diamond Centre (143 Bethlehem Road) is worth while. All sorts of creative jewellery, imaginative and of a high standard, is on offer: take a look, for example, at galleries along the main city centre streets. The King David Hotel has shopping arcades where some of the best in this field can be seen and purchased. Look out too for fine fashions, especially swimwear, in which Israel excels (swimwear giant Gottex is based here). Leather goods are another local strong point, including sandals, which are reasonably priced.

The silversmith's art

Bargain-price tapes and worry beads

One century ago
'In 1873 it was calculated that the Jerusalem Jews, who then numbered only a few hundred in all, were increasing at the rate of 1,200 or 1,500 souls per annum. The Russian persecution gave a great impetus to the movement. I suppose that the present Jewish population of the Holy City cannot be reckoned at less that 40,000 souls. And they are no longer a timorous, oppressed minority, but something more resembling the masters of the city.'

The Future of Palestine, Major C R Condor, 1892

Nightlife

Dress code
Whatever the event or venue, informal or casual dress is the norm in Israel. It often startles foreign visitors at official events to see Israeli dignitaries without jacket or ties. Televised Knesset proceedings likewise show members of Israel's parliament – including the Prime Minister – wearing open-neck short-sleeved shirts. For his important treaty signing ceremony with King Hussein of Jordan, the late premier Yitzhak Rabin wore a baseball cap. However, sloppy, scruffy clothing is not favoured, and immodest or provocative dress is definitely considered unacceptable.

What's on
For more ideas of what's on during your stay, ask the tourist office for copies of the current *This Week in Israel*, *Events in Jerusalem* and *The Jerusalem Tourist Guide*.

Nightlife is clean and wholesome

No sex please ... It might be thought that this capital city of religion and faith would go to sleep at an early hour. That is far from being the case. The city is full of life and there is masses to do right around the clock. However, nightlife does tend to be of a clean and wholesome variety. Raunchy nightclubs are few, and risqué acts frowned upon. Drama, ballet, concerts and bright and cheerful folklore shows are constantly available. The only exception is the sabbath (Saturday), when Jerusalem does become quieter than many other Israeli towns.

Evening air The heart of after-dark Jerusalem is the Nahalat Shiv'a area around Ben Yehuda Street and Zion Square. Along the pedestrian streets, crowds stroll in the open air and outdoor cafés are packed with people talking, relaxing and snacking, often to music, far into the night. From certain doorways comes the throb of popular music – late-night discos appealing mainly to the young.

Top of the pops Some evening entertainments are unashamedly touristic, but top quality, nevertheless. Among them comes the outdoor Son et Lumière at the Citadel (Tower of David), a superb show telling the history of the city in a magnificently appropriate setting (nightly except for Friday; take a sweater; tickets from hotels or the Citadel entrance at Jaffa Gate).

Song and dance Slick Israeli/Jewish folklore shows are put on in the big hotels. Often there are specials, such as a dramatised performance of a Yemenite wedding. Folk shows are put on at the YMCA, on King David Street, and at the Khan Theatre, in an old Turkish inn south of Yemin Moshe. Open-air concerts and shows are mounted during the summer at the Sultan's Pool amphitheatre below Yemin Moshe.

Arabian nights If you have seen the Israeli shows before, or want a change, take a trip into East Jerusalem for clubs and restaurants that put on the Arab version, with lilting oriental music and exotic (but again, not erotic) dance shows.

Practical points

THE JERUSALEM CIRCLE LINE סובב ירושלים

Information The Jerusalem tourist office is at 17 Jaffa Road (tel: 02-258844). It has masses of leaflets, ideas for guided tours, and copies of the latest editions of *This Week in Israel*, *Events in Jerusalem* and *The Jerusalem Tourist Guide*. Staff speak English and are helpful.

Getting around The Old City of Jerusalem is compact, with major sights just a few paces from each other. Outside the walls, by far the best way to get from one sight to another is on bus No 99, which follows a round-town circular route every two hours (Sun–Thu 10–4; Fri and the evening before public holidays 10am and noon). This gives you the freedom to get off at any point of interest, take a look round, and board the next No 99 bus to continue.

City buses in general are frequent and inexpensive. Bus drivers speak English, and stops have brief route details in English. For local bus information tel: 02 304 704 (English spoken). Services run from 5.30am to midnight, except on Friday (when services stop for the sabbath an hour before sunset) and on Saturday (no service until after sabbath ends, an hour after sunset). Services on Jewish holidays are the same as for the sabbath. From the city's main Jaffa Road bus station, buses leave every few minutes to towns and cities all over Israel. To Tel Aviv costs 11 NIS and takes an hour.

Regular taxis (called 'special taxis'), which generally wait outside hotels, are expensive. Agree the fare in advance or insist that the meter is used (Jerusalem cab drivers are notorious for overcharging). Cheaper *sherutim* (singular: *sheru*t), shared taxis which stick to a particular route, depart from set locations.

Business hours Banks are open 8:30–12:30 Sunday to Friday, and 4–6 on Sunday, Tuesday and Thursday. In tourist areas, some open 8:30–5:30 Sunday to Thursday, and 8:30–12:30 Friday. Main post offices open 8–6 Sunday to Thursday. Post office local branches open 8–12:30 and 3:30–6, but mornings only on Monday, Wednesday and Friday.

Guided walks
Numerous firms offer guided walking tours. Their leaflets are displayed at the tourist office and big hotels. The tourist office itself runs guided walks, free of charge. Ask them for dates and times.

111

Return to sender
'How much better informed the public now is than 20 years ago, when my letters were shelved in an English country post office, because they were directed to me at Jerusalem, and the postmistress said in explanation that she thought "all that was done away with" '.

Major C R Conder, 1892

Emergencies
Police 100;
Ambulance 101;
Fire 102; Tourist
Police 391250.

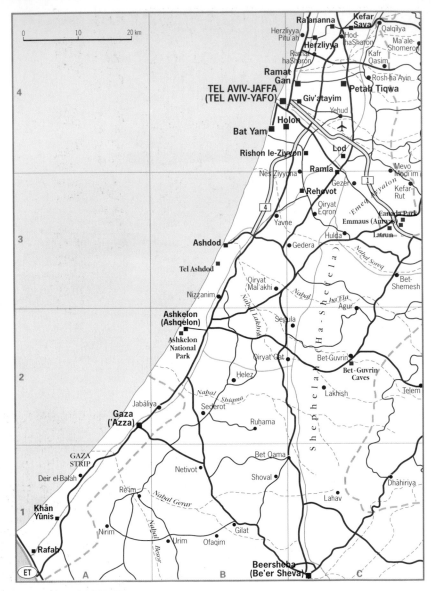

112

ET

Tel Aviv and the Coast The Mediterranean has dominated Israel's life and civilisation throughout the ages. Psychologically as well as physically, Israel faces west, for commerce, culture and communication. Almost the entire population lives on a narrow strip along the coast. Most of Israel's wealth comes from this busy, densely populated strip and from the farms of the well-watered Sharon plain, running north to south just inland from the sea. For the visitor wanting to combine beach life with exploration of the country's unrivalled array of ancient sites, it is convenient that (apart from the Negev desert) few places in Israel are further than 20km from a Mediterranean beach.

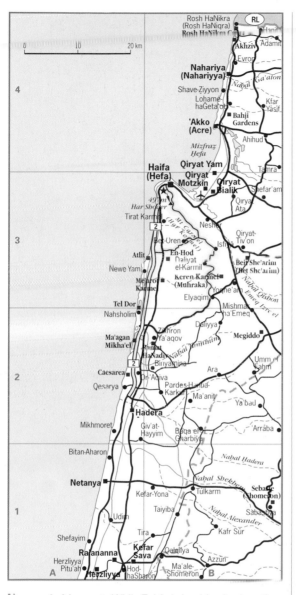

New and old resorts While Tel Aviv is a big city, bursting with energy, there is a string of quieter resorts, such as Netanya and Herzliya, up and down the coast. Here accommodation and leisure facilities tend to reach a far higher standard than anywhere else in the eastern Mediterranean. It is also possible to stay by the sea without being in town at all – for example, at a kibbutz hotel. Few resorts, whether in the town or the country, date back further than a few decades, and most are purpose built. Yet nearly all have a historical site near by, remnants of some earlier town – Phoenician or Jewish or Roman – which stood there thousands of years before, including the star attractions of Caesarea and Akko.

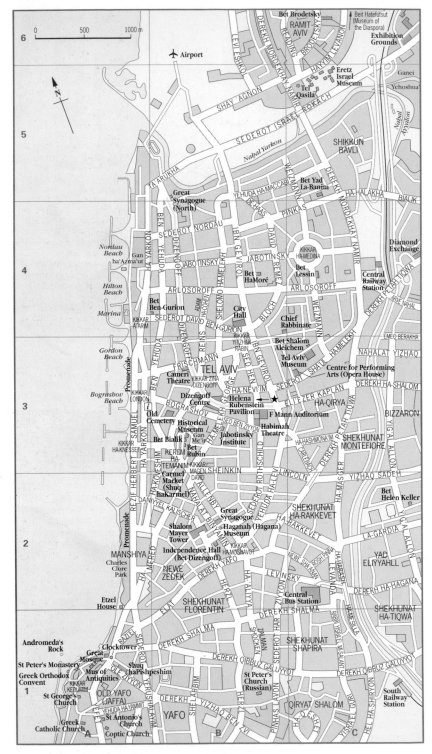

Tel Aviv

A century ago it wasn't here. The largest Jewish city ever to have existed has sprung up beside the Mediterranean with dizzying speed. The sense of liberation and excitement in the air is almost palpable. Tel Aviv has pulled fragments of a nation from the world's ghettos and Jewish quarters and, like a crucible, fused them together once again. A quarter of Israel's population lives in the city and its suburbs, which together form a hectic, dynamic conurbation dominating the country's cultural life.

Tel Aviv plays, Haifa works, Jerusalem prays. That is the popular summary of Israel's three cities. It is certainly true that, in Tel Aviv, very few pray: signs of Jewish observance, or of any other religion, are scarce. This is a breezily materialistic, pleasure-loving city. For round-the-clock entertainment and sheer *joie de vivre*, this is the place.

On the other hand, Tel Aviv at leisure will not appeal to everyone. It is a touch civilised. The city has dozens of first-class galleries and museums. People going out for the evening head to symphony concerts or stage plays, though there are jazz and rock venues too. Buskers in the street, almost without exception, play the violin: their repertoire is mainly classical or East European folk music. You probably won't, in any part of town, see anyone drunk. Nightclub acts tend towards satire, not strippers. Day and night, it is the vast beach and its waterside promenade which pull the biggest crowds of all.

An East Mediterranean city Tel Avivians compare their home town grandly to New York or Paris. True, there are smart shops and good restaurants, but the lively avenues and big squares, the broad sidewalks shaded from the sun, the outdoor tables and exuberant (but crime-free) street life, and the little backstreet shops with a pre-war feel, add up to an inescapably East Mediterranean feel. A more accurate comparison might be with Athens (but without the pollution), for Tel Aviv, like the Greek capital, is newly built, yet echoes with history. And, again like that city, it represents the joyful rebirth of a Mediterranean land swallowed up for centuries by the Ottoman Empire.

Death of a Peacemaker: Yitzhak Rabin (1922–95)
As Sabbath ended on 4 November, 1995, gunshots rang out at the Rally for Peace in Tel Aviv's Kings of Israel Square. As he left the podium bullets struck and killed Prime Minister Yitzhak Rabin. This distinguished general who, in 1967, led the Six-Day War victory and marched into a reuinified Jerusalem, was already a national hero when he embarked upon his task to create peace treaties between Israel and the PLO and her Arab enemies. At the next election, Binyamin Netanyahu was elected prime minister.

A Yitzhak Rabin memorial day is to be held every year on 12 Heshvan, the Hebrew date of his death, anf Kings of Israel Square has been renamed Yitzhak Rabin Square.

115

Mediterranean ambience

Follow the flag
All down Israel's Mediterranean coast, swimming conditions are indicated by coloured flags on the beach. White shows that swimming is safe where a lifeguard is on duty. Red shows that swimming could be dangerous, but is permitted at the discretion of the lifeguard on duty. Black means no swimming at all.

On the beach
Opposite the Dan Hotel, where now sunbathers laze, a ship carrying 850 clandestine Jewish immigrants finally came to rest on 22 August 1939. The overcrowded *Parita* had spent 42 days wandering at sea avoiding British craft intent upon preventing Jews from reaching Palestine.

Space to enjoy a swim or a stroll

▶▶▶ Beaches   *114A2–4*

A glorious 8km of wide, soft white sand runs beside the heart of the city. It is only a 10-minute walk from deckchair to Dizengoff, the main central avenue. More spectacular is the broad beachside **Promenade▶▶▶**, paved in swirling patterns, stretching from North Tel Aviv nearly into Jaffa. For most of the distance, busy Herbert Samuel Boulevard runs parallel. From 6am to 2am, you will see swimmers in the water and joggers on the promenade. And, facing west, the beach and promenade are perfect for sunsets. In the evening, buskers play the violin, sometimes even joining to form string quartets. Well past midnight, thousands of people still stroll or sit here in the tender night air.

Yet the water looks soupy, the undercurrents are powerful and the sand is dotted with oil. Join the Israelis, who happily swim and surf under the watchful eye of the lifeguards, and you will need to take a shower at the end of the day, wiping the oil off your feet with detergent-filled brushes provided at beach access points. Use towels, shoes and clothes that are not special favourites.

North of the main beach The bay by the harbour is dominated by noisy music from a café-bar. Next, Nordau beach divides into enclosed men-only and women-only areas, mainly for the religious (men can use women's beaches if accompanied by a woman). Two more small bays lie below the Hilton Hotel.

Marina and public pool This agreeable pay-to-enter swimming and sunbathing area, below the Carlton Hotel, has lawns, shade and good amenities.

Main beach and promenade This starts at Kikkar Atarim (or Namir), an ugly plaza with unenticing cafés. About 100m beyond, a far more agreeable, traffic-free section lies below the Sheraton Hotel, with open-air tables. Then the boulevard sweeps down to the promenade and a string of up-market sea-view hotels. The low-rise **Dan Hotel**, despite a garish exterior, is considered the city's best. Below it, the gardens of **Kikkar London▶** face the sea, and **Yotvata Dairy Restaurant** attracts big crowds day and night. The prestige **Opera Tower** apartment block is the latest landmark. Beach and promenade, less opulent south of this point, fade away just before rubbish-strewn **Charles Clore Park▶**.

South of the main beach The boulevard turns away from the sea by a mosque, but the promenade resumes beside a shore of heaped, rough rocks. Finally there is a pleasant little sand beach with a bar, but bathing is forbidden. Here the part-old, part-new **Etzel Museums▶▶** tell the story of the Irgun Tzvai Leumi (see page 119). Where the beach and walkway end, a road continues southwards into Jaffa (see page 124) with its busy port and its fine views back to Tel Aviv.

▶ **Ben-Gurion House** 114B4

17 Ben-Gurion Boulevard
This was the home of Israel's charismatic and powerful first prime minister, David Ben-Gurion (1886–1973) and his wife, Paula. The small and simply furnished house has been preserved as it was during their lifetime, and is full of personal memorabilia, items of political and historical interest and a library of 20,000 volumes.

▶ **Bialik House (Beit Bialik)** 114B3

22 Bialik Street
Haim Nachman Bialik (1873–1934), revered as the greatest modern Hebrew poet, designed this house, with its Moorish echoes, as his home (1926–33). Kept unchanged since his death, it contains pictures, letters and memorabilia that tell the story of his life and work.

▶▶▶ **Carmel Market (Shuk HaCarmel)** 114B2

This big daily market extends along narrow HaCarmel Street (off Allenby Street) and adjoining lanes. Despite the lack of traffic, it is noisy with stallholders' cries and the crush of people walking, talking and haggling. You will find stalls selling CDs, shoes, clothes, garlic, fruit, vegetables and bagels. Some stalls have only nectarines or olives, others lie buried in fresh herbs. In parallel Yomtov and Godera streets, stalls are loaded with meat. Here the robust younger generation mingles with greybeards and their headscarfed wives, and Eastern Europe meets Jewish Arabia. In the adjacent run-down **Yemenite Quarter▶▶** (or Kerem HaTemanim), many of the simple houses still keep their overhanging balconies and small courtyards.

Opera Tower
This prestige apartment tower, with its shopping complex, cinemas and restaurants, stands on the beachside boulevard on the site of Israel's first Knesset (parliament building) at 1 Allenby Street. The War of Independence made occupation of the Jerusalem Knesset impossible until December 1949. Later, the Tel Aviv Knesset building was used as the city's opera house until a magnificent new opera house was opened in October 1994.

Bauhaus
Large tracts of 1920s Tel Aviv consists of 'workers' residences' constructed by the Histadrut labour union in the inexpensive, functional Bauhaus design. The war destroyed Germany's Bauhaus buildings, leaving Tel Aviv with the finest collection anywhere of this 20th-century style – over 3,500 buildings in total. The Museum of Art (see page 130) runs a free weekly Bauhaus bus tour with English commentary. They will pick you up at your hotel – to book, call the Tel Aviv Museum of Art, tel. 03 695 7361.

117

Carmel Market's inviting stalls

Early town planning
When Tel Aviv's avenues were first laid out, they say, the plan was to make them in the shape of a *menorah* (the seven-branched candelabrum that once stood in the Temple and that is now the symbol of the state). Instead, the builders diverted what is now Ben-Gurion Boulevard towards their favourite beachside bar.

Traditional crafts at the Eretz Israel Museum

The first streets
Some of the first streets in Tel Aviv were laid on sand just north of Jaffa, in the area called Neve Tzedek, located behind the Dan Panorama hotel, and south of one of the city's tallest buildings, the Shalom Tower, a district of quiet streets lined by small two-storey houses. While many are scruffy and run down, others have been smartened up, as gradually the merits of the neighbourhood are being rediscovered.

▶▶ **Eretz Israel Museum** *114C5*
2 University (or Haim Levanon) Street, Ramat Aviv
Take a No 25 bus out of central Tel Aviv to travel north of the Nahal (river) Yarkon to this immense and imaginative national museum on the site of an excavated *tel* (settlement mound). Eretz Israel means 'Land of Israel', and in a dozen separate areas and pavilions the museum covers various themes spanning 3,000 years in the history of Israel's material culture and ethnography. It is a good idea to buy the inexpensive site map on arrival, which makes it very easy to find your way around. The museum literature also recommends two possible routes through the grounds, one short (half a day) and the other long (a full day), though even this is barely adequate if you want to examine the pavilions in detail. Many exhibits were actually discovered here and are displayed *in situ*. Between the pavilions and the open-air exhibits there are pleasant lawns and trees, plus a good restaurant and snack-bar.

Among the best exhibits are **Roman winepresses▶**, **Byzantine mosaic paving▶▶** and two **ancient roads▶** discovered one on top of the other. There is a superb **Planetarium▶▶**, but the commentary is in Hebrew only, unfortunately. The **Numismatics Pavilion▶▶** displays coinage across the millennia from shells to shekels, including biblical weights (of which the shekel is one). The **Nehushtan Pavilion▶▶** explains ancient mining, with useful information about Timna (see page 251). The **Folklore and Ethnology Pavilion▶▶** shows the unchanging traditions of Jewish ritual objects and apparel from ancient times to the present day. At the **Man and His Works Pavilion▶▶**, which is devoted to traditional handicrafts, you can see a glassblower at work and the workshops of a blacksmith and potter.

The grounds also include a whole archaeological site, **Tel Qasile►►►**, one of several *tels* on Tel Aviv's northern boundary. This was the first archaeological site to be excavated by Israel (in 1949): 12 settlement phases were found, with remnants of a temple and houses containing domestic objects, dating back to 1150 BC.

►► Etzel Museums   *114B3*

These three museums, known collectively as the Etzel Museums, tell the fascinating story of the Irgun Tzvai Leumi guerrilla organisation (1937–48), also known as Etzel, which took on the British Army (except during World War II) and helped to bring about the creation of the State of Israel, though using tactics condemned by the Haganah and official Zionist movement (see page 44). From 1943–48, its leader was Menachem Begin, later Israel's prime minister.

The plain white **Beit Jabotinsky►►►** building (opposite the Dizengoff Centre), covers the pre-1948 history of the organisation. Secret operations which attracted world-wide headlines are here explained with chilling step-by-step clarity, including the blowing up of the British headquarters in Jerusalem, at the King David Hotel (July 1946) when 91 people died, the destruction of the British Officers' Club (March 1947) when 17 people died, and the breaching of Akko Fortress (May 1947) when 30 Irgun and Lehi prisoners escaped.

A second museum, located beside the beach, close to Jaffa, is housed in the interesting **Etzel House►**, restored 'in memory of the liberators of Jaffa', and reveals Irgun's activities during the 1948 War of Independence. A third museum is located in **Beit Yair (Yair House)►**, at 8 Avraham Stern Street. This covers the history of the Lehi movement (also known as 'the Stern Gang'), the hardline splinter group that refused to co-operate with the British during World War II.

► Haganah Museum (Beit Haganah)   *114B2*

23 Rothschild Boulevard

Beit Eliahu (Eliahu House), home of the founding commander of Haganah, Eliahu Golomb, is a memorial to his life and times. Models and tableaux bring to life the history of Israel's armed forces, from their clandestine origins in 1907, through the creation of diverse undercover groups and up to the creation of the Israel Defence Forces in 1948.

► Historical Museum of Tel Aviv-Jaffa   *114B3*

27 Bialik Street

This round-fronted Bauhaus building, once Little Tel Aviv's Town Hall, looks across a small square, with a fountain, and recalls the creation and growth of the new city (see panel) using a mixture of old photographs, models and a film.

Little Tel Aviv
The beginnings of Tel Aviv lie in small Jewish neighbourhoods which were technically still part of Jaffa. The city really took off in 1921 when it was granted a charter as a separate town. A whole new district was immediately constructed a little further north, around Bialik Street, the nucleus of the first new Jewish city to be built in modern Israel. Its town hall in Bialik Square later became the Historical Museum. Full of socialist theory, the city's founders declared there would be no commerce or private business at all in Tel Aviv: everything would be run by the municipality. This dream bit the dust as entrepreneurial immigrants flocked in and opened the corner kiosks which are still such a feature of the city. As the town expanded, this original centre became known as Little Tel Aviv.

Patriotism rules at the Haganah Museum

A shady seat

A cross between a public garden and a street, there is a boulevard with a difference that curves right through the heart of Tel Aviv. It starts as Sederot Rothschild (Rothschild Boulevard) close to the Shalom Tower, continues, after Kikkar HaTizmoret and Kikkar HaBimah, as Sederot Hen, and becomes Sederot Ben-Gurion, which turns to reach the sea at Kikkar Atarim. For its entire length the two carriageways are separated by a broad sandy walkway shaded by leafy trees. Benches every few yards offer a chance to take a break from the noise, from sunshine and from sightseeing.

▶▶ **Independence Hall** 114B2

16 Rothschild Boulevard

The city's first mayor, Meir Dizengoff, lived in this austere bunker-like concrete building. On 14 May 1948 his home was the venue for the historic declaration that brought the State of Israel into being. The house has since become a fascinating museum (part of the Eretz Israel Museum, see page 118) recalling that momentous day, and the events which led up to it. Many other exhibits are concerned with the establishment of the city of Tel Aviv.

Among many extraordinary displays is a photograph showing sections of the sand dunes north of Jaffa being awarded by lot to anyone who wanted them, another picture of the United Nations (UN) in session in November 1947 voting to partition Palestine, and a third showing the meeting at which David Ben-Gurion announced the creation of Israel. Intriguing maps include one showing which countries voted for partition, and another showing the borders of the Jewish state as proposed by the UN – which was to consist of three small sections located between Tel Aviv and Haifa.

Alongside the hall in which the proclamation was made, the **Hall of Documents**▶▶▶ is a small annexe displaying a collection of original documents. One shows the draft proclamation with the name of the country still undecided – just days before the announcement. Pencilled-in possibilities included Zion and Western Eretz Israel.

Commemorating the founding of Israel

In the street outside, the rather impressive white memorial and fountain is known as the **Founders' Monument**▶. It names those who founded the city, and depicts the simple story of Tel Aviv in three bas-relief panels: labourers levelling the sand by hand and starting to build while harassed by snakes and jackals; some important early landmark buildings, including the first Hebrew secondary school; and the fully established modern city showing the port, art museum, theatre, the home of the national poet Bialik, and tower blocks behind.

מוזיאון ארץ־ישראל, תל־אביב Eretz Israel Museum, Tel Aviv

היכל העצמאות
Independence Hall

0600

Entrance Ticket כרטיס כניסה

Walk **Dizengoff Street**

No city-centre avenue conjures up the life and atmosphere of Tel Aviv so well as Dizengoff, named after the city's first mayor. To walk the full length – stopping to window-shop and see the sights – could take a morning, or longer still if you break for refreshment – maybe a falafel-in-pitta lunch or a fresh juice at one of the many snack-bars. As it continues northwards, the street's character changes to reflect different faces of the city and its people. The street's shaded west side is the more appealing (for map see page 114).

Dizengoff starts behind the modern **Mann Auditorium►**, home of the Israel Philharmonic Orchestra, and the national **Habimah Theatre►**, focal points of the city's thriving highbrow culture. **Dizengoff Centre** is Tel Aviv's main indoor shopping centre. **Dizengoff Circle►►►** (correctly, Kikkar Zina Dizengoff, named after the mayor's wife) is a popular, often crowded, plaza with cinemas and cheap eateries, as well as an area raised above the street where a gaudy multicoloured **fountain►** puts on a weird fire-and-water show to computerised music (11am–1pm and 7–9pm daily).
    From the Circle northwards, for several blocks, the street has a pleasant atmosphere, busy and crowded, and lined with snack-bars, juice-bars, fashion boutiques and jewellery stores, shaded by large trees.

Multicoloured fountain, at the centre of Dizengoff Circle

After the **Arlosoroff** junction things quieten down, as Dizengoff enters the more prosperous **North Tel Aviv** area. There are more food shops, while clothes stores take on a pricier, more exclusive look. Cafés become cooler and more stylish. Beyond the pleasant **Nordau** junction, Dizengoff narrows down, and close to the street's north end, around **Yirmehahu** junction, there is another little cluster of stylish boutiques and eating places. Just beyond this point, the Nahal HaYarkon (River Yarkon) marks the official city limit.

The tree-shaded pavement cafés of Dizengoff Street's northern stretch

■ **Little over a century ago Hebrew was not a spoken language at all. Most non-Jews thought it was a dead language, like Latin, and most Jews thought it was reserved strictly for prayer and ritual. Then Eliezer Ben-Yehuda arrived in Palestine from Lithuania. For him, it was imperative that Jews should speak their ancestral tongue in their own land.** ■

122

One of the people
Eliezer Ben-Yehuda was not the only East European Zionist who wished to re-establish the Hebrew language, the difference was that he actually went to Palestine and caused the language to be spoken. The Russian Zionist, Asher Ginsburg (1856–1957), also had a vision of Hebrew as the everyday language of the Jews, wherever they lived in the world. He ardently wanted the State of Israel to be created, but only as a spiritual and cultural centre for world Jewry. He himself did not envisage moving there. His vision attracted few followers, and he was an aloof wealthy character, living an almost aristocratic lifestyle – belying his pen-name of Ahad Ha'Am, literally 'One of the People'.

Nobel Laureate, Shmuel Yosef Agnon

Max Brod

Ben-Yehuda's 'crazy idea', as some described it, struck a chord with many people. By 1910, there were demonstrations calling for Hebrew to become the Palestinian Jews' official language. In 1924, the first Hebrew university opened. In 1966, a novelist writing in Hebrew, S Y Agnon, won Israel's first Nobel Prize for Literature.

New language, old language Today, as you walk in the bustling, lively streets of Israel's cities, passing newspaper stands piled high with different dailies and weeklies, all expressing varied viewpoints, or as you browse in the popular bookstores, listen to the radio or watch television, you will encounter Hebrew everywhere.
The early Zionists naturally assumed that Yiddish, the Jewish language based on medieval German and spoken by two-thirds of all Jews before the Holocaust, would be Israel's national language. True, the country does have

some Yiddish publications, just as it has Russian and English papers. But above all the life of Israel is conducted in Ivrit, as modern Hebrew is called. This is so closely based on biblical Hebrew that any Israeli schoolchild can read the ancient scriptures with ease. Similarly, Moses, King David or Solomon would be able to read a modern Israeli newspaper. Yet Ivrit includes many European (especially French and German) constructions, and much English-based vocabulary, making it a functional modern working language for everyday use.

The revival The inspiration behind Hebrew's renaissance was Eliezer Ben-Yehuda (1858–1922), who came from Lithuania to Palestine in 1881. This fanatic announced on arrival that he would not talk to his Yiddish-speaking wife and child except in Hebrew. He spoke to puzzled shopkeepers in Hebrew, wrote the first Hebrew dictionary and in 1890 founded the Hebrew Language Committee, later to become the Academy of the Hebrew Language, final arbiter on all matters of vocabulary. At first dismissed by the Zionist authorities as a harmless crank, he eventually led a mass movement they could not ignore.

Dots, capitals, roots A semitic language, written from right to left, Hebrew is hard to render into Latin letters. For one thing, it has no upper or lower case (capital or small letters), and words such as 'the' ('Ha') are joined to nouns as prefixes. For another, it has effectively two alphabets – one used in printing and one used for handwritten script. Then, more difficult, the all-important dots and dashes underneath consonants, used to indicate vowel sounds, are rarely shown. Sometimes vowels are barely pronounced (as in *K'far* or *Ketar*, village). Lastly, there is no agreed way of expressing Hebrew sounds in English. The guttural H is often written Ch. The sound Ei is also written E or Eh (as in Eilat). The letter *tzadik*, pronounced TZ, is often written as Z or even S (as in Sefat or Masada). The common word Beit – a house or institution – can be written Bet or Beth.

A nation of readers and theatre-goers Israel is reckoned to have more bookshops per head than any other nation. A UNESCO survey claimed that the proportion of Israelis who 'regularly buy books' is the second highest in the world (surprisingly, Iceland came first), way ahead of the USA or Britain. The world's literature, classic or modern, is avidly read in Hebrew translation. Shakespeare is constantly performed on the stages of Tel Aviv or Jerusalem, as are other great playwrights and contemporary Israeli works. The longest running play on the Israeli stage was not a comedy but Arthur Miller's *All My Sons*.

Writers of today Israel has produced a crop of novelists, dramatists and poets of its own (though few were born in Israel): in 1966, Shmuel Yosef Agnon (1888–1970), writing in German, Yiddish and Hebrew, was the first Israeli to win the Nobel Prize for Literature. A far better-known Israeli author is Amos Oz (born 1939), whose Hebrew novels and short stories have been widely translated, as have those of other distinguished Israeli writers such as Max Brod (1884–1968) and Ephraim Kishon (born 1924).

On the stage
HaBimah means 'the stage'. The platform on which the Torah is read aloud in a synagogue is also called the *bimah* and Israel's national theatre is called simply Habimah Theatre. It is housed in a large round modern building (in Kikkar HaBimah) beside the Mann Auditorium, the superb 3,000-seat concert hall (in Kikkar HaTizmoret) that is home to the renowned Israel Philharmonic Orchestra.

123

Israeli humorist, Ephraim Kishon

Pot luck
Inside the Jaffa Museum you can see a copy of the Harris Papyrus, which describes the conquest of the town in 1500 BC by the men of Pharaoh Thotmes III. Under their general, Tehuti, they entered the town by ship, concealed in hundreds of large earthenware cargo pots. Tehuti ceremonially announced himself to the governor of Jaffa, saying he had fled Egypt with a huge stolen treasure. Delighted, the governor invited him to a banquet while the pots of treasure were unloaded. Tehuti accepted, killed the governor over dinner and seized the palace, while his men attacked the city.

מקור
מנהלת נמל יפו
עוסק מורשה מס' 545000283

רשיון כניסה חד-פעמי להולכי רגל
129421 חשבונית מס'/ קבלה מס'
1.00 שקל חדש
המחיר כולל מע"מ
עפ"י תקנה שפורסמה בקי"ת מס' 5152 מיום 12.12.88
הרשיון מותנה בתנאים שמצד שני
תאריך

The historic port city of Jaffa

► ► ► **Jaffa (Yafo)**   114A1

The oldest still-working port in the world has become a suburb of the world's newest city. Approached along the seashore promenade or boulevard, only a short distance separates Jaffa from its neighbour, Tel Aviv. Inland, the two are joined and, since 1950, have been a single municipality. In 1960, the Jaffa Development Corporation set out to revive the squalid remnant of the town, and turned it into a place of entertainment and leisure. On Friday and Saturday evenings the atmosphere can be wonderfully vivacious and animated, as the crowds gather by the Clocktower or in Kedumim Square, to stroll and talk in the balmy air, or to eat at outdoor restaurants. The view along the seafront to Tel Aviv is superb.

Modern Jaffa conveys little sense of its long history. The earliest remains here date back to the 18th century BC. In the 12th century BC, Jaffa became part of the Israelite kingdom, and the Old Testament makes mention of the town several times. Under Solomon it was developed as the principal port for the Jewish capital, Jerusalem. The 12th and 13th centuries AD saw frequent invasion as successive Crusaders, including Richard the Lionheart, were beaten off. From that time, up until the British entered Jaffa in November 1917 (with the exception of Napoleon's destructive foray in 1799), Jaffa was resolutely Arab, and, despite its ups and downs, remained a busy port until modern times.

The 20th century led to far-reaching change, in some ways bringing Jaffa's history to an end (other than as a leisure district of Tel Aviv). By the start of the century, a few Jewish refugees had settled among the Arabs of Jaffa. They were made unwelcome, and, in any case, they aspired to better housing.

In 1909 a group called Ahuzat Bayit built a suburb on barren sands north of the port: that was the start of Tel Aviv. From then on, the building never stopped. In 1921, 1929 and 1936 Jaffa's Arabs rioted against the Jews, each time killing several people. The response of the British Mandate authorities was to cut avenues through the tangle of narrow streets, better to control civil disturbances, and a new port was constructed in Tel Aviv. It soon replaced the port at Jaffa; within months of the 1936 riots, the ancient port was closed down.

The bizarre 1947 UN Partition Plan placed Jaffa in an Arab state, and Tel Aviv in a Jewish one. Following the

Archaeological finds date Jaffa's origins to the 18th century BC

Docklands
Jaffa's historic docks, famous throughout the ages, have been turned into a curiously down-market, but atmospheric, pay-to-enter family entertainment area. The quays are lined with big old waterside warehouses, some of which have been converted to contain cheap shops and stalls or restaurants overlooking the harbour. In the water are pleasure boats (some with eating places on board) and a few fishing trawlers.

1948 Proclamation of the State of Israel, Jaffa's Arabs launched a full-scale military attack on Tel Aviv. They were defeated and many fled, tearing reprisals. Large areas of insanitary alleys and lanes were swept away. Today only a small number of residents are Arabs – Christian and Muslim – but Jaffa retains an oriental flavour, though that comes largely from the many Jews from Arab countries who live here.

The centre of activity is **Kedumim Square►►►**, a pleasant open plaza paved in pale stone. Around the square are places of entertainment, a nightclub, eating places and a large Catholic church. Steps dive below street level to the **Visitor Centre►►►**, in fact a simple little museum revealing what lies under the square – mainly walls and structures dating from around 300 BC. Off the square is the **Artists' Quarter►►►**, as it is known, a strangely quiet, picturesque district of narrow lanes with attractive Turkish-style dwellings.

The green **Abrasha Park►►**, rising from the square, is part of Tel Jaffa. At its summit there's an observation point with superb sea views. There is more history at the **Jaffa (or Antiquities) Museum►►**, a small museum (part of the Eretz Israel – see page 118) with an astonishing range of finds spanning the millennia, though it is difficult to follow the layout of the five halls and their contents. Just below it, close to the waterfront, rise the minaret and two colourful domes of **Mahmoodiye Mosque►**. Close by stands the un-Arabic looking **Clocktower►**, Jaffa's famous landmark, erected in 1906 to honour the rule of Turkish sultan Abdul Hamid II.

On the other side of Yefet Street are the squalid but busy streets of non-tourist Jaffa. Off Beit Eshel Street, near the Clocktower, you will find the atmospheric alleys and lanes of the extensive **flea market** (Shuk HaPishpeshim) – which is Jewish, not Arab, and open every day except for the sabbath.

Attractive Turkish-style dwellings in Jaffa's Artists' Quarters

125

Who returned?

Although every Jew has the right to choose to live in Israel, in practice most immigrants have been refugees, driven from their homes by force or under pressure of persecution or discrimination. Some 61 per cent have come from Europe and 18 per cent from Africa (almost all of these came from North African Arab states which expelled Jews from their homes; the others left South Africa after the start of apartheid). Some 15 per cent came from Asia, notably those who fled penniless from Yemen, while only 6 per cent have come from the Americas. Currently the population is being increased by thousands of new arrivals every year migrating from the former Soviet Union. Between 1989 and 1994 (latest figures) about 550,000 former Soviet Jews settled in Israel, adding over 10 per cent to the total population of the country.

Old and new

Tel Aviv was the Hebrew title of Theodor Herzl's seminal Zionist work, *Altneuland* (literally, 'Old-New Land'). The name is a play on words: a *tel* is a mound made by civilisations piled one upon the other. The word implies great antiquity. *Aviv* means springtime and newness. So the city's name could mean Hill of Spring, or Old and New. According to the Bible (Ezekiel 3 and 15), this is not the first town to be called Tel Aviv: there was one in ancient Babylon.

▶▶▶ **Museum of the Jewish Diaspora (Beth Hatefutsoth)** *114C6*

At Tel Aviv University (Gate 2), Ramat Aviv

Ranging over several floors of an unattractive modern building, but set in pleasant parkland in the University grounds, this museum is one of the most interesting in Israel and is excellent for an understanding of the country and its people. To gain a full appreciation takes a full day – perhaps longer – and photography is not allowed (cameras must be left at the desk).

In a succession of separate rooms, each dedicated to a particular theme, visitors wander down the generations, glimpsing the life of Jews in 80 different nations around the world (and 'speaking 100 different languages', according to a display caption), scattered since the destruction of the Temple in AD 70. The overall theme is the combination of Jewish diversity with Jewish commonality. The thesis of the museum is that it was their tenacious adherence to traditions – especially observance of the sabbath, rituals and festivals, and the constant focus on the idea of Eretz Israel – that enabled the Jews to remain as a single people and eventually to return to their homeland. Hand-in-hand with this uniformity of tradition and belief, a great deal of diversity developed in the different Jewish communities.

This 'uniformity with variety' is explored in scores of intriguing displays of ritual objects and clothing, books, photographs, models of housing and synagogues, videos, sound recordings and much else. The rooms are entitled **Family▶** and **Community▶▶**; **Faith▶▶** and **Culture▶▶**; Among the **Nations▶▶**; the **Return to Zion▶▶▶** and **Remembrance ▶▶▶**. There is also a particularly interesting room devoted to the theme of **Synagogue Architecture▶▶▶**. More recent periods are covered in **Jewish Theatre▶▶** and **Jews in Arts and Sciences▶▶**. In many exhibits, modern Jewry and Reform Judaism are contrasted with more ancient forms – frequently the links and similarities are striking.

Various **short films▶▶▶** deal with Jewish life in Eastern Europe, Greece and Morocco. A longer audio-visual show, called the **Chronosphere▶▶** (about 30 minutes) explores the Jewish Wandering, or Diaspora. Other films are shown on such subjects as Yiddish and the other Jewish lan-

guages. A number of fascinating and ingenious push-button displays and tableaux bring to life important episodes in Jewish history.

Some of the sections on the Yiddish-speaking world in **Eastern Europe before the Holocaust►►►** are painful to observe, revealing, as they do, the vibrant population and culture that was eliminated by the Holocaust. The **Jewish music►►►** of different places and periods can be heard, including the rousing pioneer songs of the socialist Second Aliyah (1904–14).

Within the museum, the **Dorot Jewish Genealogy Centre►** runs an ambitious project to record the family data of as many Jews as possible from all over the world, for the benefit of future generations and for the purpose of reuniting dispersed family members, and also simply to give people the chance to see if anything is already known about their family and its history.

For deeper research, there are also study areas where you can view films on topics related to diaspora life. The museum can also advise on particular subjects, and has a musicologist on the premises.

On the ground floor there's a pleasant, clean self-service cafeteria with good food, and customers are frequently entertained by traditional Jewish music played by invited performers. The museum's shop sells an interesting and unusual range of CDs and tapes of Jewish music.

The right to return
'Every Jew has the right to immigrate to Israel.'
– *The Law of Return*, 5 July 1950

Mystical symbols adorn the ceiling of this mid-17th-century synagogue from Poland

127

Tower of Peace
The curiously named Shalom Tower (Migdal Shalom, or 'Peace Tower') is an unattractive skyscraper dominating southern Tel Aviv. Consisting mainly of offices, it also has shops and snackbars on the ground floor, and a top-floor observatory (132m) with a restaurant. On the third floor is Mayerland, a small funfair-style recreation area, and the Israel Wax Museum, with over 100 models of figures from Israel's past.

► **Old Cemetery**   114B3
Trumpledor Street, off Pinsker
A high wall of stone blocks, in contrast to Tel Aviv's more typical concrete, encloses the city's original cemetery, founded in 1903. Many Zionist leaders, politicians and founders of the State – Nordau, Arlo, Zoroff, Dizengoff, for example – as well as poets Bialik and Tcherninchovsky, lie here. The tombs, packed extremely close together, can be hard to locate; the inscriptions are in Hebrew, as are the dates, which, in the Hebrew form, use letters instead of numerals.

► **Rubin Museum (Beit Rubin)**   114B3
14 Bialik Street
One of several interesting buildings along Bialik Street, the heart of the 1920s district known as Little Tel Aviv, this former home of the distinguished artist, Reuven Rubin, is now an enjoyable museum of his paintings and drawings. There are also frequent temporary exhibitions.

Old Cemetery, Tel Aviv

Walk Old Jaffa

This is an easy stroll around a small area. Old Jaffa today exists mainly as a tourist attraction, yet it has plenty of charm, and plenty to see, and could make a full day of unhurried strolling and exploring (for map see page 114).

Start at the 20th-century Ottoman Clocktower▶ (see page 125), in Yefet Street, which looks like an incongruous piece of Victoriana. Around it there is a strong Middle-Eastern feel; yet many of the 'oriental' snack-bars, such as the Tunisian café, turn out to be Jewish and kosher. Turn right at a sign to the 'Old City of Jaffa'. Pass by the domes of the Mahmoodiye Mosque▶. Mifratz Shlomo (no entry for vehicles) rises up, with a wooded park on both sides. To one side lies a little square with the Jaffa Museum▶▶ (see page 125) in an old stone building. Behind it, pass the old Hammam▶ (Turkish bath-house), now a theatre-restaurant, and climb to Abrasha Park▶▶, on the slope of a *tel* (settlement mound) excavated 1955–74. Descend the hill, crossing a wooden bridge, to the traffic-free and beautifully paved Kedumim Square▶▶▶ (see page 125).

Meander through the Artists' Quarter▶▶▶, off the square. Street names here are based on Zodiac signs: for a simple route, follow Mazal Dagim (Pisces) to the end, and double back on Mazal Arie (Leo), which reaches a length of ancient city wall▶▶. Emerge at the foot of broad steps, but cross straight over to narrow Shimon Habursekai Street.

Follow this, passing 'Simon the Tanner's House' at No 8, home of a family who claim that St Peter stayed in this house.

Go downhill on Mazal Keshet (Sagittarius). To visit the port▶ (see page 125), turn left at Nativ HaMazalot (Zodiac) and go down covered steps to the waterside. Return along Nativ HaMazalot, below lofty buildings, including the Greek Orthodox church and Catholic St Peter's. Take a path into the delightful HaMidron Gardens▶, passing below the domed former Jews' shelter (now a restaurant) and above the evocative pale minaret of the Sea Mosque. Reaching the Mahmoodiye Mosque, return to the Clocktower.

Old Jaffa's traffic-free lanes invite unhurried exploration

Healthy take-away
Fresh juices are made to your order at dozens of stands all around the city centre. The 'menu' generally runs the gamut of fruit varieties, including watermelon, peach, kiwi, prickly pear, orange, or a cocktail of several mixed together.

Expressionist mural, Helena Rubinstein pavilion

▶▶ Tel Aviv Museum of Art 114C3

27 Shaul HaMelech Boulevard

The imposing modern building of Israel's leading art museum is a world-famous showpiece of 20th-century art and aesthetics. From the architecture of the museum itself – with its exterior sculptures and light, open interiors – to the distinguished exhibitions of 20th-century painting, video, photography, music and film, this is an important focal point of modern high culture. **Permanent exhibitions▶▶▶**, representing the major 20th-century schools of painting, are arranged in a series of rooms, and include works by Braque, Klimt, Kandinsky, Picasso, Léger and Mondrian. **Temporary exhibitions▶▶▶**, often long-term, cover contemporary painting and photography, often on loan from leading international galleries and museums.

The Tel Aviv Museum of Art specialises in 20th-century art and sculpture

There are also **special exhibitions▶▶▶** covering subjects relevant to Israel's history and culture – for example, the latest finds from major sites such as Masada.

Despite specialising in the modern, the museum does not ignore everything that occurred before 1900. There are collections, temporary and permanent, of the art of past centuries, and many of the evening **concerts▶▶▶** feature classical music – while others feature jazz. The **Helena Rubinstein Pavilion for Contemporary Art▶** (6 Tarsat Boulevard) is part of the Museum of Art (same ticket valid). It shows work by guest artists from Israel and abroad.

As an unusual diversion from the usual type of museum visit, the Museum of Art offers a free guided **Bauhaus tour▶▶▶** by bus through the 1930s areas of Tel Aviv, a showcase for this simple and functional architectural style. The tour takes all morning (the bus will pick you up at your hotel). Although the tour is free, the Museum will charge its usual entrance fee; when the tour is over, you can visit the museum without further payment. Tel Aviv is a fascinating city of many different architectural styles – including art nouveau and Orientalist, but it is these modernist (or Bauhaus) apartment blocks, many influenced by Le Corbusier, that give their character to the 'White City'.

■ Visitors are soon made aware of certain obvious facts about Israeli music. For one thing, most buskers play classical violin music. For another, the country's contemporary pop music is absolutely dire. Less obvious is that traditional Jewish folk rhythms from Eastern Europe, North Africa and the Middle East are fusing with other Mediterranean styles and starting to produce a genuine new Israeli music. ■

A mix of traditions Not only have Jews fled to Israel from Eastern Europe, North Africa and Arabia, they have also brought their instruments and musical traditions with them. Indeed they have come from every continent, bringing the multitude of diverse styles which can be heard today in Israel.

Memories of the *shtetl* For many, the most recognisably Jewish music is the lilting clarinet-and-fiddle of *klezmer*, the sound of celebration and festival in the destroyed Jewish world of Eastern Europe. Few of the old players have survived, but the style lives on. Most *klezmer* today comes from America, though you will hear plenty of it in Israel, including a variant called Hasidic rock. Similarly, traditional oriental Jewish music has settled in Israel, become more upbeat and is growing in popularity.

New sounds Israel has not done well in the pop and rock field. Its repertoire is limited to rousing, repetitive, singalong tunes, from religious, kibbutz and army life. The bland, smooth harmonies which it submits to the Eurovision Song Contest are (unlike those of most contestant countries) just the thing that many Israelis actually like. However, a new style is emerging, strongly influenced by Greek rhythms. You will often hear Greek tapes and records played – they are very popular – but you will also hear new Israeli recordings that join traditional Jewish musical ideas to a Greek style which reflects Israel's East Mediterranean location.

A symphony of orchestras In classical music, Israel really excels. People say, only half in jest, that every police station and every works canteen has its symphony orchestra. Certainly there are an astonishing number (the Tel Aviv suburb of Ra'anana, for example, has its own), including several of high standing. At the national level, Israel's Chamber, Symphony and Philharmonic Orchestras, and its National Opera, are all acclaimed worldwide – a remarkable achievement, given that the population of Israel is only five million.

Musical movements
Music is such an integral part of Jewish life that almost everyone can play an instrument, often to professional standards. One Israeli joke has it that two in every three Russian immigrants arrives with a violin case tucked under their arms. What about the third? He's the pianist.

Classical busker

Accommodation

Shabbat and festivals
Although things grind to a stop for Shabbat (sabbath) each week from Friday afternoon to Saturday evening, and also on certain festivals and holy days, the one place where you can still expect to find things working more or less as normal is a hotel. Only at religious hotels (which make a point of informing guests of the restrictions on arrival) will you find that there are no reception staff on sabbath – but even here you will usually be able to get a meal.

Hotels line Tel Aviv's coastal road

All mod cons plus a sea view Altogether, Tel Aviv, including its suburbs, has a total of over 6,000 hotel rooms ranging from the de-luxe to the budget category. Charming old hotels of character, however, are not the thing in Tel Aviv. This is a new city, and almost all its hotels are modern, comfortable, well equipped and close to the seashore. At most of them, a superb buffet breakfast comes as standard. Some Tel Aviv hotels aspire to (and reach) a high level of service and facilities, whilst remaining relaxed and informal – children are made welcome. Widely accepted as the best in the city is the Dan Tel Aviv (on the corner of Frishman and HaYarkon). This is just about the best location, too, for beach access, eating out, entertainment and city centre shopping. Even if you cannot afford the Dan, it is a good idea to stay in this area.

In the right place The main hotel district lies along HaYarkon Street, between Trumpledor and Ben-Gurion junctions. Here you will find the Dan Tel Aviv, Carlton, Moriah Plaza, Ramada Continental and Sheraton hotels. These are all on the sought-after west side of HaYarkon. But there are also hotels on the other side of the street, or in side turnings. Among the best are the Basel, Astor and City: a few paces further from the beach and lacking the very finest sea view, these are nevertheless comfortable, convenient and more modestly priced.

Friday night special
Many hotels, even those that are not especially observant of Jewish ritual, offer something special for Friday night dinner, the big meal of the week for Jewish families. Usually, there are candles by the entrance so observant Jews can light them at the start of Shabbat (sabbath). *Hallah* (the tasty sabbath bread) and *kiddush* wine will be on the table. Typically, the main dish will be *cholent* (pronounced chilunt), the meat stew popular on Friday night among East European Jews.

Off the beaten track A few beach hotels lie outside this hotel district. A little further from the centre of things, they can represent good value for money. Examples are the Hilton, north of the main beach but overlooking a sandy bay, and the family-oriented Dan Panorama, opposite Clore Park at the southern end of the main beach. A free shuttle minibus connects the Dan Panorama to the Dan every few minutes throughout the day.

Eating out and shopping

Out and about Sightseeing, strolling or shopping, you will pass dozens of places – some smart, some simple – offering cakes, pastries and falafel or shwarma in pitta crammed with salad. Acclaimed for cakes and snacks, Café Levana (182 Ben Yehuda) is a youthful favourite. The many juice stands are a delight, and offer a delicious and healthy meal: some squeeze or liquidise more fruits than you knew existed. Street nibbles include bagels (bigger and breadier than the familiar Ashkenazi bagel) and nuts – plain, salted or honey-roasted.

Dinner Most big hotels have restaurants. In the hotel area – near Dizengoff Circle, in Ben-Yehuda Street, and along HaYarkon – eating places span the range from elegant French cuisine, to pizzerias, to cheap-and-cheerful eateries. Spicy, tasty Yemenito cooking can be sampled in the Yemenite quarter, for example at Shaul's Inn (Eliashiv Street). Beside the sea, queues form at Yotvata Dairy Restaurant; if you can't wait, there are pizza and burger places to either side of it! The huge outdoor London Restaurant fills the traffic-free promenade section north of Frishman – its prices reflect the lovely setting, but it has a big menu, big portions, friendly service and live music to accompany the food.

Where to shop, what to buy Tel Aviv's main shopping streets are Dizengoff and Ben-Yehuda, but the city's smartest shopping centre is in the Opera Tower (corner of Allenby and the promenade), with fine fashions, music, jewellery and high-quality Judaica for sale. Kikkar HaMadeina, the big circle in the north of the city, is a designer label zone. For creative, elegant clothes, jewellery and Judaica, check out boutiques in the northern Dizengoff Street. The southern part of Dizengoff is good for shoes and sandals. If you are wealthy enough to want diamonds, there is no better place than the Israel Diamond Exchange, Maccabi Boulevard, Ramat Gan. At the opposite extreme, try Bograshov Street for low-cost street fashion, while for unusual gifts and crafts take a stroll in Carmel Market.

English	Price	Hebrew	Arabic
HUMMOS	7	חומוס·פול	حمص·فول
HUMMOS +	12	חומוס מיוחד	حمص مميز
SALADS	3	מבחר סלטים	سلطات متنوعة
FISH		سمك وألوان דגים לפי משקל	
SHISHLIK	23	ששליק	شيش
MOJADDARA	4	מוג'דרה	مجدرة
KIDNEYS	23	כבד	كبده
CUBBEH	3	קובה	كبة
LIVER	23	לבבות	قلوب
CHIPS	6	צ'יפס	شبس
KEBAB	20	קבב	كباب
RIBS	30	צלעות	ضلوع
SHRIMPS	35	גמברי	ربيس
KALAMARI	35	קלאמארי	صيدن
LOBSTER	30	לובסטר	كلكت
SOFT DRINKS		משק·קלים	مشروبات
ICE-CREAM	5	גלידה	بوظة
SEASONAL FRUITS	5	פירות העונה	فواكه الموسم
ORIENTAL SWEETS	2	ממתקים מז'	حلويات شرقية
BEER	5	בירה	بيرة

133

Not kosher, but tasty
Only a handful of Tel Aviv eating places attain a really high standard, despite the ubiquitous 'gourmet' boast. Even so, most are perfectly adequate for an enjoyable evening out, and a surprising number offer live entertainment. Observant Jews need to know that the majority are not kosher. The tourist office has restaurant listings, such as *Tel Aviv Menus*.

Cheap and cheerful cafés line Dizengoff Street

Night owls

Like other big cities, Tel Aviv has its share of all-night stores and services. Five supermarkets, a dozen gas stations and (more surprisingly) half-a-dozen little confectioners who specialise in nuts and candies stay open in the Tel Aviv area. There are also a dozen different locations where you can rent a video for 24 hours from an automatic machine. Details and addresses of late-night stores are listed in *This Week in Tel Aviv*, obtainable from the tourist office or in hotels.

Tel Aviv's nightlife is livelier than in the capital, Jerusalem

Just hanging around

For an easy and relaxing evening, sometimes the best thing of all is to walk, talk and sit out of doors. Scores of cafés and bars (often misnamed 'pubs') open until well after midnight on Dizengoff, Ben-Yehuda, HaYarkon and the waterfront promenade.

Nightclubs The racy end of late-night Tel Aviv is mainly concentrated in the south and east of the city centre, along and off Allenby Street, and close to Jaffa Port. In the same area there are some 20 nightclubs for the youth market, offering disco, techno and house music, and most kick off after midnight. Another 20 or more specialise in various ethnic music styles – generally Oriental, Turkish or Greek – often with a stage performance, and mostly aimed at adults, rather than disco-hungry teenagers.

Live music Most big hotels have bars with easy-listening live music (often just a piano) until the small hours. For something more special, there are performances almost every evening by the New Israel Opera (Tel Aviv Performing Arts Centre, 19 Shaul HaMalech Boulevard, tel: 03 692 7777), the Israel Chamber Orchestra and Israel Music Conservatory (19 Streiker Street, tel: 03 546 6228) or the Israel Philharmonic (Mann Auditorium, tel: 03 528 9163). Other important concert venues are the Tel Aviv Museum of Art (tel: 03 696 1297) and Noga Theatre (7 Jerusalem Boulevard, Jaffa, tel: 03 681 6427). Big-name rock concerts are often staged in the open air at Yehoshua Gardens (close to the University, tel: 03 521 8210).

Dance and drama Tel Aviv is home to most of Israel's quality theatre. Simultaneous English translation (on headphones, every Tuesday) makes a play at the Cameri Theatre (on the corner of Dizengoff and Frishman, tel: 03 527 9888) enjoyable and accessible. Performances here consist of classics and serious modern drama. Yiddish-speakers will enjoy the Israeli Yiddish Theater, frequently on stage in Tel Aviv, usually at the ZOA House (tel: 03 695 9341). The Habima Theatre (Habima Square, tel: 03 296071) is the home of Israel's National Theatre Company. For performances of modern or classical dance, find out what is on at the attractive Suzanne Dellal Centre, home of the Inbal and Bat Sheva dance companies (tel: 03 510 5656). The Hasimta Theatre, in Old Jaffa (tel: 03 683 4709) puts on performances by Israeli artists in a café-theatre ambience.

Practical points

Information The tourist office, at the New Central Bus Station (tel: 03 639 5000), can answer questions, provide free maps and assist with bookings. Racks display dozens of leaflets with information and ideas, including copies of the latest editions of *Tel Aviv Today* and *This Week in Tel Aviv*, both of which contain useful listings, telephone numbers and advertisements.

Getting around Buses, in or out of town, are cheap. Journeys within Tel Aviv cost about 4 NIS. Bus stops have brief route details in English, and all bus drivers speak English. For local bus information call Dan Buses, 03 639 4444 (English spoken). Services run between 5am and midnight, except on Friday (services stop an hour before sunset for the sabbath) and Saturday (no service until the end of sabbath, an hour after sunset). Buses leave every few minutes from the city's two bus stations to towns and cities all over Israel. From Tel Aviv to Jerusalem costs 17 NIS (enquiries to Egged, tel: 03 537 5555).

Far more expensive are taxis (called 'special taxis'), which generally wait outside hotels. Ensure that a firm agreement is reached on the fare in advance of your journey, or, far better, insist that the meter is used (check before setting out, for instance at your hotel desk, what the fare should be to your destination). It takes some time to work out the routes of the cheaper *sherutim* (singular: *sherut*), or shared taxis, but they are convenient, and can be hailed on main streets anywhere along their set route.

Emergencies Unlike almost any other city in the world, crime is not a problem in Tel Aviv. Violence is very rare. Do take precautions, nevertheless, against simple theft (for example, of bags on the beach). Noisy, horn-tooting young people are probably the worst hazard you will encounter. In an emergency, call: Police 100; Ambulance 101; Fire 102; Rape Centre 03 523 4819.

People of the bus
Amazingly, considering the small size of the country and its population, Tel Aviv has the largest bus station in the world. It opened in 1993 and looks and feels like an airport terminal. Comfortable air-conditioned buses leave here frequently for destinations all over the country, from 5am to midnight. One million passengers a week pass through – one fifth of Israel's total population. To serve them, the bus station houses hundreds of shops and restaurants. As if that were not enough, Tel Aviv actually has two bus stations! The other, a simpler terminus, is beside the railway station. Egged, the main bus line, despite operating solely within Israel, is the world's second largest bus company (after Greyhound, in the USA).

Popular transport

■ While the whole world may have heard of the Ten Commandments given by God to Moses, few realise that the scriptures contain a total of 613 different commandments (or *mitzvot*) concerning every aspect and nuance of behaviour. Attempting to obey them is 'religious observance'. Ignoring them completely is to be 'totally secular'. Most Israelis fall somewhere between the two, and regard the *mitzvot* not as commandments but as traditions. ■

Observant Israelis

16 per cent of women regularly attend *mikveh* (ritual baths).

22 per cent of men keep their head covered at all times.

25 per cent regularly wear the *tefillin* (prayer boxes containing scriptures).

55 per cent can read from a prayer book.

66 per cent mark sabbath with some kind of ritual, usually the lighting of candles.

66 per cent eat only kosher food at home.

71 per cent fast all day on Yom Kippur.

72 per cent light Hanukka candles.

78 per cent attend a *seder* (ritual dinner) at Passover.

90 per cent keep kosher part of the time.

92 per cent circumcise their sons according to Jewish ritual.

98 per cent have a *mezuzza* scroll on their doorpost.

– Guttman Institute of Applied Social Research (1994)

Burning yeast before the Passover

A Jewish state The Diaspora Museum in Tel Aviv suggests that Jewish religious observance, especially of the sabbath and of festivals, kept the Jewish people as a single nation throughout the Diaspora years and enabled their return to the Jewish homeland. Yet ironically, or perhaps logically, religious observance among Jews is at an all-time low in their homeland. Although the basic rituals are taught in school, many Israelis know little about the traditional religion of their people. Even so, they remain Jews and proud of the fact. This is the Jewishness without God that many Zionists dreamed of creating.

A secular Zion In the early years of this century, the pioneering Zionists who made the journey to settle in Palestine and struggled to re-create the Jewish homeland were almost without exception socialists and atheists. They whole-heartedly rejected religion, just as they rejected every other inheritance from the past, even family life. They considered the Jewish people to be no more, and no less, than a nation exiled from its land, and defined Jewishness in purely cultural, historical terms. Instead of the biblical injunction to be 'a light unto the nations', they wished only that Israel would be 'a nation like any other'. That is the view that prevails in Israel today.

The people of Israel The existence of Jews as a separate people rests on their attachment to Israel, which lies at the heart of the Jewish religion. Unlike Christianity, which is based on an idea (of God in Man, the Messiah), Judaism is literally a question of getting down to earth. At the corner-stone of the religion is Abraham's perception of Israel as the promised land, the land to which the Jews returned after the exodus from Egypt, the land conquered by Joshua supposedly in fulfilment of God's promise. These events are not mythical but historical (if embellished). The only sacred place in the world, for Jews, is Temple Mount in Jerusalem. Synagogue prayers, today as always, refer to the Jews simply as Israel. For millennia, Israel meant the land of the Jews, of the Jewish religion, and of the Temple. That is why diaspora Jews wanted to return to Israel, and why even the most secular Jews in Israel are part of, and the product of, a religious heritage.

The not-so-great divide A recent nationwide survey of Hebrew-speaking Israeli Jews showed that 21 per cent consider themselves to be 'totally secular'. About 39 per cent are 'strictly observant' or 'observant to a great extent'. In between are the roughly 40 per cent who pick and choose which customs to keep and which to ignore. To some extent, the divide is illusory, because Jewish festivals, such as Hanukka, Pessah (Passover), Purim, Sukkot and so on, are now as much national as religious holidays, observed even on secular kibbutzim. Shabbat (sabbath) still brings the country to a standstill – for religious and secular alike. Survey figures show that being religious or secular are not absolutes: most Israelis obey some religious commandments, seeing them simply as part of their inherited traditions.

A cause for conflict The big sabbath shut-down rankles with some Israelis, especially in a predominantly non-religious city like Tel Aviv. There is resentment that the orthodox authorities, backed by religious political parties (which generally hold the balance of power in parliament), can wield such a pervasive influence over the life of the secular. Examples range from the lack of any form of civil marriage to the fact that El Al, the state airline, cannot fly on the sabbath. But no government which depends on religious party support can risk liberalisation. Anger about this has led many Israelis, including the many who are observant to some degree, to regard 'the religious' with contempt. The antagonism is mutual.

A vote for pluralism
It is partly due to Israel's electoral system that the religious/secular divide is so sharp. The legal power of Orthodox religious authorities – for example, to define who is a Jew or to carry out marriages – was established in 1948, and cannot be altered except by the Knesset (Parliament). If much-discussed plans to tinker with the proportional representation rules are enacted, requiring parties to garner a certain minimum percentage of the vote before gaining a Knesset seat, the unpopular religious parties would disappear from government, losing most of their influence, credibility and state funding. Non-orthodox and partly observant citizens would then be in a position to win much needed civil rights and respectability.

Lighting Hanukka candles

137

▶▶▶ **Akko** *113B4*

This large, industrial Arab town (population 38,000), sitting on a spit of land projecting from the Galilee coast, contains at its heart a striking Old City with thick, sturdy fortifications and imposing towers. These superb 18th-century **ramparts▶▶▶**, now breached by newer roads, were originally entered only through the Land Gate, not far from the shore, or the Sea Gate, on the harbourside. Today access to the top of the walls is from the steps by the law courts.

The historic waterfront quarter, a mass of stone structures, beautiful archways, evocative alleys and green-roofed mosques, makes a magnificent sight. There is squalor, too, and you will find groups of youths hanging around, and unwashed children in the dirty squares and alleyways. In the past, Akko (known to the English as Acre) figured large on the map of the world and even today carries the mark of its former standing. Above all, though later restored and reconstructed, the walls and stonework recall an era of bloodthirsty medieval struggles between the Crusaders and the Arabs for control of the land of Israel.

Akko's history dates back far beyond those times. Remnants of a Canaanite settlement on the site of the **Tel▶** (settlement mound) 2km inland have been dated to 3000 BC. Taken, lost and retaken by Egyptian pharaohs, it became a Phoenician city. Joshua, the Israelite leader, was unable to conquer it in 1300 BC and the Israelite tribe of Asher, in whose territory Akko was, also failed. The Phoenicians were eventually expelled in 640 BC. The town passed between Persians, Assyrians and Egyptians, and in 219 BC became part of the Seleucid kingdom of Syria,

Akko: modern port and Crusader city

which wisely allowed it to remain an independent city-state. When the Hasmoneans forced the Syrians out of the rest of Israel in the 2nd century BC, they too were unable to take Akko, which survived as a non-Jewish town. Rome succeeded in conquering it, and it served as their campaign base for crushing the First Jewish Revolt (AD 66). Akko remained a busy port under the Byzantines, and after the 7th-century Arab conquest became the seaport of Damascus.

After years of trying, the Crusaders eventually took Akko in 1104, made it the stronghold of the Knights of St John and renamed it St Jean d'Acre (Saint John of Acre). When the Arabs took Jerusalem (1187), Akko became capital of the Crusaders' Kingdom of the Holy Land. The town's finest spectacle is still the wonderfully preserved **Crusader city►►►**, headquarters of the Knights Hospitallers, a vast and impressive complex of offices, halls, a refectory and hospice, now lying underground because the 18th-century Citadel was raised on top of it. Built largely in the 12th century, in the transition from Romanesque to early Gothic, the Crusader city's stone paved floors and vaulted ceilings retain a simple but majestic elegance and dignity.

From antiquity, Akko flourished as a port, and for a thousand years it was the biggest and busiest in the eastern Mediterranean. It was also notorious as a place of vice and decadence, which worsened under the Crusaders as the town grew. Densely populated, it was divided into quarters given over to different 'nationalities' – in fact mostly Italians from the city-states of Genoa, Pisa, Venice and Amalfi. These districts were often in conflict, sometimes breaking into open warfare. The population was mainly Christian, and there were dozens of churches.

In 1187, Salah ed-Din wrested Akko from the Crusaders; in 1191 it was reconquered by Richard the Lionheart. When the fifth Crusade reached Palestine in 1290, full of naïve zeal about driving Islam out of the Holy Land, they slaughtered the Muslim traders resident in Akko – much to the chagrin of the town's Christian citizens, who were more interested in commerce than conquest. The massacre caused the Mameluke Sultan Qalawun to attack the city mercilessly, carting off thousands of Christians as slaves. The Knights Templar fought on until the massive

Akko's Gothic arches have lasted much longer than the fragile Crusader kingdom which built them

The great escape
During the British Mandate, the authorities put Akko's medieval citadel to use as a high-security prison for Jewish guerrillas: several were hanged here. In a spectacular raid on the citadel in May 1947, the Irgun group dynamited a hole in the ancient wall, went inside, overpowered the guards and freed 30 Irgun and 11 Lehi prisoners. The citadel now contains the Museum of Heroism, honouring the prisoners who were held or executed here.

Akko's beaches
Just outside the walls, Akko has one extremely dirty and unappealing public beach. For something a little better, head further south from the city to Hof Argaman (or Purple Beach). This lies a 15-minute walk along the seafront; alternatively, you can drive along the Haifa road as far as the Argaman Motel. You must pay to use the beach, but it has good facilities and an excellent view of the city.

wall of their fortress was brought crashing down, symbolising the end of two centuries of Christian rule in Palestine.

From 1291, Akko was resolutely Arab, sinking into almost total obscurity and poverty. Druze emirs revived it in the 17th and 18th centuries, and between 1775 and 1805, under Ahmed el-Jazzar (literally, 'the Butcher'), there was much grandiose building. The Crusader city was covered and above it the mighty Citadel▶ was constructed. Later, the British made use of this as a prison for Jewish guerrillas: a poorly laid out museum▶▶ inside contains photographs, papers, and the gallows on which the Jews were executed. Beside the Citadel, on the site of the Crusaders' Cathedral of the Holy Cross, stands the Ahmed al Jazzar Mosque▶, with its geometric marble patterns, tall minaret and rococo architecture. Close by in Ahmed's handsome Turkish baths▶▶, a museum covers the story of the town, explaining how, in 1799, the British came to Ahmed's aid helping to repel an attack on the town made by Napoleon.

Under Ottoman rule, the walls of Akko were restored and new defences were constructed. Despite this, the British seized Akko in 1918. The residents staunchly defied both the British and Jewish presence in Palestine. In 1948 Akko came fully under Jewish control for the first time in its history.

Wandering around the Old City, you will find much of interest: the *souk*▶, the narrow streets full of exotic life and fragrances; the huge *khans* (enclosures built as caravanserais), notably the columned Khan el-Umdan▶▶ by the water, with the landmark clocktower beside it; the agreeable quayside▶▶ with its fish restaurants. Also of interest is the Strauss Ice Cream factory, south of the town, where the tour and free sample are most enjoyable. Some 2km north of Akko, the exquisite Bahá'i gardens▶▶ contain the burial shrine of Bahá'u'lláh (literally, God's glory, 1817–92), the title of the founder of the Bahá'i religion. Here, too, is the cottage in which he resided for the last years of his life, having been exiled to Akko in 1868. The shrine is the holiest place in the world for members of the Bahá'i faith (see page 152).

Above and below: Ahmed al Jazzar Mosque

■ **The new country of Israel was won after a hard struggle, involving determination, courage and a certain amount of ruthlessness. Born of centuries of yearning, Israel is still immensely grateful to the men and women who brought it into being. Some were intellectuals, others soldiers, others farmers who tackled swamps and deserts. They are everywhere honoured. City streets, towns, kibbutzim, even hills and valleys, not to mention sons and daughters, have been named in their memory.** ■

Creators of a nation The rebirth of Israel is regarded by many Jews, and not a few Christians, as one of the greatest events to have occurred in two millennia. For some it is nothing less than the hand of God at work. Others see it as the result of painstaking struggle by individuals of courage and vision. And for yet others, it is a combination of both of these:

after all, according to the Bible story, even when God gave the Land of Israel to the Jews, they still had to go out and conquer it for themselves. All those who made this modern, political and diplomatic miracle happen tend to be regarded with sincere admiration by Israelis.

The early days Few towns are without a boulevard, main street or central square named after Theodor Herzl (1860–1904), founder of the Zionist movement. His successor as Zionist leader, Chaim Weizmann (1874–1952), who became the first president of Israel, also has many mentions. The hard-liner who led the Revisionist group within the movement, Vladimir Jabotinsky (1880–1940), is also recalled as a hero, as is Josef Trumpledor (1880–1920), founder of the Hehalutz Zionist movement in Russia, decorated for bravery by the Russian and British armies, who died defending a Galilee farming settlement from Arab attack. More recently, David Ben-Gurion (1886–1973) was the tough and shrewd Zionist veteran who became Israel's first prime minister. All were born in Eastern Europe.

Writers and scholars Eliezer Ben-Yehuda (1858–1922) gained huge admiration for reviving and revitalising the Hebrew language. Shmuel Yosef Agnon (1888–1970), was the first Hebrew writer to win the Nobel Prize for Literature. Haim Nachman Bialik (1873–1934), author of many early Zionist songs and also considered the greatest modern Hebrew poet, is another name held in the highest esteem by Israelis.

Above: Vladimir Jabotinsky
Left: Theodor Herzl

The founder of Zionism Theodor Herzl (1860–1904), born in Budapest, grew up to be cosmopolitan, intellectual and entirely non-religious. He spoke several languages and read for a doctorate at Vienna University in a period of daily anti-Jewish rioting in the city. Finding work as a journalist, he was made Paris correspondent of the Austrian *Neue Frei Presse*. In 1895 he witnessed the public humiliation of the Jewish army captain Alfred Dreyfus, who – in a wave of anti-Jewish feeling which swept France – was convicted on a trumped-up charge of treason on evidence known to have been forged. The sight had an electrifying effect on Herzl. He at once wrote *Der Judenstaat* (The Jewish State) and in 1897 convened the first Zionist Congress. This called for 'the creation for the Jewish people of a home in Palestine'. He campaigned tirelessly to further that cause until his untimely death. Within 50 years his extraordinary dream had come true and his body was transferred to Mount Herzl, in Jerusalem, in 1948.

Gaza

Just down the coast from Ashkelon and Ashdod is another ancient city of the Philistines which regularly features in the news. Gaza (Azza in Arabic) is a noisy, crowded and squalid city. Its principal sight is the Great Mosque, originally a 13th-century Crusader church. Even if you wanted to see this, Gaza is not recommended for a visit. Despite its 'independent' self-governing status, as part of the Palestinian Autonomous Authority, the whole Gaza Strip remains dangerous and troubled, hostile to Israelis and Jews and anyone who might be thought Israeli. No overnight accommodation is open to outsiders. Measuring 50km by 6km, the Gaza Strip consists of dry, near-desert terrain and yet is one of the world's most densely populated areas. Most of the 650,000 residents are the people (and their families) who were on the losing side in Israel's 1948 War of Independence, or as it is known to the Arabs, 'The Catastrophe'. Many fled their homes, or were driven from them at the end of that war. In the 1967 Six Day War, the Arabs again lost, and Gaza was occupied by the Israelis until 1994, when the Autonomous Areas came into being.

142

▶▶   **Ashkelon and Ashdod**   *112B2–B3*

These two modern, rapidly growing, industrial beachside towns (with a combined population of 165,000), were founded in the 1950s on the sand dunes not far from the Gaza border, and are major absorption centres for new immigrants. There is a boomtown feeling in the air, as construction work carries on at a frantic pace (often using Arab labour from across the frontier). Ashdod's successful port is now second only to Haifa's.

Paradoxically the two towns also have a long history. Both were among the five Philistine cities on Israel's Mediterranean coast (Joshua 13: 3). When the Philistines captured the Ark of the Covenant they took it first to Ashkelon, then installed it in the temple of Dagon in Ashdod. A multitude of conquerors came and went during the centuries, including Egyptians, Assyrians, Persians and Romans. The towns were taken by the Crusaders in the 12th century, and then retaken – but largely destroyed in the process.

Ashdod▶▶ has a beach and a couple of modest hotels, but plans to turn it into a big holiday resort seem fanciful. Its earlier settlements were at **Tel Ashdod**▶, 5km south. Later it became an Arab village, hostile to Jewish immigration, with a British army base; during the 1948 War of Independence, the Egyptians advanced this far into Israel before being forced to retreat.

Between the two towns stretch 15km of dunes and citrus groves. **Ashkelon**▶▶, though sprawling, has more appeal for visitors. Its pleasant sandy beach and waterside hotels lie at the southern end of town near **Ashkelon National Park**▶▶, a popular picnic area with remnants of several periods. The ruined churches, fortifications and collapsed towers, whose rather forlorn fragments of stonework lie on the sand, were built by Crusaders. Within the site, the earliest remains date back to Canaanite and Israelite times, and there are Roman ruins. North of the park is a 3rd-century Roman tomb.

This part of Israel's Mediterranean coast lies surprisingly close to the desert and to southern Israel, which are within easy reach for day trips.

Right: Ashkelon
Below: Roman statue of Isis

▶▶   **Atlit (also known as Ma'apilim**
         Atlit Camp)   113B3

*About 1 km from the sea, around 8km south of Haifa
beside an exit from Highway 2 (signposted 'Apilim').*
Notorious Atlit Camp was the British detention centre,
established in 1938, used for holding illegal Jewish immigrants to Palestine during the pre- and post war period.
During this time, when Jews were trying to escape from
Nazi Europe, a succession of more-or-less unseaworthy
and overloaded ships put ashore on Israel's beaches. The
occupants were rounded up by the British authorities,
brought here and held in crowded dormitories until they
could be deported. Tens of thousands of would-be immigrants passed through the camp.

Now you can walk between the high barbed-wire fences
where Holocaust survivors, including children whose
parents had died in the extermination camps, were
detained. Some were returned to Germany or other parts
of Europe, and many were forwarded to other British
prison camps in, for example, Cyprus or Mauritius. This
camp was restored in 1970, but of the original 80 dormitory
huts only two remain. These are filled with models to give
some idea of the life and conditions endured by the
inmates. The camp is dominated by the Disinfection
Building where detainees were stripped naked on arrival,
segregated by sex, and herded in to be sprayed with
disinfectant liquid from showers, in an uncanny
resemblance to the Nazi gas chambers. Also on the site is
a ship in which some of the illegal immigrants arrived.

Atlit is geared to group visits, of which there are many,
but individuals are also welcome with advance notice. A
very moving audio-visual is shown to visitors.

▶   **Bat Yam**   112B4

This beach resort, 5km south of Tel Aviv, is effectively a
suburb of its larger neighbour. It is attractively located,
has a good, well-maintained beach and many leisure facilities including a sports centre, swimming pools, three art
galleries and several moderately priced hotels.

*Atlit's sunset
beauty belies its
tragic history*

The last castle
Now within a military base,
the huge ruined castle
which can be seen perched
on a promontory near Atlit
was built by the Templars
in 1200 following their
expulsion from Temple
Mount in Jerusalem. They
called the new fortress
Pilgrims' Castle. After the
loss of Akko in 1291, the
Templar presence in the
Holy Land looked unlikely
to survive. The fall of
Tortosa Castle, in Syria, in
the same year left only
Pilgrims' Castle at Atlit in
their possession, and the
Templars decided to leave
before being driven out.
The castle subsequently
fell into ruins. It was
excavated in the 1930s, but
is not open to the public.

Alexander Zaid

The statue of Alexander
Zaid, on the highest point
of Beit She'arim, honours
a founder of HaShomer
(the Watchman), the undercover organisation which
provided armed guards for
Jewish farmers and that
evolved into the Hagannah
(see page 42). Zaid is said
to have discovered the
Beit She'arim necropolis
while secretly patrolling in
1936. He was eventually
killed during the 1938 anti-
Jewish riots.

*Beit She'arim, site of
the Sanhedrin, or
Jewish Supreme
Court*

▶   **Beit She'arim**   *113B3*

This archaeological site at the foot of Mount Carmel,
some 20km east of Haifa, contains the remnants of a
Galilean town which acquired enormous importance in
Jewish religious life in the centuries after the destruction
of the Temple in Jerusalem. With the crushing of the Bar
Kochba Revolt, in the 2nd century AD, Beit She'arim grew
to be a large, religious town. Rabbi Yehudah Hanassi
moved here with his seminary, and under him it became
the seat of the Sanhedrin, the 'supreme court' of Jewish
Law. Hanassi spent his time here writing and codifying
the Mishna (still known today as the Oral Law), which
was to become part of the scriptural works which
Orthodox Jews consider to be God-given.

Hanassi was buried in the **Necropolis▶▶** (or
Necrophos), a remarkable network of underground
tunnels, stairways and caves. These catacombs were
already well known as a burial site, but after Hanassi's
burial, they became the most important Jewish burial
place in Israel, taking over from the Mount of Olives,
which the Romans had closed to Jews. The Necropolis
was, and is, entered through landscaped courtyards. Of
the 20 burial chambers inside, two are currently open to
visitors. Inside, it is eerie and atmospheric. The decorated
sarcophagi – now empty – have inscriptions in Hebrew,
Aramaic and Greek. There is also a museum inside the
larger of the two catacombs.

Above ground, there are traces of private dwellings and
other structures, all dating from the period of the 2nd to
4th centuries AD. They include ruins of a **synagogue▶**, a
large **basilica▶**, a **glass factory▶** and an **oil press▶**.
These ancient buildings are all that now remain of the city,
which was almost completely destroyed by the Romans
in the 4th century.

■ **Some Jewish holidays date back to the Bible, while others commemorate various events in the history of the Jewish people. Many are national holidays celebrated by all Israelis, whether religious or secular. Their date varies from one year to the next. Christian festivals also attract large numbers of visitors as do, to a lesser extent, Muslim festivals.** ■

Spring and summer Passover (Hebrew: Pessah), the seven-day festival of abstinence from bread or leavened food, commemorates the Exodus from Egypt. It is mainly a family affair. The big moment is the *seder* ritual festive meal, when the Haggadah (Exodus story) is read aloud. Christian Holy Week, with processions along the Via Dolorosa in Jerusalem, occurs at about the same time. Holocaust Day, Remembrance Day, Independence Day and Jerusalem Day, recalling the pain and joy of 20th-century events, follow soon after. Lag b'Omer (April/May) is a day of picnics, one month after Pessah. Shavuot (49 days after Passover) celebrates Moses receiving the Torah; it is traditional to eat dairy products. The Tisha b'Av fast (July), when people gather at the Western Wall, is the day on which both the First and the Second Temples were destroyed.

Autumn The month of Tishri (September/October) starts with Rosh Hashana (New Year), a happy but thoughtful time. The 10 Days of Awe which follow, are also a time of reflection, ending with the solemn fast of Yom Kippur. A joyous note returns with the seven days of Sukkot (Tabernacles), a harvest celebration that commemorates the years spent by the Jews wandering in the wilderness after the Exodus from Egypt.

Winter Hanukka ('Dedication') recalls the Maccabean victory in 167 BC and the 'miracle' that occurred when the Temple was rededicated (one day's lamp oil lasted for eight days). People light *hanukkiot*, the 8-branched candelabrum, starting with one candle, and adding another each evening until, on the last night, all eight are aflame. Fried foods and doughnuts are eaten at this time. Christmas draws huge crowds, especially to the city of Bethlehem. Purim (February/March), a zany day of dressing-up and fun, recalls the Jewish escape from an ancient Persian plot to kill them. The story of Esther is read in synagogues, and children try to drown out the name of the villain, Haman.

Merry Christmases
In Israel, Christmas does not come just once a year: it is celebrated on different dates by different Christian sects. The Catholics, Latin churches and Protestants proclaim the birth of Christ on December 25. The Eastern Orthodox churches celebrate his birth on January 6th and 7th. The Armenian Church has its Christmas on January 18th and 19th.

145

Top: lilies for Christ's Resurrection Left: the fruit and palms for Sukkot, the Jewish harvest festival

▶▶▶   **Caesarea**   _113A2_

Anyone for golf?

For visitors or Israelis who fancy a round of golf, Caesarea Golf Club has no rival; not because it is so good, but because it is the only golf course in Israel. Established in 1980, the club has an 18-hole course covering 160 hectares, including 25ha of grass – no mean achievement in this terrain. The course is open all day, every day of the week, including Saturday – in fact, Saturday is the most popular day and it is advisable to make a reservation.

Ein Shemer

A short drive inland from Caesarea, lying just off the cross-country road that runs from here to the Sea of Galilee (via Afula), Ein Shemer is an interesting kibbutz, still with the protective enclosing wall that all kibbutzim once had. Calling itself The Old Yard, Ein Shemer has a museum and video about the history of the settlement. One of the kibbutz members is the famous artist-blacksmith Hofi, who can knock up a little work of art out of iron in just a few minutes.

Caesarea: Corinthian capital (right) and theatre (below)

One of the great cities of the ancient world, Caesarea was a port from the 4th century BC onwards, and the Roman administrative capital of Judaea for hundreds of years. As an archaeological site it is dramatic, extensive and accessible. Excavations began within three years of the founding of the State of Israel, and still continue. Today, one sees an area of superimposed walled cities – Herodian, Roman and Byzantine – overlaid in part by the Gothic remains of a medieval Crusader fortress town. The best-represented periods, dominating the site visually, are the Roman and Crusader cities. A short distance from the archaeological site, modern Caesarea consists of a coastal area of high-quality holiday and leisure facilities, including hotels and restaurants, as well as some of Israel's best and most expensive private housing.

The first port at Caesarea was set up by the Phoenicians, and conquered 100 years later by the Greek army of Alexander the Great. In 22 BC, the Roman city was born under Herod. This large walled town encompassed the enormous 20,000-seat **hippodrome▶** (or race track), which remains unexcavated, and a splendid **theatre▶▶**. The water supply was carried in on a fine beachside **aqueduct▶▶**, the ruins of which remain impressive. Through taxes and trade, the town became a source of wealth for Herod and for Rome. It attracted large numbers of Jews and pagans, and was above all a cosmopolitan and commercial town. From AD 6, Judaea became a Roman province, with Caesarea as its administrative centre; it was here that, in AD 69, Vespasian was proclaimed emperor. Around this time, according to the Acts of the Apostles, St Philip baptised the Roman centurion Cornelius, and later set up a Christian community. In the year 135, following the defeat of the Bar Kochba Revolt, the great scholar Rabbi Akiva was tortured to death at Caesarea.

The town continued to be an important Christian

Minaret in Caesarea, relic of Turkish rule

centre, and the seat of a bishop, right through the Byzantine period. New walls were erected, enclosing a much more compact area, and the port town prospered. The **Byzantine street**▶▶, lined with shops, is the evocative remnant of this era.

After the Persian invasion of 614, the commercial life of the town came to a complete end, and it fell into obscurity. A succession of Muslim rulers held the town until the arrival of the Crusaders in 1099. Not until 1101 did they turn their attention to Caesarea, but in that year they moved in and began to revive the site, constructing numerous substantial new buildings, reusing many pieces of Roman and Byzantine masonry. In 1254, the Crusaders (under the French King Louis IX) constructed their imposing **fortifications**▶▶▶, of which the splendid walls and moat of the Crusader citadel survive. They enclose only a small, rectangular part of the ancient Caesarea which can be reached by passing through a Gothic gatehouse into the ruined city. Dusty walls and arches, vestiges of houses with their water cisterns, and skeletal remnants of other buildings are sufficient to kindle the imagination. The three apses of the Crusaders' cathedral remain standing.

The Crusaders' presence was abruptly terminated in 1275 by the Mamelukes, and again the city fell to ruin. During the four centuries of Turkish rule, up to 1917, there was increasing decay and destruction, apart from an odd episode in which Muslim refugees from Bosnia were accommodated on the site. They built the 19th-century **mosque** beside the Crusader cathedral, and put up warehouses by the **Old Harbour**▶▶, which had originally been constructed by Herod and later reconstructed by the Crusaders. Today the attractions of the harbour district include several inexpensive eating places, and a pleasant pay-to-enter beach area.

A tale of two cities
'If you hear that Caesarea thrives, but Jerusalem suffers – believe it. If you hear that Jerusalem thrives, while Caesarea suffers – believe it. But if you hear that both Jerusalem and Caesarea are thriving – don't believe it.' This ancient saying reflects the rivalry between the two great 'capitals' of Judaea. Jerusalem was the spiritual, Jewish capital. Caesarea was the temporal, Roman capital. Caesarea attracted pagans, and was devoted to wealth and luxury. Jerusalem was pious and dominated by the Temple. Caesarea became an early stronghold of Christianity. Jerusalem was the bastion of Judaism. Even today, Jerusalem remains the religious and national capital, while Caesarea has the country's wealthiest inhabitants, best housing and most secular atmosphere.

Kosher food

■ The non-Jewish slang use of the word kosher – as in 'a kosher business deal' – is very close to the real meaning. Other Hebrew words related to kosher mean such things as honest, wholesome, to legalise a doubtful situation, to be worthy of an honour, to succeed. The word kosher itself does not only refer to food. It means that things are right, correct, and as they should be, and in particular, that they satisfy the requirements of Jewish law. ■

Forbidden foods

'The camel, because he cheweth the cud but parteth not the hoof, he is unclean unto you. And the rock badger, because he cheweth the cud but parteth not the hoof, he is unclean unto you. And the hare, because she cheweth the cud but parteth not the hoof, she is unclean unto you. And the swine, because he parteth the hoof and is cloven footed, but cheweth not the cud, he is unclean unto you. Of their flesh ye shall not eat, and their carcass ye shall not touch. Whatsoever hath no fins nor scales in the water, that is a detestable thing unto you. And these ye shall have in detestation among the fowls; they shall not be eaten, they are a detestable thing ...'
– Leviticus 11: 4–13

148

A right way The body of Jewish law and ritual concerning food and drink is called *kashrut*. On restaurant menus and in food shops, you may notice the three Hebrew letters of the word 'kosher'. That is to let people know, especially religious Jews, that all the food sold there is acceptable to eat. If it is not kosher, food is usually called *trefa* (or *treif*, in Yiddish), meaning impure, incorrect.

Some examples Certain foods are utterly forbidden, such as pork and shellfish. Commercially prepared foods may be acceptable if free from forbidden ingredients – they generally require the seal of rabbinical approval to ensure compliance. Meats must be from animals killed in the prescribed manner so that they have not a drop of blood in them: Jews must never consume any blood. The biggest problems relating to *kashrut* come from the biblical injunction that 'You shall not seethe a kid in its mother's milk.' Perhaps this was meant to be taken literally; perhaps it was meant metaphorically as a way of saying that, even when animals are killed for meat, they should not be humiliated or treated with contempt. Over the years, however, this has come to be defined as a law that forbids eating dairy products and meat products at the same time – or even within several hours of each other. For the strictly Orthodox, they cannot even be cooked in the same pans; for the more strict, they may not be eaten off the same plates; for the stricter still, the utensils may not even be cleaned in the same sink or dishwasher. It also means that cheese cannot be made with animal rennet, that you cannot put milk in your coffee after a meat meal, and that there is very little call for cheeseburgers in Israeli fast-food bars.

The good part None of this matters unless you are an observant Jew. It has no disadvantages except for people who simply cannot live without a pork chop or prawn cocktail. Food in Israel, despite *kashrut*, tends to be very good, and the whole country is full of vegetarian or 'dairy' restaurants (where fish is usually served as well).

*Top: Sabbath bread
Above: 'kosher' sign*

Arguably the most appealing and agreeable of Israel's three large towns, Haifa is a city of views, beautifully situated on a promontory projecting into the Mediterranean and rising steeply to the south on the slope of the attractive Mount Carmel upland. A popular Israeli saying has it that Jerusalem prays and Tel Aviv plays, but Haifa works. The city has industrial areas on the north-eastern side, a university, a science and research institute of worldwide importance at the top of the Carmel slope, and a major port almost in the town centre.

Haifa is also a town with a mixed population: while predominantly Jewish, there are many Druze, Muslims and Christian Arabs here. Between the different groups, there seems to be no strife or friction at all, merely a pragmatic desire to work together amicably and have a peaceful life. The city is also the world centre of the Bahá'i community (see page 152), whose Shrine of the Bab, with its gilded dome, makes a striking landmark.

Haifa also has considerable attractions of interest for the visitor too. The Mediterranean shore, extending alongside the western sections of the town, has a good, long beach▶ and promenade, within sight of the Haifa–Tel Aviv highway. The beach curves around the headland, almost reaching the **Old City▶**, a mainly 18th and 19th-century harbour district at the foot of the hill. Up the slope lies **Hadar HaCarmel▶▶▶**, the city centre. Here you will find scores of inexpensive eating places, including Sephardic snack-bars selling Middle Eastern dishes.

The city centre Herzl Street is the busy main thoroughfare, for shopping or eating. Parallel to it runs a pleasant pedestrian mall, Nordau Street, which has a quieter atmosphere and scores of open-air restaurant and café tables. As the city heads up the steep Carmel hill, a striking feature is the **stepped alleyways** linking street to street. Further up, near the crest of the hill, **Central Carmel▶** is the more stately well-to-do residential and academic neighbourhood. A **funicular railway▶** with six stations, from Kikkar Paris at the bottom to the hotel district of Central Carmel at the top, joins the three sections of the city centre.

History Archaeological studies show settlements on and around present-day Haifa dating back to the 10th century BC. The busy port town with a large *yeshiva* (a school devoted to the study of sacred texts) was taken by Crusaders in 1099, and largely destroyed.

Herzl's dream
Theodor Herzl, the 19th-century founder of Zionism, once said that he had a dream – no metaphorical Utopian vision, but a real sleeping dream – in which he saw Haifa transformed, with white buildings rising up the hill and great liners in the harbour. His dream has come true with astonishing accuracy, though in Herzl's fantasy, the liners were cruise ships. In today's Haifa, a century later, they are cargo vessels laden with goods.

149

The Technion
Another dream of Herzl's was that Israel would one day possess a centre of scientific research that would be the envy of the world. Haifa's Technion (the Israel Institute of Technology), the country's first university, opened in 1924, with Albert Einstein as its first president. Even before the creation of the State of Israel, the Technion had made major leaps in knowledge and technology in the fields of construction, water management and agriculture. In 1954, the Technion moved to its present Mount Carmel campus. Since then it has made great advances in aviation, chemistry, agriculture, electronic communications and medicine. Its medical school, engaged mainly in developing new techniques, is a world leader.

Haifa, city of views

Map: Haifa

Exodus

Originally called *The President Warfield*, the 1,800-tonne river steamer renamed *Exodus*, packed with Holocaust survivors, set sail in early July 1947 from the French port of Sète in an attempt to reach Palestine. On 18 July, on the approach to Haifa, British sailors boarded the ship, overcame the crew, killing three passengers and injuring 28. The British government ordered all passengers returned to the French port. On arrival, the refugees refused to disembark, and the French refused to use force against them. They remained on board until the British decided to take them back to Germany, where they were forcibly removed from the ships in September, to be transferred to camps for displaced persons.

Bahá'i Temple, Haifa

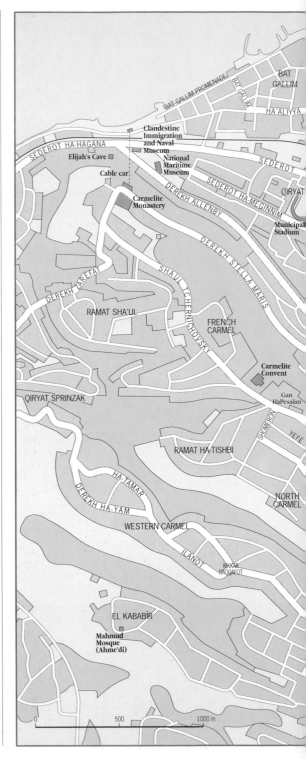

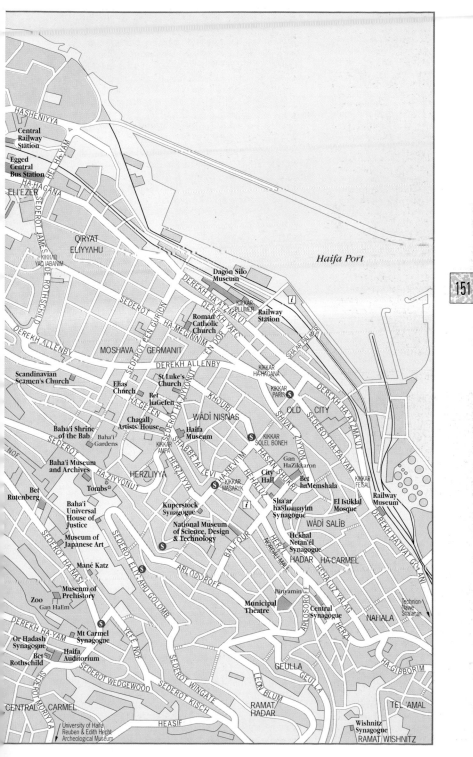

HASHENIYYA

Central
Railway
Station

Egged
Central
Bus Station

ELI'EZER

HA-HAGANA

HEL HA-YAM

SEDEROT JAMES DE ROTHSCHILD

QIRYAT
ELIYYAHU

KIKKAR
YAD LABANIM

DEREKH ALLENBY

SEDEROT BEN GURION

MOSHAVA GERMANIT

Scandinavian
Seamen's Church

Baha'i Shrine
of the Bab

SEDEROT HA-NOF

Bet
Rutenberg

Baha'i Museum
and Archives

Baha'i
Universal
House of
Justice

Museum of
Japanese Art

Mané Katz

Zoo
Gan HaEm

DEREKH HA-YAM

Museum of
Prehistory

Or Hadash
Synagogue

Bet
Rothschild

SEDEROT MORIYYA

Mt Carmel
Synagogue

Haifa
Auditorium

CENTRAL CARMEL

Elias
Church

HA-GEFEN

Chagall
Artists' House

Baha'i
Gardens

Tombs

HA-ZIYYONUT

HERZLIYYA

SEDEROT ELIYAHU GOLOMB

YEFE NOF

SEDEROT WEDGEWOOD

HE'ASIF

St Luke's
Church

Bet
HaGefen

Dagòn Silo
Museum

DEREKH HA-ATZMA'UT

DEREKH HA-YAEC

DEREKH HA-MEGINNIM

EN DOR

Roman
Catholic
Church

DEREKH ALLENBY

HA-NEVI'IM

SHABBETAI LEVI

KIKKAR
AMPA

HERZLIYYA

Haifa
Museum

WADI NISNAS

KHOURI

SEDEROT WINGATE

SEDEROT KISCH

ARLOSOROFF

BALFOUR

National Museum
of Science, Design
& Technology

Kuperstock
Synagogue

KIKKAR
MASARYK

HA-NEVI'IM

HA-HALUZ

Municipal
Theatre

LEON BLUM

RAMAT
HADAR

Binyamin

KIKKAR
PLUMER

Railway
Station

Haifa Port

i

KIKKAR
HA-HAGANA

KIKKAR
PARIS

SHIVAT ZIYYON

HASAN SHUKRI

City
Hall

Gan
HaZikkaron

OLD CITY

SEDEROT HA-PALYAM

Bet
haMemshala

Sha'ar
haShamayim
Synagogue

Hekhal
Netan'él
Synagogue

HERZL

MORDAI HAEL

HADAR

ARLOSOROFF

GEULLA

El Istiklal
Mosque

WADI SALIB

HA-CARMEL

Central
Synagogue

GEULLA

DEREKH HA-ATZMA'UT

KIKKAR
FEISAL

DEREKH HA-TIYAT GOLANI

Railway
Museum

REHALUZ YALAG

NAHALA

HA-GIBBORIM

Technion-
Nawe
Sha'anan

TEL 'AMAL

Wishnitz
Synagogue

RAMAT WISHNITZ

University of Haifa
Reuben & Edith Hecht
Archeological Museum

The Bahá'í faith
Followers of the Bahá'í religion believe in a single deity, in the essential unity of all human beings and religions, and in the continuous revelation of an evolving, yet fundamentally unchanging, divine truth through a series of prophets ('Divine Educators'). In particular, adherents worship the 'Martyr-Herald' (or 'the Bab') who announced his beliefs and his mission in Iran in 1844 and was executed in 1850 (aged 31) as a result, and the 'Founder of the Faith' ('Bahá'u'lláh'), who was exiled to Akko in 1868 and died there under house arrest in 1892. Haifa is the administrative capital of the religion and the Universal House of Justice is its supreme institution. But while the magnificently beautiful shrine of the Bab is in Haifa and is seen by more visitors, the lovely shrine of Bahá'u'lláh, at Bahjá, near Akko (see page 140), is actually the more sacred site.

Carmelim – a new region
The warm, green and wooded Mediterranean hills of Mount Carmel, the wine country around Zichron Yaakov, and the narrow coastal plain flanked by a long ribbon of sandy beach, have together been dubbed Carmelim by Israelis. This most beautiful part of Israel's coastal strip, reaching from Haifa to Caesarea, contains an exceptional legacy of history and culture but thas barely been discovered by tourists.

Haifa survived only as a quiet village until the 19th century when its port grew to accommodate steamships. The first half of the 20th century saw a huge amount of development and Jewish settlement. The Technion (the scientific research institute) was founded (see page 149), various Zionist-run commercial and manufacturing enterprises were opened and Histadrut (the all-pervasive workers' union which to this day remains a pillar of the Israeli establishment) based itself in the town. Haifa also became the principal entry port for clandestine Jewish immigrants to Israel.

The **Clandestine Immigration Museum▶▶▶** (204 Allenby Street), close to the beach and a little out of the heart of town, catches the eye of every passing motorist – it is the building that incorporates a whole real ship. Inside, the museum combines the functions of memorial and archive, recording, through displays, documents, lifesize models and exhibits, the whole organised struggle that brought 107,000 'illegal immigrants', including Holocaust survivors, to Israel from Europe during the years 1934 to 1948. Some heart-rending exhibits detail particular events, such as the story of the 1947 clandestine ship *Exodus*, carrying over 4,500 Holocaust survivors who on arrival at Haifa were held by the British authorities and then sent back to Germany. The real refugee ship on display shows what the interior would have been like.

Almost next door is the **National Maritime Museum▶** (198 Allenby Street), a record of shipping throughout the ages. Opposite, on the other side of Allenby and up steep steps, is **Elijah's Cave▶▶**, sacred to the devout of four religions – Jewish, Christian, Muslim and Druze. All four attach improbable stories to this atmospheric cave. A steep staircase of 300 steps cut into the hillside continues up and across an attractive heath with superb sea views, to the handsome **Carmelite Monastery▶▶▶**. Inside, a circular domed chapel encloses another reputedly holy and miraculous cave where Elijah is said to have lived and died. The easy way to reach the monastery is to take the cable-car from close to the Clandestine Immigration Museum.

The conspicuous gilded dome rising grandly over central Haifa belongs to the exquisitely beautiful **Shrine of the Bab▶▶▶**, completed in 1953. This is, without doubt, the best cared-for and most elegant holy site in Israel, and inspires an awareness of its sanctity even in non-religious visitors. The rather meditative, private style of worship takes place in two small and silent white rooms, laid with rich carpets, separated by a transparent curtain from the inner sanctum (built in 1909) which houses the remains of the Bab, predecessor of Bahá'u'lláh, founder of the Bahá'í religion (do not enter these shrines without invitation and on no account after noon if you are not of the Bahá'í faith). Across the street the glorious **Bahá'i Gardens▶▶** and the splendid white **Universal House of Justice▶**.

Haifa Museum▶ (26 Shabtai Levi Street) brings together a wide range of exhibits on ancient and modern art, folklore, ethnography, and Jewish ritual art. Almost opposite is **Chagall House▶**, another art museum hosting special exhibitions of work by contemporary artists.

► **Herzliya** *112C4*

This resort, named after the 'father of Zionism', Theodor Herzl, lies 15km north of Tel Aviv. Herzliya proper, a short distance inland, is a busy working town quite separate from the small seashore development correctly called Herzliya Pituach. This has a wide swathe of superb white beach backed by a few tall and luxuriously equipped hotels and apartment blocks. To spoil this idyll, waste water from the hotels pours directly onto the sand and oil can also be a nuisance. Better avoided is the grubby oil-coated pay-to-enter beach which lies through the big arch off central De Shalit Square.

► **Lod (Lydda)** *112C4*

More than just the place where Ben-Gurion International Airport is situated, Lod is a small town dating to the Israelite conquest of Canaan, which took place in 1300 BC. Its subsequent history, detailed in the Bible, includes centuries of rule by the Greeks, the Maccabees and the Romans. The Acts of the Apostles record that St Paul came here and miraculously healed a bedridden man. It is also claimed as the birthplace of St George, the Roman tribune sacred to Christians and to Muslims, and he is buried here in a building which is both church and mosque, on the site of the 6th-century basilica and 12th-century Crusader church.

►► **Lohamei Hagetta'ot Kibbutz** *113B4*

The name of this kibbutz, located just outside Akko, means 'The Ghetto Fighters'. It was founded in 1949 by Holocaust survivors and former ghetto resistance fighters. Their **Holocaust Memorial** makes a striking sight from the road, and they keep a remarkable **museum►►►** of historical material on the Nazi death camps and ghetto resistance in Germany, Poland and Lithuania. Other displays cover the pre-Nazi Jewish world of Poland and Lithuania, Nazi blueprints for the mass extermination of the Jews, a plan of Treblinka death camp, thousands of works of art by concentration camp inmates, photographs of the Warsaw Ghetto Uprising, and much more.

Behind the scenes
Perceived by most visitors simply as one of Israel's quieter beach resorts, Herzliya has a successful 'clean industries' zone generating an income of US $300 million, and accounting for 25 per cent of Israel's science-based exports.

153

Lod, claimed as the birth and burial place of St George

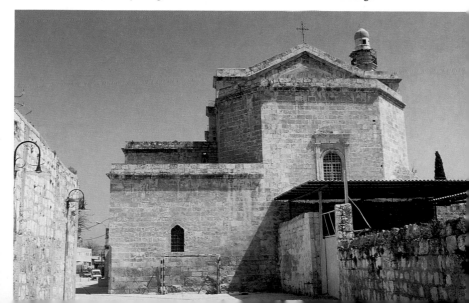

Dunes and swamps
Israel's coastal strip is a region of infertile dunes which, apart from the Carmel upland, used to be backed by the hot swampy Sharon plain. Right into this century, the area was notoriously unhealthy and unworkable. On top of the other problems, it was inhabited by crocodiles. The great Levantine highway of the ancient world, later to become the Romans' Via Maris (the Coast Road), had to divert away from the swampy, treacherous coastal hinterland. The British Mandate authorities were the first to set about drainage and bridge-building to make the area more accessible. With the founding of the State of Israel, a mammoth effort was made to build new towns along the coast. The marshes were drained and the main north–south highway put through. The Sharon plain has since been turned into one of the world's most productive citrus-growing areas.

Right and below:
Carmel National Park

▶▶▶ Mount Carmel   113B3

Some of the most beautiful countryside in Israel falls within the Carmel National Park. The Carmel range – consisting of the Carmel escarpment itself, and the smaller Mehallel, Shoker and Sumak peaks – rises from the surrounding coastal lowlands in the form of a triangle whose northern apex pushes into the sea at Haifa and whose sides plunge down to the Kishon valley and Yizre'el Plain on one side and to the Mediterranean Sea on the other. The base of the triangle fades gradually into the lower Sharon countryside, creating an attractive landscape of rock and abundant, varied scrub, rolling across the Mediterranean hinterland.

Despite the name, Mount Carmel is no mountain. The highest point, only 546m, hardly projects above the rest of the Carmel ridge along which runs the road from Haifa. The range covers a tiny area (23km from end to end, and only 10km at the widest), yet it has the feel of a world apart, with a character and history distinct from that of the lower lying country all around.

In Canaanite times, these hilltops were adorned with shrines dedicated to Ba'al. The cult's appeal was such that it continued to thrive long after the Israelite conquest. Its end in the 9th century BC is described in the (presumably allegorical) biblical account (I Kings 18) where Elijah, having won a public contest to see whose god could make spontaneous fire, persuades the people to murder the 450 'prophets of Ba'al' and turn instead to the God of Israel. Since then, Elijah's name has been associated with Carmel, ironically more among the Christians and the Muslims than among the Jews.

Drive Carmel scenery

Mount Carmel's Mediterranean countryside, of limestone hills covered with fragrant evergreen vegetation, is full of historical and human interest. There are Druze towns to visit, plus religious and historical sites, an artists' village and local wine to taste (for map see page 113B3).
Allow all day

From **Haifa** take the steep road to the **University**, dominated by the intrusive **Eshkol Tower**, a monstrosity bent only on being as tall as possible. Leave the city on the tranquil hill road to **Isfiya▶**, a small town of Christians and Druze. The road winds steeply down to larger **Daliyat▶▶**, more noticeably Druze. Its main street has a fascinating Middle Eastern atmosphere, with open-fronted shops and snack-bars. **Oliphant's House▶**, a memorial to Druze soldiers who died for Israel, was the 19th-century home of an Englishman whose Jewish secretary, N H Imber, wrote *HaTikva*, Israel's national anthem. A turn leads to the hilltop monastery at **Muhraka▶** (or Keren Carmel), traditional site of the meeting between Elijah and the Ba'al prophets. Take the main road to **Zichron Ya'akov▶▶** (see page 160), where wine-tasting and a tour of the cellars is on offer at the Winery Visitors' Centre.

The open-fronted shops of Daliyat's main street

Traditional Druze skull-caps for sale in Daliyat.

On the coast, **Kibbutz Nachsholim▶** has a museum, located in a former wine-bottle factory. The kibbutz also offers simple beachside accommodation. The archaeological site of **Tel Dor▶** was a Phoenician port town thousands of years ago. Take the Haifa highway, and turn into the **Nahal Me'arot Reserve▶▶▶**, where several big caves were inhabited by human beings as far back as 200,000 years ago. These can be toured with a guide. The reserve also offers a choice of marked footpaths through lovely natural vegetation.

En Hod▶, to the north, is a hillside 'artists' village' of meandering lanes, scattered houses, pretty gardens, art galleries and numerous open-air sculptures. At the crossroads, a left turn leads to **Atlit▶** (see page 143) while the right turn winds up between beautiful rocky limestone hills to **Carmel Forest▶▶**. The sign to **Hai Bar▶** leads down a dirt track to a reserve where once-indigenous animals are being reintroduced. Continue to the junction where a left turn will take you back to Haifa.

■ In ancient Israel, wine was the usual drink before, during and after meals, but the Scriptures warned against over-indulgence. Jewish coins of the Second Temple period depict bunches of grapes. Grapes or vine leaves can often be seen in the mosaics and stone carvings of post-Temple synagogues. During the diaspora years, wine-drinking declined but, with the return to Israel, the wine-making tradition has been revived with great success. ■

Wine and ritual
'Blessed are you Lord, our God ruler of the world, who created the fruit of the vine.' This blessing over wine is said (in Hebrew) before every meal on the sabbath, starting with the Friday night dinner. A glass of kosher wine is then drunk – usually just a tiny glass of the extra-sweet Kiddush wine.

Products of the Golan Heights Winery

Sacred and profane Israelis are not big drinkers. There is no breath-testing here for motorists, simply because excessive drinking is almost unknown. Observant Jews thank God for the fruit of the vine on the sabbath, yet no one could be more abstemious. Things have obviously changed since biblical times when the people of Israel grew grapes in abundance, were fond of wine and – to judge by references in the Scriptures – sometimes drank a great deal of it.

Jews are supposed to drink only kosher wine. Rabbis decided that any contact with a non-Jew would render wine non-kosher, unless the wine was boiled. Of course, boiling is not the ideal way to preserve a wine's finest qualities, and kosher wine came to be regarded with derision by wine-lovers. There is also an ultra-sweet blended wine specially produced for Kiddush, the ritual blessing that sanctifies all sorts of occasions. Such wine seems calculated to put people off drinking – yet when the sages decreed that the sabbath be sanctified over a cup of wine, the reason given was precisely that wine brings joy and festivity.

The new approach Even Israelis do not think of themselves as a wine-producing nation. They are mistaken: in recent decades, Israel has rediscovered its great wine tradition. In keeping with the Talmudic injunction, to ensure that the wine is kosher, only Jews may be involved in its production at every stage. The most modern techniques are used, and many different grape varieties have been planted, crossed or combined, in the search for higher quality and an authentic Israeli style of fine wine.

Some have been a great success, especially the elegant dry white Chardonnay and Sauvignon Blanc and the classic, full-bodied red Cabernet Sauvignon. Blander and sweeter Emerald Riesling is the most popular with Israelis. Richly sweet Muscat is grown, as is the tangy Californian

variety Zinfandel. The main wine areas are in southern Carmel, the district south of Tel Aviv around Rishon-l'Tsion, and the Golan Heights, with smaller wineries around Ashkelon and Beersheva. Less expensive labels include the Segal and Baron wineries.

Mural celebrating Baron Rothschild's introduction of viti-culture to the Carmel region

Carmel It is said that the name Carmel probably means God's Vineyard (Kerem El). A century ago, Baron Edmund de Rothschild had the whole area, from Zichron Ya'akov down to Binyamina, planted with vines, under the direction of French agronomists. The Carmel Mizrachi Winery in Zichron Ya'akov is now the country's largest wine producer, and welcomes visitors for tours and tasting.

Rishon l'Tsion The name (also spelled Rishon le Zion) means 'First in Zion', in other words the first Jewish settlement of modern times, set up in 1882. Five years later, the struggling pioneers were bailed out by Baron Rothschild, who again planted vineyards, with tremendous success. The Carmel winery here, recently modernised, offers guided tours and tasting. Its wines have improved enormously in quality and reputation in recent years.

בן עמי

Ben Ami

UN VIN SEGAL

1 9 8 9

PRODUIT ET MIS EN BOUTEILLES PAR ASKALON WINES - CARMEI ZION Ltd. 750 ML. PRODUIT D'ISRAEL 11.5% VOL

כשר לפסח

Golan Heights winery Acclaimed as Israel's best are the wines produced on the Golan Heights, just outside Katzrin. The vineyards, tended by settlements and kibbutzim over a wide area of the Golan, are – together with the winery itself – run as a co-operative. This launched Israel's dramatic rediscovery of wine-making, and is the only wine-maker in the world to have won the Chairman's Trophy of Excellence at the trade's important Vinexpo exhibition in three successive years. Golan's soils and drainage are perfect for wine, and, because of the lack of rain, the water supply is controlled by irrigation. The wines, in a wide range of styles, are marketed under three labels: Yarden (the best), Gamla and Golan. The winery, the only one in Israel using Merlot grapes, also makes a fine sparkling dry white.

Netanya's beach

Open-air entertainment

Summer nights
Open-air entertainment takes place in Netanya's main square every night of the week (except Friday) right through July and August. The atmosphere is jolly, participatory and good-humoured. In a typical week you could expect a disco on Sunday, folk dancing on Monday and Saturday, magicians, puppets and clown shows for children on Tuesday, and community singing on Wednesday and Thursday.

▶ **Nahariya** *113B4*

The waterfront area of this resort on the Galilee coast, 30km north of Haifa, enjoys a good beach, a pleasant waterfront, a wide range of leisure amenities and a generally calm and tranquil air. Further back from the sea lies a busy working town, founded in 1934 by Jewish refugees from Germany. **Museums▶** of art, archaeology and local history can be found in the town hall. Nahariya resort makes a good base for excursions and tours of the surrounding area. Just 5km north are the seashore ruins of ancient **Akhziv▶▶**, now a National Park, once an important Canaanite, Phoenician and Israelite town renowned for the purple dye produced from its shellfish. Some 3km south of Nahariya, 4th- and 5th-century Byzantine mosaics and other archaeological finds can be seen at **Kibbutz Evron▶** and **Moshav Shavei Zion** (which also has a good hotel).

▶▶ **Netanya** *113A1*

Spreading itself comfortably alongside the seashore, but not going far inland, this large town is one of the most agreeable and unpretentious beach resorts on the Israeli Mediterranean. It has a peaceful, almost sedate, atmosphere, yet has dozens of decent, mid-range hotels and moderately priced eating places. The park-like clifftop walk gives magnificent views out to sea, and there is more than 10km of sandy beach to enjoy.

One focal point for visitors is **Kikkar HaAtzma'ut** (Independence Square), which fronts on to the clifftop above the main central section of the beach. Another gathering place is the main street, **Rehov Herzl**, where tourists and locals alike stroll in the pleasant evening air. Yet behind this leisurely façade, Netanya is a productive commercial town. Diamonds have been among its most lucrative specialities since World War II, when the jewellers of Antwerp moved here to escape the Nazis. Ask at the tourist office (Kikkar HaAtzma'ut) for details of the interesting **diamond workshops▶**, which can be visited.

►► Ramla 113C4

Almost unique in that it came into being during a period of Arab rule, Ramla was founded in 716 by Caliph Suleiman and became a large city inhabited by Muslims, Christians and Jews. In 1936 the Jews were forced out by the Arabs, who in 1948 largely fled in fear of reprisals. The population of 50,000 now consists mainly of Jews driven in turn from their homes in Arab countries, along with several thousand Israeli Arabs. It is also a centre of the Karaites, a small Jewish sect which accepts the Torah but rejects subsequent rabbinic comment. The town is attractive and friendly, with a strongly Middle Eastern character.

The **Great Mosque►** (off Herzl Street), reflecting the town's mixed history, is a 12th-century Crusader church topped by a white minaret and transformed into a mosque. The landmark **White Tower►►**, a substantial Gothic stone structure, is gaunt and square and 27m tall. Napoleon, who in 1799 stayed overnight in Ramla, enjoyed the view from the top, and General Allenby, in 1917, found it useful as a military observation post. Also known to Christians as the Tower of Forty Martyrs and to Muslims as the Tower of the Prophet's Companions, it was built in 1267 by the Mameluke Sultan Baibars. It adjoins an extensive walled area, along one side of which are remnants of a **mosque►** which dates to the founding of the town by Caliph Suleiman. Below the walled courtyard are three large vaulted crypts. Just off Herzl Street, **St Helena's Pool►** in fact has no connection at all with St Helena – it is an impressive 8th-century reservoir.

► Rehovot 113C3

Zionist leader Chaim Weizmann (1874–1952), Israel's first president, lived here at the end of his life. In his honour, the distinguished **Weizmann Institute** research centre was founded in 1944 (tours by arrangement), close to **Weizmann's house►** (open to visitors), where he died and lies buried in the garden.

Chaim Weizmann (1874–1952)

As well as being a leading Zionist, the person who persuaded Balfour to write the famous Declaration (pledging Britain's support in setting up a Jewish homeland), president of the World Zionist Organisation and first president of Israel, Weizmann was a distinguished chemist. Born near Pinsk, in Russia, Weizmann studied chemistry in Germany and Switzerland, and in 1916 was made director of the British Admiralty Chemical Laboratories. Although devoting much of his energy to diplomacy and politics, he had an international reputation in the scientific world for his discoveries in organic chemistry. He made historic advances in the study of carcinogens and his many other discoveries included the making of synthetic rubber from organic substances.

159

Independence Square, Netanya

Dor
Located on the coast close to Zichron Ya'akov, and next to Nachsholim, Dor was a Phoenician port in 2000 BC. Though seized by the Israelites, and then the Assyrians, it was recaptured by Phoenicians and remained an independent city until the Roman conquest. From the 4th to 7th centuries it was a Christian town, destroyed in the Arab conquest. Crusaders built a castle on the shore here in the 12th century, but within a hundred years it had been destroyed by the Mamelukes. Dor was revived in 1949 as a *moshav* (co-operative village), set up by immigrants from Greece. It has a beautiful beach and plenty of reminders of its long history.

The white cliffs of Rosh HaNikra

►►► Rosh HaNikra   113C4

The coastal hinterland climbs as it approaches the Lebanese border, which runs along a high ridge in Israel's northwestern corner. Rosh HaNikra is essentially just a frontier post on this ridge of mountain whose white cliffs plunge straight down into the blue Mediterranean. At the top, thrilling views run far down the country's Mediterranean shore. The border bristles with defences, yet United Nations and Israeli soldiers continually cross through the gate here.

The area's biggest attraction is the **Rosh HaNikra Caves►►►** at the bottom of the cliffs, which can be reached by cable-car. Here the sea has eaten into the soft pale sandstone like moth grubs in a woollen cloak. The cliffs are riddled with little holes and tunnels which bore through the rock from one opening to the next – and at each the azure water hammers in as if to bring the whole cliff tumbling down into the waves.

►► Zichron Ya'akov   113B2

The name means 'In Memory of Jacob', and refers not to the biblical character but to the 19th-century banker, Jacob de Rothschild. It was named in his honour by his son, Baron Edmond de Rothschild (also known as Benjamin or Binyamin). A pleasant small town on high ground at the edge of the Carmel hills, it looks down towards the sea in one direction, and into the Valley of HaNadiv 'The Benefactor' in the other. The benefactor in question was Baron Rothschild, who purchased this valley and its surrounding country in the 1880s in order to establish new settlements and bail out existing ones. His intentions were Zionist, but not always entirely philanthropic: the settlements were run as business concerns, and expected to pay their way and cover their costs.

Zichron Ya'akov was founded by Romanian Jews in 1882. They floundered and fell into serious difficulty: half of them died and the others were ready to quit. Rothschild then came in with an offer to buy up the settlement, lock, stock and barrel, and employ the residents on a salaried basis. They agreed. The baron then brought in non-Jewish agronomists from the south of France and asked them what could be produced there successfully. Their answer was wine. Other Jews came and, desperate for work, were employed here. Zichron

Ya'akov became the most important of the little wine-making towns of Israel. Today, the main attraction for visitors is a tour of the co-operatively owned **Carmel Oriental (or Carmel Mizrachi) Winery▶**. After a visit to the cellars, you can taste the several varieties of wine made here. The town centre is also worth a stroll. On the main streets, HaNadiv and Mayasdim, pioneer houses, can still be seen, and at the central junction, the pioneers' synagogue. **Beit Aaronsohn▶** (Mayasdim Street) was the home of the distinguished agronomist and botanist, Aaron Aaronsohn (1876–1917). He created and led, with his brother Alexander and sister Sarah, the Nili spy ring which operated for the British against the Turks in World War I. The group was eventually uncovered by the Turks, who captured and tortured Sarah for several days before allowing her to commit suicide. Their home, the ring's headquarters, has been preserved just as it was when the Aaronsohns met their death in 1917.

Memorial to Rothschild, the Benefactor, who turned Zichron Ya'akov into an important wine town

The road south leads through countryside planted with vineyards to another wine settlement, **Binyamina**, named from the Baron's Hebrew name. Between the two towns, an access road leads to **Ramat HaNadiv▶▶▶** (Hill of the Benefactor), the beautiful memorial park dedicated to Baron Edmond de Rothschild and his wife. In the park is their massive and dignified burial chamber, where the two lie under a single slab of black marble in a mausoleum that is open to the public.

161

Cable-car to Rosh HaNikra caves

GALILEE AND THE NORTH

▶▶▶▶▶▶ **REGION HIGHLIGHTS**

CHURCH OF THE ANNUNCIA-TION, NAZARETH *see page 193*

CHURCH OF THE BEATITUDES *see page 189*

CHURCH OF THE PRIMACY OF PETER, TABGHA *see page 202*

HULA VALLEY *see pages 178–9*

OLD SYNAGOGUE, PEKI'IN *see page 195*

ROMAN AND BYZANTINE SPA, HAMAT GADER *see page 176*

SEA OF GALILEE *see page 196–8*

SEFAT *see pages 200–1*

SYNAGOGUE, CAPERNAUM *see page 171*

TEL DAN *see pages 202–3*

See drive page 173
See drive page 194
See drive page 198

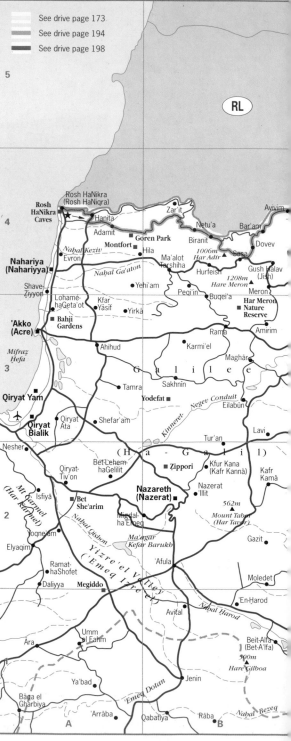

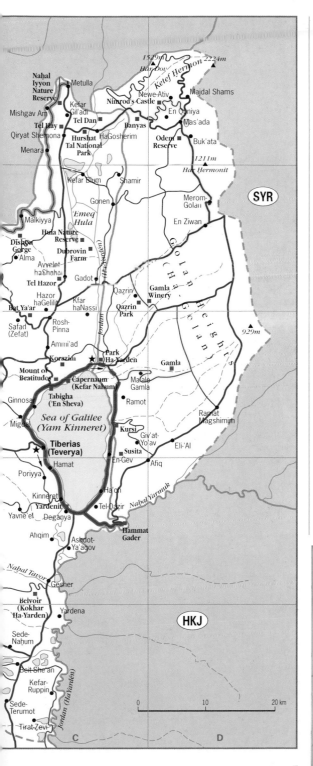

Map labels:

1529m
Har Dov — 2224m
Ketef Hermon
Nahal Iyyon Nature Reserve
Metulla
Newe-Ativ
Majdal Shams
Mishgav Am
Kefar Gil'adi
Nimrod's Castle
En Qoniya
Mas'ada
Tel Hay
Tel Dan
Banyas
Odem Reserve
Buk'ata
Qiryat Shemona
Hurshat Tal National Park
HaGosherim
Menara
1211m
Har Hermonit
Kefar Blum
Shamir

SYR

Malkiyya
Emeq Hula
Gonen
Merom-Golan
Hula Nature Reserve
En Ziwan
Dishon Gorge
Dubrovin Farm
Alma
Avvelet-haShahar
Tel Hazor
Gadot
Gamla Winery
Hazor haGelilit
Kfar haNassi
Qazrin
Bat Ya'ar
Qazrin Park
Safad (Zefat)
Rosh-Pinna
929m
Ammi'ad
Korazim
Park Ha-Yarden
Gamla
Mount of Beatitudes
Capernaum (Kefar Nahum)
Ma'ale Gamla
Ginnosar
Tabigha ('En Sheva)
Ramot
Migdal
Sea of Galilee (Yam Kinneret)
Kursi
Ramat Magshimim
Tiberias (Teverya)
Giv'at-Yo'av
Eli-'Al
Hamat
Susita
En-Gev
Afiq
Poriyya
Ha'on
Kinneret
Nahal Yarmuk
Yardenit
Tel-Qazir
Yavne'el
Deganya
Atiqim
Hammat Gader
Ashdot-Ya'aqov
Nahal Tavor
Gesher
Belvoir (Kokhar Ha-Yarden)
Yardena
Sede-Nahum
Beit She'an
Kefar-Ruppin
Jordan (HaYarden)
Sede-Terumot
Tirat Zevi

HKJ

0   10   20 km

C   D

Sign advertising the Jordan River baptismal site

The District
The Hebrew name for Galilee, HaGalil, simply means 'the District'. Originally it was HaGalil HaGoyim, meaning (more or less), 'The Non-Jewish District'. That is because, from the 8th century BC to the Hasmonean conquest in the 2nd century BC, the region was not part of the Israelite kingdom, being a possession of the Assyrians, Babylonians, Persians and Seleucids. Under Roman rule it was reunited with Judaea. Yet the name has rarely been accurate. Jews have always been numerous here, and this northern region has historically been a stronghold of Jewish nationalism as well as a centre of Jewish religious learning.

Right: Christ recruited his disciples from the fishermen of Galilee
Below: Christians from around the world come to trace Christ's ministry

Galilee and the North The hills of Galilee, on Israel's warm northern borders, are startlingly green. Here, the rocky landscape has been clothed in natural or planted forests, and farms produce an extraordinary range of crops. The northeast corner, around Dan, on the slopes of Mount Hermon and in the upper Hula valley, enjoys a wealth of plant, bird and animal wildlife.

Images of Israel as a Middle Eastern country can be misleading. Essentially this is a Mediterranean land, tied by history, culture, geography and climate entirely to the waters of the classical, Mediterranean world, rather than to the sands of Arabia. No part of Israel strikes the eye as so utterly and familiarly Mediterranean as the Galilee.

The Galilee forms a narrow band stretching from the sea in the west to the River Jordan. The east is dominated by the Sea of Galilee, while to the south it is bounded by the Jezreel Plain. The region is blessed with an exquisite climate that is a few degrees cooler than in the beach resorts further south. Snow falls on the heights in mid-winter, but fine weather lasts from May to October.

A place of pilgrimage The fact that Jesus lived in Galilee – and walked on its waters, miraculously fed the multitudes, taught that we should love one another and recruited his disciples from among the Galilee fishermen – is accepted by Christians around the world. Many travel to see the spots where all this happened. The fact that the sites have been disputed, or are symbolic rather than historically proven, seems not to matter. Stand beside the tranquil shore of the Sea of Galilee and it is easy to believe that you are indeed standing where he stood, seeing the serene landscapes where he wandered in prayer and in thought. Dozens of simple churches and grand basilicas commemorate the great moments of what the modern church would call 'his ministry'.

It is now more widely understood among Christians that Jesus was an observant Jew, learned in the scriptures and concerned only that his fellow Jews should obey the spirit, rather than just the letter, of the Law. Galilee, far from the Temple in Jerusalem, was perhaps an ideal place for his teachings. Yet within a few years of his death, after the crushing of the First Jewish Revolt and

the destruction of the Temple, the eastern Galilee was to become the greatest centre of Jewish learning. The Mishna and Talmud (commentaries on the ancient scriptures) were both written here, and two of the four Jewish holy cities – Sefat and Tiberias – are in Galilee. The region again became the focal point of Jewish culture after the expulsion of the Jews from Spain in 1492. The tombs of the great Galilean scholars and sages of the biblical and medieval periods attract numerous Jewish visitors.

Golan Mediterranean scenery also rises to the east, in the Golan hills. These sparsely inhabited uplands rise to a high plateau overlooked by the majestic snows of Mount Hermon. All this countryside formed part of the biblical land of Israel and has extensive remains from that era. Coming under Arab control in the Middle Ages, Golan formed part of Syria until Syria invaded Israel in 1967. Six days after the invasion, Syria had been defeated and driven east. Israel took the Heights and created a buffer zone, which Syria still claims as its own.

Cultural diversity For more than a century, Jews have been drawn to the Galilee as an ideal place to settle and cultivate. Many of their most difficult struggles, both with the land and with the Arabs, have taken place here. Today, there is a good degree of harmony between the different cultural groups, and certainly for a tourist it is safe (and interesting) to visit Israel's non-Jewish communities. The largest Arab town in Israel is Nazareth, most of whose residents are Christian. Several other Galilee towns have a Christian Arab population, though of course many other smaller Arab towns and villages are Muslim. Almost all the members of Israel's 40,000 Druze population live in the western Galilee and on the Golan Heights.

The Sea of Galilee

No meat and two veg
Israel has an exceptionally large proportion of vegetarians, and the Galilee, in particular, seems to have become the capital of the meatless lifestyle. Jewish dietary laws require meat and milk to be kept separate – to the point where they cannot be eaten within several hours of each other. For many, the problem of keeping meat and milk apart could be avoided most easily by becoming vegetarian. That is why, for example, nearly all works canteens in Israel are vegetarian. Many other Jews chose to become vegetarian for reasons of compassion towards animals, which is a biblical precept. As well as its famous vegetarian village (Amirim), the Galilee has a good meat-free hotel (the Sea View, near Rosh Pinna) and an unusual cheese restaurant (Ein Camonim, near Parod).

Byzantine-era frieze in the Golan Archaeological Museum

GALILEE AND THE NORTH

Who are the Druze?
Bnei Maruf, the Children of
Grace, is how the Druze
refer to themselves.
Members of this distinctive
community wear striking
black-and-white attire and
live in their own well-kept
villages scattered over
Galilee and Golan. They
originated as an 11th-
century breakaway group
from Ismailism, a branch of
Islam. The tenets of the
religion are a closely
guarded secret, with a
body of arcane knowledge
known only to the initiates
or the *Ukal*. The rest of the
Druze population are the
Juhal, the ignorant.

Israel's Druze have been
keen supporters of the
Jewish state, because it
gives them full religious
freedom, unlike any of the
other countries where the
Druze are to be found. As
a community, they have
accepted the obligations
of army service (for which,
as Arabs, they could have
asked to be exempt), and
many have distinguished
themselves fighting to
defend Israel.

*Gushing rivers and
ancient caves in
Banyas National Park*

▶   **Amirim**   162B3

High in the Galilee hills (the name means 'Treetops') this
tranquil agricultural *moshav* (co-operative village) is entirely
vegetarian. Located a short drive from historic Sefat, it
offers tremendous views to west and east, as well as
south to the Sea of Galilee. Half of Amirim's 60 families
take paying guests on a full or half-board basis, and Dalia's
vegetarian restaurant is very popular.

▶▶   **Banyas National Park**   163C5

At the foot of Mount Hermon, this lush, delightful park is
one of the sources of the River Jordan. With gushing
waters, shaded picnic tables and benches, and extensive
classical ruins, it attracts many visitors. An enjoyable footpath (about 1½ hours' walk) makes a circle through rich
vegetation, crossing and recrossing the turbulent Banyas
stream on wooden walkways, with an optional extra 1km
walk to a lovely waterfall crashing into a pool enclosed by
moist greenery.

Banyas was once perhaps the most important pagan
shrine in Israel, and the park entrance opens into an
impressive Greek archaeological site, with water pools
and statuary. Previously sacred to the Canaanite god,
Ba'al, the shrine was rededicated to Pan (Paneas in
Greek, from which the name Banyas is derived) when it
became part of the Hellenistic kingdom of Antiochus III of
Syria in the 3rd century BC. In those days the spring
poured from the mouth of a cave above the shrine; now it
emerges from a crack below. Niches around the cave
originally held statues, and scores of Greek carvings have
been discovered here.

The Romans, on taking control of Palestine, rededicated
the site jointly to Pan and Zeus, greatly enlarging it.
Herod's son, Philip, made Banyas his capital, renaming it
Caesarea Philippi and turning it into the biggest city in
northern Israel. It later passed into Arab hands and the
city died away, though held by Crusaders from 1129 to
1135. At the time of the 1967 Israeli takeover, its population was just 200.

A long two weeks
In late 1948, Israeli forces fighting desperately against invading Arab armies arrived at the Christian Arab villages of Biram (now Bar'am) and Ikrit, on the Lebanese border. They were welcomed and, to assist the soldiers, the villagers agreed to leave for an estimated period of two weeks. But the continuing state of hostilities after the war left the Israeli government wary of Arab villages on the border, and the residents were never allowed back. Ikrit was destroyed in 1951 and Biram in 1953. Many of the villagers, and now their children, live in nearby Rama and Jish, but they have not abandoned hope of returning to their homes and lands.

The remains of Bar'am synagogue

The gospel (Matthew 16: 13–20) relates that, while visiting Caesarea Philippi and walking beside the water, Jesus asked his disciples who they thought he was. Simon for the first time declared Jesus to be the Messiah (Christos in Greek), whereupon Jesus called him Petrus, saying, 'and upon this rock I will build my church.' Banyas remained important to Christians, the see of a bishop from the 4th to the 7th centuries AD. The white-domed Weli el-Hader on the hillside, built in honour of the prophet Elijah, is sacred to the Druze (see panel).

▶▶ Bar'am National Park 162B4

Dating from the 2nd century AD, the well-preserved remnants of the fine synagogue here include two walls of huge stone blocks, sturdy stone columns forming three aisles, and a handsome flagstone floor, with an arched entrance facing Jerusalem.

Until the 1948 War of Independence, the synagogue was part of a small Maronite Arab village friendly to the Jewish forces. During the fighting – which was particularly intense at this point, being close to the Lebanese border – the population were asked to leave 'temporarily', but instead their homes were largely destroyed. About 100m up from the synagogue, on higher ground, is the villagers' church and their ruined houses. Their children, now grown up, still use the church for weddings and ceremonies, and have campaigned to have the village returned to them. Many distinguished Israeli personalities have supported their cause, and the authorities now seem likely to grant the request.

Sometime, never
Among the sayings and legends attached to Banyas is the Talmudic statement that the Messiah will come only 'when the Banyas turns red.' This seems to relate to the old Yiddish expression, that you can have the present you want or do the thing you want 'When Moshiach (the Messiah) comes'.

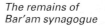

Marriage made in heaven
Over the road from Bat Ya'ar, in a pretty vale of pine and olive groves outside Amuka village, stands a small domed building housing the tomb, blackened with candle flame, of Rabbi Yonatan ben Uzziel. The building is divided into men's and women's sections. Here Hasidim and Sephardim flock to pray for a marriage partner or that they might become pregnant. Obscure and tenuous rabbinical remarks account for the superstition. Yonatan himself was very preoccupied with the importance of the marriage bond, and later rabbis commentated that the need for a wife and the way to find one, was 'deep' (*amuka* – which happened to be where Yonatan was buried). You might think that only a few hopeless cases would be found here, but among the worshippers are many pretty young women and handsome young bachelors. Glances between the men's and women's sections lead to many a friendly conversation later, and often subsequently to a wedding – thus proving the efficacy of a prayer at the tomb.

▶ **Bat Ya'ar** *163C3*

This popular activity centre, close to Sefat and Rosh Pinna, is set in a clearing in the midst of Israel's largest forest, the Birya. All planted by the Jewish National Fund, these high, refreshing woodlands consist mainly of Jerusalem pine, cedar and cypress. Offering activities and excursions ranging from an hour to a week, by pony, jeep or on foot, Bat Ya'ar is well placed for 'off-road' tours into the prolific Upper Galilee countryside. The 3-hour guided jeep tour travels along rough tracks through farmland planted with a range of crops from apples to bananas, and encounters wildlife from foxes to gazelles to bee-eaters.

The centre also puts on children's entertainment, dance and open-air music shows. It often attracts many lunchtime visitors to its timber ranch-style restaurant serving abundant salads, steaks and home-made breads with a view across the Hula Valley to the snowy summit of Mount Hermon.

▶ **Beit Alfa** *162B1*

Located between Heftsiba and Beit Alfa, two neighbouring kibbutzim at the foot of Mount Gilboa, 40km from Afula, the ruins of the Beit Alfa synagogue were discovered in 1928 during the digging of a kibbutz irrigation channel. The most striking feature of the synagogue is its beautiful mosaic floor, divided into three panels. One depicts religious emblems and the Ark of the Covenant. Another shows a zodiac circle with the astrological signs named in Hebrew, the moon and the stars, four women symbolising the seasons and a youth riding a horse-drawn chariot. The third represents the sacrifice of Isaac as described in the Bible. Unusually, the work is dated with an Aramaic inscription: 'This floor was laid down in the year of the reign of Emperor Justinus.' Justinus ruled Palestine from AD 518 to 527.

▶▶ **Beit She'an** *163C1*

This charmless little town seems modern but has in fact been inhabited for 5,000 years and is the site of Scythopolis, mentioned in Egyptian documents as long ago as the 19th century BC. Its excavations are among Israel's most impressive. In the middle of the new town, a large site contains remnants of a **Roman theatre▶** in white stone and a 5th-century **Byzantine street▶** in black. Of the amphitheatre's original 12 rows of seats (enough for 6,000 spectators), three have survived to this day.

Downhill lie the remarkable principal **Scythopolis excavations**, where work is still in progress. Steps lead to the summit of the tel▶▶, where 18 successive towns have been revealed. A circular footpath gives a good overview of the whole site, and the remains of the imposing buildings that once stood in the city centre. White and black stone make a dazzling

The Chariot of the Sun, Beit Alfa synagogue

Conserving water

The Jordan valley, from Belvoir to Beit She'an, and the Beit She'an valley, a tributary of the Jordan, have been chosen for a massive water conservation programme. Water shortages are the biggest threat to Israel's future life and livelihood. Most of the country's water comes from the Sea of Galilee, but this is proving inadequate. Winter downpours result in huge run-offs into the Jordan. The Jewish National Fund has been building a network of 40 reservoirs in the two valleys designed to capture this water and solve some of the problems, adding some 50 million cubic metres to the country's water supply.

contrast here as well. White columns, now being re-erected, lined the black-paved Byzantine **cardo**►► (main street). Black walls enclose a superb white Byzantine **amphitheatre**►►► (also seating 6,000), and there is a huge 4th-century **bath house**►► with marble columns rising from a mosaic floor. Tragically, an entire 6th century mosaic floor was stolen from the site in 1989.

►► Belvoir (Hebrew: Kohav HaYarden, literally 'Jordan Star') 163C2

A steep side road climbs to these substantial hilltop ruins of a powerful French Crusader castle. The remains consist of a five-sided outer wall, seven towers and a wide moat on three sides. Inside, a square inner castle has the remains of the storerooms, kitchen and dining room. The setting is magnificent, with views reaching across the Jezreel plain and Jordan valley to the Jordanian mountains. Built by Knights Hospitallers in 1168, the castle was twice unsuccessfully attacked by Salah ed-Din in 1182–83. A third seige, from 1187 to 1191, ended in victory for the Muslims, who magnanimously allowed the Crusaders safe retreat to Tyre. The Sultan of Damascus then ordered the castle to be partially dismantled – wisely, since Crusaders returned in 1241 but were unable to reconstruct it.

169

The basalt walls of Belvoir Castle

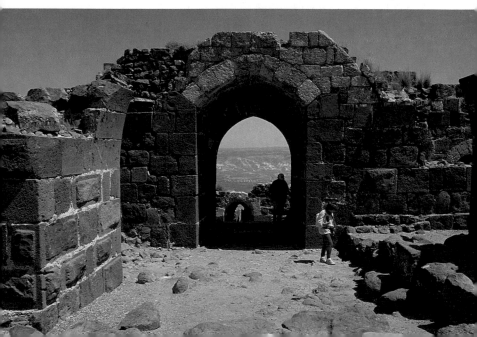

Greek Orthodox Church, Capernaum

▶▶ **Capernaum (Hebrew: Kfar Nahum)** *163C3*

Little remains of 'the town of Jesus', except for the ruins, enclosed within black basalt walls, excavated by Franciscan monks over the last 100 years. According to the gospel (Matthew 4: 11) Jesus moved to Capernaum from Nazareth to fulfil the words of the prophet Isaiah (9: 1–2), while John's gospel (6: 42) implies that Jesus was already well known in Capernaum, as were his parents (see side panel). Here, all the gospels agree, Jesus encountered first Simon and Andrew, then James and John, all of them fishermen working on the nearby Sea of Galilee. They became his first disciples. He then began preaching 'in the synagogues throughout all Galilee', or so Mark's gospel tells us, but mostly in and around Capernaum, where he performed numerous miracles.

Enlarged by refugees from Jerusalem after AD 70, the town thrived until it was completely destroyed during the 7th-century Arab conquest. Franciscans acquired the ruins in 1894 and began a programme of excavation which continued into the 1960s, turning the site into a fascinating open-air museum. On the right, inside the entrance, is an impressive frieze of carved white stone, and on the left the ruins of simple **houses▶** in black stone. Ahead rises the ugly modern roof of the octagonal St Peter's Memorial, erected over the black stone ruins, below ground level, of what the monks claim is the home of St Peter►►. Around the house are traces of several similar dwellings, all from about 200 BC to AD 700.

Adjacent stands the largest structure in Capernaum, the substantial reconstructed ruin of a fine synagogue►►► in imposing black and white marble, with Roman-style façade, pillars and carved capitals and lintels. The stonework depicts Jewish symbols, such as the Star of David and the seven-branched *menorah* candelabrum, as well as non-Jewish images, such as a half-man, half-fish. The synagogue, dating from the 2nd century AD, is not old enough to be the one where Jesus urged his astonished neighbours to 'eat of my flesh and drink of my blood' (John 6: 54), though it almost certainly stands on the same spot. For their scepticism, Jesus said the people of Capernaum faced eternal damnation.

► **Degania 'A' Kibbutz**   163C2

On the Sea of Galilee's southern shore, by the Jordan outflow, Degania 'A' (founded in 1909) is Israel's oldest kibbutz. At the gate stands a small Syrian military tank►►, one of a whole column which was halted by kibbutzniks, armed with old rifles and Molotov cocktails, during the 1948 War of Independence. Within the kibbutz, the A D Gordon Institute► (entrance on the main road) is a museum and study centre devoted to local history, archaeology and natural history.

►► **Gamla**   163D3

A rough 2.5km driveway leads to this dramatic, exposed site. Its name – meaning 'the camel' in Aramaic – derives from the humped terrain. The viewing area beside the car park gives a stark impression of the ruined city on its barren hill. Difficult footpaths lead up to the ruins. Gamla was one of many Golan towns founded after the Maccabean revolt against the Seleucids (168 BC). Some 250 years later, during the First Revolt against Rome, the people of Gamla supported the rebel Zealots. Other Judaean towns having been subdued or surrendered, Gamla's population of 5,000 was doubled as Zealots flocked here. Over 15,000 Roman troops gathered below, but most were slaughtered in the first battle, which resulted in a surprising victory for the rebels. Three more Roman legions (60,000 men) arrived to besiege the fortress town for a month before unleashing a second attack. This time Gamla was taken: thousands of residents and rebels were captured and killed, but 4,000 others chose suicide. Gamla was totally destroyed. To see artefacts from the site, and a stirring film about Gamla, visit the Golan Archaeological Museum in Katzrin (see page 182).

►► **Ginnosar Kibbutz**   163C3

Located on the western shore of the Sea of Galilee, some 6km from Capernaum, the kibbutz is home to the Yigal Allon Museum of Man in the Galilee►►, with its 2,000-year-old fishing boat►►, found offshore – exactly the type of vessel that would have been used by the disciples of Jesus (see panel). The excellent Nof Ginnosar Kibbutz Hotel, next door, has superb grounds.

Deh Gabriel
Almost opposite Degania, 'the mother of kibbutzim', stands the attractive new Beit Gabriel. On the main road beside the Sea of Galilee, this is a cultural centre open to the public, with a theatre, restaurant and auditorium for concerts and a variety of other performances.

171

The ancient boat
The small fishing vessel found at Ginnosar gives a great insight into biblical passages in which the disciples are described fishing, or cowering during a storm, or when Jesus is described preaching from a boat to a crowd assembled on the shore. The boat is 8.2m long, and 2.3m wide. It is made entirely of wood, the planks being held together by mortise-and-tenon joints. The frames were installed after the hull had been constructed, rather than the more normal practice of building the hull round the frame. It appears that the boat was crewed by five people, using a sail and two pairs of oars.

HaAm im HaGolan

All over Israel you will see bumper stickers, posters and even banners hanging from apartment balconies declaring, in Hebrew, HaAm im HaGolan (The people are with the Golan). The slogan opposes any deals with Syria which might involve giving back any part of the Golan region. Opinion polls show that only 5 per cent of Israelis are willing to return Golan in its entirety while 30 per cent would be prepared to let Syria have back some of the territory.

Basalt columns in the Hexagonal Pool at Nahal Meshushim, in the Golan Heights

A shepherd works in the Golan Heights – a scene unchanged in centuries

▶▶ The Golan Heights   163D3–D4

The high, rolling Golan hills, often known as the Golan Heights, rise steeply from the Sea of Galilee (200m below sea level) to the Mount Avital plateau (1,204m above). Airy and open, these agreeable uplands have spacious uncultivated areas of heath and grassland cut by deep plunging *wadis*, as well as some pretty farmed districts and important historical sites. A popular outing is to the Kuneitra viewpoint, which looks far into Syria.

From 1948 until late 1994, Syria officially maintained a state of war against Israel. Until the Six Day War of 1967, Syrian big guns, located on the Golan Heights, regularly bombarded kibbutz homes in Israel. When Syria invaded Israel in 1967, it rapidly lost control of Golan. An attempt to regain it in 1973 caused the Syrians to lose even more ground. In 1981, Golan was formally annexed by Israel. However, Syria still vigorously lays claim to the territory, and the Golan Heights remain a bargaining chip in Israel's quest for lasting peace with its neighbour.

In 1967, the population of the region stood at 12,000 and was almost entirely Druze (there are no Muslim or Christian villages). The establishment of new kibbutzim, and the town of Katzrin (see pages 182–3), have since attracted 12,000 Jews to the Golan, which has a considerable Jewish heritage. To the surprise of many visitors, there is no tension here, and no danger – though walkers should of course not climb into fenced-off military enclosures and training grounds.

Drive The Golan Heights *(for map see page 163)*

Israel's influence on the lower slopes, close to the Sea of Galilee and the Hula Valley is now complete, with well-established communities large and small, productive farms and holiday facilities. Higher altitudes remain relatively deserted, and the presence of army and United Nations personnel is a reminder that Syria is not far away. *Allow a full day.*

Cross the River Jordan into Golan on the unceremonious **Arik Bridge**, a simple, army construction of wooden planks. Beyond the bridge, an access road on the left leads into the pleasant **Jordan River Park▶**, where you can hire a kayak, have a picnic or visit the excavations at **Tel Bethsaida**. At a fork, turn right (signposted 'Bet Shean, En Gev'). At the next left, turn uphill. Reaching higher ground, pass the new settlement of Ma'ale Gamla, press on to a T-junction and turn left on to the Golan's high plateau road. Soon after, an unpaved road leads to the impressive, rugged site of ancient **Gamla▶▶** (see page 171).

Just before Katzrin, and indicated only by a sign saying 'Industry', the outstanding **Gamla Winery▶▶**, collectively owned by Golan's vine-growing kibbutzim, produces some of Israel's best wines, under the Gamla, Yarden and Golan labels. Feel free to drop in for a tasting. **Qasrin Antiquities Park▶▶** (see page 183) lies in woods off the road. New **Katzrin▶▶** (see page 182), a pleasant, planned modern town, is Golan's capital, containing half the region's Jewish population. Do not miss its excellent **Golan Archaeological Museum▶▶**. The delightful **Dolls Museum▶**, opposite, uses little models to portray Jewish history. Drive up to **Kuneitra Viewpoint▶**, at the crest

of Golan, to gaze across the now-abandoned village of Kuneitra, towards Damascus, 40km away. Israel seized Kuneitra in repelling Syria's 1973 attack, but has since handed it back. The UN base separating the two nations can be seen in the foreground.

Turn north towards the snow-streaked Mount Hermon, rising in the distance. You will skirt the lovely oak forest of the **Odem Reserve▶** and pass the **Druze villages▶** of Buk'ata, Mas'ada and Ein Kuniya. Zigzagging across the foot of Hermon, you will reach **Nimrod's Castle▶▶** (see page 195), **Banyas▶▶** (see page 166), and **Tel Dan▶▶▶** (see page 202), enjoying extensive views over the **Hula Valley**, before leaving Golan.

A word of warning

❏ If you get out of the car and walk in the Golan border areas, do not be tempted to climb over fences. In particular never go into an area with a blue triangle warning sign – this means that there are unexploded mines. ❏

View to Mount Hermon

■ The kibbutz (plural, kibbutzim), surely Israel's best-known institution, is dedicated to shared effort, mutual aid, communal ownership and the simple life. Only some 2 per cent of the population live on kibbutzim, yet 'kibbutzniks' play a vastly disproportionate role in Israel's national life, with top army officers, government ministers and senior officials in all fields being drawn from a kibbutz background. ■

Kibbutz hotels

Around 50 kibbutzim, which happen to be in holiday areas, have opted to make tourism a major part of their income, and 30 of these are members of the highly professional Kibbutz Hotels Chain, which has its own Tel Aviv head office. Some, like Ramat Rachel in Jerusalem, offer top-quality accommodation not unlike other city hotels; others are simpler guest houses in rural settings.

A typical kibbutz canteen where kibbutz members eat all their meals together

Many visitors first encounter Israel through working as a 'kibbutz volunteer'. For some this is rewarding, for others it is a shock, to find that this is no easy-going holiday with plenty of time off. Kibbutz life involves hard work and few luxuries, and these tightly knit communal villages are run on principles very different from those that reign beyond the kibbutz's metal gate and sturdy perimeter fence.

For outsiders who do not really want to roll up their sleeves and earn breakfast by the sweat of their brow, another way to glimpse kibbutz life is as a paying guest. Most of Israel's 270 kibbutzim have holiday accommodation, which varies in style, quality and price from basic guest rooms to large, high-quality hotels.

To look at, a kibbutz is a purpose-built village of unostentatious dwellings and public buildings. Within its grounds are footpaths rather than roads, while all around lie its fields and orchards, cowsheds, banana plantations and orange groves. Many kibbutzim also have a theatre, museum and other visitor attractions (marked on tourist maps).

The kibbutznik, though also partly a figure of fun for having such plain and unsophisticated ways, is almost everywhere revered as the ideal Israeli – forthright and hardworking, the product of a pioneer movement which literally drained the swamps, watered the desert and settled the land. Ever since these early days, kibbutzim have played a vital security

role, because of their strategic locations, public shelters and good defences.

Origins The kibbutz movement started in the Second and Third Aliyahs (1904–14 and 1919–23). Thousands of socialist Russian Jews fled to Palestine under often cruelly difficult conditions – some came all the way on foot. They were ardent Zionists who believed just as passionately in the ideals of shared ownership and the virtue of labour. The egalitarian communes they created were not like anything seen before in the world. Decisions were made communally, no one possessed any private property, and children lived together but without their parents. Though keenly aware of their Jewish identity and heritage, these early kibbutzniks were fiercely anti-religious. The first kibbutz was founded at Degania in 1909, and is still going strong (see page 1/1).

Even today new kibbutzim are being set up. In fact, more have been established in the last 25 years than in the first 25 years of the movement. Though still based on common ownership, with free education, healthcare, childcare, laundry and other services, and free meals in a communal dining room, they have diversified from farming into dozens of other ways of earning a living, including manufacturing and tourism. 'Children's houses' were scrapped as children were found to thrive better with their parents. A tolerant attitude to Jewish traditions has replaced strict secularism – and several observant religious kibbutzim have been set up.

The moshav But communal living is not for everyone. In 1920, the first *moshav* (literally 'seat'; plural, *moshavim*) or co-operative village was started, and today this is the commonest form of village or rural community in Israel. By the standards of any other country, even the *moshav* is Utopian. *Moshav* members are paid by the community for their work and live as families on their own income, but they lease their homes and land, rather than owning them, and are not allowed to employ hired labour. *Moshavim* are run by elected committees, and many free services are provided for the community by its members. A *moshav* is not the same as the similarly named *moshava* (plural, *moshavot*), which is more like an ordinary, non-communal village.

Beyond the kibbutz
The kibbutz movement has its own institutions of higher education and scientific research, as well as its own chamber orchestra, theatre groups, highly acclaimed dance group, art galleries and large publishing houses, enabling kibbutz members to by-pass the private sector in many areas.

175

Farm workers on a kibbutz in the 1930s express the pioneering spirit of the original movement

►► Hamat Gader 163C2

Blessings and curses
The track which rises from the Roman spa baths to the 5th-century synagogue ruins passes the burial site of the local Arab ruler who was given Hamat Gader in 1918 by the British Mandate forces. The inscription on his tomb reads: 'He who honours Hamat Gader shall be blessed in eternity. He who desecrates Hamat Gader shall be cursed in eternity'.

According to the Byzantine empress Eudocia, these were the finest spa baths in the whole Roman world. Even the ruins are considered among the most impressive anywhere, and as there are also modern hot baths, eating places, picnic tables and other attractions, this is a popular place for a day out. Situated in the Yarmuk Valley at the meeting point of Israel, Jordan and Syria, the surrounding area bristles with army patrols. The entrance fee is rather high. From the main car park, signposted footpaths lead through and around the pleasant, park-like grounds.

Steps descend to the extensive **Roman and Byzantine spa►►►**, for six centuries (2nd to 8th) a grand bathing resort. Much survives of the huge and opulent bath houses built in black and white stone, with numerous pillars, vaults and statues. You can walk through from one pool room to the next, passing the small Lepers' Pool, the Oval Pool (almost totally preserved), the imposing Pilaster Hall, with huge windows in the form of a triumphal arch, and others. A separate outdoor pool beside the bath houses contains oily-looking, blue-tinted water from a bubbling hot spring, veiled in clouds of pungent, sulphurous steam.

Four mineral springs and a freshwater spring emerge at Hamat Gader. A few paces from the Roman baths are the attractive **modern hot baths►►**, laid out as a series of open-air swimming pools, also smelling strongly of sulphur. The hottest is a constant 42°C, and bathers are officially advised that it can be dangerous to stay in for longer than 10 minutes – though some appear to soak in the steaming water for an hour at a time.

Remnants of an **ancient synagogue►** stand beside a high **observation point►** with good views over the lush valley. The abandoned mosque on the site is recent. In front of it is a children's play area. As an added amusement, mainly for children, there is also a curious **alligator**

*Roman baths,
Hamat Gader*

Crocodile Creek
'The crocodile still lingers in one corner of Palestine, at the north-east corner of the Plain of Sharon, under Carmel, in the marshes of the Wadi Zerka (Crocodile Wadi). One was brought to me measuring 11 feet 6 inches. I still possess its head and bones. This is the only spot beyond the limits of Africa where it is found.'

The Natural History of Palestine, by the Rev. Canon Tristram, FRS, 1892

farm▶ at Hamat Gader. A wooden walkway crosses an area of naturally warm water where dozens of alligators and crocodiles can be seen basking.

▶ **Ha'on Kibbutz** *163C2*

This pleasant kibbutz, noted for its flowers and palms, is located on the Sea of Galilee's southern shore and contains a popular holiday village and restaurant, and an ostrich farm (not merely for entertainment: the birds are sold for their meat).

Reared for meat, feathers and entertainment: ostriches at Ha'on Kibbutz

> **Praying for rain**
> If there's a drought while you're at Hatzor, pop along to the Cave of Honi HaMe'ayel, near Ayelet Hashahar. Named for a famous 'rainmaker' of Second Temple times, the cave is still considered by the credulous as one of the most effective places to pray for a downpour.

▶▶ **Hatzor National Park (Tel Hazor)** *163C4*

This, the largest *tel* (settlement mound) in Israel, consists of separate Upper and Lower sections and overlooks the southern Hula valley. In total, 21 layers of civilisation have been uncovered here, and key biblical passages verified. Joshua, leading the Jews into Canaan after the years of desert wandering, set about conquering the 'promised land'. In the 13th century BC, having destroyed other Canaanite city-kingdoms, he took on Hatzor, the largest city in northern Canaan. Its king, Jabin, rallied other local chiefs against the Israelites, and chose the difficult Hula swamps, with which only his men were familiar, for a pitched battle. Against the odds, the Israelites won a phenomenal victory, killing Jabin, and destroying Hatzor by fire. Later, the Jewish king Solomon restored the town as a fortified royal residence.

That much can be read in Joshua 11, Judges 4 and I Kings 9. Every part of those biblical accounts was confirmed in the excavations led by Professor Yigael Yadin between 1955 and 1959. He also revealed Canaanite temples and other buildings dating back 400 years before Joshua, as well as traces of structures as old as the 27th century BC. By comparison, the constructions put in place by Solomon appear almost recent. Perhaps the most remarkable discovery was King Ahab's tunnel, built in the 9th century BC, reached by 123 spiral steps down a 38m-deep shaft. The Bible records (II Kings 15) that in 732 BC the Assyrians completely destroyed the town. A large number of finds from the site, including beautiful carved stonework and ivory, is on display at the Hatzor Museum on the other side of the road beside Kibbutz Ayelet Hashahar (which has good hotel accommodation).

> **Joshua's triumph**
> 'And Joshua at that time turned back, and took Hazor, and smote the king thereof with the sword: for Hazor beforetime was the head of all those kingdoms. And they smote all the souls that were therein with the edge of the sword, utterly destroying them: there was not any left to breathe: and he burned Hazor with fire. And all the cities of those kings, and all the kings of them, did Joshua take, and smote them with the edge of the sword, and he utterly destroyed them, as Moses the servant of the Lord commanded'.
> – Joshua 11: 10–12

Yesud HaMa'ala
The first attempt to tackle the problem of draining the Hula swamp was part of a venture of almost reckless idealism. It started at a *shtetl* (Jewish village) in Poland, when several young people decided to leave together for Palestine. They bought a section of the uninhabitable, uncultivated swamp and in 1883 started to build their new village here. They named it, using an evocative phrase from the Bible, *yesud hama'ala*, ('he began to go up'), describing Ezra's first steps on the road to Jerusalem at the head of the Jews returning from captivity in Babylon. Lacking in knowledge, under attack from Arabs, and brought low by the malaria which thrived in the swamps, the young pioneers might have failed if not for the intervention of Baron Rothschild: he suggested, and provided, eucalyptus trees – which can consume vast amounts of water – to plant all around the settlement.

Hula wetland reserve

▶▶▶ **Hula Valley (Emek Hula)**   *163C4*

The green landscape of Hula, wide and flat under an immense sky, makes a glorious sight when viewed from the higher country at its margins. From this viewpoint, a number of small lakes can be seen, each lying beside the canalised River Jordan. The most southerly of these, Lake Hula, lies at the centre of an interesting nature reserve, and has an information centre about the region.

The name of the valley is misleading: there is no Hula River, and neither is this a valley. In Hebrew it is more often called Emek Hula; literally, the Hula Plain. The flatland of Hula lies in a rift basin between the steep Naftali and Golan hills, north of the Sea of Galilee. Several rivers and streams run into or through the valley, which in the Bible is referred to as 'the waters of Merom', and until the early 1950s this was a huge area of malarial swamp and fetid waterways. The Arabs used to say that through its reeds it was impossible even for a wild boar to make its way: perhaps this is an exaggeration, for wild boar certainly lived here, as did water buffalo and hundreds of bird species, some rare. The reed varieties growing here included papyrus, this being the northern limit for the wild plant, from which an early form of paper was made.

The draining and cultivation of Hula began in 1883 with the setting up of Yesud HaMa'ala village (see Dubrovin Farm opposite) by Jewish refugees who drained their settlement by planting eucalyptus. In 1934, the entire Hula valley was purchased by the Jewish National Fund (JNF), which, after the creation of the State of Israel, began to transform the swamps. The work, completed in 1957, involved changing and channelling the course of the Jordan river, and resulted in 6,000 hectares of new land being opened up for cultivation, as well as the eradication of malaria from the region.

Yet, in 1994, history took a small step backward when the JNF rediverted the waters of the Jordan into the drained marshes, deliberately reflooding some 200 hectares as part of a wildlife conservation scheme.

Even before it was completed, the original drainage work had given cause for concern about its environmental impact, and this had given birth to the Society for the Protection of Nature in Israel (SPNI) – now a powerful national pressure group with a decisive consultation role on all major environmental projects. The first act of the new SPNI was to set aside Lake Hula as a nature reserve. However, the diversity of the region's flora and wildlife was drastically reduced, while the populations of certain other species – for example, rats – exploded. Worse still, the drained terrain was transformed into a dry and peaty organic material, easily eroded by wind and liable to spontaneous fires in summer. The dried-out terrain began to sink at the rate of 75mm per year and windblown Hula peat polluted the Sea of Galilee.

The reflooding scheme is intended to enlarge Lake Hula, and a further 800 hectares of land, in a 61-km strip, will be returned to peat bog. There is public access to the area, and there are plans for a large new nature reserve where marsh fowl and animals will be able to breed. The existing Lake Hula Reserve▶▶, the country's first nature reserve, gives a good idea of how the swampland looked before 1957. There are picnic areas and an easy walking trail – partly on boards over swamp – allowing visitors to see (if they are lucky) wetland species including water buffalo, wild cats, mongoose, beaver, boar, coypu, and numerous migratory and resident bird varieties: from October to March the reserve is full of birds. The **Visitor Information Centre**▶ has a museum dedicated to explaining Hula's flora and fauna, and shows a short film about the region.

Dubrovin Farm▶, just south of the Reserve, originally part of the 19th-century settlement of Yesud HaMa'ala, has been reconstructed to show how a pioneers' fortified farm once looked. The buildings of the farmyard are ranged around a spacious enclosed courtyard. The family home, smithy and gardens are the main attractions, while many visitors go simply to enjoy the Dubrovin Farmyard Restaurant, specialising in its own smoked meats and trout, where good food is served in a rough and ready stone-built outhouse.

Dubrovin Farm – a fortified 19th-century pioneer settlement which has been preserved and restored

Kibbutz concerts
In the middle of the pastoral landscape of the Hula Valley, at a plain and simple kibbutz, a week of civilised entertainment is held every summer during the Kfar Blum Chamber Music Days. The Voice of Israel radio station, the Galilee Council and the Ministry of Education have jointly sponsored the annual classical music extravaganza since 1984. Nowadays the programme has widened, with typically around 25 concerts and some 50 musicians, a choir, and a programme that includes baroque music on period instruments, lieder and even jazz, in addition to chamber music. The Chamber Music Days take place usually at the end of July or beginning of August.

■ **The fact that Israel is turning the desert green is a cliché – and one which does not bring fully to mind the many types of terrain that exist here, or the extraordinary transformation that is taking place. Even more startling than desert irrigation schemes are the vast forest plantations and nature reserves that now occupy millions of hectares of the countryside.** ■

Who owns Israel?
Some 92 per cent of the land in Israel is publicly owned, to ensure that it remains a possession of the Jewish people as a whole. This has been a deliberate policy since 1901, when the Jewish National Fund (JNF) began to buy land from the Arabs, most of whom were absentee landowners. Almost all of Israel had been purchased before the setting up of the State, and almost all by voluntary contributions from Jews all over the world. The State owns 78 per cent of Israel directly, while the JNF owns 14 per cent. The JNF also administers most of the rest of the country's non-urban land.

Some of the oak trees of Hurshat Tal National Park were growing 2,000 years ago

A drive along Israel's border road with Lebanon shows the stark contrast between the wooded hills of Galilee and the infertile rocky landscape on the other side of the frontier, where goatherds lead their animals in the constant search for vegetation. At the time when Israel came into being, the two landscapes were identical.

Jewish households around the world are familiar with the 'blue boxes' of the Jewish National Fund (JNF), in which coins have been collected since 1901 to raise money for planting trees in Israel. During that time the JNF has planted 32,000 hectares of woodland; that is over 200 million trees. These forests, almost entirely of pine, are criss-crossed with public footpaths and riding tracks, often linking places of historic interest, and some provide considerable leisure opportunities. More importantly, their main purpose is to create topsoil and oxygen, to provide a habitat for threatened animals and birds, and to bring about a lasting change in the terrain.

One of the longest forest belts in the country is the 2,000 hectare Bar'am, Ein Zeitim and Biriya woodland, planted by the JNF in the 1950s on treeless mountain ridges surrounding the historic Galilee town of Sefat. It has been argued that it was a mistake to use only pine, and new planting includes many other tree varieties. The green

belt created by the JNF around Jerusalem on the formerly barren Judaean hills, for example, has been planted with acacia, pepper, myrtle, laurel, oak, cedar and carob, as well as pine. Areas with any natural woodland – such as Goren Park, around Montfort Fortress – are carefully tended and enlarged.

A popular JNF scheme allows donors to pay for and plant a tree in Israel with their own hands. You can do this at the JNF's Jerusalem Planting Centre, which enables visitors to make a personal contribution to the capital's green belt or to other new forests around the country.

National Parks Israel's forests are intended to change the land, the National Parks to conserve it. There are 40 National Parks in total, scattered across the country from Galilee to Negev and from the Mediterranean shore to the stony banks of the Dead Sea; some do contain beautiful woodlands, but others are stark desert and wilderness. The National Parks Authority mainly cares for areas of great historical interest – major archaeological sites, for example. Catering to millions of visitors each year, an important part of the authority's job is to open up such places to the public while protecting them from the damage that public access can cause.

Most National Parks are relatively small, such as the ancient ruins of Bar'am, Nimrod Castle, Kursi and Tel Hatzor; others cover larger areas, such as Carmel Park near Haifa, Hurshat Tal, and Masada. Other properties could hardly be called parks at all – for example, the Jerusalem city walls.

Nature Reserves The 160 Nature Reserves in Israel are something different again. Totalling about 400,000 hectares, they concentrate on protecting the country's astonishing diversity of flora, fauna and landscape. This adds up to over 3,000 species of plants (150 exclusive to Israel), 430 kinds of birds, 70 mammals and as many as 80 types of reptiles, and terrain from lush river valleys and springs like Tel Dan to dry, leafless desert, like Timna Park.

Access to forests is free at all times, but National Parks and Nature Reserves are supervised and have entry charges and opening hours (almost all open every day of the year except for Yom Kippur). They are well signposted, and equipped with restaurants and picnic areas.

Carmel Park protects sacred sites and a lovely Mediterranean landscape

For more information
If you want to plant a tree, call the Jewish National Fund (Keren Kayemet l'Israel) toll-free on: 117 022 3484. The head office of the National Parks Authority is in Tel Aviv on: 03 576 6888. The Nature Reserves Authority is in Jerusalem on: 02 536 271.

White oryx in the Negev desert

The hilltop town of Jish, in the 1st century an important Jewish stronghold, is now a Christian Arab community

The Miracle at Cana
'When the ruler of the feast had tasted the water that was made wine, and knew not whence it was (but the servants which drew the water knew), the governor of the feast called the bridegroom, and saith unto him, Every man at the beginning doth set forth good wine, and when men have well drunk, then that which is worse. But thou hast kept the good wine until now'.
– John 2: 9–10

► ► **Hurshat Tal National Park** *163C5*

Located between Tel Dan and the Hula valley, this pleasant woodland area, whose name means 'Forest of Dew' is watered by the River Dan. Scores of mighty oaks grow here – some thought to be 2,000 years old. Legend has it that 10 of Muhammad's messengers paused here for the night and, finding nowhere to tether their horses, stuck stakes into the ground. In the morning they awoke to find their stakes had sprouted into these fine trees. An artificial swimming lake, restaurant and picnic site, as well as a riverside campsite 100m away, also make this a popular spot. Adjacent Kibbutz Hagoshrim, a member of the Kibbutz Hotels Chain, has attractive park-like grounds and offers high-quality kibbutz guesthouse accommodation.

► **Jish (Hebrew: Gush Halav)** *162B4*

Today a hillside village of Christian Arabs, Gush Halav was an important town during the Second Temple and Talmudic periods, associated with the learned Jewish community based around Meron (see page 185). It was also renowned for its olive oil. During the First Revolt against Rome (AD 68), it was a rebel stronghold. Revolt commander Yohanan came from here. The tombs of 1st-century sages Shemai'a and Avtalion lie in a domed building by the road below the village. Remnants of small 3rd- and 4th-century synagogues were found 2km east of the village and at the neighbouring *moshav* or co-operative (village) of Sifsufa.

► ► **Katzrin (Qazrin)** *163C4*

This attractive, well-laid-out town, built since 1967, is now the capital of the Golan region. Its population of 6,000 accounts for half the Jews in the Golan. The name derives from the Hebrew version of *castrum*, the Roman word for a military camp, and the town makes a good base for exploring local antiquities. The **Golan Archaeological Museum**► ► has extensive displays of relics from all over the region, especially coins, domestic implements and stonework, with many relief carvings of *menorahs* (ritual candlesticks), dating from Temple times and from the

Daniel in the Lions' Den: Byzantine frieze in the Golan Archaeological Museum

Volcanic Golan
The Golan summit was volcanic until the Upper Pleistocene period (40,000 years ago), and the terrain is rich in signs of volcanic activity. Massive basalt boulders, areas of lava flow, deep craters and remnants of volcanic cones characterise the heights. The Golan's largest extinct volcano is Mount Avital, near Kuneitra. Its crater is now cultivated.

Talmudic obelisks in the Qasrin Antiquities Park

Roman and Byzantine periods. It is well worth seeing the museum's short film about the Roman conquest of Golan's former capital, Gamla. Almost opposite is the **Dolls Museum▶**, which tells Jewish history through a succession of charming tableaux made of little models.

Just outside the town on the southeastern side, a sign saying 'Industry' indicates the way to the **Gamla Winery▶▶**, a leading name in Israel's quality wines and open for tastings, though it is wise to phone ahead to arrange this. Near by are the remains of the 4th-century **Ancient Synagogue▶**, and the **Qasrin Antiquities Park▶▶**, an open-air museum with reconstructions giving an impression of life in Talmudic times alongside the archaeological site of the original town of Katzrin.

▶ ▆▆▆ **Kfar Kana**   *163C5*
St John's gospel names the (now Arab) village of Cana, near Nazareth, as the place of Jesus' first miracle: turning water into wine at a wedding feast. The Franciscans claim that their church, built in 1881, stands on the ruins of the house where the miracle occurred. It does stand on the remains of a 6th-century church or synagogue, with a 3rd-century mosaic floor beneath (with an Aramaic inscription honouring the craftsmen who made the mosaic). Other Catholic and Orthodox churches in Kana also claim to be built on sacred sites.

▶ ▆▆▆ **Kiryat Shmona**   *163C5*
The name, which simply means 'eight men ' – which includes women – commemorates Joseph Trumpledor and his seven comrades-in-arms who died defending the nearby Tel Hai settlement in March 1920. Arab attacks on Tel Hai were launched from the village of Halsa. After the defeat of the Arabs, Halsa was transformed into this (rather unappealing) development town, today populated largely by new immigrants. Even then, there was no peace, for Halsa continued to be subjected to ceaseless PLO rocket fire until the 1982 Israeli invasion of Lebanon.

Honouring Rashbi
Thousands of Orthodox Jewish pilgrims make their way to Meron every year for the joyful early-summer Hilula Rashbi procession on the eve of Lag b'Omer (the 26th day after Passover, marking the midpoint between Passover and Shavuot), carrying Torah scrolls from Sefat to Meron. On arrival, two bonfires, and countless candles, are lit at Rashbi's tomb. Riotous music and dancing and noisy picnics take place through the night. The following morning, three-year-old boys – who, until then, have been allowed to let their hair grow long – receive their first haircut.

Megiddo at the end of days
'And he gathered them all together into a place called in the Hebrew tongue Armageddon. And the seventh angel poured out his vial into the air; and there came a great voice out of the temple of heaven, from the throne, saying, It is done. And there were voices, and thunders, and lightenings; and there was a great earthquake, such as was not since men were upon the earth, so mighty an earthquake, and so great. And the great city was divided into three parts.'

Revelations 16, 16–19

► **Korazim**   *163C3*

For Jesus it would have been less than an hour's walk between Capernaum and this comfortable, hardworking farming town built of dark basalt, now all in ruins, located 4km from the Sea of Galilee's northern shore. According to Matthew's gospel (11: 21), this was one of the thriving Galilee towns for which Jesus angrily foresaw damnation on Judgement Day because its citizens did not repent after he had performed 'mighty works' there. The town continued to prosper for four centuries more, being much praised for its wheat. Its fine **synagogue►►** was constructed in the 2nd century and substantial remains can still be seen. Parts survive of the walls and floor, and of the pillars that divided the building into three aisles. Remnants of **houses►►** (some partly restored) and an **oil press** also survive. East of the site, **dolmens** confirm that the area was inhabited in prehistoric times. Abandoned in the 5th century, Korazim was revived as a Jewish village in the 16th century. Korazim Kibbutz and the holiday village of **Vered HaGalil►** are just to the west.

► **Megiddo National Park**   *162A1*

The fortified hill of Megiddo is a remarkable *tel* (settlement mound) where 20 layers of civilisation have been uncovered since excavations began in 1903. The museum has a scale model of ancient Megiddo, which is worth seeing on arrival.

The English corruption of Har Megiddo, or Megiddo Hill, is Armageddon. Here – according to the New Testament (Revelations 16) – God will gather everyone together at the end of days and pour out his wrath in earthquakes, storms and a hail of stones. The hill, long considered worth fighting for, controlled a narrow pass on the ancient route between Egypt and Assyria. Of vital military and trading importance, this highway became the Romans' Via Maris. The French (in 1799) and the British (in 1917) both defeated Turkish forces at Megiddo: one of the titles granted to Commander-in-Chief Allenby was Lord Allenby of Megiddo. In 1948, Jews defeated Arab forces here.

About 4000 BC, Canaanites took over the neolithic settlement here, and remained for some 2,000 years: a **Canaanite temple►►** and **fortifications►►** survive. In 1479 BC, Pharaoh Thutmose III attacked the city; hieroglyphics describing the battle, carved on the walls of his temple in Upper Egypt, are the first reference to Megiddo. When Megiddo was conquered by the Israelites under Joshua in the 13th century BC, the name of the town first enters the Bible. Philistines subsequently held the city for 100 years, but it was retaken by King David in 1000 BC. Solomon enlarged the city, and many vestiges remain from that period. After a 9th-century BC Egyptian attack, it had to be rebuilt by King Ahab, who added an impressive **underground shaft and water tunnel►►** 36m deep and 65m long. On the site of Solomon's Palace he built **chariot stables►►** for 450 horses, chariots and riders. In front is a large circular **grain silo►**, built in the 8th century BC. Conquered by Assyrians in 733 BC, the site frequently changed hands and was abandoned from 538 BC. A Roman camp was later set up on the adjacent site, which became the Arab village of Lejun (from 'Legion') and is now the Kibbutz Megiddo.

Sacred numbers
Kabbala is the Jewish form of mysticism based on the notion that every letter and word in the Torah contains a hidden meaning, and that much of the secret can be revealed through numerology (even in every-day modern Hebrew, letters are used as numbers: Alef = 1, Bet = 2, and so on). In this way some supposed significance was read into the formation of individual words and their total values. The prime kabbalistic work, the *Zohar*, is generally attributed to Rashbi, especially by Devout Hasidim and Sephardim, but scholars believe the book was written by several people, probably in medieval Spain, though based on earlier works stemming from Sefat and Meron.

Remains of Roman houses, Korazim

► Meron   *162B4*

In Second Temple and Talmudic times, Meron became a great centre of Jewish learning, as well as a focal point for acts of rebellion against Roman rule. In 1949 a new Meron, an Orthodox religious settlement, was founded in the same place. From that era, several 1st and 2nd century tombs survive, including the domed mausoleums, set within a walled enclosure, of the renowned **Rabbi Shimon bar Yochai**►►► (also known by his acronym as Rashbi) and his son, Eleazer. Rashbi is claimed by the Orthodox to be the author of the *Zohar* (the principal book of the mystical kabbala). Some scholars assert that Rashbi was not in fact the author of this work, although Meron, together with Sefat, can still be considered the birthplace of Jewish mysticism (see side panel). North of the tomb stands the magnificent rock-carved façade of a 2nd-century **synagogue**►, though little else remains of the building. Several other revered rabbis are reputedly buried in rock-cut tombs here, including the great 1st-century sage **Hillel**► and his less liberal rival **Shammai**, and the 2nd-century **Rabbi Yohanan** 'the shoemaker'.

Armageddon Village
The settlement of Mishmar HaEmek (literally Guard of the Plain) stands next to Megiddo, or Armageddon. Founded in 1927, it was the first modern community to be established in the Jezreel valley. The scene of much prolonged fighting, especially during the 1948 war, it is better known today for its striking Holocaust memorial.

The Good Fence
Close to Metulla is the only place where civilians (with correct documents) can cross the border between Israel and Lebanon. There are broad views over the Lebanese hills from here. On the other side lies a narrow strip of 'security zone', controlled by members of a pro-Israeli militia, and a village just across the frontier. Most of the permitted border traffic consists of Lebanese workers employed in Israel. The name 'Good Fence' comes from the Israeli medical post here, which Lebanese citizens can attend free of charge.

A wronged woman?
Magdalen has come to mean a reformed prostitute, or even a home for such women, through the association of Mary Magdalene. Yet the Scriptures give no reason to suspect her of being a prostitute. It used to be thought that the 'woman which was a sinner' (Luke 7:32), who anointed Jesus' feet and wiped them with her hair, could be identified with Mary Magdalene, but the text does not suggest this and modern scholars reject the idea. Later, Jesus encounters 'Mary called Magdalene, out of whom went seven devils' as if for the first time. The name Mary Magdalene means simply 'Mary, woman of Magdala'.

Spring comes to Mount Hermon: the view from Metulla

▶ **Metulla** 163C5

Enclosed on three sides by the northern border with Lebanon (you can see Arab labourers working the fields across the well-defended frontier), this small agricultural town has a cool, tranquil hill setting overlooked by the snowy crest of Mount Hermon. Metulla was settled a century ago on land purchased by Baron Rothschild. Since 1976, it has been best known as the HaGader HaTova (the Good Fence), an opening in the border between Israel and Lebanon through which Lebanese people pass freely to obtain medical supplies, or even to work in Israel. The town's main avenue, **Settlers Street▶**, gives visitors a chance to glimpse those early days with its Farmer's House Museum and a few surviving older buildings. The town's Canada Centre is a modern leisure complex with high-quality sports facilities, indoor and outdoor pools, squash, tennis and basketball courts, a complete football pitch and the largest ice-skating rink in Israel. Between the town and the frontier lies the Nahal Iyon Nature Reserve and the seasonal Tanur Waterfall (see page 191).

▶ **Migdal** 163C3

On a hillside beside the Sea of Galilee and within an hour's walk of Jesus' home at Capernaum, lie the ruins of ancient Migdal (the name means 'a Tower'). This was the supposed birthplace of Mary Magdalene, the woman from whom Jesus drove out 'seven devils' and who became one of his most ardent followers. Migdal was a thriving small town at least until the 2nd century; remnants of paved streets, a villa, a pool and a synagogue have been uncovered. Above the old village rises the new, which has plenty of guest accommodation.

▶▶ **Montfort Castle** 162A4

This majestic ruined Crusader fortress, soaring on a high crest enclosed by an immense natural forest, is best seen from **Mitzpe Monfort▶▶▶** (*mitzpe* means viewpoint) in **Goren Park▶**. The park, 14km inland from Nahariya, is a natural forest of oak, carob, almond, arbutus and the purple-flowered Judas tree. To reach the castle you must follow a series of steep narrow paths for about half an hour, at first down to the attractive **Kviv stream▶**, then up again to the fortress. The castle can also be approached on a longer walk, equally steep, from the village of Hila.

Built in the 12th century by French Crusaders, **Montfort Castle▶▶** is the largest ruin in western Galilee. Though some reconstruction work is in hand, the castle consists mainly of remnants of outer and inner ramparts, great blocks of fallen stone, roofless sections of sturdy walls and broken Gothic arches. These vestiges are all that survive of a once-huge fortress. Its lofty position provides a stirring view over rolling woodland. Shortly after completion, Montfort (which means 'Strong Mountain' in medieval French) was destroyed by Salah ed-Din (in 1187). The shell was then sold (in 1220) to the Knights of the Teutonic Order, who rebuilt part of the fortress and renamed it Starkenburg (Strong Castle); this they occupied only until 1271, when they were forced to leave by Baibars, the Mameluke sultan. He allowed them to take their archives and treasury, and the castle has remained abandoned ever since.

▶▶ **Mount of Beatitudes** 163C3

This lovely grass-covered hillside, rising behind the sites of Tabgha and Capernaum, has long been considered the place where Jesus delivered the Sermon on the Mount. The view from the top of the slope, taking in the calm blue expanse of the Sea of Galilee with blue-tinted hills behind, is serene and inspiring.

Did Jesus really preach his sermon here? The weight of tradition points to this as the likely hill. The church at the summit is modern; previously the event was commemorated by a church nearer to Tabgha. The official Catholic view is that the hill, and the church, must be understood only as commemorating the sermon – not marking the site. But for millions of pilgrims, this is the very hill where Jesus inspired the multitude with his message of purity of spirit, humility and peace.

The Sermon on the Mount, fully recorded only by Matthew's gospel (5: 7), marks the start of Christianity's departure from Judaism. The nine Beatitudes are Christ's assertion that nine categories of people are blessed and will receive a reward. He named in turn the poor in spirit, mourners, the meek, those who hunger for righteousness, the merciful, the pure in heart, peacemakers, those persecuted for righteousness' sake and those persecuted for

How to feel towards your enemies
'It has been said that thou shalt love thy neighbour and hate thine enemy'. These words of Jesus during the Sermon on the Mount have caused controversy, since it had *not* previously been said that people should hate their enemies. Leviticus 19: 18 states: 'Thou shalt love thy neighbour as thyself'. He adds that it is all right 'to rebuke thy neighbour' (though not in public) but 'not to take vengeance nor bear any grudge'; and 'Thou shalt not hate thine brother in thy heart' (Leviticus 19: 17–18). Some of the earliest Bible passages urge humanity and restraint with respect to enemies: 'If thou meet thine enemy's ox or his ass going astray, thou shalt bring it back to him again' (Exodus 23: 4). Christian scholars agree that Jesus himself would not have misquoted or misunderstood the scriptures, but the gospel writers may well have done so.

Jesus's sake. The remainder of the sermon praises those who lead a simple, virtuous life according to Jewish law, and much of the sermon restates ancient commandments, although he also departs from them by, for example, prohibiting divorce, redefining adultery to include looking lustfully at a woman, warning of hellfire for so much as saying 'You fool' to your brother, and adding to the original 'Love thy neighbour' the more difficult precept 'Love your enemies'. The sermon ends with a Jewish text that sums up his message: 'Be ye therefore perfect, even as your Father in heaven is perfect'.

Luke's gospel (6) briefly describes what is probably the same sermon, but says that it was delivered at the foot of the hill, 'in the plain', after Jesus had spent all night on the mountain in prayer, having chosen and named 12 of his followers as Apostles whilst there. He then descended the hill with the Apostles to preach to the multitude. Jesus 'looked up' to address the crowd, so they stood on the higher

ground, and urged them to 'love your enemies and do good to them which hate you; unto him that smiteth thee on the cheek offer also the other'.

The **Church of the Beatitudes**▶▶▶ on the hilltop, an octagonal arcaded structure under a dome, belongs to Italian Franciscans. It is one of the most attractive works of Antonio Barluzzi, architect of some of the finest 20th-century Galilean churches and basilicas. Built in 1937 (the date in the church floor being given as Year 15 of the Italian People – in other words the Fascist regime), it elegantly contrasts white and dark stone and stands among palm trees in delightful gardens. Each of eight sides of the church is dedicated to one of the eight Beatitudes, which are written in Latin inside the church; the ninth Beatitude (blessing those who suffer persecution for the sake of Jesus) is symbolised by the dome itself, reaching to heaven. Around the altar of the church are representations of the seven virtues (Justice, Charity, Prudence, Faith, Fortitude, Hope and Temperance).

Close by is the Franciscans' **Mount of Beatitudes Hospice**▶. Glorious views can be had by walking down the slope from the summit of the Mount to Tabgha. The journey takes a more circuitous 4km route by road.

The Sermon on the Mount
'And seeing the multitude, he went up into a mountain. And when he was set, his disciples came unto him, and he opened his mouth and taught them.'
– Matthew 5

The Mount of Beatitudes, where Christ laid down some of the basic tenets of Christianity

189

Mount Tabor's Basilica of the Transfiguration

The Transfiguration
'And after six days Jesus taketh Peter, James and John his brother, and bringeth them up into an high mountain apart, and was transfigured before them: and his face did shine as the sun, and his raiment was white as the light. And behold, there appeared unto them Moses and Elias talking with him. Then answered Peter, and said unto Jesus, Lord, it is good for us to be here: if thou wilt, let us make here three tabernacles.'
– Matthew 17: 1–4

► **Mount Hermon (Har Hermon)** *163D5*

The snow-covered peak of Israel's highest mountain (2,766m), is visible over much of Golan and northeastern Galilee and makes a startling and dramatic contrast to the Mediterranean sunshine, landscape and vegetation below. Only a small slice of the Hermon massif belongs to Israel, the rest forming the barrier between Lebanon and Syria. From its snows and springs originates much of Israel's water supply. **Neve Ativ►** (or the Mount Hermon Ski Centre) is a small winter sports resort high on its slopes. It has a ski lift from 1,650m to 2,000m, equipment hire, decent accommodation and reliable snow from December to April. Pistes range in difficulty, the longest run being 2.5km.

►► **Mount Meron Nature Reserve** *162B3*

Occupying a high ridge at the heart of Upper Galilee, the wooded Meron heights can be reached on steep but fairly easy footpaths from near the Druze village of Hurfeish (on the western side) or from Meron (on the eastern flank). The paths climb through attractive (though thorny) Mediterranean scrub and low woodland, where you may see several of the curious *katalav* trees with their smooth bark resembling polished copper. At the rocky wooded summit (1,208m), you will find a radar base, a tiny stone pool enclosed by a stone terrace (which is actually a 2,000-year-old winepress) and immense vistas to the north, with Sefat visible to the east.

►► **Mount Tabor (Har Tavor)** *162B2*

This striking fortified plateau, rising from the Jezreel Plain, is taken to be 'the high mountain apart' on which Jesus was 'transfigured' in the eyes of Peter, James and John. According to the gospels, 'His face did shine as the sun, and his raiment was white as the light. And behold, there appeared unto them Moses and Elias talking with him.

From a cloud came a voice, saying 'This is my beloved son, in whom I am well pleased' (Matthew 17: 1–4; Mark 9: 2–13; Luke 9: 28–36). These were almost the same words that a voice from heaven had uttered when Jesus was baptised in the Jordan (Mark 1: 11).

Over the centuries, several churches were erected on or near the site of the apparition, especially during the Crusader period, and their ruins now adorn the mountainside. The slopes are covered with vegetation, notably Tabor oak. A twisting road winds up to the top of the hill. At the summit stands the Franciscans' handsome **Basilica of the Transfiguration►►**, with its two sturdy square towers, built by Barluzzi in 1921 and incorporating the remains of 6th- and 12th-century churches. The basilica encloses three grottoes, or chapels, mirroring the three tabernacles which Peter suggested should be put here for Jesus, Moses and Elijah (Elias). The Grotto of Christ contains a mosaic pavement dating from before the year 422 (after which date it was forbidden to put the shape of the cross in any position where it could be walked upon). In the upper part of the church, a fine mosaic depicts the transfiguration. Close by stands the Greek Orthodox **Church of Elias►** (Elijah), built in 1911 on the ruins of a Crusader church. A **Canaanite shrine►** also stands on the summit.

During the period of the Israelite conquest of Canaan, the judge and prophetess Deborah (12th century BC) gathered 10,000 men here and led them in a victorious attack on the men and chariots of Sisera, one of the generals of Canaanite king Jabin of Hatzor (Judges 4).

►   Nahal Iyon Nature Reserve   *163C5*

Located 2km from the small northern border town of Metulla (see page 186), the reserve lies in the Iyon valley beside the Lebanese frontier. It offers pleasing tree-shaded water pools and seasonal waterfalls. The **Tanur Waterfall►** can be found 1km nearer to the town. It is dry in summer, gushing in winter, and the name (meaning 'Oven') is based on its shape and the impression of smoke given by its billowing misty haze.

Nebi Sabalan
From the village of Hurfeish the path up Mount Meron first skirts Mount Larom, at the top of which stands Nebi Sabalan, a large structure enclosing a small cave, together with a pilgrims' inn. Sacred to the Druze, this became a holy site in 1948. The Druze claim that their prophet, Sabalan, lived as a hermit in the cave, studying and composing religious texts. One day, Muslims discovered him and despatched a force to kill him. When they tried to climb Larom, from the Kziv stream at its foot, Sabalan prayed for divine assistance. It came in the form of a dam which blocked the stream and caused the area to be temporarily flooded – just long enough to drown his pursuers. When the water subsided, he moved on to Mount Lebanon, where his tomb can be seen today. Every year on 10 September, the Druze make a pilgrimage to Nebi Sabalan, where there are lodgings and provisions for slaughter and sacrifice.

Galilee from Mount Tabor

► ►   Nazareth (Hebrew: Natzerat; Arabic: En-Nasra)   *162B2*

The largest Arab town in Israel (population 46,500) is sprawling, noisy and chaotic. Since the time of the gospels, Nazareth has been regarded as the childhood home of Jesus. Most of the residents are Christian (though there is an adjoining new Jewish town called Natzaret Illit, or Upper Nazareth), and the town bristles with churches. Sunday, not Saturday, is the holy day here. Yet the lack of spirituality or any feeling of authenticity sometimes disappoints Christian pilgrims.

The childhood home of Jesus

Matthew 2: 23 implies that Jesus' birthplace in Bethlehem was not a temporary dwelling but the family home of Joseph (a native Judaean) and Mary (daughter of a Temple high priest, and therefore living in or near Jerusalem). In his account, they fled from Bethlehem to Egypt, and he relates that, returning with Jesus and Mary from their exile, Joseph was afraid to return to Judaea and went to dwell in Galilee, eventually settling in 'a city called Nazareth'. None of the other gospels refer to the trip to Egypt. Mark 1: 9 describes how Jesus, having already reached manhood, 'came from Nazareth of Galilee and was baptised of John in the Jordan.' According to Luke 1: 26, Joseph and Mary returned after the birth of Jesus in Bethlehem 'into Galilee, to their own city Nazareth'. John 2: 46 simply has Nathaniel, a Galilean, astonished to be told that Christ comes from Nazareth.

Right and below: Church of the Annunciation

Nazareth is not given any mention in Josephus' comprehensive list of towns and villages of the Galilee. Archaeological evidence finds scant trace of habitation at the time he refers to, although there are vestiges of older structures on the site dating from 2000 BC. From the 3rd century AD there was a Christian settlement here, destroyed by Persians in the 7th century. It was revived in 1099 by the French Crusader, Tancred, but then seized by Mamelukes in 1263, whereupon all Christians were banished until 1620. Nazareth once again became popular as a centre for Christian worship in the 19th century, when it became a focal point for Christian Arabs.

All the gospels agree in suggesting that Jesus spent most of his childhood in Nazareth, though how many years is unclear, and there is disagreement as to whether Joseph and Mary lived there before the birth of Jesus. According to Luke (1: 26), they did: he asserts that it was here that the Archangel Gabriel spoke to Mary, telling her that she was to give birth to a son who 'shall reign over the house of Jacob for ever, and of his kingdom there shall be no end.' According to Matthew (1: 20–21) it was Joseph to whom an angel of the Lord intimated these things.

Early Christians worshipped at the place which later became known as the Grotto of the Annunciation. The first of Nazareth's churches was built there, in a style that resembles a synagogue. With the shift in devotion among European Christians from Jesus to Mary, and to the image of Jesus as a baby or child rather than as a man, even greater importance became attached to the grotto where Gabriel is supposed to have addressed Mary.

Three more churches, erected in the 5th, 12th and 18th centuries, were built at the grotto before today's **Church of the Annunciation**►►► (often called the Basilica) was constructed, between 1955 and 1969. The main entrance is in Casa Nova Street, the heart of the older part of town. This pleasing modern edifice, by the Italian architect Giovanni Muzio, is built of pale stone, arranged in bands of lighter and darker shade, under a dark conical dome surrounded by delicate white stonework. Some of the walls stand on top of the ruined 12th-century Crusader walls, and the Crusaders' triple apse at the east end has been brought into the new building. Thus it ingeniously combines the past – represented by the lower levels and the grotto itself – with the present, the two being linked by stairs at the west end. A large opening in the floor beneath the dome gives a view down through the centuries to the grotto and the relics of earlier churches. The upper church is decorated by images of the Madonna and Child from around the world.

Other churches lie a short walk away, reached via teeming narrow streets and an open-air market. **St Joseph's**► (1914), in Casa Nova Street, stands above a grotto known since the 17th century as Joseph's Workshop. **Synagogue Church**►, by the market, stands on traces of a 6th-century synagogue which, despite the date, Greek Catholics claim was the one Jesus attended. **Mensa Christi Church** (1918), west of it, contains a slab of rock which Franciscans claim was the table at which the risen Christ ate with his disciples. Some 1.5km away from the centre of town, on the Tiberias road, **Mary's Well**►or the Fountain of Mary has four waterspouts set in an attractive modern circular stone surround. This is another place where some claim that Gabriel appeared to Mary, and many believe the waters to have magical healing powers. This new Mary's Well replaces the older one in the crypt of **St Gabriel's church**► near by.

Touring Nazareth
Be prepared for a possibly difficult day visiting Nazareth. The town is hot and crowded, built on a steep hill, bus services are not geared to tourist sights, and the maze of streets is short of signs. Much the easiest way to see the town and its sights is to join an organised tour. Hotels and tourist offices all over Galilee can provide details of these.

193

Greek Orthodox rites at St Gabriel's church

Drive **The Northern Road** *(for map see pages 162A4–163C5)*

The northern road takes a quiet, peaceful course along a crest of forested hills. There are good views into Lebanon, with its relatively barren terrain, and across the Galilee, where a hundred years of tree-planting have sharply altered the scenery. Along the way the drive passes a string of old pioneer kibbutzim and appealing, small-scale relics of history ancient and modern. *Allow a full day.*

Start at the high chalk cliffs of **Rosh HaNikra►►** (see page 160). On the clifftop is the scruffy frontier post with Lebanon but there are also magnificent views from here down the coast. At the foot, reached by cable-car, spectacular white caves lie half submerged in the sea. The winding road descends through natural and planted woodland towards **Kibbutz Hanita►** (founded in 1938), with its small antiquities museum. Among the trees near by is **Hanita Tower and Stockade►**, a well-preserved example of the simple wooden watchtowers used by early settlers. The border road continues east beside the frontier; for greater interest take the parallel route through attractive maple and terebinth woods around **Eilon►** and **Goren Park►►**, south of which rises **Montfort Castle►►** (see page 186).

Back on the border, **Netua►** and **Biranit►►** give great views into Lebanon. Cross the high **Har Adir** plateau, descending to the superb ancient synagogue at **Bar'am►►** (see page 167). After **Avivim**, where 11 children were killed in a PLO attack on the school bus in 1970, the **Dishon Gorge►** on the right has a drivable trail at the bottom. Suddenly ahead you will see a broad view of the Naftali hills, reaching to the Hula plain. The fence of **Mishgav Am Kibbutz** forms the national boundary; in 1980, five PLO men captured the nursery and ended up shooting a

A landscape under transformation: newly planted forests on the once-barren Lebanese frontier

2-year-old and the adult carer in front of the other children.

Continue to **Metulla►** (see page 186) via **the Good Fence►►** border crossing, so named because of the free medical clinic run there for Lebanese citizens.

▶▶ Nimrod's Castle National Park   *163D5*

The hillside fortress 3km east of Banyas was long ago named after Nimrod, the 'mighty hunter' (Genesis 10). This massive, imposing ruin dates largely from the 13th century. Built by Crusaders in 1129, it was immediately seized by Syrian Arabs. Held again by Crusaders from 1140 to 1164, it was taken and enlarged by Ayyub sultans in 1220, and by Mamelukes in 1260, but later abandoned.

▶▶ Peki'in   *162B4*

Now mainly Druze, this village has an impressive Jewish history unbroken from Temple times until 1936 (only one Jewish family – the Zinatis – remains). The revered 2nd-century Rabbi Shimon bar Yochai (see page 185), reputedly author of the *Zohar* (the mystical kabbalistic work), lived in a cave here with his son for 13 years while in hiding from the Romans. A possible candidate above the village has been speculatively marked **Rashbi Cave▶**. Walk down past the ornate **village fountain▶** and balconied houses to the attractive **Old Synagogue▶▶**, on its original 2nd-century foundations. It has a simple interior, a floor of huge stone blocks and fine stone-carving. Other historic sights in Peki'in include the olive-presses, flour mill and Jewish cemetery. Two snack-bars face each other on the main Haifa road, one 'Jewish', the other 'Druze'; but both are run by Arabs and make excellent pittas and local dishes.

▶ Rosh Pinna   *163C3*

The name means 'Cornerstone', and this settlement, set up in 1882 with Rothschild funds on the slope of Mount Canaan, was the first in Galilee. Today it is an unremark-able little town, but up the hillside is the original **settle-ment site▶**, consisting of a main street, restored pioneer dwellings and the old synagogue. The 5km of winding road from here to Sefat give remarkably good views. At the **Mitzpe HaYamim▶▶** viewpoint, both the Sea of Galilee and (hazily) the Mediterranean can be seen.

Echoes of the past

When the Israelites conquered Canaan in 1300 BC, the area which would become Galilee was shared between the tribes of Asher and Naftali. The Menasseh tribe had the Golan. The tribe of Dan was given the foot of Mount Hermon. Many of today's place names recall this remote past. The Naftali hills overlook the Hula plain. Ancient Dan lies 1km away from the Dan of today. Sefat stands atop Mount Canaan.

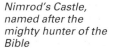

195

Nimrod's Castle, named after the mighty hunter of the Bible

Below the red line
The banks of the Sea of Galilee lie 212m below true sea level. From north to south, the lake measures 21km, and its width reaches a maximum of 13km. The total area is 170sq km. On average it is 49m deep. The lake is Israel's principal reservoir, and the National Water Carrier pipeline pumps water directly from the shore near Capernaum to smaller reservoirs across the country. The 'red line' is a theoretical water level below which the lake's surface should not drop – but it has done so frequently in recent years. In the early and mid-1990s, the level has often been about 300mm below the red line, causing anxiety about the quality of the water and the effect on its fish.

Still waters of the Galilee shore

▶▶▶ **Sea of Galilee (Hebrew: Yam Kinneret)**   *163C2-C3*

Not really a sea, of course, the exquisitely beautiful and tranquil body of water that Israelis call Lake Kinneret astonishes the eye, lying blue under a pearly sky, enclosed by hills that also seem blue-tinted. The name Kinneret comes from **ginnar**, meaning a harp, because of its shape. Certainly its size and shape are ideal; wherever you stand, whether on a distant viewpoint or on the very shore, the countryside can be seen rising steeply on the other side, while the gently lapping waters disappear enticingly around folds in the landscape.

This is, of course, no ordinary lake. It exists as much in faith and legend as in reality, and holds a central place in the hearts of millions of people around the world. This, more than anywhere else, is the land of Jesus. He lived on the lake shores, his disciples were its fishermen, many of his miraculous works were performed around its banks, and – if the gospel account is not a metaphor – he even walked on its waters. What is more, the River Jordan, of hymns and prayers and gospel songs, that richly symbolic frontier of the biblical Promised Land, flows in one end and out of the other.

Not surprisingly, many visitors find here not only water and sunshine, but also the very spirit of Jesus and echoes of his ministry. Beware, though: many pilgrim sites, even those hallowed through the centuries, rest on scant historical evidence. Theologians have decreed that this does not matter, that one should regard the sites as commemorative. But for anyone with simpler, Sunday School notions of 'The Holy Land', a few places associated with Jesus could prove quite surprising, and even disappointing. Many of the New Testament stories were never intended to be taken literally anyway, yet shrines, exquisite churches or opulent basilicas mark every spot.

Yet Israel is not a story book: it is a real country, inhabited by Jews for whom the greatest miracle is their return to this land after their 1,800-year exile. For them, the most wonderful thing of all about the Sea of Galilee is that it is a vast clean lake in a Mediterranean country with few other

Changing names
In the early Scriptures, the Sea of Galilee is called Sea of Chinneret; both Numbers 34:11 and Joshua 13:27 explain that its eastern shore forms the edge of the Promised Land. By the time of the Book of Maccabees – which was not included in the Bible – the lake is called the Sea of Ginnosar. This evolved to Lake Gennesaret in the New Testament (Luke 5:1), though Sea of Galilee (Matthew 4:18) and Sea of Tiberias (John 21:1) are also used. Sea of Tiberias seems to have been current in the 1st century – the time of Jesus – as both the Talmud and the historian Josephus use that name.

197

Oleander in full bloom

sources of fresh water. It is full, too, of edible fish – 20 different species, notably the unique St Peter's Fish – while its shores are fertile and eager to yield their produce. Most of its shoreline remains wonderfully undeveloped, but kibbutzim and *moshavim* (co-operative villages) are scattered all around the lake. Their fields grow the whole gamut of produce: apples, avocados, beans and bananas. Most people are involved in fishing or fish farming.

The lakeside kibbutz hotels make excellent places to stay – or even just to visit for a meal – with park-like settings and a more restful atmosphere than conventional hotels. Among the best and most appealing are the well-placed **Nof Ginnosar**, on the northwestern shore, and the religiously observant (though non-Jews are very welcome) **Kinar**, facing it on the northeastern bank.

On the whole, the northern half of the lake offers superb tranquillity. Most of the places associated with Jesus are here: **Capernaum▶▶** (see page 170), and, within a few minutes of it, the **Mount of Beatitudes▶▶** (see page 189), **Tabgha▶▶** (see page 202), **Migdal▶** (see page 186), the home of Mary Magdalene, and ancient **Kursi▶** (see page 198).

The southern half of the lake tends to appeal to a livelier crowd. **Tiberias▶▶** (see page 204), Galilee's little capital, stands on the edge of the water, and invites you to swim in it, ski on it or take a trip on it – either in a mock-biblical boat or in a modern pleasure cruiser equipped with disco. Or you can soak in the hot spa, famous since Roman days. At the southern tip of the Sea of Galilee, where the River Jordan pours out of the lake at **Yardenit▶** (see page 205), you can even be baptised in its waters.

Water for peace
Under the 1994 peace accord, Israel will provide Jordan with 150 million cubic metres of water per year by allowing extraction from the Yarmouk River which flows into the Sea of Galilee. Meanwhile, the amount of water now pumped out of the Sea of Galilee every single day to meet the needs of Israel's own people is more than the total for the whole year in 1948.

Drive The Sea of Galilee *(for map see pages 163C2–C3)*

This round tour of the lake offers plenty to do and see. *Allow all day and take a swimsuit.*

From the lake's biggest town, **Tiberias**►► (see page 204), head south, after 5km passing the Roman and modern spa baths of **Hamat Tiveria**►► (see page 205) and, on the hill slope opposite, two beautiful **old synagogues**► close to the tomb of Rabbi Meir Ba'al Haness, revered by many Sephardic Jews. Turn right beside the River Jordan to the **Yardenit**► baptismal park (see page 205). Almost next door, **Degania**► (see page 171), founded in 1909, is Israel's oldest kibbutz. A right turn leads from the lake to **Hamat Gader**►► (see page 176), site of extensive spa baths and an alligator farm. If alligators are not to your taste, try the ostrich farm at **Ha'on Kibbutz**► (see page 177).

Kibbutz **Ein Gev**►, founded in 1937, lies just within the pre-1967 border. This was where the first Jews in modern times cast their nets again into the Sea of Galilee. On the stony hill above is ruined **Susita**►

Green and scenic Galilee, site of many events in Christ's life

(Hebrew for 'Horse', named after the hill's saddle shape) which, as the seat of a Byzantine bishop, flourished until the 7th-century Arab conquest. Nearby **Kursi National Park**► (biblical Gergesa) contains what was once Israel's largest Byzantine monastic church. The 5th-century building, partly reconstructed, traditionally marks the place where, in the Miracle of the Swine, Jesus drove devils from a man into a herd of pigs, who promptly ran down to the water and drowned. **Kinar**►, a religious kibbutz, has a hotel and restaurant in delightful lakeside grounds.

The road recrosses the Jordan on the wooden planks of **Arik Bridge**, and straightaway reaches **Amnun Beach**►, an agreeable spot for a dip. Just minutes away, several important places in Jesus' ministry lie close together: **Capernaum**►► (see page 170), **Tabgha**►► (see page 202), and the **Mount of Beatitudes**►► (see page 188 and opposite Walk). Do not miss the **ancient boat**►►► at the Man in the Galilee Museum beside the attractive **Nof Ginnosar Kibbutz Hotel** (see page 171). Last comes ancient **Migdal**► (see page186), just 4km from Tiberias.

198

Walk In the footsteps of Jesus

Most of Jesus' ministry took place within a small area around Capernaum. This attractive countryside, dotted with churches, makes for enjoyable, easy walking. Wear a sun-hat, take drinking water, and dress modestly for access to churches. *Allow 1½ hours.*

Start by visiting Capernaum's ancient synagogue and dwellings, including the one said to have been St Peter's House (see page 171). Jesus lived at Capernaum►►, where he preached and roundly condemned the townsfolk for not taking his message seriously.
    From the site, take the access path back to the main road. Almost opposite, paths lead through the fields on to the **Mount of Beatitudes►►** (see page 188), a possible site of the Sermon on the Mount. Climb to the summit (about 1km), where the lovely domed **Church of the Beatitudes** (or Basilica), set in gardens adjacent to the **Hospice**, commands a fine view of the countryside and the lake.
    Descend on the path which heads in the direction of Tabgha (1km). You meet the road almost opposite the

*The Chapel of the Primacy
of St Peter*

grounds of the **Chapel of the Primacy of Peter.** Walk to the simple chapel which stands on the shore of the lake; this was built on the spot where the risen Christ appeared to his disciples, who were fishing on the lake. They did not recognise him until he told them to cast their nets on the other side of the boat, whereupon their nets were full. Peter then miraculously walked on the waters of the lake to reach the shore. Over breakfast Jesus thrice asked Peter if he loved him. On replying yes, Peter was made head of the Church.
    Turn along the road away from Capernaum. At once on the right are remains of the 4th-century **Monastery of the Sermon on the Mount**, held, at that time, to mark the site of the Sermon. Continue for 150m to the modern **Church of the Multiplication of the Loaves and Fishes,** the third church on this site, traditionally associated with the feeding of the multitude with loaves and fishes. Return (3km) along the quiet road to Capernaum.

The Ari

Sefat's Ari Ashkenazi Synagogue is supposed to stand on the spot where the nature-loving Yitzhak Luria, known as Our Master Rabbi Yitzhak, or the Ari (an acronym which means 'the Lion'), would greet the sabbath. The six psalms and chanted blessing which he and his followers recited have become the familiar Friday evening *Kabbalat Shabbat*. The Ari also established the popular Tu b'Shvat festival, the 'New Year for Trees', now celebrated by Jews everywhere. The Ari was Sephardi, but the congregation today is Ashkenazi – hence the synagogue's name.

▶▶▶ **Sefat (Hebrew: Tsfat or Zefat)**   *163C3*

One of Israel's most picturesque towns, Sefat stands 1,000m high in beautiful hills north of the Sea of Galilee, with superb views. This has been a great centre of Jewish learning for centuries and was, with **Meron**▶ (see page 185) a birthplace of the kabbala (Jewish mysticism). Many strictly observant Jews live here, but it is a focus of secular Jewish culture, as well. Every July, Sefat hosts its popular festival of *klezmer* (East European Jewish music).

Café-lined **Yerushalayim (Jerusalem) Street**▶▶▶, with cafés in a pedestrian section, is the old city's main street, set on the slope of a steep hill. Pick up a map at the tourist office, located a few paces from the **Davidka**▶, a home-made cannon whose noise alone is said to have helped the Jews conquer Sefat in 1948. At the hill's summit there is a park and the remains of a **Crusader Citadel**▶▶. On the northern slope, the **Israel Bible Museum**▶ is actually a collection of art depicting biblical scenes. More interesting, **HaMeira House**▶▶ has material on 19th-century Sefat. It is located near the top of **Ma'alot Olei HaGardom**▶, a remarkable flight of hundreds of stone steps sharply descending the hill. Also at the top of the steps stands the **Police Station**▶, built by the British to separate Jewish and Arab neighbourhoods. It is still pitted with bullet marks from the fighting.

North of the steps, wander among the attractive cobbled lanes, stairways and courtyards of the **Synagogue Quarter**▶▶▶. The many ornate little 16th-century synagogues (some rebuilt in the 18th century) are very much in use; they welcome non-Jewish visitors, though modest dress (cover your arms and shoulders and your

Sefat's ancient Abuhav synagogue

legs to the knee) is expected of both men and women. Do not miss the **Ari Ashkenazi Synagogue►►►**, a tiny white stone building in a quiet stone courtyard, with its ornate hand-carved ark, nor **Abuhav Synagogue►►**, with its three arks, nor **Yosef Caro Synagogue►►►**, named after the Spanish-born rabbi who arrived here in 1535 and wrote the still-authoritative work on Jewish law.

South of the steps lies the **Artists' Quarter►►**, a former Arab district taken up in the 1950s by an artists' collective. Over 50 artists live here today and this charming area is packed with studios and open-air displays of sculpture. Further south is the town's fascinating **Ancient Cemetery►►**, which has the graves of many distinguished 16th-century rabbis, as well as victims of two tragic PLO attacks – the 22 Sefat high school pupils killed at Ma'alot on a school trip, and the 11 younger children from Avivim whose school bus was attacked.

After the First Revolt (AD 66–73), the town grew as Jews fled here from Jerusalem. Crusaders drove the Jews out

and constructed the citadel in 1140 (they dubbed the town Safed – still a popular version of its name). It was taken in turn by Salah ed-Din (1188), the Knights Templar (1240) and the Mamelukes (1266). In 1517 all Israel came under Ottoman rule. Jews returned, including many expelled from Spain in 1492. The new arrivals brought with them a rich culture; they built the synagogues and, in 1578, set up the region's first printing press. An earthquake in 1759 caused great damage, after which many Sephardim (Jews of Spanish origin) moved elsewhere, but Ashkenazim arriving from Russia took their place, bringing their own brand of mysticism and Yiddish culture. In 1837, another earthquake and epidemic killed over 5,000 people, and the town went into a decline. Arabs moved in, and in the 1929 anti-Jewish riots they killed 21 Jews and wounded 80.

In the 1948 War of Independence, Sefat was an Arab stronghold with a population of 12,000 Arabs, including a fighting force of 6,000. When they entered the Jewish quarter, with its population of 1,500, mainly elderly, Hasidim, a group of 35 men of the Palmach (the élite Jewish fighting force) arrived. The fact that such a small number of men managed to defeat the Arab forces and take the whole town is now widely celebrated in Jewish history, and has gone down as the Miracle of Sefat.

The Miracle of Sefat
When the Jews won Sefat in the 1948 war, the chief rabbi of the town gave it as his opinion that the victory had been due to two things: the natural course of events, and a miracle. The natural course of events was that Jews prayed and God answered their prayers. The miracle was that the Jews were prepared to stay and fight for their city when so heavily outnumbered.

Lions and doves in the Artists' Quarter

201

How are you spelling that?
The name of the hilltop town north of the Sea of Galilee is spelt in Hebrew with the three letters, *tsadi, feh, taf,* pronounced approximately as Tsfat. Foreign efforts to say this, or transliterate it into different European languages, have led to a multitude of alternative spellings. As well as Sefat, the town's name is commonly written as Sefad, Safed, Zefat, Sfat and Tsefat.

Modern walls on
Roman columns in
the Church of the
Multiplication of the
Loaves and Fishes

►► Tabgha *163C3*

Not a village, but a small, fertile valley on the Galilee lakeshore, its name derives from the Greek *hepta pegon* ('seven springs'); the springs themselves emerge by the Chapel of the Primacy of Peter. Just 3km from Capernaum, Tabgha lies at the foot of the **Mount of Beatitudes►►** (see page 188). At the bottom of the hill (on the opposite side of the road), the **Church of the Multiplication of the Loaves and Fishes►►►** commemorates the feeding of the multitude. This attractive modern building was constructed in 1982 for the German Benedictines whose 1956 monastery stands next door. The church stands on the site of its 4th- and 5th-century predecessors, and encloses a beautiful cloister in white stone. Inside, visitors must remain quiet, which creates a tremendous atmosphere. In the transepts, exquisite **ancient mosaics►►** retrieved from the two earlier churches depict Egyptian imagery, common in the art of the Early Christian period. A mosaic in front of the altar shows the two fishes and the basket of five loaves with which many believe Jesus fed 5,000 people (Mark 8).

Next door, the small, black **Church of the Primacy of Peter►►►**, built in 1933 on traces of a 4th-century church, marks the site where Jesus appeared to his disciples after his Resurrection, according to the account given in the gospel of St John (21). The church stands in a superb setting on the shore of the Sea of Galilee, the waters brushing against it. Inside, modern coloured glass contrasts with the black basalt. The simple interior is built around the waterside rocks, with one great rock emerging from the tiled floor – this, known as Mensa Christi, is the 'table' at which the risen Christ supposedly sat and ate bread with the disciples. Beside the church, rock-carved steps lead down to the water. These steps date from the 2nd century, but many believe that the risen Christ appeared to his disciples on them. On that same occasion, he named Peter head of his church.

►►► Tel Dan *163C5*

The ancient city of Dan, standing on the largest of the three sources of the River Jordan, marked the northern limit of the Jews' Biblical Land of Israel ('from Dan to Beersheva'). It is now located within a glorious 40-hectare **nature reserve►►►**, still on Israel's northern border, with two marked paths that wander through the exotic

Josef Trumpledor
Born in Russia in 1880, Trumpledor served in the Tsar's imperial army, lost an arm in battle and was decorated for bravery, and yet still had to endure the anti-Semitism sweeping Russia at the time. He founded the Zionist Hehalutz (Jewish Pioneer) movement, and in 1912 went to live in Palestine. There he founded the Zion Mule Corps and, despite having only one arm, fought with the British at Gallipoli, after which he was again decorated for bravery. On his return to Palestine, in 1917, he joined with others to purchase and cultivate the land which they called Tel Hai, the 'Hill of Life'. In 1920, Arabs attacked the settlement, which was vigorously defended. Eight settlers died, including Trumpledor, whose last words were 'It is good to die for our own country.' His grave attracts many visitors, especially on the 11th day of the Jewish month of Adar, which has been set aside for the commemoration of Tel Hai Day.

jungle of mulberry, laurel, fig trees, wild grapes and willow to the source of the Dan. The sound of water, pouring under and over the paths, accompanies your walk. Rising above the spring, the adjacent Tel►► (settlement mound) gives a dizzying sense of history. This is the site of Laish, a city mentioned in Egyptian records of the 19th and 15th centuries BC, conquered by Joshua in the 13th century BC, and occupied by the Jewish tribe of Dan, who – the Bible notes – had a bad record as idolators. About 200 years later the city was destroyed by the Assyrian King Tiglath-Pileser III and never rebuilt.

Kibbutz Dan►, located 1km away on a panoramic ridge, looks clear across the Hula valley in one direction and up to the summit of snow-covered Mount Hermon in the other. The kibbutz runs a field studies centre with residential classes and guided walks. Its **Beit Ussishkin**►► (Ussishkin House) has an information centre and museum on the wildlife of Golan, Hermon and Hula. The displays and video can only hint at the region's fantastic variety: there are over 2,000 species of plants and 400 species of birds to be seen here.

►   Tel Hai   163C5

Just north of Kiryat Shmona, Tel Hai (the Hill of Life) is a simple encampment preserved as a museum of the pre-State Haganah underground militia. The remarkable Josef Trumpledor (see panel opposite) and others of the 'eight people' (*kiryat shmona*) – died here in March 1920 while defending from an Arab attack the land they had purchased in 1917. Trumpledor's grave at the **military cemetery**► is a place of pilgrimage for young Israelis. Just 1km north, **Beit HaShomer**► at **Kibbutz Kfar Giladi**► is a museum of the HaShomer (literally, 'the Watchman'), another early Zionist militia.

203

The Tel Dan Nature Reserve, believed by some to be the Garden of Eden

Maimonides
Rabbi Moshe ben Maimon, also known by the sobriquet Rambam, or as Maimonides, was born in Spain in 1135. The leading scientist and physician of his day, he became the personal doctor of Salah ed-Din and wrote important commentaries on biblical matters that have now become standard works. He died on 13 December 1204, and was buried as he wished, at the holy city of Tiberias.

Wish you were here?
In the year 985, Arab writer El-Mukadassi had this to say about life in Tiberias: 'For two months a year they gorge themselves upon the fruit of the jujube bush which grows wild and costs nothing, for two months they struggle with the numerous flies, for two months they go about naked because of the heat, for two months they suck sugar cane, for two months they wallow in mud because of the rain, and for two months they dance in their beds because of the legions of fleas.'

Modern fishermen follow in the footsteps of St Peter

▶▶ **Tiberias (Hebrew: Tiveria)**   *163C3*

Galilee's little capital (population 30,000) runs steeply downhill to the edge of the Sea of Galilee. The traffic-free waterfront promenade, with its palms, strolling crowds, fish restaurants and oriental-looking food stalls, has a pleasant, convivial air, and a curious mix of the plush and the tacky. There is a lot of entertainment for visitors, including evening lake cruises with dinner and dancing on board. Away from the shore, the town degenerates into squalor and appalling traffic jams. Most residents and tourists live in new districts high above the old city, but even the lakeside old quarter is marred by a mishmash of modern architecture.

History In AD 20, near the ruins of ancient Rakkat, Herod Antipas built an opulent palace and synagogue here. After initial doubts, because Herod's construction had covered old grave sites, the synagogue soon attracted numerous religious scholars. The *Mishna* was compiled here about AD 200, codifying the so-called Oral Law, the traditional interpretation and practice of the Written Law. From then until AD 429 (when it was abolished by Emperor Theodosius II), this was the seat of the Sanhedrin, the supreme court of Jewish law. The Palestinian or Yerushalmi *Talmud* (Book of Law) might be better termed the Tiberias *Talmud*, as it was written here around AD 400. Jewish life thrived until the 7th-century Arab conquest. Crusaders took the town in 1099 and Salah ed-Din in 1187. Under the Ottomans, Druze Emir Daher revived Tiberias, resettling it with Jews. The First Aliya (1882–1903) dramatically increased its population, and the town has continued to grow ever since.

Sights Remains of the black basalt **Crusader fortifications▶** can be seen on the north side of the old town. The handsome **St Peter's Monastery▶**, close to the waterfront, also stands on Crusader ruins. Off the main HaGalil Street, the **tomb of Maimonides▶▶** (the renowned 12th-century Rabbi Moshe ben Maimon, also known by his acronym as Rambam) lies beside a small garden, reached by means of steps, lined with black pillars, leading from the road. The large, rounded, pale stone tomb, set within a black stone enclosure, is the one

The tomb of Maimonides

The Tayyelet
Until 1934, the waterfront of Tiberias was densely populated, with houses descending to the edge of the lake. A huge storm in that year caused mud, water and rock to pour through the city, demolishing hundreds of homes at the foot of the hill. Many people were killed. In the aftermath the ruined homes beside the water were swept away. In their place was constructed one of the town's most appealing features, the *tayyelet*, or waterside promenade.

covered by a ramshackle metal roof. His wife's square tomb lies to one side of the enclosure, beyond which are several other imposing rabbinical tombs, including those of 1st-century Yohanan ben Zakai, the eminent scholar and founder of the Yavne Academy, and 2nd-century Eliezer 'the Great', another scholar revered for his wisdom. The white **tomb of Rabbi Akiva►►**, spiritual leader of the Second Revolt against the Romans (AD 132), can be seen higher up the hill among newer buildings.

Nearby Romans flocked to enjoy the hot baths at **Hamat Tiveria►►**, 5km south of town. Still very popular, the spa now occupies a modern complex and the emphasis is not really on health, but self indulgent pleasure; perhaps it always was so. On the hillside opposite, ancient buildings were found; relics can be seen in the **Lehman Building►**. Drive or walk up the ramp to an attractive esplanade paved with pale stone, where steps enter the domed interior of an ancient **Sephardic synagogue►**, still very much in use, and, above it on the slope, a blue-domed **Ashkenazi synagogue►**. Both provide access to the low vaulted chamber of the **tomb of Rabbi Meir Ba'al HaNess►**, the 2nd-century scholar revered by Sephardim as a miracle worker.

► **Yardenit** *163C2*
Kibbutz Kinneret's baptismal park, on the banks of the Jordan south of the Sea of Galilee, has attractive grounds and water terraces where devout Christians come to experience ritual full immersion in the biblical river.

►► **Zipori (or Sepphoris)** *162B2*
North of Nazareth, close to the modern *moshav* (co-operative village) of the same name, this remarkable **archaeological site►►►** consists of ruins from the First Temple period, remnants of a complete pre-Roman Jewish town and a Roman theatre. A reconstructed Roman villa contains its beautiful original Dionysian mosaic floor; a woman's face in the design has been dubbed the 'Mona Lisa of the Galilee'. Zipori's 12th-century **Crusader fortifications►** are a reminder that the Crusader armies gathered here in 1187 before marching to the Horns of Hittim to take on Salah ed-Din. Their crushing defeat ended the Second Crusade.

Crusader fortress rising above Roman theatre ruins at Zipori

JUDAEA AND SAMARIA (THE WEST BANK)

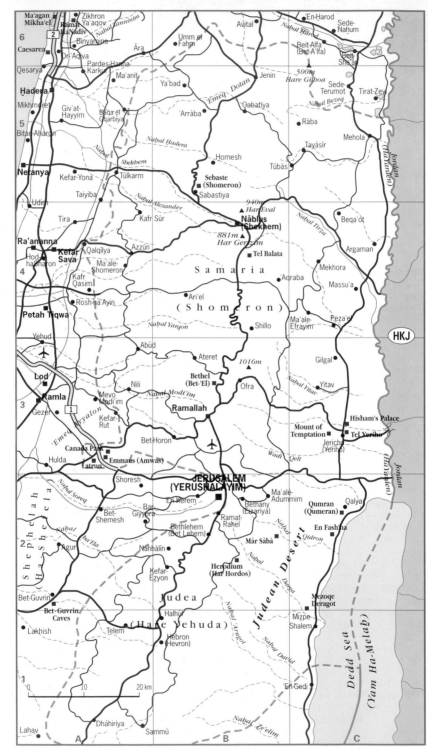

Judaea's rocky terrain is cut by wadis that run only in the rainy season

Judaea and Samaria (the West Bank)

Judaea and Samaria (the West Bank) In Hebrew, this region is known as Yehuda and Shomron. By Arab residents the area is referred to as Al Defa al Gharbia, literally, the West Bank. Much of Judaea and Samaria lies outside the State of Israel. These two ancient Jewish kingdoms have been disputed territory since 1948. Technically the territory belongs to no one and is part of no country, although, since the setting up of the Palestinian Authority in 1994 most of the region is under PLO administration.

The term West Bank (of the River Jordan) is merely a convenient shorthand: originally it included most of the State of Israel. Currently, 'the West Bank' suggests only the land placed under Israeli military rule after the 1967 Six Day War. Worldwide, it was dubbed the Occupied Territories until the handover to the Palestinian Authority; Israel refers to it as the Administered Territories (or just 'the Territories'), arguing that, under international law, only land properly belonging to another country can be described as occupied. Either way, it remains a divided, disputed region, the remnant of Palestine which ended up in neither Israel nor Jordan (see side panel on page 209 for advice on travelling in the region).

A hard place A narrow ridge of rocky hills, reaching from Galilee to the Negev, passes through Judaea and Samaria and forms the greater part of the terrain. On their eastern slopes the hills fall sharply down into the Jordan Valley. Certain parts of Judaea fall within the borders of Israel proper: Ein Gedi on the Dead Sea, Masada and Arad, and the capital itself, Jerusalem, including 'the mountains that are round about' the capital (Psalm 125: 2). 'Administered' Judaea lies south and east of Jerusalem, with Samaria to

JUDAEA AND SAMARIA (THE WEST BANK)

Judaea weeps
After quelling the Jewish Revolt and destroying Jerusalem, the 1st-century AD Roman emperor, Vespasian, issued celebratory coins showing a palm tree, a man in chains and a woman weeping, and bearing the words: *Iudaea Capta* (Judaea taken).

Disappointment
'What public relations can do for a river!' – Henry Kissinger, on seeing the west bank of the River Jordan in 1980

Land with no name
Israelis often talk about 'across the Green Line' when referring to the West Bank territories. They are also known officially by an acronym, Yesha, from Yehuda-Shomron-'Azza (Hebrew names for Judah, Samaria, Gaza). The name West Bank was first coined by the American CIA, and brought into general use by the Jordanians.

Previous page (bottom right): detail at the entrance to the Milk Grotto Sanctuary

St George's monastery at Wadi Qelt, near Jericho

its north. Together they total just 5,878sq km (less than half the size of Northern Ireland). Both districts are stony, mountainous and largely infertile, though the Samarian hills are terraced and planted with olives and other crops. A large proportion of Judaea consists of harsh uninhabitable desert, yet Judaea and Samaria lie near the heart and soul of Jewish history and heritage. Judaea (in Hebrew, Yehuda, or Judah) actually means 'the Land of Jews'. This is the country in which Abraham wandered, where he and the other patriarchs – and the matriarchs – of the Jewish nation lived and died. Jewish towns and places of pilgrimage grew around their tombs. Later, some of these became Moslem holy sites as well.

Whose land? In 1947, when the British were about to withdraw and the UN debated the future of Palestine, the Arab Higher Committee in Palestine – chief representative body of Palestinian Arabs – declared that 'Palestine is part of the province of Syria'. At the same time, the new kingdom of Jordan claimed sovereignty over all of British Palestine, while the Egyptians formed their own All Palestine Government to fill the vacuum left by the British departure. In 1948, the war between the Arab states and Israel left the region partitioned between Jordan, which annexed the entire West Bank, and the new State of Israel. With its defeat in the 1967 Six Day War, Jordan lost the West Bank, which Israel then occupied (but did not annexe).

After 1987, Israeli rule was challenged directly by the Intifada (literally 'Throwing Off'), essentially an uprising of West Bank Arab residents, some opposed to Israel's presence in the West Bank, others opposed to the State's very existence. Partly through their inability to contain the Intifada, Israelis moved towards the idea of quitting the West Bank. Prime Minister Yitzhak Rabin's government was elected in 1992 with a mandate to 'trade land for peace'. Agreement between Israel and the PLO was reached in 1993, and in 1994 the Palestinian Authority took over Gaza and Jericho as a first step. In stages, more of the land came under Palestinian rule. The argument does not stop there, however. Some Arab guerrilla groups will not contemplate any accommodation with Israel, and some Israelis cannot bear the idea of 'giving back' any part of the Promised Land.

►► **Bethany (Arabic: El Azaria, Eizariya)** *206B2*

A small town just over the crest of the Mount of Olives, Bethany is only 5km from Jerusalem. The gospels of Luke and Matthew record that, before riding into Jerusalem on his final journey, Jesus sent two disciples to Bethany to fetch 'a colt [of an ass]... whereon yet never man sat' that had been tied up for him there – presumably by Lazarus and his sisters Martha and Mary, friends of Jesus who lived in the town.

In Aramaic, *bethany* means 'house (or place) of poverty', but the Arabic name means 'the (place) of Lazarus'. Lazarus is revered by Muslims as well as Christians. When Lazarus died from an illness, John's gospel claims, he had 'lain in the grave four days already' before Jesus arrived, wept and called out 'Lazarus, come forth'. The dead man promptly got up, to the consternation of mourners (John 11).

Lazarus' Tomb►►, by the mosque, is the principal sight: difficult steps descend to a dark cavern, which leads to the low tomb where Lazarus supposedly lay – the place does not accord with the gospel description, however, and was chosen by pilgrims in the 4th century. In fact, the gospel of Mark makes no mention of Christ raising Lazarus from the dead, but he does have Jesus and the disciples going to Bethany on that day. In his story, Jesus is hungry and pauses at a fig tree. Finding it without fruit (because, as the gospel states, Passover is not the fig season) he curses the tree and tells it that no man shall eat fruit from it forever. Gullible tourists are sometimes shown what is said to be the very tree, although Matthew (21:20) says that after Jesus' curse 'the fig tree withered away'.

Jesus stayed with his friends again 'six days before the Passover' (John 12: 1), on which he was to be crucified. Once again, the various gospel accounts differ in their details of what happened on that day. John's gospel claims that Lazarus' sister, Mary, anointed Jesus' feet with 'a pound of spikenard, very costly', and wiped his feet afterwards with her hair. Matthew's gospel says that a woman came with precious ointment in an alabaster box and anointed his head. These anointments, Christian authorities have claimed, were the ritual verification of Jesus as the Messiah, since the word messiah, or *moshiach* in Hebrew, means 'the anointed', and is used several times in the Old Testament to describe Jewish kings or leaders.

In Matthew's gospel, the anointment of Jesus takes place not at the home of Martha and Mary, but in the home of a leper called Simon. Not far from Lazarus' Tomb, the ruined **House of Simon the Leper►**, formerly known as the Castle of Lazarus, was, in reality, part of the defences for a nunnery founded by Milicent, wife of the Crusader-era King Fulke. Similarly, the so-called **House of Mary and Martha►** is, in fact, the remains of the medieval nunnery itself. A blocked-off recess in the **Church of Mary and Martha►** forms another entrance to Lazarus' tomb.

According to Luke's gospel (24: 50), Bethany is also the site of Christ's Ascension and there are other Christian associations near by: about 10km out of Bethany, on the Jericho road, is the inn of Jesus' parable about the Good Samaritan (Luke 10: 25–37).

209

Travel in the West Bank
Two well-supported, well-funded and well-armed Palestinian guerrilla organisations are at war with Israel: Hamas and Islamic Jihad. Their presence in most areas of the West Bank make it dangerous to travel here. The stoning of cars with Israeli licence plates (including hire cars) is commonplace, and shootings have also taken place, resulting in the deaths of several drivers and passengers.

This being said, the main roads to popular tourist sights are considered safe and have good security cover (for example, the Jerusalem to Qumran and Jericho road, or the Dead Sea road to Ein Gedi). Arab buses will not be attacked, and the Arab-run buses based at the East Jerusalem bus station travel to towns and villages throughout the West Bank. Organised tours, though dull and predictable, are the safest way to see the sights; West Bank tours are usually organised by Arab companies, with Arab guides travelling in Arab buses. Women should never travel alone.

The PLO

■ **The Palestine Liberation Organisation (PLO) was created in 1964 with the aim of destroying Israel. Its stubble-cheeked leader, Yasir Arafat (known to the Arabs as Abu Amr, Father of War), never seen without his traditional *keffiye* head dress and a pistol strapped on to his battle fatigues, became a media figure lauded by western radical groups and Soviet-bloc client states. ■**

Changing role
'Chairman Arafat is doing his best to be a leader of a people, rather than the leader of a faction.'
– Nabil Sha'ath, the PLO's planning minister and chief peace negotiator
(December 1994)

Top and below: violent scenes such as these have diminished since Palestinian Arabs were granted self-rule

On 13 September 1993, Yasir Arafat took off his gun and held out his hand in peace to Israeli prime minister Yitzhak Rabin on the lawn of the White House in Washington. In 1994, the Israelis began the process of handing over territory to PLO rule. This has not brought an end, though, to the Palestinian war against Israel. The PLO is an uneasy alliance of guerrilla factions. As boss of the largest group, Al Fatah, Yasir Arafat may be Chairman but his policy is dictated by the need to appease rivals and keep warring factions together. Until 1993, they were bound by a common aim, set out in the PLO Covenant: to destroy Israel and set up an Arab state in all of Palestine. The Washington handshake and Arafat's *de facto* recognition of Israel have thrown the PLO into crisis. The Covenant still stands, and many PLO groups are determined to abide by it. Meanwhile, no-quarter Islamic groups are winning the hearts of those who have lost faith in the PLO yet still wish to see 'the Zionist entity' utterly destroyed. Israel's hope is that the prospect of at last having some land to rule will encourage Chairman Arafat to deal firmly with his opponents.

History In the Arab world, resolute opposition to the setting up of a Jewish state in Palestine goes back a long way and runs deep, for psychological, religious and political reasons. Before and after Israel came into being in 1948, Arab states set up anti-Zionist armed groups. *Fedayeen* (terrorist) attacks ran at a high level through the 1950s. In 1964 the Arab League (a pan-Arab intergovernmental forum) met in Cairo to create the Palestine Liberation Organisation as an umbrella for these diverse forces, and declared the PLO was 'the sole legitimate representative of the Palestinian people'. Al Fatah joined in 1967 and became the dominant faction. Through the 1970s, terrorist acts around the world sharply escalated. At the same time, the PLO set up humanitarian bodies that won support among the Palestinians. More recently, the PLO's support for Iraq's invasion of Kuwait backfired as the Arab states allied themselves with the Kuwaitis. At this point Israel seized the opportunity to work for peace with the weakened PLO.

A new era As the PLO at last reaches out for acceptance and compromise, and is duly rewarded with territory to call its own, the unrest continues. In 1987, the Intifada uprising against Israeli rule started in the West Bank and came under the wing of the violent Islamic groups.

Hamas (based in Gaza) opposes Palestinian self-government, seeing the region as part of a pan-Islamic state. It calls for the murder of all Jews. Islamic Jihad (sponsored by Iran) sees Israel as an arm of western imperialism. Members believe that those who die attacking Israel enter heaven at once. The PLO does not wish to antagonise Palestinian Arabs by coming into open conflict with such groups, although it will have to curb them somehow if it is to continue the Peace Process, and achieve the ultimate aim of securing an independent state, under PLO rule, for the Palestinian Arabs.

Arab prisoners held for acts of aggression against the State of Israel

On paper
Israel is the only Middle Eastern country in which PLO newspapers are freely available, although they are subject to the same degree of censorship as all Israeli papers. The main Arab newspapers, both published in Jerusalem and distributed throughout the West Bank, are *Al-Quds*, which is pro-PLO, and *Al-Nahar*, which is pro-Jordan.

Zionism
Arabs hostile to Israel brand it 'the Zionist entity'. Their influence enabled a vote to be passed year after year in the UN Assembly affirming that 'Zionism is Racism', a Soviet-sponsored motion only rescinded with the collapse of the Soviet bloc. In fact, Zionism is the political movement whose objective is to create (and now, to maintain) a Jewish homeland in Israel. Most political organisations and parties in Israel, even those advocating total withdrawal from the West Bank, consider themselves Zionist.

Clashes often involve youths and children

Christmas in Bethlehem

Those who wish Christmas would come more often should be taken to Bethlehem. The three sects controlling the Church of the Nativity celebrate the birth of Jesus on different days: Catholics on 25 December, Greek Orthodox on 7 January and Armenians on 19 January. The Catholic Christmas is a huge event but, to prevent crime and overcrowding, visitors require a permit to visit Manger Square, St Catherine's Church and the Church of the Nativity on 24 and 25 December. Permits can be obtained from Israel Government Tourist Offices in Israel. Seats for midnight mass in St Catherine's Church must be booked well ahead with the Christian Information Centre, Jaffa Gate, Jerusalem, tel: 02-287647.

Solomon's pools

South of Bethlehem, on the main road to Hebron, three large and ancient reservoirs are attributed to Solomon (Ecclesiastes 2: 6). Herod brought water from them to Herodion, and Pontius Pilate ran their waters into Jerusalem.

Beware of touts

On arrival in Manger Square, visitors are usually set upon by groups of would-be guides of all ages, who shout and pull at the tourists while offering their 'services'. To employ one might be an act of charity, but for a more enjoyable visit to Bethlehem, it is wise to refuse.

▶▶▶ **Bethlehem (Hebrew: Beit Lechem; Arabic: Bet Lacham)** *206B2*

For devout Christians, a visit to this Christian Arab town, located 10km from Jerusalem, is the experience of a lifetime. The focal point is the Church of the Nativity in Manger Square, known to the world as the birthplace of Jesus and praised in carols, nursery songs and poetry.

History Bethlehem first appeared in the scriptures, nearly 2,000 years before Jesus, as the burial place of Rachel, wife of Jacob, who 'set a pillar upon her grave' (Genesis 35: 19 and 48: 7). The events of the Book of Ruth took place locally, and a young shepherd boy from Bethlehem, David, son of Jesse, was anointed King of Israel here by Samuel (I Samuel 16: 1–13). The richness of Bethlemen's fields and pasture are reflected in its name: the Hebrew Beit Lechem means 'House (or Place) of Bread' while the Arabic name means 'House of Meat'.

Christian beliefs That Jesus was indeed born in Bethlehem seems probable. The gospels of Matthew (2: 1) and Luke (2: 4–7) relate what has become the traditional Nativity story (neither Mark nor John refer to the birth of Jesus). They give no details of the exact location, except that Jesus was lain in a manger 'because there was no room at the inn' (Luke), and tradition has it that a certain cave was the exact place of his birth – animals were often quartered in such places and many older Bethlehem houses have caves to their rear to this day. According to the 4th-century St Jerome, however, the cave and site had long been sacred to Adonis, the youthful god who symbolised the winter solstice. Christians later claimed, though, that Hadrian built a temple to Adonis on the site deliberately to damp down Christian belief, though there is no evidence for this.

The first church When Helena, mother of the Emperor Constantine, visited in the 4th century, she was shown the cave, told the legend and promptly ordered a church to be built. The Emperor Justinian pulled this down in the 6th century and replaced it with a larger structure. His church was left alone by the Arab invaders of the 7th century and also remained untouched in the 11th century when many churches were destroyed by invading Muslims; Jesus is named in the Koran as one of the Holy Prophets, and the destructive force of the ferocious Muslims was quelled by the thought that this was his birthplace. Justinian's church remains essentially that which exists today, except for alterations carried out by the Crusaders, who captured it in 1099. On Christmas Day in 1100, the Crusader King Baldwin I had himself crowned here.

Power struggle When the Crusaders left, the church went into decline. Warring Christian factions divided it into sections and each defended its own patch, whilst Mamelukes and others took everything of value. Later, in the bitter struggle for ownership of the church, Napoleon intervened on behalf of the Roman Catholics, securing a portion for them. Armenian, Greek Orthodox and Catholic monasteries and churches were built abutting the Church

Herodion
This magnificent archaeo-
logical site, set on a high
hilltop in the Judaean
wilds south of Bethlehem,
preserves substantial and
impressive remains of the
palace which Herod
constructed for himself in
24–15 BC. He flattened the
summit and ringed it with
defences to enclose his
luxurious circular
Mountain Palace. The
Lower Town, at the bottom
of the hill, was built for
Herod's staff. In both the
First and Second Jewish
Revolts, the palace was
seized by rebels and used
as their fortress and
operations centre. Later,
Byzantine monks built a
monastery on the slope
among the ruins of the
palace annexes. From the
summit, there is a fantastic
view of Bethlehem and the
Judaean hills.

of the Nativity, with entrances directly into it. When the
church was damaged by earthquake (1834) and fire
(1869), disagreements between the factions made it
impossible to carry out repairs or replace lost furnishings.
Under British and then Israeli rule, pilgrimages to the
church were revived. Israeli soldiers have several times
stepped in to separate fighting Christians, notably in 1984
when armed Greek and Armenian clergymen fought a
pitched battle.

Church of the Nativity▶▶▶ For nearly all visitors
Bethlehem's main attraction is the church believed by
millions to stand over the place of Jesus' birth. Despite an
unattractive, buttressed, fortress-like Crusader outer wall,
the church is a good example of early Christian basilican
construction. It is entered by crossing a large paved courtyard to reach the tiny 6th-century doorway, which
Crusaders made even smaller, apparently for ease of
defence. By contrast, the interior is large and open,
almost entirely free of any decoration or furnishing, with
two double rows of red limestone pillars under an oak

*Visitors entering the
church bow in sub-
mission and humility
through this low
door*

The Church of St Catherine

Where shepherds kept watch there is now a modern shrine

ceiling (a gift of 1482 from Edward IV of England and Duke Philip of Burgundy). During Crusader times and after, this austere interior was beautifully painted and gilded. Trapdoors in the floor open to show remnants of the **mosaic floor▶** of Helena's original church.

Site of the Nativity Beside the ornate Greek Orthodox altar at the east end, steps lead down to the **Grotto of the Nativity▶▶▶**. The marble-lined cave is small – 2.5m high and under 4m across – and rather overpowering, with its warm, heavy atmosphere of incense and lamps. Some visitors are visibly moved. Groups on religious tours often break into carols or hymns. Below the little curtain-fringed Altar of the Nativity, a large silver star overhung with lamps supposedly marks the exact spot on which Mary gave birth, though the position was chosen only in the 17th century. Across from the altar, three steps lead into the **Chapel of the Manger▶**, where Mary is said to have placed her newborn baby. The Grotto, a Greek Orthodox possession, is part of a labyrinth containing altars, chapels and the tomb of St Jerome, with separate access from the Catholic side. To the right of the Grotto is the Greek Orthodox Monastery, and to the left the pleasant 19th-century Franciscan **Church of St Catherine▶**.

The other sights Leading off Manger Square, Milk Grotto Street passes **Chapel of the Milk▶**, where, some believe, Mary spilt some milk while breast-feeding Jesus, turning the ground white. Running parallel, Shepherds' Street leads out of town to the cultivated **Field of Boaz▶▶**, where Ruth gathered the gleanings left by her future husband (Ruth 2), and beyond (2km) to the walled **Shepherds' Fields▶**, now an olive grove. A small cave in the centre has become the **Grotto of the Shepherds▶**, a shrine believed – without much reason – to be the very place where the 'shepherds watched their flocks by night'. Some 10km further south, **Herodion▶▶▶** is the well-kept remnant of Herod's majestic hilltop palace (see panel, page 213).

Out of Bethlehem on the Jerusalem side, **Rachel's Tomb▶** is an old-established place of prayer for the Jews. A large tomb here, shrouded in cloth, is supposed to cover the grave of the matriarch, second wife of Jacob. Beware of youths stoning cars on the way to all of these out-of-town sites.

► **Hebron (Hebrew: Hevron;**
Arabic El Khalil) *206B1*

Be careful if you intend to visit this notorious troublespot, a town with a large population (70,000) and a devout Islamic centre with a tradition of violence (see page 209 for advice on travelling in West Bank trouble spots). Hebron is a harsh town without warmth, bars or theatres, but it does have a powerful, fervent atmosphere. Among the world's oldest cities, occupied continuously since Canaanite times, this is also one of the four Jewish holy cities. It was here, as Genesis details, that Abraham made his covenant with God, here that Abraham and Sarah, Isaac and Rebecca, Jacob and Leah, founders of the Jewish nation, lived, died and were buried. Here David was anointed Saul's successor as King of the Jews; he made Hebron his capital before Jerusalem. As a national shrine, the town has been vitally important ever since. The Bible also calls the town Kiryat Arba, and that is the name of the heavily defended, tough-minded new Jewish district (population 5,000) which replaced the old and peaceful Jewish quarter (population 700), emptied by Arab rioters in the horrific 1929 massacre and demolished during the Jordanian occupation.

Sights The town is dominated by the fortress-like structure (largely 13th- and 14th-century, but with Herodian elements dating to 20 BC) built over the **Cave of Machpela►►►**, or Tomb of the Patriarchs (in Arabic: Haram el Khalil – literally 'Tomb of the Friend'), the tense, divided shrine where Jews and Arabs both pray. It stands on the south side of town, not far from the busy *souk*. The cave itself is sealed; 9th- and 14th-century cenotaphs in the building and courtyard are said to stand above the graves of Abraham and Sarah. Koranic script decorates the walls. The shrine has been a synagogue, a mosque and a church before reverting to the Muslims, who from 1267 to 1967 banned Jews from entering. The Yitzhak (or Isaac) Hall is still reserved for Muslims, and a synagogue has been placed between the cenotaphs of Abraham and Sarah. It is quite probable that this really is the site of their graves. Less plausible is the popular idea that Adam and Eve are also buried in the cave: Adam's footprint, Abraham's oak tree, and other doubtful tombs and relics, are among the town's sights.

215

Massacre in Hebron
Hebron had an almost unbroken Jewish presence for thousands of years up to August 1929, when Arabs besieged the Jewish quarter, killing 67 people and forcing the rest to abandon their homes. After the 1967 Six Day War a group of Jews returned and created the new Kiryat Arba district. In May 1980, as a group of Jewish students came out of the Cave of Machpela , Arabs opened fire on them, killing six and wounding 17. In 1993 and 1994, following the Israel-PLO accord, there were numerous attacks on Jews in the Hebron area. In February 1994 a Jewish doctor, Baruch Goldstein – previously considered a dutiful servant of both communities – walked into the Isaac Hall at the Cave of Machpela and opened fire on the Arabs praying there, killing 29.

Hebron's atmospheric
souk *(market)*

The walls of Jericho come tumbling down

Crossing into Jericho
The PLO-Israel accord was held up for months by the PLO's insistence that it should have its own border checkpoint on the Jericho road. Despite this, most travellers approaching the 'frontier' of Jericho's autonomous area are simply waved by without so much as a glance at their documents. About 3km before reaching the Palestinian line, near the turning for Yered Yeriho, an IDF (Israeli Army) check-point adopts a similarly low-key attitude.

Knot window from Hisham's Palace

▶▶   **Jericho (Hebrew: Yericho; Arabic: Er Riha)**   *206C3*

The lowest town in the world (250m below sea level), and the oldest, Jericho has a shabby charm, a relatively calm atmosphere, lots of places to eat and a striking abundance of greenery and flowers. It's the main centre of Palestinian administration on the West Bank, and was the first town to become autonomous.

History The 'oldest town' claims do not really apply to present-day Jericho – only the *tel* (settlement mound) on the northern boundary is ancient. This was, the Bible vividly records, the first town in the Promised Land taken by the Israelites under the command of Joshua. Following God's instructions, Joshua encircled the city; when the priests blew their trumpets, the walls came tumbling down. He then cursed the city and any man that would rebuild it. All this and more is told in ripping style in the Book of Joshua. The curse was not taken too seriously by his fellow Israelites, who immediately rebuilt Jericho as a Jewish city, and this – despite a succession of foreign rulers – is how it remained, with a few breaks, right through the millennia up to the Arab conquest in the 7th century AD, though its location varied slightly.

Jericho makes numerous other appearances in the Bible, and its life seems to have been entwined with that of Jerusalem: Temple priests had homes here, and it was said that trumpets blown at the Temple could be heard in Jericho, 36km away. In 30 BC, the city became the personal possession of King Herod, who enlarged and aggrandised it, building a winter palace here. It was the Herodian city that Jesus knew, and to which he came prior to the Crucifixion.

Herod's city was virtually destroyed by the Romans during the Second Jewish Revolt, but reappeared in its present site under the Byzantines. Arabs took control in AD 638, then the Crusaders, who were driven out in 1147. The town then dwindled away; at the British takeover it had a population under 3,000. This changed dramatically in 1948, when 70,000 Arabs, fleeing from the new State of Israel, settled here in refugee camps. After 1967 they came under Israeli rule and again fled, this time to Jordan, but in 1994, under the gaze of the world's TV cameras, Jericho became the first independent Palestinian city on the West Bank. So far, tourists are as welcome and safe as before.

Sights Most things worth seeing lie north of modern Jericho. Start at the beginnings of history with **Tel Yeriho▶▶**, where 23 layers of civilisation have been found, dating back to 8000 BC. The whole of the mighty encircling defences of Canaanite times has been excavated, together with traces of the rampart which fell at the sound of Joshua's trumpet blast. Despite its importance, however, the *tel* does not convey a great deal to the layman. At its foot, and across the road, **Elisha's Spring** (Nahal Elisha), also known as Sultan's Spring (Ein es-Sultan), provides the abundant fresh waters which have given the area its greenery and fertility. Close by, in a private house, ruins of an **Ancient Synagogue▶▶** have a lovely 6th-century patterned mosaic floor including a *menorah* (candelabrum) and the inscription 'Peace on Israel'.

Some 500m east, the ruined **Hisham's Palace▶▶** was probably built by Caliph Hisham of Damascus as a winter palace in 743; just four years later it collapsed in an earthquake. Even so, much survives, including massive columns, a sumptuous bath house, exquisite mosaics and delicate stonework. Some 2km further north, the **Mount of Temptation▶** is where Orthodox churches claim (without the least evidence) that Jesus was 'led into the wilderness to be tempted of the devil' (Matthew 4: 1–11) after his baptism. An impressive Greek monastery hangs on to its barren, rocky slope. West of town, at the start of Wadi Qelt, are the ruins of **Herod's Palace▶**, where Herod entertained during the winter months and occasionally got up to darker deeds: it was here, for example, that he murdered his 18-year-old brother-in-law, drowning him in the swimming pool.

Jesus' baptism
The River Jordan east of Jericho is where Jesus was baptised by John, according to Matthew's gospel. The reputed site (chosen by Byzantines), though signposted, has remained closed for a number of years. However, a visit is possible for members of the Greek Orthodox church at Epiphany (January), and for Roman Catholics on the third Thursday in October. The Christian Information Centre at Jaffa Gate, Jerusalem, has more details.

217

This harsh desert is typical Judean terrain

JUDAEA AND SAMARIA (THE WEST BANK)

The Samaritans

A tribe and sect descended from the tribes of Ephraim and Menasseh, which broke away from mainstream Judaism around 400 BC, the Samaritans hold that only the Torah (the first five biblical books) is sacred, rejecting all subsequent oral and rabbinic law. In that respect they resemble the Karaites. However, the Samaritan Torah contains variations from the Jewish text, including its own version of the Ten Commandments, one of which requires God's followers to build his sanctuary on Mount Gerizim. Samaritans say the original holy scriptures were altered by Ezra, for which there is some historical evidence. There are no lay teachers, and all ritual remains in the hands of the hereditary priests and Levites (assistants to the priests). Savagely persecuted by Romans, Jews, Muslims and Christians, Samaritans today number only about 600, all living at either Holon or Nablus.

Palestinian post

In 1994, the Palestinian Authority issued its first postage stamps, initially priced in the British Mandate currency of Mils, then overstamped in Jordanian currency of Fils. Significantly, the Palestinian stamps depicted locations which had not been transfered to Palestinian rule, including the Temple Mount and the Tower of David, in Jerusalem.

► ►   **Latrun**   *206A3*

This monastery, fort, wooded park and ruined village is located on the main highway, midway between Jerusalem and Tel Aviv, overlooking the Ayalon Valley. It sits in a corner of land that saw some of the worst fighting in 1948; many lives were lost as Jews struggled to keep the road to the capital open, and Arabs struggled to close it. The abandoned building on the hill above the road was the British police station which had previously overseen this troublespot and which, like many other British military emplacements and police stations, was handed over to the Arab Legion in 1948. The Ayalon Valley, now blooming with new settlements, has a long history as a battleground, not least when Joshua came this way and urged the sun and moon to remain still so as to prolong the day and give him more time to slaughter the Amorites; they obligingly did as he asked (Joshua 10: 12).

On the left-hand side of the road (as you come from Jerusalem), the attractive French **Trappist monastery►►►** of 1927 stands among its flourishing gardens and crops. It is open to visitors every day except Sunday. The monks produce good wine, spirits and olive oil (on sale by the entrance). Early Christian stonework can be seen in the monastery gardens. On top of the hill behind stand the ruins of a 12th-century **Crusader fort►**. To the right of the road is the ruined village of Amwas, known in the Bible as **Emmaus►**, where (according to the gospel of Luke) Jesus appeared to two disciples after the Resurrection. Here are the ruins of an old church, while above it are a monastery and the ruins of a Crusader-era basilica, erected on the site of a Roman villa. Here, too, the **Canada Park►** forest makes a pleasant place for a walk and a leisurely picnic.

► ►   **Mar Saba (St Sabas) Monastery**   *206B2*

The watchtower of this historic Greek Orthodox monastery lies at the end of a long road that passes through barren hills. West of it rises the sheer Kidron gorge, pockmarked with caves, in which a sect of hermits used to reside, each man in his own cavern. One of them, arriving here in AD 478, was a monk called Sabas, originally from Cappadocia. In 492 he founded the monastery on the slope opposite his cave, and became an influential figure, visiting the Emperor Justinian and persuading him to rebuild Bethlehem's Church of the Nativity. After his death, in 532, the monastery of St Sabas and the saint's grave both became popular places of pilgrimage.

In 614 the community was attacked by Persians and in 636 by Arabs, but adherents continued to arrive. One of them, in 712, was John of Damascus, who until then had been the representative of the Christians to the Ummayad rulers in Damascus. In the 12th century, Italian Crusaders stole the body of Sabas and took the remains to Italy (in 1838 Russians reconstructing the monastery also removed the remains of John of Damascus and took them to Moscow). In 1965, Sabas' relics were returned by the pope.

Only male visitors may enter the monastery; taken around by a monk, they are shown what is left of Sabas, along with the main church with its painted walls, the skulls of monks killed in the 7th century, and a fantastic view across the valley. Women have to make do with the Women's Tower on an adjacent hill – though there is another superb view from here.

▶▶ Mount Gerizim 206B4

The holy place of the Samaritans rises to 881m (2,890 feet) just south of Nablus and is reached from that city. The mountain gives glorious views over Nablus and the surrounding countryside. Below the summit are dwellings which the Samaritans use at Pessah (Passover), which they observe as a pilgrim festival, fulfilling to the letter the biblical injunctions concerning the sacrificial slaughter of sheep (at a ceremonial site just off the road). Samaritans believe that Abraham prepared to sacrifice Isaac on the same mountain.

Castles and robbers
The name Latrun has an odd history. For centuries Christians have held that it comes from the Latin *latro*, robber, and that this was the home of the 'Good Thief' crucified alongside Jesus. In fact Latrun is probably the Arabic form of the medieval French name, Le Toron des Chevaliers (Knights' Hill), so called because of the Crusader fortification built here in the 12th century. Later the fortress ruins became known as Castrum Boni Latronis (Castle of the Good Thief), compounding the confusion.

219

Surviving against the odds: the 5th-century Mar Saba monastery

Samaritan Israelis
Although Samaritans are not considered Jews, their relationship with Israel is a special one, and their religion is closely connected with Judaism. That is why the Israeli High Court has ruled that Samaritans have the right to become Israeli immigrants with full citizenship. The court was responding to a petition from Samaritans wanting to leave Nablus (on the West Bank) and live at Holon (near Tel Aviv), the other Samaritan population centre.

►   **Nablus (Hebrew: Shechem)**   *206B4*

Nablus is a beautifully located commercial and industrial town, the largest on the West Bank (population 75,000). It is also a passionate centre of Palestinian nationalism, with a recent history of violent unrest and political killing. This is a place to visit with the utmost care, after checking the current situation. Note that all the mosques and Islamic sites in the city, as well as all the hotels, are closed to non-Muslims.

Nablus is the successor to the biblical city of Shechem, demolished by the Romans in AD 70 and replaced in AD 72 by Neapolis, literally the 'New City'. Its name became corrupted to Nablus after the Arab conquest. The small **Samaritan quarter►** lies in the western part of town.

Just 2km southeast of Nablus, **Tel Balata►►** is the site of the original Shechem, the place where Abraham was told by God 'Unto thy seed will I give this land'. Here Abraham erected his first altar before heading further south. Returning from Mesopotamia, Jacob set up camp here. An unfinished Greek Orthodox church, on Crusader foundations, now encloses **Jacob's Well►►►**, set within an elaborate, arched chamber hung with lamps. This is probably the very same well dug by Jacob on land where he had pitched his tent outside Shechem (Genesis 33: 19). It is also the place where, according to a plausible account in John's gospel (4: 5–8), Jesus sat down to rest and chatted about life with a Samaritan woman. Just a few hundred metres north, a white dome covers the reputed **Tomb of Joseph►** (Joshua 24: 32), whose remains were brought here from Egypt. Formerly closed to non-Muslims, the shrine is now open to all.

▶▶ Qumran National Park 206C2

Though famous as the place where the Dead Sea Scrolls were found in 1947 (see page 222), Qumran's main interest, apart from its dramatic setting, is the mystery which surrounds this archaeological site, 20km south of Jericho. The ruins stand among the red desert rock, close to the Dead Sea. The building was constructed in 150 BC and destroyed in AD 70, and its stonework is well preserved, with several rooms still enclosed by high walls. Its watchtower gives an excellent overview of the site. The Scrolls were found in almost inaccessible caves in the adjacent hillsides. The mystery is that so little is known for sure about Qumran. Among scholars, theories and questions abound. Was it a community? There are no bedrooms. Just a library? There is a large cemetery. A military fortress, a religious retreat, a factory? Many of the Scrolls detail the practices and structure of a rule-bound community. The prevailing view is that this was a community of some 200 to 400 Essenes (see panel, page 223), and that they hid their writings in the caves to save them from the Romans.

▶▶ Sabastea 206B5

In 876 BC King Omri founded the hilltop city of Samaria, or Shomron (I Kings 16: 24). Capital of the Northern Kingdom, and notorious for abandoning Judaism in favour of Ba'al, it was destroyed in 721 BC by Persians, who built their own non-Jewish city here. Taken by successive conquerors, it was eventually left deserted. Today there is a small Arab village here and, just above it, the ruins of the ancient city. The finest of the ruins date from the Herodian period, when it was given an amphitheatre, temple and palace.

Ein Feshka
Beside this freshwater spring, some 5km from Qumran, are traces of other structures believed to be related to the Essene community. Today, the area around the spring is a small nature reserve with some unappetising water pools that are nevertheless popular for a cool dip.

Qumran's ruins continue to mystifiy scholars

Sinjil and Shiloh
Between Nablus and Ramallah is the village of Sinjil, named after St Gilles, a small town in southern France, ruled by Raymond, Count of Toulouse and St Gilles, who built the fortress here. On the other side of the road, a turning leads to the site of ancient Shiloh, where the Ark of the Covenant was housed in its Tabernacle during the early days of the Israelite conquest. From here the Ark was seized by the Philistines. Little survives from that period, though there are traces of an even older Canaanite temple, as well as some Byzantine mosaic floors.

The Dead Sea Scrolls

■ **In 1947, he didn't remember in which month, a Bedouin shepherd boy called Muhammad ed-Dhib scrambled into a cave near the (then unexcavated) site at Qumran and found strange-looking earthenware jars containing fragments of parchment and leather. It was to prove the most dramatic discovery of ancient Hebrew documents ever found.** ■

Now read on...
Scores of books have been written about the Dead Sea Scrolls, some sensational, some academic, some religious. For a balanced, intelligible overview, authoritative and academic yet accessible, read *The Dead Sea Scrolls – Qumran in Perspective* (Revised Edition), by Geza Vermes (SCM Press, London).

The caves (top) that held the Dead Sea scrolls and the jars (above) in which they were stored

What are the Scrolls? After the initial find, a dozen more Qumran caves yielded a vast hoard of ancient manuscripts in Hebrew, and occasionally in Aramaic, ranging from scraps to scrolls. Among them were two complete Books of Isaiah, parts of all the other Hebrew holy books (except for Esther), Books of the Apocrypha and Pseudepigraphia (both excluded from the Jewish Bible), and other non-biblical works such as the Books of Tobit, of Jubilees and of Enoch.

There were prophetic and visionary Jewish books not previously known, and biblical commentaries offering unfamiliar interpretations. The Temple Scroll described the Holy Temple in detail. The enigmatic Copper Scroll discusses hidden treasures. Perhaps most interesting, many scrolls – including at least one written in poetic form – spelled out the Qumran sect's customs and beliefs: the Community Rule (beliefs and rituals), Statutes (practices and laws in detail), the War Scroll (concerning the perpetual struggle between Good and Evil), and dozens more.

Important for Jews The discovery of the Scrolls, the oldest Hebrew texts ever found, revealed two complementary and contradictory things. First, that the Hebrew scriptures have remained essentially unchanged for at least 2,000 years; but second, that parts of the Bible existed in several versions. Some of the Scrolls resemble later Greek editions, some are like the Samaritan Torah, some contain the Masoretic text used today.

The Qumran scribes also worked on and from other scriptural writings, which have passed out of Jewish knowledge. Individual scribes felt free to 'reinterpret' or 'edit' texts, showing that they considered the scriptures a product of the human hand and human mind, albeit perhaps guided by God. Only after the destruction of the Temple did a group of Pharisee rabbis set the seal on a limited and censored body of holy literature, conforming to the Pharisee viewpoint, including a compilation of oral traditions, which they then declared to be the word of God. They thus created a unified, unchallengeable 'Orthodoxy' which has, arguably, served well as a survival mechanism during the Diaspora years.

Important for Christians At an early stage in the study of the Scrolls, excited attempts were made to read them as Christian documents. Some wanted to believe that Jesus was the Teacher of Righteousnesss mentioned in various scrolls, others that this was John the Baptist, or Jesus'

Professor Bieberkraut has devoted his life to conserving the scrolls

The Essenes

Much has been learned about the Essene sect from the contemporary Roman writer, Pliny, and from the Jewish writer, Josephus; both greatly admired their austerity, asceticism and firmness of purpose. The Essenes at Qumran (see page 221) were vegetarian, probably celibate, pre-occupied with a high degree of ritual purity, living communally but under a hierarchy with a Teacher of Righteousness at its head, and believing that they alone were the chosen, the 'Sons of Light', who would soon be led by the Messiah to victory over the 'Sons of Darkness'. They were vehemently opposed to the Hasmonean dynasty, to the Pharisees, the Saducees, the Romans, and to the Temple priests, whom they felt had betrayed and defiled the Temple. They revered the descendants of King David's High Priest Zadok as representing the pure line of the priesthood, supplanted by the Hasmoneans.

brother James. Several agreed that Paul was the Wicked Priest. None of these notions stood up to further study. Instead, it became clear that the Essenes – their ideas predating Jesus by a century or more – had many beliefs which reappeared in the New Testament. The hierarchical community devoted to religious study under a learned leader presaged the monastic and church system. The Essene idea of a Holy Spirit became part of Christian doctrine. Jesus' celibacy and his emphasis on sharing and communality – all these echoed Essene dogma.

Essenes practised baptism to symbolise a new beginning in religious awareness, just as did Jesus' hero and mentor, John the Baptist. Miracle cures, associated with forgiveness of sins were well-known among the Scroll writers. One of the Scrolls, the Prayer of Nabonidus (set in the 6th century BC) is about just such a cure. To this extent, the Scrolls show that Jesus' ideas were not new. It is interesting, too, that the New Testament reviles all the other Jewish groups but makes no mention of the Essenes. But Jesus himself was no Essene. Their rigid, structured and exclusive community prepared itself for the end of days, while Jesus opened his arms to the common people and a new age.

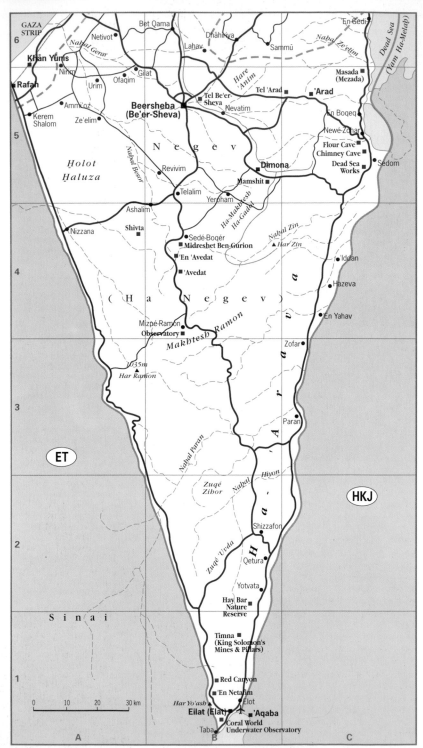

Scorched rock eroded by wind-blown sands

The South More than half of Israel is desert, including the whole of the southern half of the country, which is taken up with an awesome expanse of scorched rock and raw, naked mountains scored by bone-dry valleys. This is the Negev, picturebook desert, where the harsh dryness, consuming heat and intense light can thrill you – or kill you. Anyone exploring off the beaten track here, or even stepping out of their car for a quick look around in some desert location, will realise within seconds that it is vital to take precautions.

Life Yet the Negev is no sterile, lifeless zone. This part of Israel has its tough and resilient flora and fauna, and it has, too, a human history. Nations have thrived in the Negev, nourished by a body of practical knowledge – of how man can live in such an environment – that has been all but lost. Three thousand years ago, Nabatean trade routes ran through the Negev between the ports at Gaza and Eilat and the Nabatean capital at Petra, in what is now Jordan. Camel trains carried perfumes and goods of all types, many imported from Europe.

The Nabateans built caravanserais, even small towns such as Avdat, in the midst of this empty land. Water cisterns were placed at the foot of flood valleys to catch the run-off after rare desert rains. It has been estimated that a Nabatean settlement collected enough rain in half an hour to provide water for three years. The Romans, conquering Palestine, took over the Nabatean settlements, fortified and enlarged them. Following the Arab conquest, civilisation disappeared, leaving only the nomadic, pastoral Bedouin as the last people of the desert – until, a thousand years later, Jewish kibbutzniks arrived.

The serenity of the desert at dawn

Desert cities
Despite annual rainfall levels of less than 200mm a year, five Nabatean cities once thrived in the Negev. Taken over by the Romans and later occupied by Byzantines they continued to prosper right up to the Arab conquest in the 7th century, when four were destroyed. The fifth, Shivta, was occupied by the Arabs but abandoned two centuries later. Known as the Negev Pentapolis, the five desert cities were Avdat, Kalutza, Nitzana, Mamshit and Shivta.

Landscape The Negev, merely a region within a much larger arid desert zone reaching into Jordan, Egypt and Saudi Arabia, is a hard land consisting mainly of bare granite mountains and dry valleys scattered with sand or stones, the rockfaces streaked through with shades of red, yellow, purple and even stark black and white. Visually, it is highly dramatic. On the map, the Negev forms a vast upside-down triangle, its point at Eilat on the Red Sea, its base running across Israel from Gaza to the Dead Sea. On its eastern edge, the Dead Sea and the Arava rift valley score a deep frontier between Israel and Jordan. The rather arbitrary border with Egypt's Sinai desert marks the western side. The flatter Arava, where the main road links Eilat to the rest of Israel, is less interesting than the mountainous interior.

Leisure There is a tremendous amount to see, learn, explore and experience in the Negev – this is Israel's vast, natural adventure playground. Hiking, birdwatching, climbing, riding, jeep tours and camel tours – even sight-seeing – are excitingly different in this terrain. Although even a quick glimpse can be intriguing, you need something more than the usual brief tour taken by every visitor to Eilat to get the best of it. Far more rewarding is to stay in the heart of the desert itself – for example at Mizpe-Ramon, or at a Dead Sea spa resort, such as the lovely Kibbutz Ein Gedi. Remarkably, there is plenty to see in the Negev, including Roman and Nabatean ruins, and a reserve for rare desert animals, such as oryx and addax.

The future It is an old Zionist dream that towns will prosper in the midst of the Negev. Several kibbutzim shock the eye with their lush fields lying like vivid green rugs on the rocky desert floor. So far, though, attempts to break and harness the spirit of the Negev have met with only limited success. Some Israelis want to keep it that way. Others would like to see the whole place green and cultivated. Inevitably, some parts of the Negev will be developed. Water conservation will be advanced so that small towns, industry and agriculture can indeed flourish here, but this vast area of heat and rock will never be tamed, never lose its haunting spirit.

▶▶ **Arad**   *224C5*

Arad, the town nearest to the Dead Sea, was founded in
1962 as a base for scientists working in connection with
Dead Sea industries, and for archaeologists engaged in
researching desert and Dead Sea sites. The thriving new
town has also attracted a lot of medical staff because of
the allergy and asthma treatment that goes on here, as
well as university people from Beersheva who like living
in modern and civilised Arad. In addition, the WUJS
(World Union of Jewish Students) is based here, bringing
students engaged in Jewish studies.

The town perches on the hilly ridge just west of the
Dead Sea. Immediately noticeable is the remarkable and
tangible cleanliness of the air (despite mineral industries
on one edge). Neither is there any pollen at all – local
authorities control all planting in the area – so the place is
a boon for asthmatics. The Margoa Arad Hotel has a clinic
catering specifically for them.

For visitors, Arad makes an ideal base for touring the
northern Negev, the Dead Sea and the wild Judaean hills.
The **Visitor Information Centre** is well informed on local
antiquities and desert walks. Next door, the **Arad
Museum▶** displays collections of finds from nearby **Tel
Arad▶** (see page 250). Round the edge of the town are
several Bedouin encampments where, despite the
unrelieved aridity of the area, sheep and goats are somehow grazed. The Bedouin, who have very good relations
with the locals, find casual work in the town.

Arad Festival
Arad's usual peace and
quiet are broken in July for
the huge neo-hippy and
hippy-revival rockfest
lasting non-stop for four
days and four nights. About
200,000 visitors (most aged
under 20) gather for round-
the-clock Israeli rock and
folk music during which
some 120 performances
are staged in the town or
under the desert stars at
nearby Masada.

Opening times
Opening times differ slightly
from those in the north, and
many sites remain open on
the sabbath. Museums and
attractions in the south are
usually open 8:30–4:30, with
slightly shorter hours on Fri
and Sat.

227

▶▶ **Avdat National Park**   *224B4*

The walled, ruined desert city of Avdat stands on a rocky
ridge of high ground just off the main Negev interior road
(Route 40), 65km from Beersheva. Constructed in 300 BC
by the Nabateans (who called it Obodas, after a
king they worshipped as a god), it flourished
under Roman and Byzantine rule, but – having
become a Christian settlement – was
abandoned at the time of the Arab conquest
in the 7th century. The town has survived
remarkably well, and has benefited from
sensitive and intelligent restoration. It
retains superb relics from each period in its
history, especially from the Roman era, with
remnants of streets, dwellings, water cisterns,
houses, a Roman bath, temples, basements
and wine cellars. Its irrigation system was
studied by the Israelis in 1948, and successfully
copied at new Negev settlements.

*Byzantine frieze,
Avdat*

*Avdat's rock-cut wine
cellars and
basements*

Abraham founds Beersheba
'And Abraham planted a tamarisk tree in Beersheba, and called there on the name of the Lord, the Everlasting God.'
– Genesis 21: 33

The Negev Museum, Beersheva

Abraham's well probably dates from the Turkish period

► ◄◄◄ **Beersheva** *224B5*

The capital of the Negev stands on the desert's flat northern edge, where irrigation and water conservation have dramatically reduced the aridity. The town's picturesque Turkish old quarter still has a slightly rough and ready, dusty look. However, the sprawling newer neighbourhoods around the town, which has mushroomed in the last 10 years and continues to grow rapidly (current population: 125,000), are fresh and modern, if less atmospheric. There is also a university and a desert research centre.

The town's roots run deep into the pages of the Bible. Cave dwellings of 4000 BC and an Israelite town of 1100 BC have been found 4km east at **Tel Sheva►**, which has a museum at the site. The patriarch Abraham settled at Beersheva and purchased a well for the price of seven lambs (*be'er sheva* means both 'well of seven' and 'well of the oath'). Here he was called by God to sacrifice his son Isaac, and here he drove out the Egyptian maidservant, Hagar, with his other son Ishmael, who grew up in the desert and married an Egyptian (Genesis 21 and 22). In the next generation, Jacob left Beersheva on his own journey to Egypt. Later, Beersheva was named the southern limit of the Land of Israel (Judges 20: 1).

The **Old City►►►** dates only from 1907, when the Ottoman Turks revived the town as a Bedouin market. After 1948, the toughest type of Jewish settlers were drawn to the place and developed it. Today it is an attractive area of the city, with pedestrian streets and pavement cafés. The Old City runs to **Abraham's Well►**, an Ottoman invention with no known connection to Abraham, despite what visitors are told. In a former mosque off the main HaAtzmaut Street, the **Negev Museum►►** displays artefacts from the town's prehistoric origins.

The town's most interesting feature is the continuing Bedouin presence. However, the **Bedouin market►►**, held every Thursday, has been marred by tourism and modernisation. Permanent **Bedouin encampments►►** can be seen south of the town: big, dark tents among which human beings, camels and dogs go about their business together under the desert sky.

■ Abraham was a nomadic pastoralist. To understand something of his way of life, and that of the other patriarchs, take a look at the Bedouin who still wander through the harsh desert scenery, far from food or water and accompanied only by a herd of animals who somehow find enough pasture to survive. ■

Tribal lands Just as the people of Israel comprised 12 tribes, so too are the Bedouin divided into several tribal sub-groups, each with its own territory. In 1946, when the British created the Kingdom of Trans-Jordan (now Jordan) almost 40 per cent of its population were described as Bedouin. A report of that year stated: 'There are constant seasonal migrations of the Bedouin from Trans-Jordan into Palestine, from Arabia into Trans-Jordan, and back again'. The Bedouin are true native inhabitants of these uncultivated regions, former pagans who embraced Islam when it arrived in the 7th century.

Lifestyle Like Abraham, the 'nomadic' Bedouin do not in fact wander constantly. They have home ground and they have seasonal territories in which they pasture their herds of sheep, goat and camels. They move according to the seasons and the needs of their animals. Like Abraham, they live in spacious, makeshift tents, in extended family groups. They are subject to their own tribal laws, enforced by their tribal sheik (chief), which the state recognises as valid for minor disputes.

The future The official Israeli view of the Bedouin is that they should be housed in modern well-equipped dwellings as soon as possible, and offered tempting alternatives to the ancient but insalubrious nomadic lifestyle. New Bedouin small towns and neighbourhoods have thus come into existence. At the same time, Bedouin culture is changing spontaneously, for many tribes have started to erect their own stone dwellings for more permanent habitation on the desert margins. However, the nomadic way of life is enduring and adaptable. It is unlikely that the Bedouin will be persuaded to abandon it altogether.

Bedouin Israelis
Most Bedouin consider it in their interests to support the State of Israel. They distinguished themselves during the War of Independence, and assisted the army in later wartime desert operations against neighbouring Arab states.

229

Above: settling down for the night
Left: preparing to move on

Pillars of salt

Floating free

The depths
At 398m below true sea level, the shores of the Dead Sea are as low as you can get on the surface of the earth. It is said that the additional 400m or so of atmosphere filters out enough ultra-violet radiation to help prevent sunburn – but it is not worth running the risk of exposing yourself unnecessarily to find out whether this is true.

▶▶▶ **The Dead Sea**
(Hebrew: Yam HaMelach)   *224C6*

Dramatic rocky desert surrounds this blue lake, the saltiest on earth, and located at the lowest point on earth, at nearly 400m below sea level. It is so salty that the human body floats like a cork and you can sit in the water reading a newspaper. Try it – almost everybody else does!

The saltiest The Hebrew name means Salt Sea, and it is the high level of salts – nearly 10 times the proportion in the Mediterranean – that makes it the Dead Sea: life is impossible in these weird waters. The Jordan trickles down from the Galilee to the Dead Sea, and gets no further. The water evaporates, leaving minerals behind. The process has been going on for countless millennia, so the concentration of salt is greater than ever.

At its southern tip, mushroom-like excretions of minerals have formed a bizarre white landscape. This 'salt' is not the table condiment variety, but is composed of a mass of minerals. Saltpans in the south draw off magnesium, potassium and sulphates for a multi-million dollar industry. In this same location, the biblical cities of Sodom and Gomorrah, synonymous with moral decadence, were located. According to Genesis, when God determined to destroy them, he first allowed Lot to flee with his wife, but she looked back with regret, and was turned into a pillar of salt.

The healthiest The mineral-rich waters, together with hot springs, have given rise to a number of thriving spa resorts. These are nothing new: Cleopatra, Herod and Solomon all visited the Dead Sea for a cure. Their naturally warm waters are a proven help in the treatment of skin and rheumatic problems. It is claimed that the water is beneficial even to healthy skin. Be careful, though, when taking a dip: the salts are painful to the eyes and the mucous membranes, including lips and nostrils. After bathing, the skin feels oily and sticky. Unless you are on a cure, it is far more enjoyable to swim in a hotel pool. As a

bonus, this arid zone is almost totally pollen-free – a boon for people with hay-fever or respiratory complaints.

South to north Measuring 76km from tip to tip, and never more than 16km across, half of the Dead Sea's western shore is in Israel's Negev region and half in Judaea. The eastern shore is in Jordan. At the southern tip, erstwhile Sodom has been reborn in different guise as **Sedom**, centre of the mineral extraction industry. The bleak little hot-springs spa resort of **Zohar►** stands on the shore just up the road. From here an empty, uninhabited coast road clings to the shore, with a salty desert plain (formerly under water) and mountains to the left. **Ein Bokek►** is another small, and not very appealing, waterside spa resort with a couple of hotels and a beach. Beyond the **Masada►►►** turning (see page 242) there is **Ein Gedi spa►**, a curious concrete and glass structure in the middle of nowhere, and, a little further, **Ein Gedi►►**, a waterside bathing area.

Above it, **Ein Gedi kibbutz►►►**, set up in the 1950s by the children of concentration camp survivors in the harshest environment they could find, is now a comfortable and prosperous community. It has a popular 'inn', consisting of terraces of small, simple bedrooms in basic blocks scattered about the attractive grounds. The self-service restaurant is of good standard. Most guests are here on spa cures. Ein Gedi's fantastic setting, and its amazing achievement, the lush florid greenery of the kibbutz bursting from a hillside of barren red desert rock overlooking the Dead Sea, make it a remarkable place to stay. Below Ein Gedi, the **Nahal Arugot►►** and phenomenal **Nahal David►►►** Nature Reserve both consist of desert gulleys with footpaths running alongside their seasonal river beds (see side panel).

Beyond here, the road crosses into Judaea, and while the scene changes little, there are no further developments or interesting sights on the road until the area of **Qumran►►** (see page 221), close to the northern end of the Dead Sea.

Nahal David
In this nature reserve, a footpath follows the narrow *nahal* (seasonal watercourse), which flows with water and bursts with lush greenery, in contrast to the barren rocky cliffs either side. After some 20 minutes the path reaches a lovely waterfall splashing down from high rocks. Turn back here, or take a steeper path to the top of the waterfall, which emerges from a spring, close to which there is a cavern, called Lovers' Cave, and some ancient temple ruins. For a longer walk, leaving most other visitors behind, continue up the *nahal* past two more springs, and into the desert canyon beyond. A marked path in the 'dry canyon' takes all day to complete; above the springs can be moist and even muddy underfoot, and winter can bring flash floods. Several animal species thrive in the reserve: little hyrax (or rock rabbits) dash across the path, and there is an ibex observation point. Wild leopard live in the western part of the reserve, but are rarely seen.

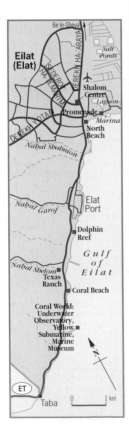

Dolphin Reef

Eilat (Elat)

Be'ér-Sheva
Salt Ponds
DEREKH HA-'ARAVAY
Shalom Centre
Lagoon
Promenade
Marina
North Beach
Naḥal Shaḥmon
Naḥal Garof
Elat Port
Dolphin Reef
Gulf of Eilat
Naḥal Shelom
Texas Ranch
Coral Beach
Coral World: Underwater Observatory, Yellow Submarine, Marine Museum
ET
Taba
0   1 km

► ► ► **Eilat**   *224B1*

The location of Eilat (pronounced Eh-lat, with the stress on the second syllable) is what makes it so special. Jagged rose-tinted mountains rise up on three sides, forming ridge after ridge of barren rock fading back into scorched wilderness. In front lies the sea, reflecting those red peaks under a blue sky like shimmering silk. The desert air is warm and dry and visitors experience a sense of immense space, of enormous distances. Eilat feels like a land apart, separated from the rest of Israel not just by the Negev desert, or by time and distance, but by attitude. It is racy, alive, with a taste for pleasure and action. This southern outpost was for years a rough sort of place with a Wild West feel to it. Even though Eilat long ago turned over a new leaf and became a civilised beach resort with a whole string of high-quality hotels, the old pioneering spirit and taste for adventure linger in the atmosphere and even in the look of the town. Even so, Eilat is not as new as it looks. It even gets a mention in the earliest books of the Bible, for Moses paused here with the Children of Israel when they were wandering in search of the Promised Land. They arrived here, but soon moved on again. Maybe that is why almost everything is open on the sabbath: Eilat must be just about the least religious town in the whole of Israel.

The town centre The heart of Eilat remains surprisingly small and undeveloped, with something of a 'settlement' look: even indoor shopping precincts, such as the **Shalom Centre►►** do not rival those in other Israeli towns. In front of it there is a plaza with dozens of café tables. Mingling with the locals you will still see a few tough, tanned outdoor types – some have driven in from desert kibbutzim. To discover the finer things in life, look in the hotels and in the beach areas, a little separated from the rest of town.

North Beach Within easy walking distance of the town centre, Eilat's main holiday district is **North Beach►►►**, which runs along the tip of the warm Gulf of Eilat (or Gulf of Akaba). The beach is of mixed sand and pebble, lined by palm and tamarisk trees, bars and water-sports rental shops. Running alongside is a very pleasant paved promenade, lined for most of its length by good restaurants. North Beach ends at the **Marina and lagoon►►►**, where a hump-backed pedestrian bridge crosses the water to another agreeable promenade area, which turns to follow the lagoon waterside, with shops and eateries alongside. Most of Eilat's leading and popular hotels are clustered around here. On the seafront beyond North Beach, the two **New Lagoons►►►** include a swimming lagoon with beaches, while the **Royal Promenade►►►** pushes the resort eastward towards the Jordan border, via the smart Royal Beach and Dan hotels.

Coral Beach To find Eilat's marine nature reserve, drive out of town and down the Taba road, following the western shore of the Gulf. After five minutes, just past the port where thousands of imported Japanese cars await collection (the port itself is an eyesore, but plays a vital role in Israel's trade with the east), is **Dolphin Reef►►►**, a delightful pay-to-enter sand and pebble bay with a good, relaxing beach bar-restaurant, and a couple of big open-air enclosures within the sea where you can swim with dolphins. If you prefer, you can watch from floating pontoons as the endearing dolphins – as well as sea-lions and turtles – play and frolic in the water. Further

> **Petra and Aqaba**
> With the opening of Eilat's Arava border-crossing into Jordan, Petra makes a superb excursion. The amazing desert capital of the Nabateans, with its temples, treasury, tombs, amphitheatre and monastery all cut out of the pink sandstone cliffs can be visited with an overnight stop. Allow time to linger in Aqaba, Eilat's unassuming neighbour on the Red Sea shore, and an entirely non-touristic Arabian town. Inclusive trips from Eilat are bookable through all hotels and cost (with a stopover in Jordan) upwards of US$165 per person.

Competing attractions

Bring the children to Texas Ranch

Coral Beach gives access to the under-water coral reserve

down the road, on the right, is the **Texas Ranch▶**, a mock Wild West town which children might enjoy.

A couple of hundred metres south, the pay-to-enter **Coral Beach▶▶▶** and its offshore waters form an unusual and important nature reserve, a magnificent underwater garden of coral and warm-water fish (see page 236). This is one of the world's leading sites for diving, and a visitors' centre on the beach is geared up to deal with divers' needs. Marked 'paths' under the water lead around the coral reef.

At the southern end of Coral Beach is **Coral World▶▶▶**, the major Eilat attraction. This comes in several sections, with a recommended route indicated by directional arrows. First come the large and impressive

aquariums, including the circular Reef Tank, which visitors view from the middle, and the Shark Pool. An outdoor pool contains turtles and rays. The walkway then reaches the superb **Underwater Observatory▶▶▶**. This is no ordinary tourist attraction, and should not be missed: spiral steps descend to viewing areas where you can literally walk around under the sea, peering through thick windows at a seabed heaving and moving with strange life-forms, like a bizarre jungle. There are no barriers or nets to keep the fish in: what you see is really living out there. The Observatory also rises high above the waves, giving magnificent views across the gulf to the red mountains of Jordan and Saudi Arabia.

Also available at the Observatory, for an additional fee, is a trip in the **Yellow Submarine▶▶**, called *Jacqueline*. This takes visitors on a one-hour journey beneath the Red Sea, giving a close view of the exotic underwater world. The 23m-long, 3m-wide submarine descends to a depth of 60m, then gradually climbs to 30m beside the coral reef wall. Passengers must check in 45 minutes before boarding to allow time for a thorough security procedure. The submarine tours run daily (except Sun) from 9am.

Finally walk through the intriguing **Marine Museum▶** for a closer look at some of the species that live here.

Taba The coast road continues from Eilat to the Egyptian frontier, established here in 1989 after a long dispute about its exact location. The beach along this stretch is poor, and the location bleak, though the views are dramatic. Just before the crossing, the Princess Hotel is one of Eilat's most remarkable resort complexes; its dining room has a huge glass wall almost touching the desert mountainside.

Crossing the border is a nuisance and can be time-consuming, with queues of backpackers and the usual careful security procedures. On the other side is the Hilton Hotel, one of Eilat's best, constructed when Taba was in Israeli hands. It has a private beach, and hotel guests have special arrangements to speed up the border crossing.

View the creatures of the deep by submarine or underwater observatory

Israeli folklore
Since Israel is hardly a half-century old, its 'folklore' is necessarily something of a recent invention, but simple traditional Jewish dances and shows based upon Jewish popular themes and customs are a popular entertainment. The weekly Israeli Folklore Evening at Kibbutz Eilot, 3km from town, makes a good night out. It is held every Saturday evening, and the price includes a typical kibbutz buffet dinner, free drinks, and transportation from Eilat to the kibbutz, as well as a singing-and-dancing extravaganza under the desert stars.

■ **The greatest treasure of Eilat is the water itself. Beneath its surface lies a whole spectacular world of colour and coral, home to thousands of exotic fish, coloured like rainbow fragments. For a closer encounter, dive in: the water is gorgeously warm (constantly around 20°C). No wonder this is the world capital for scuba and snorkelling enthusiasts.** ■

Marine reserve
Coral Beach is managed by Israel's Nature Reserves Authority. The area was studied over a period of years following the creation of the State of Israel, and declared a nature reserve in 1964.

236

Dali-esque fish drift among the vividly coloured foliage. Tiny silver shoals like iron filings dart past as if towards a magnet. There are fish with pink dots, blue stripes, yellow patches, and long feathery spikes. Is that a plant, a fish, or just a stone lying on the bottom? Seemingly all three, and it is called a stone fish. Whether for experts, amateurs or complete novices, diving at Eilat is a remarkable experience, and one not to be missed.

The reserve The Gulf of Eilat (or Akaba), part of the Red Sea, is one of the most northerly extensions of tropical seawater, and the Eilat coral reef is the most northerly in the world. Starting just below the surface of the warm, lapping waters, the coral reef is 1,200m in length, reaches to within 10m of the high-tide line and drops 6m to the sea bed at its furthest edge. The reserve extends out from this point on to the densely populated sea bed where thousands of species of tropical fish and sea animals can be seen.

Sea life The surface of a coral reef is a mass of living animals (mainly stony corals), while the rest consists of fossilised or dead corals from previous generations. The corals live for hundreds of years, growing at an incredibly slow rate, as they expand the existing colony or create new ones. Living among the hard corals are several species of soft coral, looking

Eilat's coral reefs throng with colourful fish

like brightly coloured seaweeds, their delicate tendrils waving to and fro.

Pretty as they are, corals can be dangerous, and it is best to avoid being scratched by them. One variety called fire coral (not a true coral but a similar lifeform) gives a burning sting that marks the skin. Sharing the sea bed with the corals are weird molluscs and other invertebrates such as giant clams and sea anemones. Other plant-like animals move around at night, including the sea lilies, sea urchins and different kinds of starfish which

Scuba hire

Scuba equipment can be hired from several firms in Eilat, mostly along the Coral Beach area. The tourist office and most hotels have the names of diving hire companies.

Warning

Wear sneakers or plastic shoes in the water. Swim, don't walk, except where indicated on marked pathways. Don't touch anything at all underwater, whether it seems to be a plant, fish, animal or rock. Some of these are in fact highly venomous creatures whose poison can injure or kill.

Diving at Eilat (left) leads to close encounters with Dali-esque fish (below)

hide during the day. Day and night, the coral throngs with dazzlingly coloured fish. Pretty damsels and clowns, butterflies and parrots, blues and cleaners can be seen during the day, while darkness brings out the uglier, highly poisonous varieties, such as the lion, scorpion and stone fish. Most coral-dwelling fish are exceptionally thin, enabling them to slip in and out of the coral construction.

Snorkel and scuba It is possible to get a good look at all these creatures without even getting wet, either from the Underwater Observatory (see page 235), or on a glass-bottomed boat tour. For a closer, more rewarding encounter, get in the water at the Coral Beach marine reserve (see page 234), one of the best places anywhere in the world for diving. If you want to scuba dive, bring your licence and log book to hire equipment locally. If you want to learn scuba, just bring a medical certificate.

Desert walks and drives

■ **The Negev is no theme park. This is raw and dangerous wilderness, yet majestic and beautiful. No visit to southern Israel would be complete without an off-road excursion into this haunting rocky terrain. The best introduction is by means of a guided tour in a 4-wheel-drive jeep (in the tourism jargon, these desert tours and excursions are always referred to as 'safaris').** ■

Walking ideas
Experienced hikers thinking of tackling a short outing in the southern Negev should ask the tourist office for their free booklet *Routes and Trails in Eilat Mountains*.

If you are hungry for something challenging, rest assured that an all-day trip into the desert, even with a group and a guide, will be something to remember. The vehicles do not offer pampered luxury: mostly the ride is rough, with a certain amount of clinging on for dear life. As if that were not enough, there are two-day, even three-day trips, with nights spent under the stars. Trips on horseback, or even by camel, are available, and it is also possible to see the desert on foot, perhaps combined with jeep touring: for this, it is even more important to have an experienced guide, except on short marked trails.

Desert encounter On closer inspection it is easy to see that the desert is not totally barren. Isolated acacia trees spring from the solid rock. Red-berried mistletoe clings to the branches. Tiny sand-birds dart about. Ibex sprint with ease up near vertical cliff-faces. Caper bushes hang from granite clefts: the edible part is the flower bud, but the caper fruit can be eaten too – it tastes like mustard and, so Bedouin say, improves virility.

Desert safaris reveal that life exists in the wilderness

Around Eilat A quick 4-wheel-drive trip into the desert is a popular excursion for Eilat tourists. There are outings that last an hour or two, or all morning or all day. Most jeep tours, or 'desert safaris', make their way into the wilderness from the Coral Beach area. There is plenty to see even within just a few minutes: the incongruous, lush spring of **Ein Netafim**►► where animals and birds gather; the vivid sandstone of the amazing **Red Canyon**►, where there is an easy one-hour marked walking trail between the

07-335377 ☎
057-586229

DESERT SHADE
THE CENTER FOR DESERT TOURS

rockfaces; and **Mount Yoash►►** for a panoramic view reaching into four countries – Israel, Egypt, Jordan and Saudi Arabia. Either do-it-yourself or guided trips on noisy 'fun buggies' – small motorised all-terrain vehicles – can be a lot of laughs but you will miss out on the magic, silence and beauty of the real desert experience.

The Arava Part of the Syrian-African Rift, the Arava is a deep lowland at the eastern edge of the Negev, marking the border with Jordan. A main road runs along it from Eilat to the Dead Sea, and this offers the easy way to penetrate the desert while staying on a modern highway (virtually free of traffic, however). Sights along the way include **Timna►►** (see page 251) and, just a little further north, the **Hai Bar Reserve►►** (see page 240). For the more intrepid, there are several simple-to-follow three- to four-hour walking trails that follow desert canyons, signposted off the road, such as **Wadi Sh'horet►►**, **Nahal Barak►►** and the **Amran Valley►►**.

Central Negev Several firms, notably the excellent market leader, Desert Shade (tel: 07 335377), run a range of long and short off-road drives, some combined with walks, in the immense and magnificent Makhtesh Ramon crater, near Mizpe-Ramon. Here you will find Nabatean and Roman ruins, strange flora, the tracks of strange fauna and spectacular other-worldly scenery. Other trips through the desert go to Avdat, the ruined Nabatean city, and to Sde Boker, the desert kibbutz where former prime minister David Ben-Gurion once lived. It can be cool in these higher regions out of season (even cold – snow is not unknown).

Eastern Negev Walks and drives from Ein Gedi include explorations of the Dead Sea hinterland, and hikes up the steep, stony footpath to Masada (see page 242). There is also a great hike from Ein Gedi along the enclosed valley trail of the Nahal Arugot nature reserve to a waterfall and pool in the midst of desert.

The majestic landscape of Sde Boker

239

Take water!
On any trip into the Negev, summer or winter, it is essential to carry adequate supplies of drinking water – you will need about one litre per person for every hour spent in the desert.

Get back to where you once belonged
'At all times one should live in Israel, and not live outside Israel, even in a place the majority of whose population is Jewish.'

Maimonides (The Laws of Kings, 5: 9–12), 1197

'I call upon you, our brothers and sisters in the Diaspora, to send your children here.'

Ezer Weizman, President of Israel (Independence Day speech), 1997.

*The upper Zin ravine,
cut by the Ein Avdat*

Dinner guests
Numerous guided trips in
the desert offer dinner or
tea in a real Bedouin tent
with a real Bedouin playing
host. The Bedouin consider
the whole thing just a game
in which they win a few
shekels from the gullible
tourists, and the experience
bears little resemblance to
an authentic encounter with
nomads. For all that, it is
interesting and enjoyable to
sit on the floor in a huge
tent, eating meat and pitta
bread or being poured a
cup of tea by a Bedouin in
full traditional attire.

►► **Ein Avdat National Park**   *224B4*

The Ein Avdat, or Avdat spring, runs through the upper Zin
ravine in the midst of the Negev. To either side the ravine
walls rise to crests of striking white chalk and dark flint. The
spring and its surroundings form an oasis, bursting with
plant life, an island of startling lush greenery surrounded by
harsh, though spectacular, aridity. Trees even grow in
places around the spring, and at the head of the ravine
there is a single 250-year-old pistachio tree. Desert animals
and birds also gather here for food and drink. Two marked
walks, one of three to four hours' duration, the other of one
to two hours, provide the opportunity to explore the area
thoroughly. The longer route involves some steep climbing
and the use of metal ladders. The shorter walk is much
easier, while taking in all the main sights.

►► **Hai Bar Reserve**   *224B2*

On the Arava road, 35km north of Eilat, a side road leads to
the right into this curious desert enclosure which mixes
nature reserve and zoo, combining entertainment with
serious conservation. Visitors may only explore the
reserve by means of guided minibus tours, which include
a walk. In big, open-air enclosures, or roaming freely, a
wide variety of desert creatures can be seen. Most or all
have been at some time native to the Negev; the reserve's
objective is to breed these animals for reintroduction to
the wild, and to disperse some species throughout Israel's
other 280 nature reserves. Many species live here that are
not usually found in zoos and which most visitors will
never have come across before. For example, you will see

the ongar (or Asiatic wild ass), an elegant, pale, nervous little wild donkey like a miniature horse; the grey Somalian wild ass, precursor of the donkey; the oryx and white oryx, antelope-like animals that routinely cover 40km in a night in their search for a few acacia leaves and that can live for prolonged periods without any water at all. The walk takes you through the smallish Carnivore Enclosures, where the species include the lovely fennec, like a little golden fox, the sand cat, the ancestral wild cat and the caracal, like a small lioness, as well as lynxes, wolves, hyenas and leopards. Also on view are rodents, snakes, lizards and birds of prey.

A well-camouflaged caracal

► ▬▬▬ Mamshit (Arabic: Kurnub)   224B5

Mamshit is the most northerly of the five walled and fortified Negev cities of the Nabataeans and is located some 6km from Dimona, southeast of Beersheva. Mamshit was changed little during the Roman and Byzantine periods, and so preserves many elements of its original character. The fine pale-stone ruins possess to this day a certain magnificence and grandeur: there are remnants of the main street, of houses, arched lintels, stables, an imposing flight of steps and two Byzantine churches. Several tomb chambers have been excavated at the cemetery, outside the town.

The nearby Camel Ranch is a fun desert-encounter holiday base, providing accommodation in a Bedouin tent, with Bedouin hosts who entertain with good food and traditional music. Guests can set off with guides to explore the desert by jeep, camel or on foot.

Over the border
The Negev continues, without any change, across the Egyptian border into the Sinai, where several intriguing sights can be found within easy reach of Eilat. Highlights are Ein Hudra (a beautiful oasis), the Nawamis (well preserved Bronze Age burial sites), St Catherine's Monastery and Mount Sinai. In the other direction, trips can be made to Petra, the rock-carved Nabatean desert capital.

Mountain-top Masada

▶ ▶ ▶ **Masada National Park** *224C5*

A ruined mountaintop fortress in the desert, overlooking the Dead Sea, Masada has become a potent symbol for the state and people of Israel. Israeli soldiers are sworn in here with the words, 'Masada shall not fall again'.

Reaching the site From the car parks, visitors climb dusty Snake Path to the mountain top – the walk takes around an hour. Alternatively, the cable-car swiftly carries visitors up the great golden wedge of mountain, a marvellous ride with magnificent views, leaving 80 steps to be climbed to the site entrance.

Reaching the top the easy way

History The small Hasmonean fort at Masada assumed its present form under King Herod (40–4 BC), who constructed the palaces and fortifications as a desert retreat. He did not make use of it, but a Roman garrison was always stationed here. In AD 66, the knife-bearing Sicari, or Zealots, captured Masada from the Romans at the start of the First Jewish Revolt (AD 66–73). As the revolt was crushed in other parts of the country, Zealots made their way here. Eventually the Romans besieged Masada with 15,000 men: traces of their camps can be seen at the foot of the mountain. The Zealots and their families numbered about 967. The Romans built a ramp up the western side of the mountain, and breached the wall on the first day of Pessah in the year AD 73. They found everyone dead, except for one woman and her children. She related what had occurred. When defeat seemed inevitable, the Zealot leader, Ben-Yair, made a rousing speech praising death above defeat and dishonour.

Ten men were selected by lot to kill everyone else. Every family group lay down together, and all were killed. Finally the 10 killed each other, one last man killing himself. She alone had decided to choose life.

The Romans occupied Masada again briefly. Byzantine monks resided here in the 5th and 6th centuries, after which the site was abandoned.

Visiting the site Snake Path Gate passes through the citadel's original guardroom into the site, which consists of a vast space, open to the sky, steep and rocky in places, with several ruined structures, the whole encircled by ramparts. A black line on all structures shows the height that remained standing until reconstruction work began in the 1980s. Turn right to follow the fortifications; the walls here are low, giving an impressive view across the flat red and white terrain to the Dead Sea. You will reach a small **quarry▶**, spacious **store rooms▶**, which held a year's supply of stores in big jars, and a **lookout▶▶**. Just beyond, projecting northward on a rocky crag, is the **Northern Palace▶▶▶**, Herod's immense private dwelling. Built on three levels of mixed large and small boulders, it retains corridors with several large and small rooms leading off. There is also a splendid **bath house▶** with traces of mosaic and frescoes, and several hot and cold pools. In front of the bath house, the **upper terrace▶▶** of the Northern Palace villa gives a fantastic view.

The marked path next follows the perimeter of Herod's Northern Palace, above a vertiginous precipice. From here the **Roman ramp▶▶** can be seen (on the Arad side). Leaving the palace on the southwestern side, there is an **administration building▶** and a **mikvah▶** (ritual bath), close to the **storerooms' watch tower▶▶▶**, which gives a clear overall impression of the entire site, its buildings and its layout.

Now follow the western rampart wall, where there are a number of interesting structures, including a **synagogue▶**, the oldest ever found. The **observation point▶** here marks the point where the Roman ramp reached the citadel. This is close to the Byzantine western gate, the point of entry for walkers from the Arad side (the walk up the ramp takes 20 minutes). The **Western Palace▶▶** here has a complex of small rooms, including baths, with mosaic decoration. Close by is a small Byzantine **church▶**.

A longer tour through the large, open southern section of the citadel reaches **bakeries▶**, **large pools▶** for bathing, a neat, circular **columbarium▶** (or dovecote) and a **water cistern▶**, probably all of the Herodian period.

Visiting Masada
Masada is signposted from near the southern end of the Dead Sea and from the desert town of Arad (45km east of Beersheva). It can be approached from either direction, but both roads end at car parks at the foot of the mountain (after visiting Masada you must return the way you came). Here, shops, eating places and toilets are available. A visit to the site takes several hours. Recommended routes round the site are signposted. It is a good idea to wear a sun-hat and take drinking water. Masada is open daily, from sunrise. The last cable-car down leaves at 4pm.

243

History lesson under the stars
A *son et lumière* in the extraordinary setting of Masada is as dramatic as you might expect. Using the latest in light and sound techniques, the show is staged in an amphitheatre at the foot of the Masada mountain and brings to life the story of the citadel from Herod's construction to the Roman conquest. The amphitheatre lies on the Arad side of Masada and the show takes place every Tuesday and Thursday at 9pm.

Roman under-floor heating

■ That Israel has 'made the desert bloom' is a cliché. Before Israel was created, much of this land was tough stony heathland, swamp and dunes. Travellers in the 19th century spoke of the appalling poverty of the land and its people. Early Zionists threw themselves into the task of reclaiming all this land, draining the Hula, planting the hills of Galilee and Carmel, and irrigating the Negev. ■

Israel in the time of plenty
'For the Lord thy God bringeth thee into a good land, a land of brooks of water, of fountains and depths that spring out of valleys and hills; a land of wheat, and barley, and vines, and fig trees, and pomegranates; a land of olive oil and honey; a land wherein thou shalt eat bread without scarceness, thou shalt not lack any thing in it.'
– Deuteronomy 8: 8

Milk and honey Was Israel ever a land of milk and honey? When the British took it over from the Turks, it consisted largely of infertile and arid terrain, supporting a total population of under 700,000 who scraped the most meagre of livings. Yet the Bible records that, 3,500 years ago, fields of corn, vineyards and oak forests ran from Jerusalem to the sea. It seems likely that, as the generations passed, more and more forest was cut down to make way for fields. Without the tree cover to bind the soil, storms washed the surface away. Overgrazing by sheep and goats made it difficult for trees to re-establish themselves and the land became impoverished.

Reclamation The British and the early Zionists together started the process which proved that the land could be drained, improved, planted and cultivated – or in Zionist terminology, redeemed. The new State of Israel continued with the task of reclaiming poor land. Kibbutzim and *moshavim* – communal settlements, whose occupants were usually willing to undertake difficult tasks for little reward – played a vital role in this process, and still do. Scientific research has also contributed. The Rothschilds brought in agronomists from the south of France to help replant the Carmel as a vineyard region. Millions of trees have been planted by the Jewish National Fund.

The rewards These efforts have paid off. Israel is now completely self-sufficient in agriculture, and exports large quantities of produce. Previously uncultivated areas are now intensively farmed. The range of crops grown is astonishing, with bananas, apples, avocados and oranges growing alongside each other. The Sharon Plain has become one of the world's most productive citrus regions. Galilee farmers have prospered on terraced fields of grain. Cotton, cereals and beet thrive in the

Top: corn, vetch and poppies – typical roadside wildflowers. Right: turf production

Jezreel Plain. The sun-baked Arava, on the Negev border with Jordan, supports thousands of hectares of tomatoes and vegetables. Vineyards again flourish on the slopes of Mount Carmel. Careful planning, mechanisation and skilful use of water account for much of the success.

Water, water everywhere All over Israel, the land is being irrigated, mostly by the underground drip-feed system which was invented here and is now used all over the world. The system allows tiny drops of water to cover a wide area, being channelled directly to the roots of crop plants, to achieve maximum effect using a scarce resource – and water is very scarce indeed. The National Water Carrier pumps water from the Sea of Galilee to reservoirs all over the country. New reservoirs are always being built. Forty new reservoirs, built mainly to catch the run-off after storms, have been constructed in the Beit She'an and Jordan valley areas south of the Sea of Galilee. Much of the water used for irrigation is brackish – not clean. It has been found that this actually yields much better results.

Natural riches Land reclamation is not all about agriculture. Israel has some 300 nature reserves, and an extraordinary variety of flora and fauna, including over 2,000 plant species, hundreds of types of resident birds and almost 100 different kinds of native animals. By setting aside over 1600sq km for wildlife reserves, it is hoped that this abundance and diversity will flourish and become common throughout the country.

Milk and honey
'If the Lord delight in us, then he will bring us into this land, and give it us; a land which floweth with milk and honey.'
– Numbers 14: 8

Ben-Gurion University research station: testing the tolerance of various plants

The road south of Mitzpe-Ramon crosses the floor of the huge Makhtesh, or crater

►► **Mizpe-Ramon** 224B4

Mizpe-Ramon means 'Ramon Viewpoint'. The settlement was built in the 1950s in the optimistic belief that it would grow into a prosperous desert city. It hasn't yet, and remains a rather bleak one-horse town. It does, however, have one astonishing treasure: Ramon Viewpoint.

The Makhtesh The town has a setting that few places can rival, standing on top of a dramatic cliff with an extraordinary view, a sight that simply compels awe. Spread out below the cliff is the immense desert canyon called Makhtesh Ramon or Ramon Crater (a *makhtesh* is a gigantic canyon-like crater formed not by a river but by huge natural cracks in the Earth's surface), at 400sq km the world's largest. On the far side the canyon rises to barren mountainous uplands. The whole scene is raw, vast and unspoiled. If standing in the open air, on the teetering brink of a 1,000m drop, does not appeal, go into the town's clifftop **Observatory►►►**. This semicircle of glass, projecting over the cliff edge, gives a glorious opportunity to linger safely over the view.

This gigantic cut into the surface of the globe has been uniquely valuable to geologists, providing a window into the planet's earliest history. The strata at the bottom of the canyon date from 200 million years ago, and successive bands of colour on the cliffs show the aeons rising to reach our own era. In its dizzying timescale, and in its sheer physical size, Makhtesh Ramon puts humanity into perspective. Mizpe-Ramon's **Visitor Centre►►►**, adjacent to the Observatory, houses an excellent exhibition explaining what has been learned from the canyon, together with displays of what has been found in it, and an audio-visual show about its creation.

Exploring the Makhtesh For rugged and experienced individualists, well-equipped with maps, local knowledge and plenty of drinking water, there are several hiking trails through the Makhtesh. For a safer adventure, with all the benefits of having an experienced and capable companion at your side, book on to a guided 4-wheel-drive tour, which

Hamsin
An annoying feature of the Negev climate is the Hamsin, the uncomfortably hot and dry wind which blows occasionally in April, May, September and October. The name comes from the Arabic for '50' – supposedly the number of days the wind will blow once it starts.

can be combined with a walk. On a Makhtesh tour, foot paths and tracks reveal the astonishing character of the terrain. One trip passes through a dazzling white limestone ravine, narrow and echoing, the rock slashed and riddled with holes by rough weather in seasons long past. Leopard tracks run across the paths, and multicoloured lizards bask on the stones. Bedouin signs, made of stones or tied into a bush, are translated by your guide. Visiting the remnants of past civilisation and the natural wonders within the Makhtesh is like finding lost treasure: such places lie all around, but are hard to locate without a guide. En Saronim►►, not far from the main road, is a 2,000-year-old caravanserai. Such camel-train stopovers appear every 25km or so, the distance a loaded camel can walk in a day. Near by is a gracefully arched water cistern, cool and fresh, which once held 100,000 litres of water. It could still be used today. Another high point is Ktsra►►, where there is a ruined Nabatean fortress; from the hills above, vistas open up across landscapes of sometimes formless chaos, a world of chalk and flint, black and white swirling shapes, ridges, edges and clefts, leading to the incongruous sight of snow-covered peaks in Jordan.

Around the town Other sights near by include the popular Alpaca Farm►, which makes for an interesting outing, entertaining for children. Not just alpacas, but other unexpected animals, large and small, are reared here for various purposes: llamas, angora goats, angora rabbits, camels, Pyrenean sheepdogs and Welsh border collies. The animals are all harmless to humans, though sometimes alpacas show their irritation by spitting at visitors!

Desert delights
Walkers in the desert should cover up against the sun, and take care to avoid some of the less-welcoming inhabitants: highly venomous yellow scorpions, vipers, black widow spiders, and the sand flea, whose bite is said to be able to kill a dog.

247

The view from Mizpe-Ramon looks far across an awesome scene of arid desert

Bird migration

■ **Israel just happens to lie at the junction of several important bird migration routes between Europe, Asia and Africa. Literally millions of birds – especially birds of prey, storks and pelicans – pass overhead twice a year. The time to see them is between February and May and from September to November, and one of the best places to come for birds is Eilat. ■**

Taking to the air
It is possible to take wing yourself in a motor glider, arranged by Eilat's International Birdwatching Centre (07 374276). With the engine turned off, you drift silently in the sky among the flocks, enjoying a close-up view of the migrating birds.

Bird highway More than 150 different species of bird pass through Israel on their migration routes. Bird-watchers recently counted 750,000 birds of prey alone passing over Eilat – fully 10 times as many as in the world's other great birdwatching area, the Bosphorus. The birds' main 'corridor' is the Arava/Jordan Valley, which takes them from Eilat, via the Dead Sea, to the Galilee, after which the different species take different routes into Europe and Asia. The Arava/Jordan Valley forms part of the Syrian-African rift which guides the birds between continents on their long journey. On reaching Eilat after their lengthy flight from Africa, millions of the smaller birds touch down for a rest on the saltpans beside Eilat and the fields of Kibbutz Eilot, 3km from town.

Watching the birds Free birdwatching walks depart from Eilat three times a week, led by a qualified guide (Sun, Tue and Thu, starting at 8:30am from Marina bridge; bring a hat, water and binoculars). The walks last three hours and follow an easy path via the beach to the extensive salt ponds and Kibbutz Eilot fields. For those who prefer to go on their own, a marked trail takes a similar route. The best times to watch birdlife are early morning and late after-noon. Numerous ducks and small waders such as plovers and sandpipers, some migratory, some resident, will be seen. An interesting colourful bird to watch out for is the little green bee-eater. Coots, herons, stilts and flamingos wade in the shallows. Birds of prey, such as falcons and hawks, try to pick off the smaller birds; kites scavenge the less fortunate. In the Eilot fields, wagtails, warblers and pipits scamper down below, while millions of swallows and swifts fly overhead.

Pelicans (top) and twitchers (below)

▶▶ **Sde Boker (Sedé-Boqér)** 224B4

This desert kibbutz attracted the attention of Israel's rugged, no-nonsense first prime minister, David Ben-Gurion, and he resolved to settle here with his wife, Paula. They became members in 1953. The kibbutz itself is a hardworking community cultivating fields and orchards, and manufacturing adhesive tape. Members, totalling just a few hundred, live in plain white bungalows, some draped with dazzling purple bougainvillaea. The Ben-Gurions' 'hut'▶▶▶ was only slightly superior to those of the other kibbutzniks.

A guided tour of the house, unchanged since the 1960s, reveals the little details of this gigantic character. His library, for example, contains 5,000 volumes on everything from the Bible to Yoga – but not one novel. In the kitchen is a list, pinned up by Paula, detailing her husband's medication and menus. We see that the pair slept in separate – and very different bedrooms. his stark and spartan, hers adorned with personal mementoes and photographs; apparently this was where she sat dreaming of living somewhere more comfortable.

A 15-minute drive from the kibbutz, you will find **Ben-Gurion College▶**, a centre for desert studies and part of Beersheva University.

Here, the college's solar energy centre is open to the public. At the end of a pathway through a pretty, natural garden, lie the **tombs of David and Paula Ben-Gurion▶▶▶**, marked by massive stone slabs set side by side on a clifftop overlooking the Wilderness of Zin, the barren heart of the Negev, where bleached cliffs plummet to a stony plain riven by wadis. **Ein Avdat▶▶** begins at the foot of the cliff (see page 240).

see page 240

The Ben-Gurions at Sde Boker

Having visited Sde Boker in 1953, David Ben-Gurion wrote to the kibbutz expressing his huge admiration for the enterprise and his envy of the life of its members. Later the same year he retired from politics, aged 67, and moved with his wife Paula to Sde Boker, both becoming kibbutz members. He was asked to return to public life in 1955 and agreed to do so, while remaining a kibbutz member. In 1968, Paula died, aged 76, and David returned to seclusion on the kibbutz. He died in 1973, aged 87, and was buried alongside Paula near Sde Boker.

249

David Ben-Gurion (left) and the hut (below) to which he retired after 13 years as Israel's prime minister

Ben-Gurion's dream
'It is possible to settle even millions of Jews in the Negev. Some day two million can be settled there based on agriculture. If so, another three million can be based on industry.'
– David Ben-Gurion, 1935

Desert fruits
Scientists at Ben-Gurion University are working with Negev farmers to use brackish water from deep desert aquifers. The water, previously thought unusable, is proving highly effective for fish farms, tomatoes, and exotic new crops like argan, which produces a cholesterol-free cooking oil, and pitaya, an edible cactus fruit which Israel has started selling to European supermarket chains.

Timna National Park

▶▶   **Shivta (Subeita)**   224A4

Located in the desert, about 60km south of Beersheva, this impressive site is remarkable as the only Nabatean city to escape being sacked and destroyed by the Arabs. Like others in the Negev Pentapolis (see page 226), the town was originally founded as a stopover on the Nabatean caravan route to Petra. It was taken over and improved by the Romans, later to be Christianised and occupied by the Byzantines. By the 4th century it had become a substantial community, despite the arid setting, thanks to the Nabateans' knowledge of water conservation. It continued to thrive until the Muslims invaded in the 7th century and settled here without causing much damage to the existing structures. However, as Nabatean know-how on water and irrigation was lost, the town went into decline and was abandoned completely in the 9th century. Shivta's desert location, well away from the main road, enabled it to survive the centuries relatively unscathed. Buildings survive up to two or even three storeys high, each with its water cistern. You can also see a wine press, paved streets, three churches with marble-clad walls, and a mosque.

▶   **Tel Arad National Park**   224C5

Some 20 minutes' drive west of the new city of Arad, these remnants of an ancient walled Canaanite and Israelite settlement, of 3500–1500 BC, lie on a desert hillside set back from the road. This was already an old, handsome and wealthy city when its king joined the struggle to keep Moses and the Children of Israel out of Canaan. Later Israelite settlements on the site were smaller and simpler. Tel Arad's setting is glorious: gentle, undulating sand and rock, speckled by the dark tents of the Bedouin (who administer the site). Ruins of streets, houses, wells, sacrificial altars, a synagogue and a palace have been uncovered in two separate excavation areas, vividly illustrating desert life in those times. From the site is a view towards modern Arad, a striking blanket of green thrown over the desert.

▶▶ Timna National Park 224B1

Renowned as one of the great Arava copper mines of ancient times (Timna was once known as King Solomon's Mines) this is now a huge area (60sq km) of desert scenery and historic ruins set around the dry Wadi Timna and enclosed by a semicircle of hills. Lying off the main Arava highway, 30km north of Eilat, and reached by a long access road, the Timna National Park is desert pure and simple consisting of bare red sandstone and limestone with a few acacia trees and tumbleweed, though an artificial lake has been added as an extra diversion for visitors. The park is big enough and interesting enough to occupy a whole day.

About 2km into the park, turn right for the **mushroom rock▶**, so called for its shape, and the **copper smelting plant▶**, which dates from the 14th century BC and belonged originally to the Egyptians. Dwellings, workshops and stores survive and a temple site of the same period near by was probably built for the use of miners.

Continuing on, the road reaches the extensive **copper mines▶▶▶**, characterised by sandstone arches, caverns, shafts and tunnels. Archaeological work in the 1960s showed that copper had been worked here as long ago as 3000 BC. The Bible records that Solomon exported copper from a port at Ezion-geber (near Eilat), and derived great

Temple used by Egyptian miners, the first to exploit Timna's mineral wealth

Israel's flag
Israel's national flag is the same as the Zionist flag raised at the First Zionist Congress in 1897. The design, worked out by David Wolfsohn, subsequently World Zionist Organisation president, simply placed the Star of David in the centre of a Jewish prayer shawl. 'That is how our national flag came into being,' he said. 'And no one expressed any surprise or asked whence it came, or how.'

Copper at Timna
The name King Solomon's Mines is misleading because, although Solomon exploited this and other mines, Timna was known and used many centuries before (and after) his reign. Copper mining continued at Timna under the Romans, and the Arabs also extracted from the site. Mining was resumed here from 1958 to 1976, but proved unviable. In 1980, copper mining started again at another site about 2km south of Timna and the mine is still in operation.

Yotvata in the city
If you are fond of Yotvata's imaginatively flavoured milk products, you can enjoy them in Tel Aviv, at the excellent Kibbutz Yotvata restaurant on the waterfront.

King Solomon's Pillars

wealth from the proceeds. In a crevice at the bottom of a cliff, reached by means of rock-cut steps from the mine, **rock drawings▶▶**, attributed to 12th-century BC Egyptians and Midianites, depict war scenes in which charioteers and archers fight with men armed with axes and shields.

The road continues to the artificial lake (with a restaurant and picnic area) and beyond, to the most enjoyable feature of the park, the natural phenomenon known as **King Solomon's Pillars▶▶▶**. Having nothing to do with Solomon, these rocky structures result from the erosion of a 50m-high sandstone hill, at the foot of which, on the east side, is a 13th-century BC temple dedicated to Hathor. The pillars are gigantic columns forming just part of a jumble of weird and weatherbeaten rocks, monumental in size and eroded to fantastic shapes, that can be climbed on, in or through. Steps have been carved up the massive formations, sometimes by man, sometimes by centuries of wind. The red stone is covered with its own red dust. Openings between the rocks suddenly look out on to immense desert mountains and the dry plain.

▶ ▶ **Yotvata**   *224B2*

Many of Israel's favourite milk products come from Kibbutz Yotvata in, of all places, the Negev desert. Their chocolate milk, sweet and savoury yoghurts and flavoured cream cheeses, for example, are big hits with young and old alike. The kibbutz has had some bright ideas for dairy snacks, including tubs of curd cheese with olives and *za'atar* (a delicious herb condiment). Passers-by on the Arava road nearly always make a point of stopping here for a bite in the **Yotvata Tourist Restaurant▶**, though this is just an ordinary self-service cafeteria. It also has a picnic area and a children's play area under palm trees, as well as the more interesting **Yotvata Visitor Center▶▶** (with a permanent exhibition on the flora and fauna of the Negev). Set back further from the road is **Ye'elin Holiday Village▶**, with a pool and pleasant chalet accommodation in the shade of acacia and palm trees. Ye'elin has its own big cafeteria, open to non-residents, which is better than Yotvata's.

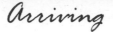
Getting there

Entry formalities Visitors to Israel do not require a visa but their passports must be valid for at least six months from the date of arrival. Travellers are normally granted a three-month stay. However, those entering by land from Egypt or Jordan may be allowed only one month (visitors wishing to extend their stay must apply for a visa through the Ministry of the Interior; expect a certain amount of delay and frustration as Israeli bureaucracy is not fast-moving).

On arrival (and departure) in Israel visitors should be prepared for a longish wait at passport control. Security is a big issue in Israel and every visitor is closely questioned by highly trained staff who will also scrutinise carefully all documents. Answer all questions frankly – and do not try to be humorous. For those travelling to or from Israel by air this formality will usually be performed as part of the check-in procedure. Travellers entering the country by private car are, in addition, asked to empty the vehicle of all luggage and the vehicle is thoroughly searched. Cameras may be opened, so film should be removed before passing through security checks. An entry permit – form AL17 – will be inserted in your passport, to be returned on departure.

Haifa, the biggest and busiest of Israel's ports

By air Israel has two international airports: Ben Gurion, which lies 60km from Jerusalem and 20km from Tel Aviv (and is known as Tel Aviv Airport), and Ovda, located in the Negev desert, about 60km from Eilat (bear in mind that Ovda offers virtually no facilities). A new international airport for Eilat is planned.

El Al, Israel's national airline, offers frequent non-stop departures from London, regional UK airports and major European cities. They also fly direct to Israel from New York and several US and Canadian cities. Although not always the cheapest option many travellers choose non-stop El Al flights for security reasons. All the food served on board is kosher. British Airways and several major US airlines also offer scheduled flights direct to Ben Gurion airport.

In addition, numerous charter airlines fly to Israel, many direct to Eilat. These flights vary widely in price, so it pays to shop around. July and August, and the periods around the major Jewish and Christian festivals, are the most expensive times to travel to central and northern Israel, while the winter months are the high season for Eilat.

For details of all El Al flights, call:
- UK House, 180 Oxford Street, London W1N 0EL (tel: 0171 957 4100)
- 120 West 45th Street, New York, NY 10036 in NY, tel: 212 768 9200; everywhere else, tel: 1–800 223 6700.

Catering to the visitors who come to Israel from all over the world

By sea Israeli ports are frequently included in the itineraries of cruise ships. There are sailings from ports in Italy, Greece and Cyprus to both Haifa and Ashdod. The popular inexpensive sea route from Piraeus, in Greece, takes about 58 hours.

By land There is, as yet, no border crossing between Israel and either Lebanon or Syria. Travellers may cross to and from Egypt at Taba (Eilat). There are three crossing points between Israel and Jordan: at Arava (just outside Eilat), at the Allenby Bridge (east of Jerusalem) and the Sheikh Hussein Bridge (south of the Sea of Galilee). Border procedures are slow and bureaucratic, and exit fees are levied.

Departure Air travellers should reconfirm their reservations 72 hours before scheduled departure times. Those travelling with El Al may reduce the long check-in time to just one hour by checking in their hold baggage at certain special El Al offices 24 hours before departure – notably the office opposite the Tel Aviv North railway station.

A departure tax is payable, and this is often included in the price of pre-paid tickets. Where this is not the case, it is payable at check-in. Those arriving and departing from Eilat do not have to pay.

VAT repayments On leaving Israel, visitors may claim back VAT paid on individual purchases of greater than US$50 in value, paid for with non Israeli currency (see Money Matters, page 258) at shops designated by the Ministry of Tourism and displaying a sign to this effect. The cash can be refunded on the spot in US dollars through the Bank Leumi office located in the departure hall at Ben Gurion Airport and at Haifa Port. The purchase receipt must be produced and the goods should be packed separately in your hand luggage. At all other points of departure the amount of the refund will be stamped in your passport, and sent by post to your home address.

The calendar
❏ No fewer than four separate calendars are in use in Israel – the Jewish and Muslim lunar calendars, plus the Julian and the more familiar Gregorian (Western) solar calendars. For all everyday and business purposes the last is used. The remaining three are mainly of religious significance. However, the terms AD (*Anno Domini*, the Year of Our Lord) and BC (Before Christ) are not used; instead years are measured as Before the Common Era or during the Common Era (BCE and CE). Fortunately, the Common Era is deemed to have begun at the birth of Jesus so there is no need for conversion! ❏

Climate

Climatic contrast is one of the striking features of Israel, which compresses four climate zones into a space half the size of Switzerland, ranging from Mediterranean to Saharan. All four can be experienced in a 20-minute drive through Judaea.

For much of Israel, the year is dominated by two seasons – the hot, dry summer and the cool, wet winter. January temperatures in Jerusalem can drop to around 5°C. The Galilee enjoys a short and delightful spring (in March and April) before the hills are slowly parched by the sun. Most of the country's rainfall occurs between November and April, with the area around Mount Hermon experiencing up to 1,000mm a year, while Eilat, in the south, receives less than 50mm.

The hottest areas are Eilat, with winter temperatures around 20°C, the Negev, the Jordan Valley below sea level, the shores of the Sea of Galilee (in high summer) and the Dead Sea. A strong, dry, easterly wind – known as the *Hamsin* – blows during the brief spring, and again in the autumn, raising temperatures and tempers.

It is worth remembering that the relatively short days of winter, coupled with reliance on solar heating, can leave some accommodation rather chilly.

National holidays

The system of public holidays in Israel is complex, as there are Jewish, Christian and Muslim festivals to be observed. Additionally, there are differences within the Christian community between the observance of Western (Roman Catholic and Protestant) churches and Eastern (Greek and Russian Orthodox and Armenian) churches. Jewish, Muslim and some Christian festivals are timed according to the lunar calendar and their dates in the more familiar Gregorian calendar vary from year to year. It is well worth checking for festival dates before you depart for Israel, as a lot of time can be wasted while shops and services are closed. Tourist sites are frequently affected.

256

JERUSALEM (YERUSHALAYIM)

☂ January & February
☀ May–September

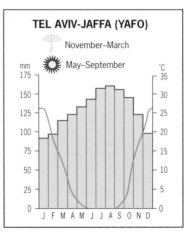

TEL AVIV-JAFFA (YAFO)

☂ November–March
☀ May–September

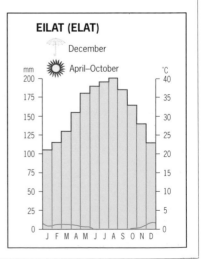

EILAT (ELAT)

☂ December
☀ April–October

The sabbath almost literally brings Israel to a standstill. The only exception to this is the southern Israeli seaside resort of Eilat, where, as a concession to tourism, most businesses seem to ignore the sabbath. Elsewhere Jewish shops and services close on Friday afternoon and reopen on Saturday evening or Sunday morning. At these times, there is effectively no public transport. If you are driving, you should avoid the ultra-orthodox areas of Mea She'arim, in Jerusalem, and Bnei Brak, near Tel Aviv, whose residents are hostile to sabbath drivers. The celebration of all Jewish festivals begins at sunset on the preceding day. Likewise they end at sunset on the festival day. Christian shops and services are generally closed on Sunday. Muslim shops and services are closed on Friday

The following list includes only those festivals when some or all shops and services will be closed. The dates are given according to the Gregorian (i.e. Western) calendar.

1 January (New Year's Day, Western churches); 6 January (Epiphany); 7 January (Christmas, Eastern churches); 14 January (New Year's Day, Eastern churches); January/February (Muslim New Year); March/April (Good Friday and Easter Sunday); March/April (Pessah, Jewish Passover, first and seventh days only); April (Muhammad's birthday); April/May (Yom HaAtzma'ut, Jewish Independence Day); 40 days after Easter (Ascension); 50 days after Easter (Pentecost); May/June (Yom Yerushelayim, Jewish Day of Liberation of Jerusalem); May/June (Shavuot, Jewish Feast of Weeks); July/August (Tisha b'Av, Jewish fast commemorating the destruction of the Temple); September/October (Rosh Hashanah, Jewish New Year); September/October (Yom Kippur, Jewish Day of Atonement); September/October (Sukkot, Jewish Feast of Tabernacles, first and eighth days); October (first day of Ramadan); October/November (Id el-Fitr, last three days of Ramadan); 24 and 25 December (Christmas, Western churches); December/January (Id el-Adha, Muslim Feast of Sacrifice).

Time
Israel is two hours ahead of Greenwich Mean Time (GMT) and seven hours ahead of Eastern Standard Time. Israeli Summer Time, a source of much controversy locally, is three hours ahead of GMT and operates from mid-April to the end of September.

When to go
Although beach resorts are packed in the summer months, the weather then is not necessarily at its best, being oppressively humid on the Mediterranean coast and almost unbearably hot on the Dead Sea and at Eilat. The brief spring and autumn are perhaps the most comfortable times to visit Israel. Winter in Eilat can be delightful, with clear blue skies and temperatures usually in the lower 20s. The periods around the great Jewish and Christian festivals are expensive and crowded. Easter/Passover in spring and Sukkot in autumn are both lovely times of year, but go just before or after the festivals to avoid the crowds.

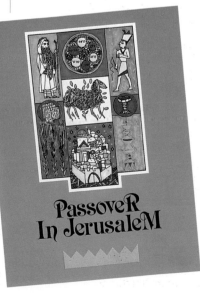

PassoveR In JerusaleM

Money matters
Currency The unit of currency is the New Israeli Shekel (NIS), known simply as the shekel, divided into 100 agorot. There are banknotes of 10, 20, 50, 100 and 200 shekels denomination. Coins are issued in denominations of 10 and 50 agorot and 1, 5 and 10 shekels.

Changing money Money may only legally be changed through a bank, many of which have branches in the larger hotels, or through a licensed money changer. Only a few of the latter remain and in Jerusalem many are to be found near the Damascus Gate of the Old City. They may give a better rate of exchange. The relative weakness of the shekel makes it preferable to change money in small amounts in Israel rather than abroad.

Credit cards Most major credit cards are freely accepted in Israel and credit card companies usually give a good rate of exchange.

businesses to accept this. The US dollar is most favoured but sterling and Deutschmarks are readily accepted. Many shops quote prices in dollars. Change will be given in shekels, so it is advisable to bring notes of small denomination. No VAT is applied to hotel, airline, car rental and other bills paid in overseas currencies or by credit cards.

Opening times
Shops Traditional hours are Sunday to Thursday, 8:30am to 1pm and 4pm to 7pm; Fridays and days preceding Jewish holidays, 8:30am to 1pm. These days, many stay open all day. Additionally, many shops close on Tuesday afternoons, most hairdressers close on Monday afternoons and travel agents close on Wednesday afternoons.

Banks Generally open 8:30am to 12:30pm Sunday to Thursday, 4pm to 6pm on Sunday, Tuesday and Thursday, and 8:30am to noon on

Eurocheques and cashpoints
Although Israel is not part of Europe, Eurocheques are widely accepted. Holders of Eurocheque cards (and Mastercard) can obtain cash from automatic tills at many branches of Bank Hapoalim.

Payment in foreign currency Goods and services may frequently be purchased with foreign currency, although there is no obligation on

Friday. Some banks are open for longer hours in the afternoon and branches in hotels may keep hours to suit their guests.

Museums and archaeological sites
Usually open Sunday to Thursday, 9 or 10am to 4 or 5pm. Typically they

open mornings only on Friday and are closed all day on Saturday (any exceptions are noted in the individual entries in the A to Z section).

Post offices Hours vary considerably. Some main post offices are open from 7am to 10pm while others are open Sunday to Tuesday and Thursday, 8am to 6pm; Wednesday, 8am to 1:30pm; Friday, 8am to 1 or 2pm. Sub-post offices open Sunday to Tuesday and Thursday, 8am to 12:30pm and 3.30 to 6pm; Wednesday, 8am to 1:30pm; Friday, 8am to 1 or 2pm.

Petrol stations These are usually open all day and into the evening. However, only a few stations on main roads remain open on Friday afternoons and Saturdays, so remember to fill up before sabbath starts.

Government offices Usually open to the public from Sunday to Thursday between 8:30am and 12:30pm.

Pharmacies A list of pharmacies open on a rota basis outside normal business hours is published in the *Jerusalem Post*. It can also be obtained from hotels, or from Magen David Adom (the Israeli equivalent of the Red Cross).

Customs and courtesies
Israelis are remarkably casual in their dress and behaviour, though immodesty in both sexes is frowned upon. Nor are they sticklers for politeness, regarding excessive displays of courtesy with disdain. You should not, therefore, take it amiss if your own attempts to be polite are disregarded – you must abandon the habits of a lifetime and accept that Israelis simply do not queue patiently or hold open doors for each other.

However, visitors should pay attention to the customs of the sabbath and religious festivals. Smoking in public should be avoided on these days and it is prohibited in certain places, including the public rooms of some hotels.

Religiously observant Israelis leave their cars at home on the sabbath and festival days. For information concerning conduct in places of worship see page 268. Photography is forbidden within the enclosure at the Western Wall.

Another feature of life in Israel is that daily life starts early (about 6am) and carries on until late (many restaurants and bars are open past midnight).

see page 268

259

Car rental

To rent a car it is necessary to produce your driving licence and be over 21, with at least one year's driving experience. Many international car hire companies are represented here and it is possible to book a car before departure from home, to be collected at the point of arrival in Israel. Several Israeli companies, which are just as good and can be much cheaper, also have offices abroad (for example, Eldan; tel: 0181 951 5727 in London). Rates are seasonal and highest in July and August. Car hire desks at Ben Gurion airport are open 24 hours a day.

Driving

An excellent road network, lovely and varied scenery and short distances make touring Israel a pleasure. However, as in all areas of life, Israelis can be impatient and are not afraid to take risks when they are behind the steering wheel. Caution is required. Rush hours in the major cities are hectic and traffic jams frequent.

Traffic drives on the right and the rules of the road are broadly similar to those of North America and Western Europe. International, easy-to-understand traffic signs are used and signposting is in Hebrew, Arabic

Petrol prices are slightly higher than many visitors are used to

and English. Seat belts must be worn by all passengers at all times. Driving under the influence of alcohol is prohibited. Traffic approaching from the right has priority except on main roads marked with a sign bearing a yellow square with a black and white border. These roads have priority over all side roads. All vehicles driving on interurban roads must use their headlights (sidelights are not enough) *at all times* between 1 November and 31 March.

Emergencies Breakdown assistance can be obtained from the Automobile and Touring Club of Israel (MEMSI). The club offers free assistance to members of affiliated motoring organisations, such as the AA. Patrols operate round the clock but a charge is made for assistance given between 5pm and 8am. Towing is free for distances under 25km. Car rental companies often include short-term membership in the price of hire, or have their own emergency arrangements.

Parking This is strictly regulated in most town and city centres. Cars can be legally parked only in streets where the kerbs are painted in blue and white stripes. A parking card (*cartise*) allowing 5 hours of street parking must be purchased from a post office or street kiosk and displayed on the windscreen.

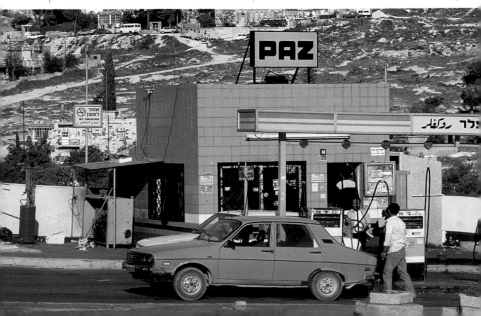

Between 7am and 5pm a car may be so parked for one hour. From 7pm to 10pm a longer period is allowed and appropriate parking cards must be displayed. Overnight parking on blue and white striped streets is not regulated – but turn on your alarm clock! If you wish to park for long periods in city centres it is best to find a car park. Where kerbs are painted red absolutely no parking is allowed and drivers risk having the car towed away or wheel-clamped – often within minutes of arrival.

Petrol Filling stations supply standard grade petrol (91 octane), premium grade (96 octane) lead-free and diesel fuel. Prices are generally a little higher than in Europe and the USA.

Speed limits In built up areas: 50kmh; elsewhere: 80kmh for cars, 60kmh for cars with trailers and 70 kmh for motorcycles.

Public transport
Air Israel's domestic airline, Arkia, operates scheduled flights between Tel Aviv, Jerusalem, Haifa, Rosh Pinna and Eilat. Since distances are short, flying is not a cost-effective means of transport. Depending on demand, chartered flights to other airfields, such as Masada, can be arranged through Arkia and other private charter companies. Further details are

available from travel agents and Israel Government Tourist Offices.

Train Train services are run by Israel Railways. The main route links Tel Aviv and Haifa, with some trains continuing north to Nahariya. There is a limited service on the scenic line between Jerusalem and Tel Aviv, although the bus is faster. Fares are lower than for bus travel but stations are often inconveniently situated away from city centres.

Above: a station on Haifa's underground
Below: Jerusalem railway station

Bus Buses dominate the public transport scene in Israel. The nationwide Egged bus company (the name means 'linked together') provides a cheap, comprehensive and efficient network of over 3,000 routes which connect even the most isolated kibbutzim with the wider world.
The buses are clean, comfortable and, for the most part, air-conditioned.

Services start at about 5am and continue through the day until early

Bus passes also allow discounts on museum entry and restaurant bills

Travelling by bus is part of the Israeli way of life

evening. Only the major routes between Tel Aviv, Haifa and Jerusalem continue until about 11:30 pm. Services also stop for the sabbath on Friday evening and for religious festivals on the evening of the preceding day. Buses are often full, and it is well worth booking in advance at Egged offices or bus stations. Town buses stop only when required, and passengers wishing to alight must press the bell to alert the driver. Bus drivers all speak English – it is part of their training.

There are several money-saving ticket options. The Israbus pass allows the holder to travel on all Egged buses for a specified period (7, 14, 21 or 30 days). It also entitles the holder to a range of discounts on tours, car hire, museum entrance fees and restaurant bills. Multi-fare

discount passes are valid for a month on urban routes only, and permit the holder to make a specified number of journeys at a discount price. They can be used by more than one person. A simple return ticket will also give worthwhile savings. Apart from anything else, passes save you from having to queue for tickets, which can be a time-consuming and frustrating business, well worth avoiding at busy, downtown bus stations! Tel Aviv city buses are run by Dan, and Egged passes are not valid there.

Various Arabic bus companies operate from the east Jerusalem bus station, serving Arab towns and villages in Judaea and Samaria (The West Bank). Their buses are painted blue and white or green and white. Arabic buses tend to be crowded, cheap and rickety but can be very useful for visiting these areas. They do run on Saturdays, unlike their Egged counterparts.

הנסיעה באוטובוס

Beware the taxi driver – some are out to take advantage of the trusting passenger

An easy and inexpensive way to see the sights is by taking an Egged guided tour in English. The national bus company runs trips lasting from half a day, to a week spent visiting all the country's places of interest. Information and bookings can be had at any bus station in Israel, or from Egged's head office in Tel Aviv, tel: 03 537 5555.

Taxi and *sherutim* So-called 'Special' (ie non-shared) taxis have a poor reputation among tourists and locals alike. The drivers are often unhelpful and overcharging is frequent. Yet they can be a boon at times, so you will have to adopt strategies for ensuring that you do not get ripped off. One thing you can do to protect yourself is to check what the correct fare should be at your hotel, or at a tourist office, before you set out, and insist that the meter is turned on before departure. If the meter is 'broken' – an amazingly frequent occurrence – agree the fare before getting in.

The *sherut*, or shared taxi, is the preferred choice of locals. These large cars, or minibuses, carry up to seven passengers, plying fixed routes within, or between, towns. All passengers pay a flat-rate fare (usually 20 per cent more than the bus) and may alight at any point on the route. *Sheruts* operate from taxi ranks and depart as soon as they have collected seven passengers; this rarely takes long as they are very popular. Fares are

officially fixed, with supplements for night journeys, and the drivers are generally helpful and honest, if not always friendly. The correct fare can be established by checking with fellow passengers or at the tourist office. *Sheruts* often run on sabbath and festival days, but expect to pay a fare supplement. The addresses of *sherut* ranks can be found in the local telephone directory under 'Taxi-cabs'.

Boat Regular ferry services operate across the Sea of Galilee between Tiberias, Ein Gev and Capernaum. Excursion boats can be chartered on the lake – for details, ask at local tourist offices. Red Sea excursions can be booked in glass-bottomed boats, and there are ferries between Eilat and Taba. Details can be had from hotels or local tourist offices.

Ferry boats offer tranquil trips across the Sea of Galilee

THE JERUSALEM POST

FRIDAY. MARCH 3. 1995 ● II ADAR 1. 5755 ● I SHAWAL 1. 1415

Media

Israel has a thriving and extensive press, publishing in Hebrew, Arabic and many European languages and covering the full gamut of opinions. The *Jerusalem Post* is an English-language daily newspaper (no edition on Saturday) sold throughout Israel. It carries a full entertainment listings section on Fridays. A few periodicals are also published in English – for example, the *Jerusalem Report*, a monthly current affairs magazine, and the *Israel Economist*. British papers and magazines and the *International Herald Tribune* are usually available the day after publication. The Arab press produces some English-language publications, which are more readily obtainable in East Jerusalem.

Radio Kol Israel (Voice of Israel) broadcasts news in English every day at 7am, 1, 5 and 8pm on short wave (1170 kHz in the south and 576 kHz in the north). The 1pm bulletin is followed by a 15-minute magazine programme. The BBC World Service (1323 kHz) and Voice of America (1269 kHz) can also be received and are much listened to by Israelis.

English-language news is broadcast by Channel 1 on Monday to Thursday at 6.15pm, Friday at 4.30pm and Saturday at 5:30pm. In addition, cable television is available in most hotels, and shows CNN news. TV schedules appear daily in the *Jerusalem Post*. Jordanian television is avidly watched by Israelis to gain an Arab slant on current events. Syrian television can be seen in the north of the country.

Post offices

These display a sign showing a leaping white stag on a blue background. As well as stamps, they sell telephone tokens (Hebrew: *asimonim*) and telecards, and they provide fax, telex and telegram services. International phone calls can be made here and some post offices also sell street parking cards (they also collect payment of bills, parking and traffic fines).

Main post offices in major cities are open from 7am to late (see page 259 for other post office opening times)

Typical main post office

and their fax, telex and telegram services are often available round the clock. The post office at Ben Gurion Airport is open 24 hours a day. Post boxes are either yellow (local mail) or red (all other destinations). Stamps, telephone tokens and cards can be purchased at hotels and street kiosks. Stationery, souvenir and bookshops also sell stamps. Visitors may receive mail through the *post restante* service offered at main post offices (Jerusalem: 23 Jaffa Road; Tel Aviv: Rehov Mikve Yisrael Street). Information can be obtained by phoning the Postal Authority's toll-free number: 177 022 2131.

Telephones
Israel's telephone company is called Bezek. Calls from public telephone boxes must be paid for with telephone tokens (*asimonim*) or a telecard. Both can be purchased from post offices and hotels. Street kiosks sell tokens at a slightly higher price. Telephone charges vary according to the time of day, with the highest rates in the morning. Unused tokens will be returned at the end of the call. International calls can be made from hotels (very expensive) or from public telephone centres where staff can advise you on the cheapest times to call.

International calls can only be dialled from public payphones by using a telecard. However, reverse charge (collect) calls can be made from such phones by dialling 188, which puts you through to the international operator. You must insert one token to get through, but this is returned at the end of the call. Some Arab states, technically at war with Israel, do not accept reverse charge calls.

Public telephone centres
Remember that some public telephone centres are closed on Friday afternoons and Saturdays. Centres are located at 3 Koresh Street and 236 Jaffa Street, Jerusalem; 13 Frishman Street, Tel Aviv; Bezek Offices, Old Commercial Centre, Hatmarim Boulevard, Eilat; 14 HaAtzma'ut Square, Netanya; Bezek Offices, Midrehov Promenade, Tiberias.

Telephone services
Information: 144
International operator: 188
Time: 155
Telegrams by phone (up to 50 words): 171.

International dialling codes
United Kingdom to Israel: 00 972
United States or Canada to Israel: 011 972
Israel to the United Kingdom: 00 44
Israel to the United States or Canada: 00 1

When telephoning to or from a foreign country omit the first zero of the local dialling code.

Language
The official languages of Israel are Hebrew (Ivrit) and Arabic (Aravit) with Hebrew being by far the most widely spoken. Most people dealing with tourists can speak, or at least understand, some English, and this is particularly true of hotel staff. If this fails it is always worth trying another language, as many Israelis are multi-lingual – French and Russian are very widely spoken, for example.

Signposting is usually in Hebrew, Arabic and English.

Basic vocabulary
hello (literally: Peace!) *shalom*
goodbye *shalom*
yes/no *ken/lo*
please *bevakesha*
thank you (very much) *toda (raba)*
sorry/excuse me *sliha*
where is ...? *aifo?*
restaurant *mis'adah*
museum *muzaion*
church *knaissia*
hotel *malon*

265

Crime

Israel is one of the safest countries in the world, and experiences very little violent crime. A midnight stroll in any of the major cities is safer than it would be in broad daylight in most North American or European equivalents (although locals are keen to discourage walking alone in East Jerusalem and parts of the Old City after dark). Violence may not be a problem, but theft can be, and it undoubtedly pays to take a few elementary and commonsense precautions:

● always carry money and valuables in an inside pocket or in a bag with a secure strap;
● never carry your money and travel documents in the same wallet or bag;
● never leave valuables visible in a parked car or unattended on a beach;
● do not flaunt valuable jewellery;
● pay particular attention to expensive cameras and video cameras.

World headlines give the impression that terrorist attacks are frequent in Israel. In fact, owing to the high level of security, they are rare – some European countries suffer worse terrorism – and there is very little danger of being caught up in such an incident. However, anyone wishing to visit the Israeli-held West Bank, or the Palestinian Autonomous Areas, should keep abreast of events in order to avoid any local disturbances.

It is always a sensible precaution to travel by Arab bus or by taxi in these areas, rather than in an Israeli-rented car, with its tell-tale yellow number plates. If in doubt about your itinerary, check with tourist offices (see page 272), hotel staff or Israeli fellow-travellers.

Police

In Jerusalem a special unit of the Tourist Police operates from the Kishle Police Station inside the Jaffa Gate of the Old City. These officers speak English, French and German and will deal with all problems concerning tourists, ranging from crime to lost companions. They also use the services of volunteers who speak other languages. Unfortunately, this unit operates only in Jerusalem.

Embassies and consulates

Israeli embassies abroad
● 2 Palace Green, London W8 4QB (tel: 0171 957 9500).
● 3514 International Drive, Washington DC 20008 (tel: 202 364 5500).
● 50 O'Connor Street, No 1005, Ottawa, Ontario K1P 6L2 (tel: 613 567 6450).

Embassies in Israel
● United Kingdom: 192 Hayarkon Street,

63405 Tel Aviv (tel: 03 524 9171/8); 1 Ben-Yehuda Street, Jerusalem (tel: 02 510 0166).
● United States: 71 Hayarkon Street, 63903 Tel Aviv (tel: 03 519 7575); 27 Nablus (or Shechem) Road, Jerusalem (tel: 02 253 288).
● Canada: 220 Hayarkon Street, 53405 Tel Aviv (tel: 03 527 2929).

Emergency phone numbers
Ambulance: 101
Police: 100
Fire: 102

Health

The standard of health care provided in Israel is among the best in the world and most doctors speak adequate English. In an emergency any hospital will offer treatment. You should take your passport, insurance documents and money for payment with you. Do not forget to keep your receipts so that you can get reimbursed by your travel insurance.

For out-of-hours, non-emergency medical attention the *Jerusalem Post* lists duty hospitals and pharmacies. Magen David Adom, the Israeli equivalent of the Red Cross, has first aid stations in many towns.

Urgent help can be obtained from English-speaking doctors 24 hours a day, seven days a week by calling Torcm, a private health care centre at 7 Mem-Gimmel Street, Jerusalem, near the main bus station (tel: 02 652 1748). Take your passport and insurance documents.

Lost property
Serious losses should always be reported to the police, who will give you a copy of their report for your insurance claim. Loss of a passport should immediately be reported to the embassy of the issuing country, and stolen or lost credit cards and travellers' cheques should be immediately reported to a bank displaying the logo of the issuing company, or direct by using the company's emergency telephone number.

Private thoughts at Jerusalem's most holy Jewish site, the Western (or Wailing) Wall

Camping

There are camp sites throughout
Israel, including several near
Jerusalem, offering accommodation
in cabins, chalets and caravans as well
as for tents. Facilities usually include
shops and/or restaurants, round-the-
clock security and a swimming pool.
Information concerning locations,
booking arrangements and tariffs can
be obtained from Camping Holiday
Villages, 112 Mishmar Hashiva, Tel
Aviv (tel: 03 9604 524). The Union can
also offer camping packages with a
choice of hire car or unlimited-use bus
pass.

Disabled travellers

Israel Government Tourist Offices
provide a fact sheet entitled *Holidays
In Israel for the Disabled* (see page
272 for addresses).

Electricity

The power supply is 220 volts AC.
Wall plugs are of the small three-pin
type, and a suitable adaptor is
necessary for many European
and American appliances.

*Symbol of the Israeli state and
Jewish faith, the* menorah

Places of worship

There are many places of worship
in Israel, representing dozens of
different world religions and sects.
A high proportion are also major
tourist attractions and visitors
should take care to behave and dress
with consideration for worshippers
when sightseeing. Modest dress is
essential for both sexes: shoulders,
arms and legs should be covered,
skirts should be at least knee-length
and women should not wear
trousers when visiting mosques or
synagogues. Men should cover their
heads in synagogues (paper caps are
provided for those with no hat).
Women should carry a hat or scarf to
cover their heads, if required, in
churches and mosques. All visitors to
mosques should remove their shoes
before entering.

Visitors arriving during services
may take part if they wish. Those
who do not should maintain a quiet
demeanour and ensure that they do
not interfere in any way with the
proceedings.

All large Israeli towns have
synagogues representing the
various orthodox and progressive
viewpoints. There are also Masorti

ZION RESTAURANT מאכלים לזרחיים ותימניים · לאפות

מסעדת ציון

כשר KOSHER

Enjoy Coca-Cola Coke

Coca-Cola

Attitudes towards tipping are changing. Tourist-oriented restaurants now expect it

(Conservative) synagogues in several towns. The main synagogue in large cities usually follows the Ashkenazi orthodox rite.

There are numerous mosques throughout Israel's Islamic neighbourhoods.

Most of Israel's Christian population is Greek Orthodox. The Christian Arabs are Maronites. Many other Christian denominations have churches in Israel; Roman Catholics are particularly well represented. Various Protestant sects have churches in the main towns. In Jerusalem, for example, Anglicans, Baptists, Lutherans and Seventh Day Adventists all worship.

Tourist offices (see page 272) have details of local churches and times of services.

Tipping

In keeping with Israel's classless society, not to mention the total lack of any attitude of servility, Israelis do not normally expect to give or receive tips. Unfortunately, in some places catering to foreign tourists, tips have come to be expected, however, and serving staff will sometimes even inform you of the fact. Ten per cent of the bill is more than adequate. Where service is already included, no tip is required. It is not necessary to tip taxi drivers unless they have been especially helpful. It is, though, customary to tip hairdressers.

Toilets

Public toilets are few and far between. Some leave much to be desired, and little to the imagination! They are usually marked with the sign '00', plus a male or female symbol. Most restaurants, museums and cinemas have modern, clean toilet facilities, as do some of the bigger shops. Often, the best bet is to use the toilets in the larger hotels' public areas. Attendants do not normally expect a tip.

Student and youth travel

The Israel Student Tourist Association (ISSTA) can help with cheap flights and accommodation, a variety of tours, safaris, work camps and the renewal of student identity cards. There are many offices around the country, including: Hebrew University, Mount Scopus, Jerusalem (tel: 02 826116); 31 HaNevi'im Street, Jerusalem (tel: 02 252 473); 50 Dizengoff Centre, Tel Aviv (tel: 03 525 1977); 2 Balfour Street, Haifa (tel: 04 8669139).

If you want to take part in an archaeological dig, you should contact either the Youth Section Promotion Department at the Ministry of Tourism (23 Hillel Street, Jerusalem; tel: 02 237311) or the Israel Antiquities Authority (PO Box 586, Jerusalem; tel: 02 560 2627).

270

> ❏ Working as a volunteer on a kibbutz is an inexpensive and interesting way to see something of Israel and learn about its society, but be warned it is more work than play. Most of Israel's 300 kibbutzim and *moshavim* use volunteers who get full board and pocket money. They generally do menial labour and unskilled tasks unless they have some qualification that the community can make use of. For all that, most volunteers come away thinking the experience was valuable. For information contact the Kibbutz Representative, 1A Accommodation Road, London NW11 8ED (tel: 0181 458 9235); or the Jewish Agency, Kibbutz Aliyah Desk,110 East 59th Street, New York, NY 10022 (tel: 212 318 6130).❏

Hitch-hiking

Hitching is legal everywhere in Israel and is a form of transport widely practised by all sorts of people, not just tourists. Vast numbers of off-duty soldiers, carrying weapons as they are required to do, hitch around the country. Getting lifts is quick and easy, as people who stop usually take more than one person. There are known hitch-hiking spots on the major roads – you can recognise them by the soldiers hitch-hiking – which are almost like bus stops, with drivers stopping every couple of minutes to pick people up. To hitch a lift do not hold up your thumb, simply point your index finger.

Women travellers

Women can travel alone safely in Israel, but they should, of course, maintain the precautions they would usually adopt at home. Lone women may occasionally experience a certain amount of comment from male passers-by, especially teenage boys. This is best ignored, as a response might be misunderstood. As everywhere modest dress and discreet conduct will minimise hassle. In Arab areas women may receive more persistent and unwanted attention from men; emulation of the extreme modesty of Arab women can be helpful. Wearing a headscarf, in addition to very modest dress, can alleviate the situation. Locals advise against walking on the ramparts of Jerusalem's Old City alone,

though in fact women visitors often do this, and incidents are extremely rare. Women hitch-hiking alone, or with another female companion, should maintain a spirit of caution, and having got inside a car with strange men, it is best to behave and talk with great modesty and reserve.

CONVERSION CHARTS

CONVERSION CHARTS

MEN'S SHIRTS

UK	14	14.5	15	15.5	16	16.5	17
Rest of Europe	36	37	38	39/40	41	42	43
US	14	14.5	15	15.5	16	16.5	17
Israel	36	37	38	39/40	41	42	43

MEN'S SUITS

UK	36	38	40	42	44	46	48
Rest of Europe	46	48	50	52	54	56	58
US	36	38	40	42	44	46	48
Israel	46	48	50	52	54	56	58

DRESS SIZES

UK	8	10	12	14	16	18
France	36	38	40	42	44	46
Italy	38	40	42	44	46	48
Rest of Europe	34	36	38	40	42	44
US	6	8	10	12	14	16
Israel	32	34	36	38	40	42

FROM	TO	MULTIPLY BY
Inches	Centimetres	2.54
Centimetres	Inches	0.3937
Feet	Metres	0.3048
Metres	Feet	3.2810
Yards	Metres	0.9144
Metres	Yards	1.0940
Miles	Kilometres	1.6090
Kilometres	Miles	0.6214
Acres	Hectares	0.4047
Hectares	Acres	2.4710
Gallons	Litres	4.5460
Litres	Gallons	0.2200
Ounces	Grams	28.35
Grams	Ounces	0.0353
Pounds	Grams	453.6
Grams	Pounds	0.0022
Pounds	Kilograms	0.4536
Kilograms	Pounds	2.205
Tons	Tonnes	1.0160
Tonnes	Tons	0.9842

271

CONVERSION CHARTS

MEN'S SHOES

UK	7	7.5	8.5	9.5	10.5	11
Rest of Europe	41	42	43	44	45	46
US	8	8.5	9.5	10.5	11.5	12
Israel	41	42	43	44	45	46

WOMEN'S SHOES

UK	4.5	5	5.5	6	6.5	7
Rest of Europe	38	38	39	39	40	41
US	6	6.5	7	7.5	8	8.5
Israel	38	38	39	39	40	41

Tourist offices

There are branches of the Israel Government Tourist Office (IGTO) in all the larger towns and places of tourist interest. They display a sign showing the letter 'i' in white on a blue background. They can provide a wide variety of information in English about accommodation, excursions, local sights and events. Free town maps are available, as well as a free weekly English-language magazine called *Hello Israel*, which gives a round-up of news and entertainments listings for the whole country. In addition, offices in major cities produce their own local listings magazines.

The following are the main IGTO offices you are likely to need:
● 17 Jaffa Street, Jerusalem (tel: 02 625 8844);
● Jaffa Gate, Jerusalem (tel: 02 628 0382);
● New Bus Station, Tel Aviv (tel: 03 639 5660);

● 18 Herzl Street, Haifa (tel: 04 666521);
● Arava Highway Corner, Yotam Road, Eilat (tel: 07 6372 111).
There is also an office at Ben Gurion airport. Addresses and telephone numbers for other tourist offices can be obtained at any of the above.

IGTOs overseas

● Israel Government Tourist Office, 180 Bloor Street West, Suite 700, Toronto, Ontario M5S 2V6, Canada (tel: 416 964 3784).
● Israel Government Tourist Office, UK House, 180 Oxford Street, London W1N 9DJ, United Kingdom (tel: 0171 299 1111).
● Israel Government Tourist Office, 800 Second Avenue, New York, New York 10117, USA (tel: 212 499 5650 or 800 596 1199).
● Israel Government Tourist Office, 6380 Wilshire Boulevard, Los Angeles, California 90048, USA (tel: 213 658 7462 or 658 7240).

נוסד 1882

כרמל מזרחי

HOTELS AND RESTAURANTS
ACCOMMODATION

The Israeli Ministry of Tourism lists over 300 places to stay throughout the country, from pilgrim hostels to luxury hotels. Details can be obtained from IGTO offices anywhere in the world (see page 272). There is no hotel grading system, but most hotels in Israel reach an exceptionally high standard, and price is generally a reliable guide to a hotel's facilities and level of service.

Hotel prices are usually quoted in US dollars and it is worth charging all services to your account and settling your bill in hard currency (pounds sterling or US dollars, for example), or by credit card, so as to obtain VAT exemption (see page 255 and Money Matters, page 258).

Kibbutzim Most of Israel's 300 kibbutzim have guest accommodation. This varies enormously in style, quality and price; some only offer a couple of basic guest rooms, while others are comparable to high-class hotels. In the case of the latter, guests are accommodated away from the kibbutz living and working areas – though a free tour is always on offer, giving a fascinating glimpse into the day-to-day workings of a textbook utopia.

Some 30 kibbutzim, located in holiday areas, are members of the highly professional Kibbutz Hotels Chain, which has its own Tel Aviv head office (see below). These are well placed all over the country and always located within a few minutes of beaches, main towns, historic sites or resorts. For many people, the peaceful setting, informality and lack of traffic make kibbutzim preferable to staying in town hotels. Bookings can be made through travel agents, or direct through the Kibbutz Hotel Chain in Israel (Kibbutz Hotel Reservation Centre, 1 Smolanskin Street, PO Box 3193, Tel Aviv; tel: 03 5246161); or in the US (Israel Hotel Reservation Center, 20 South Van-Brunt Street, Englewood, New Jersey; 07631, tel: 201 816 0633).

Apart from these better kibbutz hotels, scores of kibbutzim and *moshavim* (co-operative villages) offer inexpensive guest accommodation on a bed & breakfast basis. Most cannot be booked except by calling the kibbutz direct, but a group of about 30, mostly in Galilee, can be booked through the Kibbutz Hotels Chain (ask for Kibbutz B & B Country Lodging). Many are in peaceful, off-the-beaten-track locations and a car is essential. *B & B in Israel* by Dov and Shirley Gilon (published by B B Gilon Ltd, Gedera) is a useful handbook available in Israel that lists the best of the budget kibbutz guestrooms as well as rooms in private homes.

Hostels The Israel Youth Hostels Association runs high-grade hostels throughout the country offering dormitories and family rooms to guests of all ages. Meals are usually provided, as well as a self-catering kitchen. Further details can be obtained from the Israel Youth Hostel Association, PO Box 6004, Jerusalem (tel: 02 655 8400).

Christian hospices There are Christian hospices of various denominations near most Christian sights. They offer simple, clean, well-maintained and very inexpensive accommodation, either with full board or on a lodging-only basis. It is not strictly necessary to be a pilgrim, or even a Christian, to use them. However, it is vital to abide by the rules of the hospice which often include a curfew and an early start. Advance booking is essential. Full details, including prices and facilities, can be found in the leaflet *Christian Hospices in Israel* published by the Ministry of Tourism, from tourist offices or the Christian Information Centre in Jerusalem, tel: 02 272 692.

The big chains The best Israeli hotels nearly all belong to chains. However, these are not always the familiar international names. While Hilton, Sheraton, Hyatt and Holiday Inn do exist in Israel, the highest standards of all are set by Israeli companies. These include the top-of-the-range Dan Hotels, with nine locations (bookable in the UK, tel: 0171 439 9893; in the US, tel: 212 752 6120; or in Israel, tel: 03 527 1430); Isrotel, with seven establishments, five of them in Eilat (to book in the UK, tel: 0181 997 6423; in the US, tel: 201 816 0830; in Israel, tel: 03 517 8989); Radisson Moriah, with seven hotels (to book call toll-free, in the UK, tel: 0800 374 4111; in the US, tel: 800 333 3333, in Israel, tel: 177 353 2 004).

Hotel price grading Hotel rates vary widely according to the week and the season. The price categories given here are an approximate guide, and are per person per night sharing a double room, including full Israeli breakfast:

- ●budget £
- ●moderate ££
- ●expensive £££

JERUSALEM – OLD CITY
See also page 106.

Within the walls, there are small, very inexpensive Arab hotels and guesthouses (£) around Damascus Gate, and Christian hospices (£) in the Muslim and Christian quarters.

JERUSALEM – NEW CITY

East Jerusalem

There is a string of low-budget Arab hotels (£) all the way up Salah ed-Din Street.

American Colony (££–£££) 1 Louis Vincent St, Nablus Road (tel: 02 6279777). Arguably Jerusalem's best hotel, despite the variable rooms and slightly less than encyclopaedic range of facilities. A former pasha's palace, this beautiful old oriental building has real charm and style, as well as a good pool, lovely terrace, and superb (non-kosher) breakfasts and buffets.

Capitol (£–££) Salah ed-Din Street (tel: 02 282 5612). Decent rooms and public areas, air-conditioned, facing the Mount of Olives.

City Centre

Most of the top-class luxury hotels, including members of international chains, are located on King David, Keren Hayesod and King George V Streets.

Belt Shmuel (£) (tel: 02 203456). Non-orthodox Jewish hostel and cultural centre (open to all) beside city walls, comfortable, friendly, regular evening entertainment (folklore, etc), attractive garden.

Dan Pearl (£££) Zahal Square (tel: 02 622 6666) Elegant, attractive stone-and-glass low rise, this is one of the most comfortable hotels in the city, close to Jaffa Gate and with good views of the old city.

Jerusalem Inn (£) 6 Histadrut Street (tel: 02 251294). Good, clean city-centre low-budget hostel accommodation.

King David (£££) 32 King David Street (tel: 02 620 8888). The city's stately and dignified number one luxury hotel, a legend as well as a piece of Israel's history, and the place where you are most likely to meet visiting heads of state, stars and tycoons (see page 90 and 106).

Laromme (£££) 3 Jabotinsky Street (tel: 02 756666). A modern, popular luxury hotel overlooking Old City, which offers good value in its class.

Radisson Moriah Plaza (£££) 39 Keren Hayesod Street (tel: 02 569 5695). Immaculate large comfortable modern hotel, with elegant rooms, rooftop swimming and numerous facilities, 15 minutes' walk from the Old City and the main sights.

Sheraton Jerusalem Plaza (£££) 47 King George Street (tel: 02 6298666). Excellent modern hotel with great views and a superb restaurant.

Tirat Batsheva (££) 42 King George Street (tel: 02 6232121). Good mid-range modern accommodation in the city centre.

Windmill (£) 3 Mendele Street (tel: 02 5663111). Popular, mid-range, comfortable place, 15 minutes' walk from the Old City, 25 minutes from the city centre.

YMCA (or Three Arches Hotel) (£) King David Street (tel: 02 625 3433). Standing opposite the great King David Hotel, and arguably just as grand and imposing, the YMCA has basic, small, but adequate, rooms and a good range of facilities, especially for sports. More expensive than other hostels and hospices.

Further out

West of the city centre, the **Park Plaza** (£££) 2 Wolfson Boulevard (tel: 02 6528221) and the **Jerusalem Renaissance** (£££) 6 Wolfson Street (tel: 02 528111) are first-class hotels close to Herzl Boulevard, the Knesset and the major museums.

Hyatt Regency (££–£££) 31 Lehi Street, Mount Scopus (tel: 02 5331234). Dramatic modern building (the six-storey atrium has waterfalls and lush vegetation) covering a huge area and overlooking the city from Mount Scopus on the east side; masses of artwork, luxurious rooms, good restaurants and superb sports facilities. Relatively inexpensive for its class.

Kibbutz Mitzpe Ramat Rachel Hotel (££) D N Tsfon Yehuda, 90900 Jerusalem (tel: 02 6702555). This excellent, well equipped hotel (see page 107) is part of the only kibbutz within the city limits (though technically not part of Jerusalem) and it makes a green haven after the noise and traffic of Israel's capital. Guests have access to kibbutz facilities which include a big grassy playground and a heated (all-year) swimming pool, as well as plenty of hotel amenities. Great views to Bethlehem. Easy and frequent access by bus from city centre.

Neve Ilan Hilltop Resort (££) (tel: 02 5339339). A 15-minute drive along the main Tel Aviv highway, set in a quiet airy location, this pleasant modern hotel has large gardens, excellent sports facilities and a decent restaurant.

TEL AVIV AND THE COAST

See also page 132.

In Tel Aviv, and right up Israel's Mediterranean coast, there are numerous modern, well-equipped hotels ranged along the beachfronts of popular seashore areas. They do not vary much in architecture, service and facilities, but standards of comfort are generally high.

Tel Aviv

The main beach and city hotel area is Hayarkon Street, between Trumpledor and Ben-Gurion Streets. This is where you will find the main high-quality hotels, as well as several catering to those on smaller budgets. Bargain basement places and hostels are scattered over the whole area west of Dizengoff Street.

Adiv (£) 5 Mendele Street (tel: 03 522 9141). Decent, simple, low-cost hotel near the sea in the main hotel area.

Ambassador (££) 56 Herbert Samuel Esplanade (tel: 03 510 3993). On the corner of Allenby Road, facing the seafront, and opposite Opera Tower, this is a well-placed modern low-rise. Most rooms have a sea-facing balcony.

Astor (££) 105 Hayarkon Street (tel: 03 522 3141). Fronting the busy beachside highway, and on the corner of Frishman, this comfortable, well-placed, mid-priced hotel has a good restaurant. Handy for the city centre and across the street from the beach.

Aviv (£) 88 Hayarkon Street (tel: 03 510 2784). Good modern cheap hotel with bar downstairs, on very noisy part of Hayarkon, but with sea views and only two minutes' walk from the beach.

Basel (££) 156 Hayarkon Street (tel: 03 524 4161). Reliable, well-liked, reasonably priced modern hotel set back just a few paces from the main beach area.

Carlton (£££) 10 Eliezer Peri Street (tel: 03 520 1818). Located a little to the north of the main beach, overlooking the yachting marina, this large, landmark hotel is in the highest classification.

City (££) 9 Mapu Street (tel: 03 524 6253). An appealing, popular hotel just a couple of minutes' walk from the main beach area; comfortable and reasonably equipped.

Dan Panorama (££) 10 Kaufmann Street (tel: 03 519 0190). A little away from things, facing Clore Park and not near the best part of the beach, this hotel offers luxurious accommodation at lower rates and has a strong bias towards children and families. A free shuttle bus runs throughout the day to the Dan Tel Aviv.

Dan Tel Aviv (£££) 99 Hayarkon Street (tel: 03 520 2525). Said to have been the city's first hotel, this is still most people's first choice for comfort, service and convenience. Though it is large and modern, it is, surprisingly, not impersonal, with masses of facilities and superb sea views (rooms on the street side without the sea view are cheaper).

Dizengoff Square Hostel (£) 13 Ben Ami Street (tel: 03 522 184). Next to Dizengoff Square, this modern, well-equipped hostel with accommodation from dormitories to private rooms (with bath) could hardly be closer to the heart of Tel Aviv.

Florida (£) 164 Hayarkon Street (tel: 03 524 2184). It may be on the wrong side of unsightly Kikar Namir, but the Florida is not far from the beach, and within walking distance of the heart of the city, this small, modest hotel is comfortable and reasonably equipped, with air-conditioned rooms and private parking.

Grand Beach (££) 250 Hayarkon Street (tel: 03 543 3333). Well away from the city centre and feeling a little remote but not far from the less-impressive northern beaches and park, the hotel represents reasonably good value for money.

Hilton (£££) Independence Park/Hayarkon Street (tel: 03 520 2222). On a seafront ridge overlooking the shore, but well to the north of the main beachfront area, and not in the best location for either beaches

or city. The building has been thoroughly renovated and this is a luxury hotel up to the usual Hilton standard.

Holiday Inn Crowne Plaza (£££) 145 Hayarkon Street (tel: 03 520 1111). High-quality modern luxury beachfront hotel, close to unappealing Namir Square.

Moss (££) 6 Nes Ziona Street (tel: 03 517 1655). Low-priced, mid-range hotel, simply furnished and equipped, in a side road off a busy section of Hayarkon Street, five minutes walk from the beach.

Ophir Hostel (£) 43 Dizengoff Street (tel: 03 525 0947). The hostel is in a busy part of the city centre, overlooking Dizengoff Centre, but is within walking distance of the main beach, this is a good, adequately equipped base which offers both dormitories and private rooms.

Radisson Moriah Plaza (£££) 155 Hayarkon Street (tel: 03 527 1515). A top-of-the-range international luxury hotel beside the unattractive Namir Square at the north end of the main beach, within manageable walking distance of the city centre.

Ramada Continental (£££) 121 Hayarkon Street (tel: 03 521 5555). High-standard luxury hotel but located close to Namir Square, at the northern end of the main beach, a moderate walk from the heart of the city.

Sheraton (£££) 115 Hayarkon Street (tel: 03 521 1111). A landmark on the Tel Aviv waterfront, a few paces from the beach, within walking distance of the city centre, a top-class luxury hotel.

Travellers Hostel (£) 38 and 47 Ben Yehuda Street (tel: 03 522 5184). Small but popular, clean and inexpensive hostel with attractive garden, fully equipped kitchen, luggage room and reception staffed almost round the clock. Easy walk to beach and city centre. Also at 122 Allenby Street (tel: 03 560 6656).

Akko
Argaman Motel (£) (tel: 049 916691). Modern hotel on the beach providing comfortable but simple accommodation, with a good view of Old Akko

Caesarea
Dan Caesarea (£££) (tel: 06 626 9111). In a green parkland setting, this delightfully relaxed and luxurious resort hotel emphasises sports – including golf at Israel's only golf course, near by.

Carmel Forest
Carmel Forest Spa Resort (£££) POB 9000, Haifa 31900 (tel: 04 832 3111). Hidden in tranquil Mediterranean woodland about a mile and a half south of Kibbutz Beit Oren (near Haifa), the Isrotel chain has opened a luxury spa hotel all about non-stop pampering and pleasure, rather than the usual health cures and Dead Sea mud.

Haifa

High quality hotels tend to be clustered in the smart Carmel Centre district up the Carmel slope above the heart of the city. Top-rung places are the smart **Dan Carmel** (£££), HaNasi Avenue (tel: 04 830 6306) and its near neighbour, the enormous **Dan Panorama** (£££), HaNasi Avenue (tel: 04 8352222), the top floors of which have fantastic views. Both have an abundance of facilities.

Nof (££) 101 HaNasi Avenue (tel: 04 8354311). Between the two Dans, this comfortable hotel offers a high standard at a reasonable price.

Shulamit (£) 15 Kiryat Sefer Street (tel: 04 8342811). An excellent, inexpensive hotel a little bit further from the city centre.

Herzliya

Dan Accadia (£££) Ramat Yam Street (tel: 09 597070) Magnificent family resort hotel on the beachfront. Popular and lively. Very much sports and activity oriented, with lots laid on for children. Good buffets.

Sharon (££) Ramat Yam Street (tel: 09 575777) Good, comfortable modern hotel near the beach.

Nahsholim

Kibbutz Nahsholim Guesthouses (£–££) MP Hof Carmel (tel: 06 399533). This kibbutz on the Carmel coast offers accommodation in very simply furnished and rather spartan terraced chalets, right on a spectacular beach. The kibbutz restaurant, however, is below average.

Netanya

There are almost 50 ministry-approved hotels in this town.

Grand Metropole (£–££) 17 Gad Mahnes Street (tel: 09 624777). Good-value mid-range holiday hotel near the beach.

The Seasons (££–£££) 1 Nice Boulevard (tel: 09 601511). One of the nicest and best hotels in this popular holiday town.

Shavei Zion

Hotel Beit Hava (£–££) Moshav Shavei Zion (tel: 04 9820391). This quiet *moshav* (co-operative village), 3km south of Nahariya, runs a remarkably high-quality modern hotel and restaurant; immaculate, with good service, attractive grounds and good facilities, including a large swimming pool.

Shefayim

Kibbutz Shefayim Guest House (£–££) Shefayim 60990 (tel: 09 595595). This kibbutz outside Herzliya runs a big, busy, popular hotel and restaurant, used almost exclusively by Israelis. The atmosphere is warm and animated, with functions and events occurring almost every evening. The rooms are well-equipped and comfort-

able. This makes a good base for much of the coast, including Tel Aviv.

Zichron Yaakov

Radisson Moriah Gardens (££) 1 Etzion Street (tel: 06 300 111). On a hilltop close to the town, this smart hotel hosts a lot of conferences. It has spacious gardens, and offers a high standard of accommodation and sweeping verdant views.

GALILEE AND THE NORTH

Amirim

Amirim guest houses (£) near Sefat. Around 30 of the families living in this beautifully located all-vegetarian *moshav* (co-operative village) west of Sefat offer comfortable guest accommodation.

Ayelet Hashahar

Ayelet HaShahar (£–££) near Kiryat Shmona (tel: 06 932302). Excellent kibbutz guesthouse offering accommodation and a lively, enjoyable holiday atmosphere, with plenty of entertainment and activities.

Beit Hillel

Beit Hillel (£). Several residents of this well-placed northern *moshav* (a co-operative village east of Kiryat Shmona) offer attractive, comfortable guest accommodation.

Ginnosar

Nof Ginnosar Kibbutz Hotel (£–££) (tel: 06 792161). Delightful, high-quality modern kibbutz hotel with comfortable rooms in several blocks set in beautiful grounds on the banks of the Sea of Galilee. Good restaurant. Well placed for sights. The Museum of the Ancient Boat is located next door.

HaGoshrim

HaGoshrim Kibbutz Hotel (£–££) (tel: 06 956231). Good, comfortable, simple rooms in guest accommodation blocks at this prosperous kibbutz, set in very attractive grounds. Pool and plenty of other facilities.

Kinar

Kinar Holiday Village (£–££) (tel: 06 732670). Attractive, efficient, religious kibbutz with good accommodation in glorious garden setting on the eastern shore of the Sea of Galilee. Pleasant, spacious public areas and restaurant.

Sefat

Ron (£) near Metzuda, Sefat (tel: 06 972590). Decent mid-range hotel with good clean rooms and restaurant, 9 to 10-minute walk from the synagogue quarter and sights.

Rimon Inn (££) Artists' Quarter (tel: 06 920666). Charming and well placed in an attractive area, this is one of the best hotels in town.

HOTELS AND RESTAURANTS

Tiberias

Several budget hostels (£) and pilgrim hospices can be found around the town. One of the very best is the **Church of Scotland Hospice** (£) (tel: 06 723769), a delightful place not far from the lake. **Galei Kinneret** (£££) 1 Eliezer Kaplan Street (tel: 06 792331). The smartest, best and most civilised place in town, by the lake in a lovely setting. **Radisson Moriah Plaza** (£££) Habanim Street (tel: 06 792233). Big, lavishly equipped modern luxury hotel in the Old City. **Ron** (£) 12 Ahad Ha'am Street (tel: 06 791350). Decent mid-range hotel in a good location with good views.

JUDAEA AND SAMARIA (THE WEST BANK)

Visitors are **not** advised to stay overnight in Palestinian areas of the West Bank.

Arad

Margoa (££) (tel: 07 951 222), and the **Nof Arad** (££) (tel: 07 957056) are conventional, modern mid-range hotels located close to one another on Moav Street, the road out of town on the eastern side. They include treatment centres for visitors suffering from respiratory conditions.

Dead Sea

Kibbutz Ein Gedi (££) Ein Gedi (tel: 07 594 222). The kibbutz runs a hotel with basic accommodation in simple, if dark, rooms in terraced blocks scattered around attractive grounds full of flowerbeds. There is a good self-service dining room. **Radisson Moriah Gardens** (£££) Ein Bokek (tel: 07 584351). Good well-equipped holiday and health hotel, with entertainment, sports, and heated indoor pool, filled with water from the Dead Sea. **Radisson Moriah Plaza** (£££) Neve Zohar (tel: 07 591591) Big, top-flight health-oriented spa hotel on the salty shore in weird, desert location. Full spa in the hotel – pools, mud baths, etc. Lots of facilities, including good restaurants.

THE SOUTH
Eilat

Most hotels in Eilat reach a pretty high standard and are catering for well-off visitors on family holidays. The cream of the selection – the Princess, Dan Eilat and Royal Beach – are probably among the best vacation hotels in the world. It is worth knowing that guests at any one hotel in the Isrotel chain may use the facilities at the others. **Adi Hotel** (£) Tsofit Street (tel: 07 376151). Tucked away near the ugly (and misnamed) New Tourist Centre, this small, modern hotel offers good value for money with simple, air-conditioned rooms with private bathroom. Breakfast room but no restaurant. The beach is about 500m away.

Club In Villa Resort (££) Coral Beach (tel: 07 334555). This aparthotel, run by the Hilton, offers pleasant two-bedroomed villas for up to six people. The villas are grouped in courtyards around the pool and sunbathing terraces. There are self-catering or hotel service options, and prices vary accordingly. Supermarket, restaurant, poolside bar, and lively evening entertainment by the pool. **Dalia Hotel** (£) North Beach (tel: 07 334004). Probably the best of the cheap hotels, with a good position near the seafront. Rooms are simple, but have air conditioning, TV and telephone. The hotel has a pool and sunbathing terrace, partially shaded by trees. Dining room, bar and café. **Dan Eilat Hotel** (£££) North Beach. (tel: 03 362 222). Right on the newer beach, east of the lagoon. A large, opulent, state-of-the-art hotel with everything and more: several restaurants, cafés and bars, live evening entertainment, including jazz, sports facilities and a huge pool area, plus lots of facilities for children, such as a 'Virtual Reality lounge'. All rooms have balconies overlooking the sea. **Etzion Hotel** (££) Hatmarim Boulevard (tel: 07 374 131). Modern hotel, close to the town centre, with simple, well-equipped rooms. Heated pool and sunbathing terrace, restaurant, mini-supermarket, disco, live entertainment, gym. **Kibbutz Eilot Holiday Apartments** (££) Kibbutz Eilot, M P Eilot 88805 (tel: 07 358816). Located 3km north of Eilat, on the main road north, the kibbutz has a small, pleasant complex of apartments set in attractive grounds surrounded by impressive desert hills. Each apartment, designed for four guests, has a shower room, toilet and simple kitchenette. Breakfast is served in the kibbutz members' dining-room. Added attractions include a children's zoo and play area, and an 'Israeli folklore evening' every Saturday, which attracts lots of visitors. A good spot for bird watchers in spring and autumn. Car essential. Handy for the Jordan crossing. **King Solomon's Palace** (£££) North Beach (tel: 07 6334111). Eilat's family favourite, a comfortable luxury hotel (belonging to the Isrotel chain) backing onto the east side of the lagoon. Crowded, informal and noisy holiday atmosphere, with many facilities, including a sports centre, a very good pool area, restaurants, lavish evening entertainment and good children's facilities. **Lagoona Hotel** (££) North Beach (tel: 07 6366666). The Isrotel chain's not-quite-so-expensive family-fun hotel. Four-storey, modern, built round a large pool and sunbathing terraces. Masses of facilities, including six cafés and restaurants. Rooms are well equipped and comfortable with balconies and air conditioning. The beach is close by.

Neptune (£££) North Beach (tel: 07 369369). This is a popular luxury holiday hotel with superb facilities set beside the North Beach promenade.
New Caesar (£££) North Beach (tel: 07 333111). Large, good-quality hotel right beside the lagoon.
Orchid Hotel and Resort (£££) Coral Beach (tel: 07 360360). Inspired by Thai architecture and set on a hill overlooking the sea, this attractive self-catering cabin complex has footpaths winding through clusters of greenery. Facilities include several restaurants and bars and a pleasant pool with waterfalls on the hilly site. Located some distance from Eilat centre, so a car would be handy.
Paradise Hotel (££) North Beach (tel: 07 335050). Modern low-rise hotel complex with tropical gardens, built round a large pool and sunbathing terraces. Two restaurants and two bars, health club and disco. Rooms are well equipped and breakfast is very good.
Princess Hotel (£££) Taba Beach (tel: 07 365555). Opulent, top price, ultra-modern hotel set amidst desert cliffs and a few paces from the narrow beach near the Taba crossing, 8km from Eilat. Free shuttle into town and to the airport. Huge atrium, marble floors, and an amazing wall of glass almost touching a rocky mountainside. Choice of restaurants and bars, and superb pool complex with facilities for children and people with disabilities . All rooms have a sea-facing balcony.
Radisson Moriah Plaza Hotel (£££) North Beach (tel: 07 361111). Large and luxurious hotel, the one that lies closest to North Beach and the promenade. Offers a vast range of facilities, with plenty for children to do, and five restaurants, two pools, a nightclub and regular entertainment.
Riviera Apartment Hotel (££) North Beach (tel: 07 6333944). This complex of low-rise flats (owned by Isrotel, and over the road from King Solomon's Palace) provides unpretentiously furnished self-catering apartments for two, four or five people. Each has a kitchenette, dining area and a spacious bathroom, with a daily cleaning service. The complex is arranged around a large pool with sunbathing terraces, a children's pool and playground. Ten minutes' walk to the beach. Cafés and a small supermarket in the building.
Royal Beach (£££) North Beach (tel: 07 6368888). Isrotel's sumptuous top-of-the-range hotel at the new eastern end of the resort, on the beachside promenade and near the lagoons. White marble reception area full of light, magnificent atrium with acrobatic sculpture, hallways made of glass with fantastic views. A dozen good restaurants and two large, palm-fringed pools with waterfalls. Children's pool and another specially equipped for people with disabilities, plus an array of other facilities.

Sport Hotel (££) North Beach (tel: 07 6333333). Comfortable, quieter-than-average hotel with two pools and many facilities, including several restaurants and cafés. Beach nearby. Childrens' activities and evening entertainment.
Youth Hostel (£) Corner of Elot Boulevard and Arava Road (tel: 07 370088). Just south of the town centre, in an unappealing location but with a sea view and within easy walking distance of everything (including main bus station). Good, modern hostel, large, with family rooms and an inexpensive dining room.

Mizpe-Ramon
Ramon Inn (££) 1 Ein Akev (tel: 07 6588822). Unusual modern apartment-hotel in one-horse desert town beside the breathtaking Ramon Crater. Rooms are spacious home-from-home suites, each with a decent kitchen/dining room. Excellent value. Bar and restaurant.

RESTAURANTS

Almost all of Israel's luxury hotels have high-quality restaurants which are open to non-residents, while for cheap-and-cheerful eating there is little distinction to be made between bars, cafés and restaurants. A good selection of these can be found with ease in any city or town centre.

Price and dining guide:

- ●budget £
- ●moderate ££
- ●expensive £££

JERUSALEM
Eldad Vezehoo (££) 31 Jaffa Road, Nahalat Shiva (tel: 02 625 4007). Great for kalamari and crabs, excellent lamb chops and sirloin steaks, the focus is on French-style food and discreet service. The restaurant has three rooms to choose from, and is ideal for an intimate evening meal.
Gilly's (££) Nahalat Shiva (tel: 02 6255955). The tops for meat and steaks served with a variety of sauces, including some based on soured cream (the ultimate non-kosher combination). A selection of Israeli salads start you off, though you could wait some time for your main course to arrive – the place is usually packed. Best turn up between 6.30 and 7 or around midnight if you want to be seated quickly.
La Gutta (£££) 16 Rivlin Street Nahalat Shiva (tel: 02 623 2322). Kosher restaurant which draws together the best of French and Moroccan cooking. Excellent starters take the Middle Eastern route, while pepper steak, trout and duck à l'orange add European flavour.

279

HOTELS AND RESTAURANTS

Oceanus (£££) 7 Rivlin Street, Nahalat Shiva area (tel: 02 624 0863). For unusual ways with fish and shellfish, look no further than this smart, well-established restaurant. The carpaccio of fish is especially recommended. The service can be erratic but the atmosphere is decidedly pleasant.

Papas (££) 16 Yoel Saloman (tel: 02 256738). A simple but sophisticated Italian restaurant, never short of discerning customers from the art and craft shops in the area, in the oldest part of 'new' Jerusalem to be settled by the Jews. There are wooden chairs and tables, whitewashed walls and a pleasant rustic approach to cooking and presentation. Excellent chicken with rosemary comes on a sizzling griddle plate, while the foccaccia bread and *antipasti* (starters) make a hearty snack.

Pepperonis (££) 4/6 Rabbi Akiva Street (tel: 02 625 7829). A one-price restaurant with a vast selection of antipasti – marinated vegetables, melon with parma ham, salami platter – followed by a choice from the blackboard. The menu changes daily but may include pork, veal, fish and beef. Very popular and with good reason.

Pundak Motza (££) Ramat Motza (tel: 02 5346713). A picturesque stopping-off place just outside Jerusalem on the magisterial climb into the city. Built from wood, the cabin-style restaurant is homely and cosy with a strong emphasis on Moroccan cuisine – great couscous, stuffed vegetables, smoked meats and fish. For a treat try the *mezze* – 15 little starter dishes that satisfy and fill.

La Rotisserie (£££) Notre Dame Guest House, New Gate, Paratroopers Road (tel: 02 6279111). A curious gastronomic find, this extremely good French restaurant is attached to a guest house frequented by pilgrims and owned by the Vatican. Located just outside the walls of the old city, the building itself is over 100 years old, though the restaurant was only established in 1978. Under vaulted ceilings, enjoy coquilles St Jacques, Châteaubriand and crêpes suzettes, and a fine selection of imported French wines. Open for dinner only Monday to Friday, lunch and dinner Saturday. Closed Sunday.

Sergio (£) The Botanical Gardens, Hebrew University, Givat Ram (tel: 02 6793904). Spot faculty professors from the Hebrew University here in the idyllic setting of the university's lovely gardens – artificial lake and all. Homemade pasta and bread, plus vegetarian and dairy food, all keep the prices low and the meals light.

Shemesh (££) Ben Yehuda Street (tel: 02 625 3232). Middle-eastern food in a buzzing spot in central Jerusalem. Salad starters of aubergine, tomato, pickles, houmous and tahina are followed, if you have room, by hearty grills, kebabs and shishliks (grilled meats).

Le Tsriff I (££) 5 Horkenos (tel: 02 6242478). The original of two thriving restaurants (see Tsriff II below). Continental food with an Israeli accent and a great range of seafood. Since 1978, its position in the centre of town has pulled in Palestinians and Israelis alike, and anyone looking for a diverse environment in which to enjoy their food. Open 364 days a year (closed for Yom Kippur in September or October).

TEL AVIV

Alexander (££) 81 Yehuda Hamaccabi (tel: 03 605 8910). Chrome, cobalt blue and a cool clientele mark out this restaurant as much for its style as for the menu, which is a mix of modern French, Italian and Israeli – the flavours are *nouvelle*, but the portions certainly aren't. See the yuppie crowd flock through the doors. Yehuda Hamaccabi has been renamed Telephone Avenue because diners cannot seem to spend an hour without talking to their mobile.

Apropo (££) 4 Tarsat Boulevard, Kikar Ha'Bima (tel: 03 526 9288); also at 75 Ben Gurion Boulevard (tel: 03 527 3208) and Opera Tower (tel: 03 517 5243). Good food, sometimes eccentric, always plentiful, the Apropo menu includes everything from 'kosher' Thai shrimps to American waffles, and satisfies all tastes in between. Each of the Apropo restaurants has its own character and appeals to a slightly different clientele, to the theatre and concert crowd, to the chic north Tel Avivis, and to tourists and beach babes respectively.

Arrcafé (£) 31 Rothschild Boulevard (tel: 03 560 9946). With the dulcet tones of Nat King Cole to welcome you through the door, it's clear that you're entering a cool zone. The wood and chrome interior is as tasteful as the delicate tarts and ciabatta sandwiches plus a wide selection of coffees served with style in unusual glasses.

Baobab (££) 43 A'had Ha'am (tel: 03 566331). No sightings of any Baobab trees here, but numerous satisfied customers. Nouvelle cuisine without the frugality: pasta, appetisers, salads, plus good service in a relaxed atmosphere. Close to the Israeli stockmarket, should you wish to invest a few shekels.

Birenbaum and Mendelbaum (£££) 35 Rothschild Boulevard (tel: 03 566 4949). Full marks to the restaurant that has made traditional East European Jewish food the in-thing again. Chopped liver, soused herrings and *lockshen* soup (chicken broth with noodles) take on a different character when served in the breezy pink-brown enclosure of this modern restaurant. A great favourite with the local legal eagles, it is an ideal place to observe Tel Aviv movers and shakers at their ease. Reservations are essential.

Bistro Picasso (££) 114 Hayarkon Street (tel: 03 524 1875). This bistro looks like a canteen, with its orange walls and wooden tables, but the food is definitely influenced by modern French. Chicken in poppy-seed jackets, liver pâté, *tarte tatin*, good wines and lively music ensure this relaxed and stylish spot close to the sea is full into the early hours.

Café Kazeh (££) 19 Sheinkin (tel: 03 293756). Ever-trendy but never unfriendly café and restaurant, which spills out on to a raised balcony on the extensive roadside and a delightful gravelled garden at the back. The menu always features delicious soups and breads, large healthy salads and good desserts.

Chimney (££) 2 Mendele Street (tel: 03 523 5215). Still pulling the locals and the tourists in, the relaxed bar atmosphere at Chimney sets a friendly tone for diners in the evening but is good for business lunches too. The food – including deep-fried mincemeat wrapped in filo, prawns in white wine and garlic, baked potatoes with sauces and salads – is ample and tasty, while the cocktails are magic. A covered terrace at the back provides a more intimate spot.

Deli Dag (£££) 13 Tozeret Ha'aretz, Nahalat Yitzhak (tel: 03 695 6216). Bustling fish restaurant in the heart of the business zone, slotted between garages and ceramic ware houses. Ask anyone with a passion for fish and this is one of the first places they'll mention. It has a well-deserved reputation for simple but superbly cooked fish – sole, salmon, St Peter's fish, mullet – and fresh salads. If you don't have time to stop, there's a huge deli-counter for take-outs.

Expresso Bar (£) 18 Yavne (tel: 03 525 2404); 57 Yehuda Hamaccabi (tel: 03 605 7521). Laid-back coffee bars for the young and funky, both serving a huge range of specialist coffees plus a small but spot-on range of fashionable sandwiches – mozarella and basil, salami and radish, prosciutto and rocket. Follow with a portion of excessively sweet desserts.

Forel (£££) 10 Frishman Street (tel: 03 522 2664). An elegant fish restaurant with high standards of cooking and service. The catches of the day, including live lobster, are brought to your table for you as a main course while either side are excellent antipasti and desserts. Marvellous wines, too – a restaurant for special occasions.

Ha'galleria Ha'levanah (££) 4 Kikar Ha'Bima (tel: 03 561 4523). Once a spearhead of light and stylish eating, the elegant White Gallery restaurant is almost an elder of the restaurant scene now. Israeli and Italian starters and main courses leave just enough room for a slice of the outstanding apple tart – a generous, caramelised confection of the plumpest fruits. Book for dinner as the post-theatre and concert crowd descend in droves. (If you have to wait, pop into the bookshop next door – a browser's paradise).

Houmous Ashkara (£) 45 Yirmiyahu Street (tel: 03 546 4547). An institution among houmous houses, and useful to remember as it is open 24 hours a day (except sabbath ie Friday evening to Saturday evening). It's houmous with everything, from broad beans to pine kernels and of course the usual pitta, pickles and salad.

Keren (£££) 12 Eilat Street, Jaffa (tel: 03 681 6565). An unpretentious two-storey restaurant serving arguably the best food in Tel Aviv. Flavourful regional dishes include liver pâté on a bed of artichokes and lentils. It's worthwhile taking the set business lunch (available on Saturday, too) for 95–120 NIS, otherwise you could pay triple to eat à la carte. Book ahead.

Maganda (££) 26 Rabbi Meir Street, Yemenite Quarter (tel: 03 517 9990). Serving traditional Moroccan and Yemenite food, this is one of Tel Aviv's better 'smart' Middle-Eastern restaurants. The buffet groans beneath the weight of delicious starters, which are followed by grills and sweet, sticky desserts. Eating on the roof terrace in summer is a delightful experience. Book in advance if you intend to eat here on Saturday night.

Margaret Tayar (££) Second Aliya Harbour (A'haliya Ha'shniya Retsif), Jaffa (tel: 03 682 4741). Couscous like mamma, or in this case Margaret, used to make. Good home cooking from North Africa with best options being the salads to start, followed by couscous and grilled fish. Brings in a cosmopolitan, arty crowd.

Namasta (£) 4 Florentine (tel: 03 681 8280). This is a hippy-chic Indian bar/restaurant in this increasingly trendy area of Tel Aviv. Indian music tinkles away in the background, and the simple wood décor is more subtle than in many such restaurants. Start with Indian spiced nuts and crisps and follow with rice, lentils and meat washed down with one of the many varieties of spicy Indian tea. Young voyagers to India looking to recapture the spirit of karma head here.

Pasta Lina (£££) 16 Eliphelet Street (tel: 03 683 6401). With a fixed price starter and main course, you'll have an eye-opening Italian experience. Salamis and rustic breads are followed by a dazzling array of antipasti – mussels, mozzarella, carpaccio, delectable salads. Then try *tagliato di manzo* – sizzling sirloin steak wafers topped with rocket, sea-salt, lemon juice and olive oil. There are other beef, veal, chicken and fish dishes, plus pasta. For dessert, the poppy seed ice-cream with chocolate sauce is unbeatable.

Remi (£££) 87 Hayarkon Street (tel: 03 524 8696). Ultra-chic Italian-style cuisine imported by way of California, in a cool airy setting (worthy of Ralph Lauren) overlooking the sea. Adventurous dishes based on rabbit, scallops and venison make a refreshing change from the traditional pasta route.

Shipudei Hatikva (£) 37 Ezel Street (tel: 03 378 014). This is a simple, clean place in the less-frequented south of Tel Aviv but which the locals know serves outstanding salads, kebabs, shwarma (doner kebab) and falafel. Immediate service with no frills. If this place is full, do not despair, the street is teeming with similar choices.

Spaghettim (£) 18 Yavne Street (tel: 03 294464). Business-like by day, Bohemian by night, this bright modern restaurant serves 40 variations of pasta and sauce, so you keep coming back to try the next one on the menu.

Suzanna (££) 9 Shabazi Street, Neve-Tzedek (tel: 03 517 7580). Modern Middle-Eastern describes the style at this delightful restaurnat near the Suzanne Dellai theatre complex. Iraqi, Moroccan, Tunisian and home-grown dishes served in rustic earthenware pots are best shared – you won't go hungry here. Dine inside or out: the ochre, wood and wrought iron décor makes either a pleasure.

Takamaru Sushi Barú (£££) 10 Ha'Arbaa Street (tel: 03 562 1629). Enormous, painted Japanese characters hang against the brick and metal interior of this trendy upwardly mobile restaurant. Tel Aviv folk have taken to Japanese cuisine with a passion, and no wonder – here is pure, clean-tasting and authentic food in every conceivable sushi combination, as well as tempura, yakitori, and teriyaki dishes. Kimono-clad Israeli staff are on hand to guide the novice round the menu. Also at 118 Hayarkon (tel: 03 527 8858).

Tandoori (£££) 2 Zamenhof Street, Dizengoff Square (tel: 03 296185). One of a successful chain also to be found in Jerusalem, Eilat, Tiberias and Herzliya Pituach. Tandoori always produces a stylish meal, though anyone coming from a country used to spicy food may find the heat a little lacking. Shrimp dishes are excellent if pricey and the cocktails are an enjoyable occidental attraction. Conductor Zubin Mehta pops in to eat and say hello to glamorous owner, Reena Pushkarna, when he is in town.

Tapooah Ha'zahav (£££) 1 Karl Netter Street (tel: 03 566 0931). This turn of the century house renovated by the much acclaimed owner/chef, Israel Aharoni, is a pastel haven of violet and blue with a cuisine that merits lyrical praise. Mixing French and oriental influences, the elegant menu offers baby lamb in filo pastry, and queen of puds or orange *crème brulée*. The business lunch here represents the best value meal in town.

Tnuva (££) 34 Ben Gurion Boulevard (tel: 03 527 2972). A consistently delicious fish and dairy restaurant which has never been matched by its other branches.

Open until the small hours, the daily pasta dish is almost irrelevant when the menu is so huge. Everything from a yoghourt and granola breakfast to brochettes of mixed cheeses or trout with almonds, it is all fabulously fresh and generously served – in fact, one portion will often satisfy two hungry diners.

Tel Aviv outskirts

Fabio (££) 11 Oppenheimer Street, Neve Avivim, Ramat Aviv (tel: 03 641 5555). A favourite with politicians, industrialists and the chic yuppie residents of Ramat Aviv, this very appealing Italian restaurant serves fresh pastas, pizzas and a carefully selected choice of starters. Great pannacotta (egg custard) for dessert, too.

Gargantua (£££) 5 Sadnaot, Industrial Zone, Herzliya Pituach (tel: 09 589722). The robust and omnipresent Leon Elkalai is owner/chef of this popular Bulgarian/ Turkish restaurant. The meat dishes are equally robust and flavourful.

Reviva Ve'Silia (££) 34 Sokolow (in the shopping centre), Ramat Hasharon (tel: 09 549 6845) The chefs at work in the open kitchen are fascinating to watch in this sparkling new café/restaurant. Baguettes full of melted mozarella and prosciutto are a definite winner as are less obvious salad combinations and cakes to die for. Treat yourself to a bag of almond biscuits when you leave. Attracts a moneyed, suburban crowd. A second branch is at 1 Ha'Misdayim.

Haifa

La Chaumière (£££) 40a Ben Gurion Boulevard (tel: 04 8538563). If you ever feel the need to eat snails, this is one of the only places you will find them in Israel. The darkly furnished, plant-filled French bistro also serves a mean *filet mignon*, fine *fois gras* and excellent seafood and gratin dishes.

Jacko (£) 12 Hadkalim Street (tel: 04 8668 813). This thriving Middle-Eastern canteen, in the heart of Haifa's Turkish market, lures diners from Tel Aviv for the evening, such is its reputation. Traditional Middle Eastern mezze begin the meal (try the ikra – fish eggs), followed by whatever happens to be fresh that day – shrimps, kalamari, sea bass or perhaps sole. Fast service and welcoming to children.

Shwarma Hazan (£) Jaffa Street, by the port. A fast-food joint serving the best *shwarma* and salads in Haifa. Noisy and popular, it is easy to spot because it is the biggest of the 20 or so *shwarma* shops down this street. Not for a special evening out, but certainly convenient and clean.

GALILEE

Dag Al Ha'Dan (££) Kibbutz Ha'Gosherim, Route 99, north of Tiberias (tel: 06 959 608). If you are travelling north, don't fail to take in this charming cabin style fish restaurant, hung with fishing nets. The centrepiece is the pool from which you select your dinner. Trout is a speciality, served with nuts and garlic, or butter and garlic, and starters include hot avocado with aubergines and melted cheese.

Ein Kamunim (££) Acco-Amiad Road, near Amiad, Lower Galilee (tel: 06 989680) The sheep and goats have disappeared from this converted barn, but their cheese remains the theme here. In fact you can eat cheese to saturation point: hard, soft, plain or spiced. A fixed price brings you an enormous selection of salads; wine is included and replenished frequently.

Ha'bayit (££) Lido Beach, Tiberias (tel: 06 792564). A delightful Chinese restaurant entered by stepping across a bridge over a little stream. Once in, you can head upstairs to one of the separate dining rooms or out on to the terrace.

Misedet Dalia (£) Moshav Amirim, 7km south of Suful (tel: 06 000340). Members of this *moshav* (co-operative village) are lucky to have this vegetarian restaurant on site. It serves light, modern dishes without a hefty pulse in sight.

The Pagoda (££) Lido Beach, Tiberias (tel: 06 725513). Chinese and Thai cuisine at the Lido Beach by the lake.

Sachne (££) Nir David Kibbutz, Gan Ha'shelosha (tel: 06 488060). Waterfalls, hot springs and tropical flora make this a beautiful stop.There are few better places to eat fish, meat, salads and pasta in the open air. Afterwards, a stroll around the gardens to walk off your meal, followed by a dip in the 35°C pools, is glorious.

San Remo (££) Kikar Ha'atzmaut, Afulla (tel: 06 522458). Fish lovers from miles around come to this well-above-average restaurant. The salads that appear on your table as you arrive include plentiful supplies of houmous, aubergine, peppers, sweetcorn and artichoke. If you have any room left, the fish is best simply grilled with a squeeze of lime over the top. Home-reared fish, such as the Nile Princess, red mullet and St Peter's fish, make a change from more predictable trout and salmon

THE SOUTH
Eilat
Au Bistro (£££) Eilot Street (tel: 07 6374333). Romantics head here for good French food. Secluded, small, clean and friendly, with seafood and meat specialities.

Beigel Nash (£) Beit Ha'Tamar (tel: 07 371443). As its name suggests, anything on a bagel is the theme of this popular café. Pizzas, pastas, fish, salads – everything comes on a bagel – except meat, which is not served in here at all.

The Dolphin Reef Pub (£) Dolphin Reef (tel: 07 374293). This thatched beach hut, with tree stumps to sit on and cushioned booths to curl up in, offers a menu ranging from simple seafood – such as shrimps in garlic and white wine – to more beefy meat meals. It is also perfect for a light snack of houmous and salads. The restaurant is open late (except in December and January), and occasionally has live music – the dolphins apparently love it.

El Gaucho (££) Ha'arava Street (tel: 07 331549). The 'grill man' is flown in from Argentina especially to perform his wonderful ways with beefsteak. This restaurant provides satisfying helpings, though you could skip the main course and just have a meal of Argentinian starters – such as *empandas* filled with cheese and beef, or spicy sausages. Catering to a young and noisy crowd, the waiters act the part in embroidered waistcoats and dashing red sashes.

The Golden Duck (£££) Neptune Hotel (tel: 07 369 369). Chinese and Thai flavours skilfully reproduced at one of Eilat's most beautiful restaurants. The black lacquer and mint green interior is a cooling antidote to the hot and sour soup and the chef is on hand to recommend and advise on the most suitable choices.

Kapulsky's (£) North Beach (tel: 07 376510). Cakes in abundance from the experts: rum babas, black forest gâteaux, chocolate mousses, cinnamon pretzels – they are all here to tempt the sweet-toothed, though some lower calorie versions are sometimes available too. Standards are always reliable and the menu does include salads and soups as well.

Last Refuge (£££) Coral Beach (tel: 07 373627). This is one of the first places a seafood lover should come to. Rustic and comfortable, it is hung with fishing nets and oil lamps and serves top-quality food.

The Lotus (£££) Caesar Hotel (tel: 07 376389). Vying with The Golden Duck for the title of Eilat's best Chinese restaurant, the lattice potato baskets and the radish and carrot cutting skills of the chefs are a delight. Split levels keep the atmosphere cosy and intimate but it is ideal for groups, too. Though expensive, the Lotus offers better value than many central Eilat restaurants.

Mandy's Chinese (££), Coral Beach (tel: 07 6372238). Much loved and long-established Chinese restaurant, right on the beachfront. Every dish is someone's favourite and locals and tourists alike mark it down as one to visit again.

Tandoori (£££) The Lagoona Hotel, North Beach (tel: 07 333666). A much larger (and kosher) version of the Tel Aviv flagship restaurant (see page 282). Lavish interior and food to match.

Teddy's (£) opposite Shulamit Gardens Hotel (tel: 07 373949). A vast western-style pub with wooden floorboards, that heave to the pulse of live music. Burgers and fries are the order of the day.

Index

Principal references are given in **bold**.

285

INDEX

INDEX AND ACKNOWLEDGEMENTS

Acknowledgements

The Automobile Association would like to thank El Al Israel Airlines and tour operator Twickers World for their help in researching this book.

The Automobile Association would also like to thank the following photographers, libraries and associations for their assistance in the preparation of this book.

JON ARNOLD PHOTOGRAPHY 11 Judaean Desert, 21 Mt Hermon, 26 Egyptian tanks, Negev, 28a Sheckels, 60a Jerusalem, Holy Sepulchre, 80 & 81 Herodian Wohl Arch Mus, 83 Ruins of City of David, 90 Jerusalem, Tombs in Kidron Valley, 97a Jerusalem, Mt Zion Church of Dormition, 99a Jerusalem, Torah Scroll Western Wall, 124 Jaffa harbour, 125b Jaffa window, 128 Tel Aviv old cemetery, 129a Jaffa street name, 130b Tel Aviv Mus of Art, 136a Passover, 136b Burning yeast, 147 Caesarea, 153 Lod Church of St George, 160 Rosh Ha Nikra, 172a Golan Heights, Hexagonal Pool, 185 Korazim houses, 197 Sea of Galilee, 205b Zippori Roman theatre & fort, 207a Wadi Qelt. Judaean Desert, 208 Wadi Qelt. St George's Monastery, 213a Bethlehem, Church of Nativity, 225a En Avedat Negev, 226 Ibex, 228b Beersheba, Abraham's Well, 229b Bedhouin camp. Sinai Desert, 229c Bedhouin & camel, 237b Coral World, Eilat, 239 Negev Desert of Zin, 242a Masada, 246 & 247 Negev Makhetsch Ramon, 249b Ben Gurion's house, 251 Timna Nat Park Remains of Temple, 263b Sea of Galilee; THE BRIDGEMAN ART LIBRARY 36/7 Victory of Constantine over Maxentius - the Battle of the Milvian Bridge, from the True Cross Cycle (fresco) by Pierro della Francesca (1419/21-92) San Francesco, Arrezo, 36 Baptism of Constantine by Pierre Puget (1620–94) Musée des Beaux Arts, Marseilles/Giraudon; MARY EVANS PICTURE LIBRARY 14/15 'Ben-Schemen' colony, 29b Alexander the Great, 30/1 Israelites march, 30 Red Sea re-forms over Pharoah's army, 31 Moses with Ten Commandments, 33 Matthatias kills desecrator of Temple, 37 Hadrian, 39 Saladin watches defile of Christian Captives, 40b Sulieman I, 41b Zionist settlement at Machnajim, 42a Field marshall Viscount Allenby, 43 British peacekeepers, 70b Foundation of the Temple, 122b Shmuel Yosef Agnon, 175 Farm workers on Kibbutz; HULTON DEUTSCH COLLECTION LTD 22 Begin, Carter & Sadat at Camp David, 27b Clinton, Rabin & Yassar Arafat, 42b Arab brigands, 44b Ben Gurion, 122c Max Brod, 123 Ephrain Kishon, 141a Vladimir Jabotinsky, 210/11 Demonstration, 210 Palestinian demonstrator, 211a Arab prisoners, 211b Gaza Strip barricade, 249a Ben Gurion; ISRAEL GOVERNMENT TOURIST OFFICE 131a Tel Aviv Hexchal Hatarboot, 145b Succot at Wailing Wall, 214a Bethlehem St Catherine's Chapel; THE ISRAEL MUSEUM, JERUSALEM 222b Pottery from Qumran, 223 Prof Bie Berkraut; JULIAN LOADER 8 Children; MAGNUM PHOTOS 13 Refugees in Tel Aviv; THE MANSELL COLLECTION LTD 141b Theodor Herzl, 216 Walls of Jericho; P MURPHY 32/3 Citadel Mus, Jerusalem, 82 Biblelands Mus, Jerusalem, 118 Tel Aviv Eretz Israel Mus, 126/7 Diaspora Mus, 170 Capernaeum Greek Orthodox Church, 232 Eilat Dolphin Reef Beach, 242b Masada cable car, 250 Timna Nat Park; NATURE PHOTOGRAPHERS LTD 230a Dead Sea Salt Rocks (H Miles), 244/5 Wild flowers (R Tidman), 248a White pelican (P R Sterry), 248b Raftor Watch Point (R Tidman); REX FEATURES LTD 23 Israel Government; SPECTRUM COLOUR LIBRARY 137 Man, child & candles, 215 Hebron, 236b Eilat fish; TONY STONE IMAGES Cover: Jerusalem people in market.

All remaining pictures are held in the Association's own library (AA PHOTO LIBRARY) and were taken by P Aithie with the exception of the following pages: 34a was taken by D Mitidieri, 16/7 was taken by T Harris, 99b, 148a were taken by C Lees, Spine, 5a, 5c, 9c, 10b, 16, 17a, 20/1, 20, 24, 29a, 34b, 38/9, 42/3, 44a, 46, 50a, 53a, 55b, 59a, 68, 72, 73a, 73b, 75, 78, 84, 85a, 85b, 87, 88a, 88b, 89b, 91b, 94b, 95, 97b, 98, 100a, 100b, 101a, 101b, 104, 106b, 108, 109a, 110, 122a, 229a, 261b, 263a, 267, 271 were taken by A Souter, 74a was taken by W Voysey

Contributors

Revision copy editor: Penny Phenix
Original copy editor: Christopher Catling
Revision verifier: Andrew Sanger